SLEEPWALKING THROUGH HISTORY

ALSO BY HAYNES JOHNSON

Dusk at the Mountain (1963)
The Bay of Pigs (1964)
The Working White House (1975)
In the Absence of Power (1980)
Fulbright: The Dissenter (1968)
with Bernard M. Gwertzman
The Unions (1972) with Nick Kotz
Army in Anguish (1972) with George C. Wilson
Lyndon (1973) with Richard Harwood

FICTION
The Landing (1986)
with Howard Simons

SLEEPWALKING THROUGH HISTORY

AMERICA IN THE REAGAN YEARS

HAYNES JOHNSON

W. W. NORTON AND COMPANY
NEW YORK · LONDON

The text of this book is composed in Times Roman, with the display set in Augustea.
Composition and manufacturing by the Haddon Craftsmen Inc.
Book design by Charlotte Staub.

First Edition

Library of Congress Cataloging-in-Publication Data

Johnson, Haynes Bonner, 1931–
Sleepwalking through history : America in the Reagan years/by Haynes Johnson.
p. cm.
Includes bibliographical references and index.
1. United States—Politics and government—1981–1989. 2. United States—History—1964– 3. Reagan, Ronald—Influence. I. Title.
E876.J64 1991
973.927—dc20 90-38623

ISBN 0-393-02937-9

W.W. Norton & Company, Inc.
500 Fifth Avenue, New York, N.Y. 10110
W.W. Norton & Company, Ltd.
10 Coptic Street, London WC1A 1PU

1 2 3 4 5 6 7 8 9 0

TO THE MEMORY OF

FREDERICK LEWIS ALLEN,
RICHARD HOFSTADTER, and
THEODORE H. WHITE

Who showed the way

AUTHOR'S NOTE

Quotations in this book are taken directly from transcripts of oral history interviews, from primary and secondary public sources, so identified, and from tape-recorded interviews in Washington and around the country. Unless otherwise cited textually or in source notes, quotes in the narrative that begins with Ronald Reagan's inaugural day on January 20, 1981, are from my interviews.

—H. J.

CONTENTS

It was a period of moral slump, the backswing from the idealism and sacrifices of war. Men's thoughts could not indefinitely maintain themselves on that lofty plane. . . . People were unhappy, restless. They craved a change.

—Samuel Hopkins Adams, on the Harding era

Reagan runs continuously in everyone's home movies of the mind. He wrests from us something warmer than mere popularity, a kind of complicity. He is, in the strictest sense, what Hollywood promoters used to call "fabulous." We fable him to ourselves, and he to us. We are jointly responsible for him.

—Garry Wills, on the Reagan era

PROLOGUE

Each decade creates its own myth, Murray Kempton observed in *Part of Our Time,* his memoir about America in the 1930s, while succeeding decades wait with knives in hands to kill the old myths and carve new ones suitable for their times. The same can be said of America in the 1980s. It was an age of illusions when America lived on borrowed time and squandered opportunities to put its house in order. Not since the laissez-faire years of the twenties had America experienced such a decade—and a decade that will extract a heavy price from Americans unborn. In their impact on social, economic, political/governmental life, and on the attitudes and personal values of Americans, the eighties were the most important years since World War II.

The myth of the eighties was that the United States of America, the greatest power the world has known, economically and militarily, a society favored with material riches beyond measure and a political system whose freedoms made it the envy of every nation on earth, had fallen into a state of disintegration and with Ronald Reagan recaptured what it had lost: optimism; strength; enterprise; inventiveness. Most of all America wanted to believe it had recaptured a sense of success. Success for the nation, success for the individual: In the public mind, the two were indivisible.

By 1990 Americans had special reason to think the myth had become real. From China to Eastern Europe each day brought evidence of hunger in totalitarian lands for American democratic values of freedom, the right to protest and express unpopular views. Each outpouring of citizenry in Beijing, East Berlin, Warsaw, Budapest, Prague, Bucharest, and even Managua and Moscow itself affirmed belief in the United States as the world's leading symbol of democracy. Furthermore, after nearly half a century the United States was clearly the victor in its global ideological struggle with the Soviet Union. Riven with internal dissent, its productive capacities weakening and threatening collapse, its alliances crumbling, the Soviet system by the nineties no longer could claim to be a viable model for the future.

Yet neither could America assert as strong a claim to preeminence as in the past. While the American *idea* of freedom and democracy had prevailed, its own economic power had diminished, making dealing with international crises more difficult. New questions existed about whether America was still capable of achieving its goals and fulfilling its ideals.

How the United States was transformed from world's leading creditor nation into world's leading debtor, how its new debts mortgaged the nation's future, how the eighties ended with the greatest promise internationally in half a century and with a greater challenge for America to win the peace after the cold war, how the domestic and foreign policies of the eighties left America more vulnerable in the nineties to problems involving energy and hostage taking and relationships with terrorist third world states, how the most conservative administration of the century ended America's age of reform, how the American people and their leaders and political institutions appeared to be sleepwalking through history, and how the nation traveled from the New Patriotism to the New Greed all within a mere decade form the central thread of this story.

It is also the story of how an America yearning for reassurance about its place in the world invested great faith in a Hollywood actor turned politician and suspended judgment on his leadership in hope that his promise would be realized. At a time when Americans desperately wanted to believe again, Reagan presented himself as the political wizard whose spell made everyone feel good.

In the myths of the eighties he was the greatest mythmaker of all, and the most striking of his myths was his own life. He was a man who emerged from a family background of pain, privation, and humiliation, living on the margin, who went to California and remade himself and his world. As Napoleon said of himself, Ronald Reagan was his own ancestor. He invented himself. It might even be argued that he invented an age. For better or worse perhaps he did, and for years to come Americans will be dealing with the consequences of it.

BOOK ONE

WASHINGTON JAN. 20, 1981

CHAPTER 1

THE CAPITAL

Only the old curmudgeon was disenchanted. Barry Goldwater, the real founder of the revolution, pronounced his unhappiness after observing the round of preinaugural parties that marked the coming to power of Ronald Reagan. "When you gotta pay two thousand dollars for a limousine for four days, seven dollars to park, and two dollars and fifty cents to check your coat at a time when most people in this country just can't hack it, that's ostentatious," he grumbled aloud. His wife, overhearing him, tried to soften the remark. Barry was just being "antisocial," she told a reporter as she nudged the senator along to another event, but as usual, the man who had first marshaled the ideological forces that seventeen years later resulted in a great shift in national political power was only expressing a blunt, impolitic truth.

Not since Andrew Jackson's inauguration, when the hero of New Orleans marked the ascendancy of popular democracy in America by throwing open the White House to mobs in muddy boots, had Washington witnessed such a spectacle.

It was an outpouring of wealth and privilege. At National Airport, corporate jets were parked wing to wing on the tarmac. The airport was unable to accommodate the private planes seeking space. They touched down, dropped off invited inaugural guests, then departed to bring back more. One group of Indiana Republicans traveled to Washington in an elegant railroad car once owned by J. P. Morgan. Limousines were the preferred symbol of status. "They give you a feeling of pride and accomplishment," explained a Republican national committeeman from Salt Lake City. "They give you a feeling of enthusiasm for your leaders."

So brisk was the limousine business that all available ones in the capital area were quickly leased. Calls went out to dispatch others from as far south as Atlanta and as far north as New York. They poured into the city, vanguards of a new era bearing special inaugural plates with names of the corporations that had leased them. Gliding up to museums and galleries and other public buildings, they discharged women in designer dresses and diamonds and men in formal wear. Society page writers, with press entry credentials to the private festivities, strained for metaphors to describe the display of affluence. Hotel coat racks, laden with mink, "looked like furry beasts." At Sunday brunches in Georgetown, "furs swallowed the beds." At a black-tie-and-boots Texas party, "a perfumed herd of thousands drank beer and wore emeralds."

As always, money did not necessarily equate with manners: Four hundred people mobbed one town house in Georgetown where a reception honored Michael Deaver, virtually unknown in Washington but said to be extremely close to the Reagans and designated deputy White House chief of staff. The catering business had never been better. "There are ten times as many parties this inaugural as last time," said Jeff Ellis of Ridgewell's, a firm that had been waiting on Washington's social-diplomatic set for generations. Ridgewell's alone served more than four hundred thousand hors d'oeuvres during the preinaugural parties. "I've never seen anything like this," Ellis remarked happily. "These people have really fine taste. Rather than shrimp salad, they want the whole shrimp."

It was the costliest, most opulent inauguration in American history, and some of the scenes gave credence to critics who likened it to "a bacchanalia of the haves."

At Union Station, a once-grand terminal built at the turn of the century in the Roman imperial manner as gateway to the capital but now badly deteriorated, tables were piled high with gourmet food. Aroma of the food inside proved irresistible to some of the poor huddling outside. They mingled with the crush of thousands in formal dress seeking admittance and penetrated security. "As the ragged outcasts hurriedly stuffed their stomachs and pockets with the highest of French cuisine," one commentator wrote, "the Reaganites were indeed letting them eat cake."

Critics had a field day. They chortled at such signs of a bread and circuses atmosphere as evidence that the Reagan inauguration represented a marriage of the New Right with the New Rich. They ridiculed the display of material possessions as insensitivity in a time of economic hardship. They delighted in contrasting the new group's promise of public frugality with its practice of private extravagance. They especially disparaged the lavish tone set by the First Lady-to-be, whose inaugural wardrobe was reported to have cost twenty-five thousand dollars (an amount that would purchase a year's supply of food stamps for fifty needy citizens, liberals and do-gooders noted dourly) and whose new handbag alone cost more than sixteen hundred dollars.

Andy Warhol, the pop culture artist celebrated for his oft-quoted remark "In the future everyone will be world-famous for fifteen minutes," came down from New York to attend a preinaugural party. "A couple of years ago, with all the parties, I said Washington was getting like Hollywood," he quipped. "Now it really is." Another television age icon, Johnny Carson, the TV talk show host and master of the one-line put-down, also noted the numbers of Hollywood entertainment celebrities present. "Well," he said, "this is the first administration to have a premiere."

Not all the criticism was so insubstantial. The nation's big-city mayors, concluding their annual session in Washington as the inaugural ceremonies were to begin, heard the Democrat Henry Maier of Milwaukee sum up a mood of apprehension about changes the new Reagan administration might bring.

Maier was an old tiger among the mayors, blunt and outspoken. For twenty years he had led his city through a series of tumultuous events that mirrored those of the nation. It had been an extended roller coaster ride from promise of urban revival in the early sixties to urban destruction from racial riots in that same decade of disillusionment, from hopes for a new beginning in the seventies to the economic and political letdown that characterized their ending.

Now, on the eve of the Reagan years in the eighties, Maier erupted emotionally as he addressed his fellow mayors. "I say to you if you say we can live without federal help, God bless you. Some of us are on the brink of catastrophe. . . . We have city after city on the verge of collapse. Now we're being told, as we are about to be booted down the hill further, that we ought to allow them to boot us, take it in good grace, and I have only one thing to say to you." He pounded angrily on the table and shouted: "To hell with that!"

On Capitol Hill another Democrat from Wisconsin, William Proxmire, issued critical statements. While Reagan promised austerity in government, Proxmire said, the president-elect's inaugural committee practiced conspicuous consumption. Proxmire's theme was familiar. Since coming to the Senate in 1957 as a lawyer with a master's degree in business administration from Harvard, he had earned a reputation as an expert in government operations. Nearly every politician in Washington railed against governmental waste and fraud, expressing platitudes but offering few specific proposals for solutions, but Proxmire's criticisms carried real weight. This time they went beyond the usual waste-and-abuse complaints. These were illegal acts, he charged. He was convinced that the Reagan inaugural committee falsely claimed that private contributions paid for inaugural costs and that hidden inaugural expenses, especially real costs of Pentagon employees on loan to the committee from the Defense Department, were deliberately concealed. His charges drew scant attention.*

People's inaugural it was not. Four years before, all events were open to the public, and most of them free. Where prices were charged, the cost of tickets had been limited to twenty-five dollars. Now events were restricted to invitation-only guests, and prices ranged from one hundred dollars per admittance to two thousand dollars for a box. Some boxes were priced at ten thousand, and oversold at that, as were all the nine white-tie-and-tails inaugural balls.

Inaugural planners had no doubts about the signal being sent the country. As one of them said, the Reagan inaugural was a symbol of

*Two and a half years later the U.S. General Accounting Office informed Congress that "much of the support provided by the Department of Defense for 1981 inaugural activities was without proper legal authority" and that the actual Reagan inaugural cost was $16.3 million, more than twice what officials had stated and nearly five times that of the Carter inauguration. "Lack of a statutory base for this support has resulted in practices questionable on policy as well as on legal grounds," the GAO's report said.

"class and dignity"—and of free enterprise at its best. Private contributions would assure that Reagan's inaugural paid for itself.

That theme of free enterprise unshackled and governmental regulations struck represented the promise of the Reagan presidency. In Washington and across the country on this forty-ninth American inaugural day, believers in that hope outnumbered doubters. "This is what America's all about," murmured a Cuban-American entrepreneur from Culver City, California, as he looked at the throng of expensively dressed celebrants attending a preinaugural event. "It looks like a bunch of people who want to get back to what America really means." Another Californian, a San Francisco lawyer who proudly called himself a conservative, could barely restrain his enthusiasm. "It's sort of an expression of joy," he told a reporter. "Finally something we've worked for has come to flourish. It's like a flower coming up in the spring."

CHAPTER 2

THE LOSER

On the morning of the inauguration clocks in the capital were set on eastern standard time, but eyes of officials were focused on those showing time zones in Germany, Algeria, and, ten thousand miles away, Iran.

Jimmy Carter, the thirty-ninth president of the United States, endured another sleepless night as his presidency came to an end. In terms of personal frustration, it was excruciating. Carter was passing into history as one of the most hapless American leaders. No matter how earnestly or intelligently he applied himself to problems of governance, he seemed fated to failure. He had sunk lower in the public opinion polls than any president before him, lower even than the disgraced Richard Nixon, who had been forced to resign under threat of impeachment nearly seven years earlier. Now, in his final hours in the White House, Carter was given one last chance to recapture some of the goodwill that marked his own inauguration just four years ago.

He had not been to bed for two days, and showed it: He looked ravaged, his face gray and puffy and careworn. Most of the time he worked at his desk, wearing the cardigan sweater that he once employed in a nationally televised address as a symbol of how the nation could conserve energy and still be comfortable with lowered room temperatures. It was a sweater that later became a subject of ridicule when energy conservation failed and a crisis over consumption of fuel ignited angry, often violent confrontations across the country. Occasionally he catnapped on one of the small couches near the fireplace in his Oval Office, covering himself with blue blankets brought by White House stewards. Telephones lay on the floor beside him so he would be certain to take important calls from throughout the world personally. Some of the time he was alone, as figuratively he had been for most of his presidency, and always he continued to glance at the big grandfather clock by the door as the hands ticked away his time in office.

Typical of his meticulous attention to detail, an admirable trait that even trusted aides conceded he carried to excess, he made detailed handwritten notes on a small pad so there would be no question that he knew exactly where things stood: "1:50 A.M., 2:23 A.M., 2:30 A.M., 2:40 A.M., 2:45 A.M., 3:05 A.M., 3:16 A.M., 3:40 A.M., 4:20 A.M., 4:35 A.M., 4:38 A.M., 5:00 A.M., 5:10 A.M., 5:20 A.M., 6:05 A.M. . . ." Minute after minute, hour after hour, the president of the United States continued to record careful notes of conversations, details, figures that alternately reported indications of progress or failure, stirring in Carter conflicting feelings of exhilaration and despair.

Finally, at 6:35 A.M., word came that he had been eagerly awaiting. The last major snag over release of Americans held hostage in Iran was resolved. The hostages would be flown from Iran to Algiers, then transported to American bases in Germany before heading back to the United States.

For weeks, as the secret negotiations over the hostages proceeded, Carter hoped to be able to greet the liberated Americans personally on their homecoming. He made plans to fly directly to Germany to be there when they set foot on Western soil and in the last exhausting twenty-four hours had even discussed the possibility of taking the commercial supersonic Concorde flight, so much faster than his own Air Force One. Time and events ordered otherwise, but it appeared that on this inaugural day he would still be able to announce the good news publicly before his term ended and thus repair some of the damage the taking of hostages had done to his presidency. Already his speech writers were drafting the text of a televised address he intended to make to the nation before the ceremonies began at the Capitol.

At 7:00 A.M. the president placed a call to President-elect Ronald Reagan in Blair House, the official presidential guest residence across the street from the White House, to brief Reagan on latest developments in Iran. Minutes later Carter was informed that his call to Reagan had been taken by aides, who said Reagan "had had a long night, was sleeping, and was not to be disturbed."

"You're kidding," Carter replied.

"No, sir, I'm not," the aide said.

The president jotted down another note in his book: "I place a call to Governor Reagan to give him the good news, and am informed that he prefers not to be disturbed, but that he may call back later. I respond that I will call him when the hostages are released."

Upon awakening at 8:31, an hour and a half later, Reagan returned the call.* The release of the hostages was imminent, Carter informed his successor. The planes to carry them to freedom were on the runway.

Only recently that prospect had seemed near impossible. Iran's "final proposal" for release of the hostages, relayed through diplomatic channels to Washington, was for U.S. payment of twenty-four billion dollars in gold, cash, and other guarantees. Financially the price was too high even to consider; politically it was unthinkable. It smacked of ransom, and that, Carter knew from painful experience, the public would never tolerate. His defeat rested in no small part on the public perception that he was weak in dealing with Iranian terrorism, a belief reinforced by the presidential campaign rhetoric of his opponent, who had repeatedly accused him of appeasement and vowed never to deal with international terrorists. Five days before the inauguration Iran made another overture, setting off desperate, around-the-clock efforts to close the deal before the inauguration.

At 6:35 in the early-morning hours of inaugural day a phone call from his chief negotiator in Algiers, Warren Christopher, informed Carter that final papers had been signed at 6:18 that morning. The way was cleared for the release.

*Reagan's aide Michael Deaver later described that Blair House scene. "When I walked in, Nancy was getting her hair done. I said, 'Where's the governor?' Without moving her head, she said, 'I guess he's still in bed.' 'In bed,' I repeated. 'If it was me, if I was about to become president of the United States, I don't think I'd still be asleep at nine o'clock [*sic*] on the morning of my swearing in.' I opened the door to the bedroom. It was pitch-dark, the curtains still drawn, and I could barely make out a heap of blankets in the middle of the bed. I said, 'Governor?' 'Yeah?' 'It's nine o'clock.' "

The president was ebullient. "That's great, Chris," he said.

In the end, Carter hoped, with the hostages freed, the country would appreciate that his policy of dogged patience, month after month, in dealing with the hostage problem had been vindicated. He had become obsessed with the hostages. He knew each of them by name, studied their careers and family backgrounds, read the personal letters they wrote from captivity, met with their wives and children, visited family members in their homes around the country, and came to hold for them, as he later wrote, "deep personal feelings that were almost overwhelming." Now, at last, it seemed over.

Still, there was more melodrama to come. This time it was played out not in official privacy but before a watching world.

The day before, at 4:44 o'clock in the morning, the president had gone to the White House press briefing room to announce a tentative hostage release agreement. Considering so absorbing a story occurring even as presidential power was transferred in Washington, the response of American television networks was inevitable. Camera crews and teams of correspondents were dispatched to Algiers.

Signals of hope were broadcast, along with reports of setbacks. On inaugural eve, prime-time network fare was filled with scenes of gaiety from Washington and forty-one other cities where special celebrations honored Reagan's inauguration; then all three networks interrupted their broadcasts to air a dramatic ninety-minute live special on the supposedly unfolding hostage release.

In dim lights of darkened airport runways in Algiers, beamed back to the United States by relays from Algerian television to communications satellites orbiting 22,300 miles above the earth, shadowy scenes of jet aircraft were shown. Planes landed and moved toward cameras positioned to record their arrivals. The incessant roar and whine of the engines made it difficult to hear what network correspondents were broadcasting from the scene, but there was no mistaking their excited tones. "We do have a plane now!" a CBS correspondent shouted to network anchorman Dan Rather back in New York. "Yes, there is a plane at the end of the runway!" The plane moved steadily toward the camera, then continued on, and finally took off and disappeared. Another appeared in the eye of the camera. Again the correspondent said, "Here they come, Dan," and again the plane moved out of sight.

The belief, as reported, was that the hostages were aboard. In one surreal scene, lasting a full thirty minutes, cameras focused mutely on one mysterious plane standing on the runway, its doors tantalizingly closed but presumably just about to open.

There was to be no denouement that night, but the dramatic way in which the episode was reported from the Mideast, along with cutaway scenes of the faces of anxious members of hostage families waiting in homes across the United States, generated an air of extraordinary drama. It guaranteed an even greater viewing audience for the inaugural day events of Tuesday, January 20. Not since the funeral of the assassinated John F. Kennedy in 1963 had Americans been so riveted before their television sets. Never in all the previous inaugurations had a president come to power under such intensely publicized circumstances.

Ronald Reagan's inauguration brought together two contradictory but complementary strains of pessimism and optimism present in the United States in 1981: a deep sense of frustration, compounded by a series of political, economic, and military failures at home and abroad that struck at the nation's self-confidence and self-esteem, and a corresponding yearning to believe that a more successful period of national strength was dawning. By the time the American people granted Reagan the ultimate democratic gift of national power, the country had weathered a period of instability and failure. President after president had come and gone in swift succession, leaving in their wakes the wreckage of four straight failed presidencies and an underlying current of doubt about America's purpose and future. John Kennedy was murdered. Lyndon Johnson was driven from office by the Vietnam War. Richard Nixon was forced to resign under threat of impeachment after the Watergate scandal had destroyed his presidency and sent many of his aides to jail. Gerald Ford became the only person to succeed to a broken presidency without even having been elected vice president, an opportunity presented when he was appointed to succeed Spiro T. Agnew after Agnew's plea bargain on criminal income tax evasion charges had forced *him* to resign the vice presidency. Then Ford became the first president since Herbert Hoover to be turned out of office by the voters.

Nor was this catalog of national turmoil confined to the White House. In the same period national leader after national leader—liberal and conservative, Republican and Democrat, northern and southern, black and white—was suddenly and often violently removed from the scene. Martin Luther King and Malcolm X, representing two poles of black thought and experience in the rural South and the urban North, one an apostle of nonviolence, the other advocating a more martial approach, were assassinated. Robert F. Kennedy and George Wallace, representing opposing views on race and the role of the state, also became victims of violence. One was slain; the other was effectively removed from national life by an assassin's bullet that severed his spine.

When added to the loss of so many other national leaders, silencing of these powerful and disparate voices created a void. Political constituencies were shattered; an already strong climate of national cynicism was reinforced; vitality of the political process was numbed. Americans became conditioned to expect less of their leaders and personally to invest less emotion in them. The person in whom they placed trust could suddenly be taken away, leaving a sense of hurt, unfulfillment, or betrayal—or all three.

The pervasive sense of pessimism that enveloped the country was something new in the American experience and especially new in the experience of Americans in this century.

In the decades leading up to the 1980s Americans might have argued whether the United States was exceptionally good or exceptionally bad, but that America was exceptional there was no question and no debate. It was the universe, the California of the Western democracies, the place where everything started. America had long since ceased to be the colony. It was the colonizer, and grudgingly recognized as such elsewhere. Europeans did not like to concede this when their old established order began to crumble in the wreckage of the First World War, but from 1914 on they could see that if it were in America in 1915, it would be in Europe by 1917. As their empires dwindled and disappeared, they could not help noticing that their children, for generation after generation, increasingly resembled corresponding generations of American children. America, the importer of European styles and elegance, had become the exporter of its own culture. Its music, films, jeans, cars, planes, radios, and products from electric toasters to toothbrushes, even its slang and informal life-style were emulated elsewhere. As increasing affluence and amounts of leisure time gave opportunities for greater numbers of previously insular Americans to travel, the experience reinforced an already strong sense of national superiority. Americans returning home from trips abroad expressed astonishment that civilized countries could have such appalling roads, inefficient telephone systems, crude plumbing facilities. The American literary critic and sometime expatriate Edmund Wilson once remarked that he had experienced more sublime thoughts while sitting in an American bathroom than in any European cathedral. Countless fellow citizens shared the thought.

Belief in America's uniqueness was the bedrock foundation of American faith, constantly expressed and deeply held throughout this century. It was this conviction of America's destiny that led the jingoistic Senator Albert J. Beveridge of Indiana to raise his glass at the herald of the new century and offer the toast: "The twentieth century will be American. American thought will dominate it. American progress will give it color and direction. American deeds will make it illustrious." That belief, too, led Henry Luce, among others, to speak confidently forty years later of the continuing glories of the American Century as the United States was about to enter the Second World War. Five years later, on September 2, 1945, after loss of three hundred thousand American lives, more than a million total casualties, expenditure of a quarter of a trillion dollars in national treasure, and a fivefold increase in national debt, that conviction became an article of unquestioned faith upon signing of peace accords on the decks of the battleship USS *Missouri* in Tokyo Bay. For the rest of their lives, those aboard the ship that day remembered the rush of emotion and fierce pride they experienced as the moment of signing the peace document coincided with the sound of a steady rumble that increased into a triumphant crescendo when a thousand U.S. planes, a fragment of America's might, broke out of gray cloud banks, darkened the skies, and swept low in formation over the huge ship. Never since have Americans felt more proud of their country, never so certain about its rightness, never so secure in its place in the world.

For Americans, belief in their country's uniqueness was based upon something more solid than self-inflating myths fueled by Yankee arrogance or Yankee naiveté. Actual achievements, from production of nuclear submarines that navigated beneath polar icecaps to spacecraft that safely carried men to lunar landings, from discovery of vaccines that eliminated such ancient scourges as polio to scientific advances that were beginning to unlock mysteries surrounding the formation of life, were tangible evidence of national worth. Nor were these achievements limited to technological successes. There were political successes as well, and the American record of righting wrongs, of being the most self-correcting society when it came to confronting abuses of power and protecting and extending rights of individuals and minorities, was as exemplary as it was unparalleled. Their tendency toward cockiness aside, Americans in the main meant no offense by their claims to superiority. They were, after all, the heirs to Western civilization and with some reason could be excused for concluding that out of such a diverse intermingling of racial, religious, and cultural threads was being woven an extraordinarily rich new national tapestry that would be the wonder of the world.

It was not, as so often alleged, crass American materialism alone or swaggering pride in Yankee ingenuity that prompted this belief. At the core of American thought lay a certainty that what America represented—its values, its moral compass, its larger meaning—was right and best. This view was especially uniformly held in the years immediately following the Second World War, when the United States stood supreme on the world stage. Americans then, and for decades to come, sincerely took it for granted that a better world was being made out of a combination of American know-how, American political will, American military power.

Measured by history's clock, the emergence of the United States as preeminent world power was swift. In 1940 the representative American statesman was still an isolationist. By 1950 the United States was garrisoning its defeated enemies, Germany and Japan, and willingly assuming global burdens and responsibilities on a scale undreamed of by the Greeks or Romans. By 1960, at the zenith of its strength, the new generation come to power with John F. Kennedy, boasting with him that they were born in this century and tempered by a harsh war and uncertain peace, reveled in its eagerly assumed mission of world leadership. By 1970 the seeds of disillusionment were sown and the beginnings of doubt were taking hold. By 1980, on the advent of the Reagan era, a more subtle and pernicious national climate had formed. For perhaps the first time many Americans wondered if the United States had passed its peak.

Symbolically, the hostages became the common element in both the new pessimism and the national hunger for restoration. They also reflected the perceptions of strengths and weaknesses the public had formed about the outgoing and incoming presidents. Those perceptions, in turn, were strongly shaped by television images. They were still being formed as the final drama played out this inaugural day.

By January 20, 1981, a mass audience without parallel in history had been joined with the advancing techniques and technology of the television industry. Now more people had access to television than telephones, and the number of television sets manufactured daily worldwide equaled the number of children born each day. A global audience estimated at 2.5 billion people watched television; the reach of the television camera extended into homes spanning 160 countries. Nowhere was television's presence more intrusive than in the United States. Ninety-nine percent of all American homes had at least one television set, and it was estimated that adult Americans spent nearly seven hours each day before the tube. (One government survey concluded that by middle age an average American would have spent nearly eleven years before a television set.) Technology, in the form of direct-broadcast earth-orbiting satellites transmitting through dish antennas instantaneously into living rooms everywhere, made all this possible and ever more invasive. Public appetite for the new and dramatic, fed by the increasing ability of television networks to record everything from lunar landings to distant wars and coronations in splendid daily isolation, made such intensive coverage inevitable. It virtually ensured that spectacle would triumph over substance.

Since the 1950s, when television began to wield such influence over American life, there had been nothing to match the extended real-life melodrama of the hostages. They became the latest, and most telling, example of the way in which television may be employed to affect—and in this instance alter—attitudes about politics, world events, and the exercise of power.

The taking of fifty-two American hostages in Iran on November 4, 1979, exactly one year to the day before the 1980 presidential election, came at a critical political juncture in the presidency of Jimmy Carter. Images of American captives driven by taunting mobs shouting "Death to America," set against a background of American flags being burned, for benefit of television audiences filled U.S. television screens. Those images quickly became graven in the American consciousness. Through television the hostage story became part of American daily life.

Americans awoke to see menacing pictures of the Iranian leader Ayatollah Ruhollah Khomeini, an old man garbed in black robes, his grim features framed by a long snow-white beard, as he leveled invective against the United States. Networks began and ended their daily telecasts by numbering each day since the hostages had been seized. By the morning of the inaugural the broadcasts were enumerating "Day four hundred forty-four." From early morning to evening network newscast, day after day, month after month, reminders of Iran were constant and inescapable. Television news programs were broadcast under such running titles as "America Held Hostage." Local as well as national telecasts ended with pictures of the American flag rippling in a breeze and the muted sound of the Liberty Bell tolling. Public passions were whipped into a frenzy of mass emotions unexperienced since the beginning of World War II.

As the hostage story continued to be highlighted, the television networks discovered that their broadcasts on Iran were attracting enormous new audiences. Competition for new aspects of it intensified. Politically the president discovered something, too.

Attacks on Carter personally by Iranian leaders, beamed back to America by television, had a dramatic effect on the president's political standing. The hostage "crisis," as it was everywhere proclaimed—a misnomer, for at best it was a self-induced crisis that affected national behavior and attitudes in a manner unworthy of a mature world power—gave Carter a stature he had failed to achieve in three previous years in office. Overnight he became the personification of the nation, the rallying point for Americans at home to respond to insults abroad. The result was the most stunning reversal of political fortunes in American history.

Two months after the hostages were taken, Carter's rise in popularity was the largest recorded in four decades of the Gallup poll, eclipsing even the soaring approval rating accorded Franklin Roosevelt after Pearl Harbor.

When the hostages were seized, Carter seemed a doomed political figure. It appeared likely he would not even win his party's nomination for a second term, something no other sitting president seeking renomination in the twentieth century had been denied. On the weekend of the hostage seizure, the Gallup poll, the standard for measurement of American opinion since 1936, showed Americans disapproved of the way Carter was handling his job by nearly two to one.

By the same two-to-one margin, Democrats polled that weekend said they preferred Edward M. Kennedy of Massachusetts as their presidential choice. That weekend, too, telephone interviewers for ABC operating from Radnor, Pennsylvania, asked Americans whom they wanted for president a year in advance of the election. Of those holding an opinion, 29 percent picked Kennedy as their presidential choice, while 17 percent favored Carter. Trailing far behind, with only 9 percent support, was Ronald Reagan.

Not since Harry Truman had a president seeking reelection confronted such seemingly hopeless political odds. Not any one thing had gone wrong for Jimmy Carter. Everything had. No scandal had stained his administration. His emphasis on human rights and desire to set a high ethical tone for government were exemplary, and a record of solid achievement existed, most notably the signing of peace accords between the bitter enemies Israel and Egypt. Yet problems, real or fancied, were omnipresent. Carter seemed incapable of resolving them.

Iran's collapse into revolution, shutting off the flow of oil from there, appeared to be a final blow. Gasoline prices, and consumption, rose rapidly as dollar-a-gallon charges were recorded for the first time in the country's history. The gasoline price spiral continued upward, raising the specter of shortages and rationing to carefree Americans. Nothing seemed to be working. Inflation roared on. By the time the hostages were taken, the U.S. inflation rate approached a 14 percent annual level with no end in sight.

Another specter haunted the nation: recession. The United States thus faced the unprecedented prospect of the worst of both worlds, inflation and recession *simultaneously,* stirring fears that events were slipping out of control. Homeowners grappled with effects of new tight-money policies instituted that fall, when the Federal Reserve Board raised the prime interest rate to an unheard-of 14½ percent, affecting all borrowing from banks.

On Capitol Hill a sullen mood prevailed. All of the federal government seemed to have come unraveled. Internally the administration seethed with dissent. Morale plummeted. Carter was shunned as if he had the plague. "He hasn't a single friend up here," a southern Democratic senator remarked privately at lunch in the Senate Dining Room. "Not one soul."

That this friendless, luckless Amcrican president, so widely perceived as a figure of impotence and ineptitude, would be able to stage the nation's most spectacular, if brief, political comeback seemed a hopeless prospect. But he did, and the manner of his reversal of fortune said much about the exercise of power in the media age, when media strategy and mass opinion polling became vital instruments in the gaining and holding of power. Carter's success demonstrated how even the weakest president, one with ineffectual media communications skills, can nonetheless use the mass media to dominate the news to his own advantage. Conversely, it showed how powerfully a more capable media performer might employ the news media, especially television, to his political advantage.

There was no miracle to his extraordinary act of political levitation. Carter canceled all political events, including a previously accepted debate with Edward Kennedy in Iowa, wrapped himself in the aura of the White House and the flag, and let the networks and Iran do his work for him. They did. His approval ratings in the public opinion polls soared. He swept aside all Democratic opponents, most notably Kennedy, whom he crushed in the early presidential primaries, and appeared headed not only for the nomination but possibly reelection was well.

Then he fell again in public esteem when he produced what the country instantly recognized as a true calamity: a dismally humiliating failure after a secret U.S. military attempt to free the hostages ended disastrously on the night of April 24 at an isolated base, code-named Desert One, in the Iranian Dasht-e-Kavir Desert, 270 miles southeast of Teheran. Everything went wrong. A violent, blinding sandstorm caused one of the rescue helicopters to turn back after its gyroscope overheated and failed, leaving its pilot flying blind and unable to see any landmarks even on the artificial horizon normally provided by the gyroscope. Another helicopter was forced down onto a dry lake bed during the same storm when one of its rotor blades malfunctioned. It never made it to Desert One. The mission was aborted when a third helicopter developed a hydraulic failure upon landing. Its hydraulic pump had burned out and would have to be replaced. No spare was available; none had been brought on the mission. The chopper was deemed unsafe to fly. For want of a pump, the mission was scrubbed.

The final calamity was crushing. During the withdrawal in the dead of the night, one of the remaining helicopters accidentally crashed into a C-130 cargo plane loaded with members of the Delta military rescue team and exploded, igniting fifty-caliber machine gun bullets aboard and sending Redeye missiles pinwheeling erratically from the plane into the darkness. A giant inferno lighted the skies above the desert and touched off alarms in Teheran and Washington.

Americans again awoke to discover their television screens filled with bad news. The president, his manner sorrowful as he spoke of "mechanical failures," gave the news to the country via television from the White House: Eight U.S. soldiers were dead, five others severely burned, seven aircraft destroyed. The television cameras gave the scenes from the Mideast: charred American wreckage and burned American bodies lying on the desert sands.

For Americans this latest debacle became another symbol of a muscle-bound country whose might amounted to naught, proof that America had become the Gulliver of the age, a giant stuck in the sand. Iranians, the primitive, modern-day equivalent of the tiny Lilliputians, had snared the mighty giant America with their tangle of threads. They also snared Jimmy Carter.

At home, economic conditions worsened as interest rates headed toward 21 percent, the highest since the Civil War. Despair, even panic, crept into economic forecasts. Sober people suggested that imposition of highly unpopular wage and price controls might be necessary, and even those might not work. In New York the influential Wall Street economist Henry Kaufman glumly observed, "There is nothing in income, fiscal, or monetary policies to suggest a way out."

The public, so supportive of the president for those first months, became critical of his performance. Carter began to slide in the opinion polls. For months he had listened to every proposal on how to free the hostages. Some of them were preposterous, ranging from delivering the shah for trial in Iran to dropping an atomic bomb on Teheran, but he had weighed them all and found none workable. All diplomatic attempts, public and private, to free the captives had failed. All entreaties to allies came to naught. All secret missions to Paris and Mideast meetings with supposed contacts of the Iranian regime produced nothing. A United Nations mission formed in February to release the hostages only brought more frustration when it ended dismally. Even Carter's attempt to demonstrate a tougher foreign policy stance after a Soviet-sponsored coup in Afghanistan—he imposed an embargo on sale of grain to the Soviet Union, proposed sharply increased U.S. defense spending, and let it be known he was prepared for war if necessary—did not help him politically. By April, when he launched the hostage rescue mission, for the first time Carter trailed his likely Republican opponent, Reagan. A *New York Times*/CBS News poll then showed Reagan leading him slightly by four percentage points.

Operation Rice Bowl, as the rescue mission was officially named in secret, seemed certain to doom Jimmy Carter's presidency. Yet even then it was not over. The disaster in the desert became a catalyst for actions that were to have fateful effect on national and international events long after Carter himself was gone from Washington.

The next morning secret planning began for another rescue mission—officially dubbed Operation Snow Bird*—only this time it was

*For detailed information on Operation Snow Bird, see Steven Emerson's *Secret Warriors* (New York: G. P. Putnam's Sons, 1988), but for a broader discussion of covert planning in the

driven by even greater desire for secrecy and fierce determination to demonstrate success after humiliating failure. A Joint Special Operations Command formed secretly in the Pentagon brought together paramilitary Army, Navy, Marines, and Air Force personnel who would work as a team, not separate entities. In the aftermath of the Desert One failure, with the Pentagon internally blaming the CIA for failure to provide adequate advance intelligence inside Iran, focus shifted from the CIA to the Pentagon for conducting additional covert operations. Soon a wide range of "black ops," or ultrasecret covert operations, worldwide in scope, was being launched and managed out of the Pentagon.

Snow Bird planning proceeded, in deepest secrecy, against the backdrop of the presidential election campaign. By September, Snow Bird was deemed operational, but with a critical missing ingredient: no knowledge of the hostages' location. After the failed rescue mission, the hostages had been dispersed throughout Iran and U.S. intelligence had been unable to pinpoint their exact locations.

Sinking though Carter was, Reagan strategists knew that Carter could still be saved by a successful end to the hostage ordeal. "One of the things that we had concluded early was that a Reagan victory would be nearly impossible if the hostages were released before the election," Michael Deaver recalled. "There was nothing we could do about it. We did, however, begin talking up the idea in August of an 'October surprise.' This had the effect of making anything Carter did before Election Day seem calculating and political."

Location of all the hostages was never determined. Snow Bird never flew. There was no surprise. Carter was defeated.

Carter's hopes for redemption through liberation of the hostages in his remaining hours in office rested on the goodwill of the ayatollah half a world away in Iran and the clocks relentless ticking away his presidency in Washington.

By 8:35 that morning he was informed that planes bearing the

---

last years of the Carter administration that assumed greater scope in the U.S. secret war on terrorism in the Reagan years, the indispensable history is David C. Martin and John Walcott's *Best Laid Plans: The Inside Story of America's War Against Terrorism* (New York: Harper & Row, 1988).

hostages were on rain-slicked runways in Teheran, cleared for take off. Then more delay. An hour and fifteen minutes later a telephone report from Christopher in Algiers: "Takeoff is not imminent, but I can state for certain that it will be before noon."

An hour and five minutes later, 10:45 now, Carter was still in the Oval Office, still unshaven and unchanged for the inaugural ceremonies that were about to begin. His wife, Rosalynn, appealed to him to get ready. The Reagans were due to arrive in just fifteen minutes for the traditional coffee in the Blue Room. Then they all must leave for the Capitol, where the oath of office signaling transfer of power would be administered at high noon as prescribed by the Constitution.

Reluctantly the thirty-ninth president walked briskly down the corridor toward the family quarters, where he quickly shaved and changed into a formal morning suit, the style preferred by Reagan in contrast with the business suit Carter wore at his own inaugural. It was rented. Standing in the presidential bathroom for the last time, combing his hair, he looked at himself in the mirror. He later wrote that he wondered whether it was cumulative stress from four years in the presidency or physical exhaustion from the last few days of the hostage ordeal that made him appear to have aged so much.

Reagan reflected on the physical change, too, when he saw Carter in the Blue Room. "Did you get a look at Carter?" Reagan asked Deaver later. Deaver had, and was shocked. Carter's face was "absolutely ashen," and "he had dark circles under his eyes and it was obvious he had not slept all night."

Soon they entered the long black limousine, bulletproofed and bearing the seal of the president of the United States, and departed from 1600 Pennsylvania Avenue. Even then the grip of the hostages had not loosened on Carter.

Carter thought Reagan affable but oddly incurious as the limousine bore them along Pennsylvania Avenue. Reagan cracked a few jokes but asked no questions about the hostages. There was nothing Reagan could do about them then anyway; they were still Carter's problem, and Carter was still obviously dealing with it. While their vehicle moved slowly toward Capitol Hill, the outgoing president took and placed repeated phone calls. All dealt with the hostages.

Left behind in the White House Situation Room, Carter's aide

Hamilton Jordan juggled two phones as he watched the clock and the television screen showing the preinaugural ceremonies beginning at the Capitol. One of the phones was connected to the presidential limousine. Another was linked to an intelligence officer monitoring the two Algerian planes carrying the hostages in Teheran. The last message relayed to the president in the limousine was encouraging: "The planes have been told to taxi to the end of the runway."

It was possible they could take off before noon while Carter was still president.

Minutes later the White House operator came back on Jordan's phone.

"Mr. Jordan, the president wants you."

"Any news, Ham?"

"No, sir. The reports are that they're actually in the planes on the runway. It could be any minute now."

"That's what you . . . told me five minutes ago!"

"That's what they're telling us."

More minutes passed, and again the president was on the line. He was inside the Capitol now, preparing to leave the building for the outdoor ceremony, which was being staged on an inaugural platform built on the West Front.

Any news? Nothing.

Carter had one last hope. He had instructed his personal aide Phil Wise to notify him the minute the planes took off. If that news came before the stroke of noon, his Secret Service detail would immediately pass him a note on the inaugural platform. Then he could step forward to the microphones and make his last act as president of the United States the announcement that the American hostages were finally free.

CHAPTER 3

THE WINNER

When Ronald Reagan stepped into the limousine to accept the cheers of crowds lining his inaugural route, he was at once the nation's most familiar public figure and the least known. His disarming manner, ruddy Irish good looks, and melodious voice betraying just an edge of raspiness were recognizable everywhere.

For more than forty years Reagan had been Hollywood's version of the genial boy next door, the all-American nice guy. Cocky without arrogance, wisecracking, and fun-loving, he appeared to embody what the country identified as American virtues: informality; humor; patriotism. He had played the part so well so many times that it was hard to separate role from reality.

Perhaps they were, in fact, inseparable. Perhaps, also, at his core there was something unknown or unknowable about Ronald Reagan. Evidence abounds that behind the smiling mask the public saw lay more complicated personality traits: ambition; coldness; courage that emerged in difficult circumstances; a gambler's instinct that led him to cast aside caution and take high risks. He was much more than he seemed to detractors, who continually disparaged him, and much less than his partisan followers believed him to be. "People consistently underestimate him and he will consistently surprise you with his depth," said Robert C. Walker, who helped him become California governor in 1966 and stayed with him until 1980. "He is taken by many people who don't know him well to be superficial. He's not superficial."*

To a singular degree, those who were in a position to observe him best—his children, his only brother, his early girl friends, his devoted aides—testified repeatedly how hard it was to know him.

"It is very difficult in looking back over my relationship with him ever to know exactly how he felt. . . . He's a very difficult guy to figure out what he's really thinking," typically said Paul R. Haerle, a lawyer and Reagan's personal appointments secretary during the first gubernatorial term. "You really always wonder, no matter how close you are to him, if you really know him, as he really is deep down inside. So you don't know."

Lyn Nofziger, a rumpled, irreverent former California newspaper reporter who became Reagan's press secretary in Sacramento and stayed with him for years in various roles, reflected on the same impenetrable quality he had observed. "It's a funny thing about Ronald Reagan," he said. ". . . I always felt for a long time that there was a kind of a veil between him and the rest of the world. You could never really get in next to him. I finally decided, after he became governor and time had gone by, that what you saw was what you got. That you had, in fact, the real Ronald Reagan. That he had become a little aloof, a little careful because as an actor, with all the publicity, and people after you, you have to guard your private life very carefully if you are going to maintain a private life. I think that he just naturally had built a kind of fence between him and the outside world."

Two girl friends, who dated him long before the Hollywood days, both spoke of an elusive quality in Reagan, one remarking, "We were seeing quite a bit of each other, but I always had the feeling that I was with him but he wasn't with me. He was always looking over his shoulder, scanning the crowd."

His older brother, Neil, called Moon, as Ronald was nicknamed Dutch during their childhood, was asked during a University of Cali-

*Unless otherwise attributed, all quotations from Reagan aides and Reagan himself in this and the next chapter are from transcripts of tape-recorded interviews from a Reagan Gubernatorial Era oral history project conducted by California university scholars in 1979, a year before Reagan became president. See Notes and Sources for further amplification of these revealing sources.

fornia oral history interview if he thought other close Reagan associates interviewed were correct when they uniformly volunteered comments about his aloofness and frustration at their inability to know him. "Yes," he said, "but that's not true [just] of Ronald Reagan. That's true of the whole group. The motion picture business does that to you. . . . I always say that Ronald is my mother's boy and I'm my father's boy; but he is my father's boy in not being demonstrative."

It was not Hollywood, though, that shaped Ronald Reagan. As his brother said, "He's really not a demonstrative guy. I don't know how to put it. He was a great swimmer, but I taught Maureen [Reagan's first child] to swim before she could walk. He didn't bother with her. . . . I taught her to swim. . . . I can't picture him doing that. . . ." Asked if he could envision his brother taking time out to help other children, Neil Reagan said, "No, no, no, not at all. He's more the type that thinks they should be on their own."

With Ronald Reagan there is no need to practice psychiatry without a license. The factual record of his life presents fascinating continuities and discontinuities. The discontinuities are obvious.

Like many formidable egoists, he was the son of an unsuccessful father and strong mother. His father, Jack, raised an orphan and become a drifter, was an alcoholic, not, by the available testimony, a mean or brutal drunk, but a man given to such binges of drinking that he could not keep a job.

Many children of alcoholic parents survive by withdrawing into themselves and creating their own reality. They invent themselves. Some learn to deny reality. Something similar seems to have happened with Reagan. He mastered, or was forced to learn by harsh circumstances, the ability to disconnect himself from his background and early environment. He exhibited character traits resembling those associated with what psychiatrists sometimes call the indestructible child, the child who becomes capable of sustaining and surmounting any amount of misfortune. In time he became a person seemingly able to absorb blows and defeat with astonishing resilience. He drew upon a rare unquenchability of spirit.

"As a kid I lived in a world of pretend," he himself said later. "But by the time I was eight or nine I felt self-conscious about it. People made fun of me. . . . 'What are you doing, kid? Talking to yourself?' Enough people make enough cracks like that, and a sensitive boy . . . begins to feel a little silly. . . . So from then on he doesn't pretend openly. . . . That was the way it was with me, anyway. I had a great imagination and I used to love to make up plays and act in them myself . . . but I soon got self-conscious."

Reagan's instinct to stand apart was formed early, a natural result of his experience.* His mother, Nelle, is said to have worried that her son's ironclad control led him into two worlds, one public, the other private, enabling him to suppress reaction to his father's drinking. Even as a child he seems not to have discussed his feelings with others, including Nelle. Yet she was clearly a formative influence on him. Strong-willed and drawn to the make-believe world of the theater (she and her husband rented play scripts and performed before townspeople in a room above the town's only bank), Nelle Reagan was sustained by a belief in religious fundamentalism as a zealous Disciple of Christ, and she pressed upon her son the need to perform graciously in public.

Not surprisingly, Reagan's world of pretend led him to identify with superhuman heroes, such as Edgar Rice Burroughs's Tarzan and John Carter of Mars (and later Louis L'Amour's strong, silent western types possessed of extraordinary strength and able to outshoot and outfight anyone). He identified, too, with ballyhooed sports heroes of his boyhood and early adult years, Jack Dempsey, Babe Ruth, Red Grange, drawn larger than life in the tabloid culture of the twenties.

Reagan's desire to be an admired central figure was manifested when he became a lifeguard during summers in Illinois. "You know why I had such fun at it?" he once remarked of that lifeguard period. "Because I was the only one up there on the guard stand. It was like a stage. Everyone had to look at me."

In his first job out of college he demonstrated natural facility at broadcasting play-by-play descriptions of major-league baseball games from Station WHO in Des Moines. This was in the pretelevi-

*Neil Reagan gave a revealing example of this when he described how "Dutch" liked to spend time alone with his birds' egg collection rather than associate with other groups of boys their age in the town pool hall, as Neil liked to do: "He would never do anything like that. He would rather be up there gazing at his birds' eggs."

sion radio days when only the most fragmentary information—a ball, a strike, a hit, an out, a run, an inning, a new pitcher, a pinch hitter—was available from Western Union telegraph tickers. As a radio announcer broadcasting hundreds of miles from the stadium, Reagan was forced to rely on his own imagination to make up scenes that had just occurred.

While Ronald Reagan spoke publicly with nostalgia about his small-town upbringing, the degree to which the American Midwest was his credential rather than his essence was striking. His pioneer credential was the new America of California, not the old one of the Midwest, and he came by it as naturally as if he had crossed the plains and mountains by ox wagon from Illinois.

His own life was riddled with contradictions. He claimed to speak for family stability, self-reliance, continuity, church, country. Yet he didn't stay at home or remain married to his first wife, and he failed to forge harmonious relationships with his children, producing bitterness and estrangement among his family. He didn't acknowledge vital assistance in federal grants and programs, target of his ridicule in a thousand campaign speeches, that enabled his father, Jack, to survive the depression through a New Deal WPA job and his hometown ("literally flushed with an infusion of government money") to grow and prosper.

He didn't attend church with regularity. He hadn't gone overseas to fight in the great war of his generation, though as the writer Garry Wills reported, he talked as if he had, falsely claiming to have photographed Nazi death camps for the Signal Corps. His wife then, the actress Jane Wyman, reinforced such mythology in interviews by describing the hardship of having her husband "off to war."*

Reagan actually remained in Hollywood, assigned to an Air Force team making military propaganda films at the Hal Roach Studio, dubbed Fort Roach by its personnel. He had received one mili-

*Garry Wills's superb book *Reagan's America: Innocents at Home* (New York: Doubleday & Company, Inc., 1987) recounts how fan magazines treated Reagan as if he were away for the war. They described Jane Wyman (whose real name was Sarah Jane Mayfield, or Fulks; the record does not seem clear) as a lonely service wife who bravely "endured her husband's absence." As *Modern Screen* magazine wrote, "It's nine months now since Ronald Reagan said, 'So long, button-nose,' to his wife and baby and went off to join his regiment." The "regiment" was at the Hal Roach Studio near their home.

tary deferment at the request of Warner Brothers to make a "patriotic" film. A second deferment request was denied, and he was called to active service four months after Pearl Harbor.

The public saw Reagan as the strong, silent, courageous John Wayne cowboy type, the John Wayne who in perfect Hollywood fashion became the prototypical heroic American, not the real Marion Michael Morrison/Wayne whose true rural Iowa background was one of poverty and unhappiness and whose experience as a cowboy began when he was picked to play the part in Hollywood. Reagan's own heroes all were similarly fearless types. Yet he himself had a fear of flying and suffered from what he once described as a "lifelong tendency to claustrophobia." For a long time after entering public life he refused to travel by airplane. No matter how great the distance, he traveled only by car or train.

Reagan's public portrait was of immense affability. Yet he had a hot temper that occasionally flared in private, though almost never in public. Once, while governor, he became "extremely angry" during a luncheon with his personal staff and members of his cabinet. He was so infuriated that he took off his glasses (which he didn't wear in public), threw them on the table, and shouted, "Damn it to hell, if this is true and they haven't been shown to me, by God, I want to know why!"

This outburst was prompted when an adviser said members of his staff deliberately had kept figures from him that affected a state tax withholding controversy. His anger startled those present, but they weren't surprised at his reaction. They knew him to be bitterly opposed to withholding taxes.

The public Reagan appeared to be open. Yet he had a penchant for secrecy. In 1939 and 1940, when he turned out film after film for Warner Brothers, he made several serial espionage-adventure movies playing Lieutenant Brass Bancroft of the U.S. Secret Service and seems to have taken to the role of secret agent. One of those Bancroft serials provided the earliest example of how Reagan's acting life resembled his later political career. In reviewing a new Reagan/Bancroft thriller on July 4, 1940, the *New York Times* critic wrote:

> A new spy scare hit Broadway yesterday with the arrival of *Murder in the Air*. However, Ronald Reagan and the Warners' FBI [*sic*]

> agents have the situation well in hand. After some 60 minutes of highly incredible melodramatic incident, the government's prized "inertia projector" is rescued from foreign hands and the saboteurs are either killed off or jailed. (The "inertia projector" is an instrument which fouls electric current at the source; its amazing practicality is illustrated when it is focused on the plane in which the enemy agents attempt to flee the country.)

Substitute "particle beam" for "inertia projector" and "missiles" for "planes," and there, more than forty years earlier, was the essence of Ronald Reagan's so-called Star Wars plan, or Strategic Defense Initiative, with its incredible fail-safe space shield that would save Earth.

It was during that pre-World War II period that Reagan appears to have been contacted for the first time by the FBI. His name, "Ronald Reagan, Warner Brothers Studio, Hollywood," was included in a list of eleven people forwarded by Washington FBI national headquarters to a special agent stationed in Hollywood. He was listed as someone the FBI believed "might be of some assistance to the Bureau." As president of the Screen Actors Guild Reagan became a secret informer for the FBI and was assigned a number, T-10, as a confidential informant. This was in 1947, during anti-Communist witch-hunting days of the House Un-American Activities Committee. It set the stage for the Joseph R. McCarthy period of character assassination that followed in the early 1950s.*

His brother, Moon, who followed him to Southern California and became senior vice-president of the McCann-Erickson advertising agency in Los Angeles with wide contacts in the movie colony, had begun spying for the FBI then. He said he persuaded Ronald to do so, too.

As Moon tells it, one night he received a melodramatic midnight phone call from his brother. Dutch wanted to see him immediately. His brother said he was calling from a Nutburger pay phone at the corner of Sunset Boulevard and Doheny Avenue after returning from

*The FBI documentation is the result of detective work by author Anne Edwards, who obtained FBI documents relating to Reagan through Freedom of Information Act requests. She describes them in *Early Reagan: The Rise to Power* (New York: William Morrow and Company, Inc. 1987). For more elaboration of the FBI connection, see Dan E. Moldea's *Dark Victory: Ronald Reagan, MCA, and the Mob* (New York: Viking Press, 1986).

a board meeting of a film group, one that Moon previously warned his brother the FBI suspected had been infiltrated by Communists or fellow travelers. "So I put a pair of trousers on and a shirt and drove up the hill," Moon said. "Here he is parked. I got in, and . . . he says, 'You wouldn't believe it. It just came to me tonight. We have a rule that if a board member misses two meetings without being excused, you're automatically off the board. There's a gal out at the such-and-such studio had missed two board meetings, and so they were off, and now we've got to find somebody else. It suddenly dawned on me that over the last several months every time one of these cases came up, she had just the individual that would be excellent as a replacement. I managed to filch the minute books before I left. I can show you the page where *her* board members [supposedly Communists] became a majority of the board, with her replacements.' "

Moon looked at his brother and said, "Junior, what do you suppose I've been talking about all these weeks and weeks and weeks?"

As for Reagan's Midwest upbringing, the strains of American history that coursed through the town he considered home, Dixon, Illinois,* a farming community one hundred miles west of Chicago on the Rock River, do not seem to have influenced (or interested) him in the slightest. There Abraham Lincoln and Jefferson Davis, the two men who were to lead the nation against itself and result in the creation of a new one, served as officers during the frontier uprising of the Black Hawk Indians in 1832. There, before the steps of the new country courthouse on a broiling summer day in 1856, Lincoln spoke for two hours and urged his fellow citizens to elect the newly formed Republican party's first presidential candidate, the grandiloquent Californian John C. Frémont, "the Pathfinder" of the West and opponent of slavery, the issue then threatening to tear asunder the Union.

There, too, was the birthplace of the great-grandfather of the most famous, and tragic, twentieth-century Native American figure

*He was actually born in Tampico, Illinois, population eight hundred, in a second-floor apartment which had no indoor toilet facilities and stood over a bakery converted from a bar. The town was one block long, with a general store, a grain elevator, a Civil War cannon mounted on wooden standards in a small park adjoining the railroad depot, and coal bins stationed along tracks that ran through town. The Reagans lived on the other, poorer side of the tracks.

Jim Thorpe, the great athlete whose Olympic medals were taken from him and who became an alcoholic. If Reagan was aware of these facts, or interested in them, he does not seem to have remarked on it.

Unlike other midwesterners, who took pride in tracing their roots from New England and identified with the ethical standards they brought west with them, or southerners, who gloried in ancestral associations and regional myths, Reagan evidenced no sense of geographical identity or family tradition. Like many Californians, he carried little hereditary baggage. What counted then was today, now, not yesterday, last week. He was, in this sense, a perfect representative of California as it had evolved by the 1980s and especially of Hollywood, America's world of make-believe.

Here, he was, a president from the Middle West, but not really so; a politician who began as a liberal New Deal Democrat but became the symbol of the new Republican conservative era. He was western, not eastern, in thought and impulse and action; a man who professed to lead a moral crusade without holding great moral convictions. He called himself a conservative, but he was a conservative of a new class, not of the old. He was a consumer instead of a preserver, a raider instead of a protector.

Reagan's sense of entitlement was Californian in another respect: in being liked; in being preeminent; in lack of concern for the absence of inherited or earned credentials.

He was not intellectually curious, not deeply read, and acted from instinct rather than reflection. Despite rhetoric about his conservative ideology and the wave of political conservatism supposedly sweeping America, he was not an ideologue. He was the vehicle around which conservative forces could and did rally, the magnet that attracted a coterie of conservative journalists and writers and ambitious young economic theorists who proclaimed sacred dogma and argued theoretically pure positions.

But these were not Reagan's chosen associates any more than were the religious true believers who saw Reagan's potential as spokesman. Yet their efforts on his behalf provided one more paradox: It took the support of the self-proclaimed Moral Majority of born-again Christians to give the United States its first divorced president.

Unlike these zealots, Reagan in personal relationships adopted a more tolerant view of personal behavior. His friends were people like himself, successful self-made men who enjoyed the good California life created through their own efforts. Like Reagan, many of them had left behind humble origins to come west to find their destiny. They, too, had invented themselves. Their proudly displayed trappings of success, Mercedeses and Jaguars, oceanfront and desert vacation hideaways, were emblems of worth. Reagan's administration in Washington would be a savings and loan administration as it had been in California and would be staffed by many of the same people.

Reagan shared their traits in his attitudes about government. Presidents who immediately preceded him, Carter, Nixon, Johnson, Kennedy, took a hands-on approach to government. Reagan was hands-off. He was more interested in being popular than in being recognized as dealing with hard problems of governance; he preferred to reign rather than rule. Reagan was not cut from the cloth of those who through will and talent bend history to their wishes, creating new forces and movements along with standards and values. For all his ideological rhetoric, Reagan skimmed the waves. He did not plunge deeply beneath the surface. While he professed to hold Franklin Delano Roosevelt as his presidential model, his true preferred presidential type was Calvin Coolidge. Reagan's political instinct was not toward FDR-style activism but toward Coolidge-like isolation, not reform but laissez-faire.

Every president of substance before him had been a builder and, at best, a creator. Reagan's impulses were to abet creative impulses elsewhere. He was not interested in the execution of policies as such. His interest was in enforcing certain general principles: combating communism; reducing government; cutting bureaucracy; removing constraints on free enterprise; turning over the forces of government to outsiders; "privatizing" public services.

Ronald Reagan was weightless in a sense that set him apart from those presidents who came to power with a strong impulse to govern. His impulse was to govern *against* the government. He seemed to take it for granted that he could appoint people of dubious qualification and expect that government would work well. Either he didn't examine things sufficiently to enable him to gain knowledge of the immense difficulties of governing in a democracy, or he simply didn't care.

He did resemble Franklin Roosevelt, however, in two important respects. "Mr. Justice" Oliver Wendell Holmes's famous characterization of Roosevelt—a second-class mind but a first-class temperament—applied equally to Reagan. And Reagan, like Roosevelt, represented the forging of a new political force in America. The man who gave the impression of an anecdotal rambler, a public entertainer instead of a public educator, also headed a political coalition never before formed. Old New Dealers, old unionists, old actors, old socialists, old Communists, old isolationists, New Right fundamentalists and Puritans, new exponents of laissez-faire, new ideologues, new radicals, new internationalists; southern Democrats, western Republicans, descendants of midwestern prairie populists and southern rural evangelists—all these had gathered behind Reagan and made possible his opportunity to lead America in the eighties.

One central question surrounded Ronald Reagan as he rode to power on January 20, 1981. Had he stumbled his way onto the national stage through historical accident, or was he actually more responsible for the forces of change than he was commonly credited for? Was it possible that this old grade B Hollywood actor, this spouter of slogans and teller of apocryphal stories, had in him elements of political genius? That is, genius of the political leader who effectuates change so effortlessly that people are unaware fundamental change is occurring?

In this the answer lay in California. Just as California for generations had symbolized the dream that lured Americans west, the desire to create a classless and casual American culture beyond the mountains, so Reagan's California past was to become the nation's political future.

CHAPTER 4

THE NEW AMERICA

The rise of Ronald Reagan as a political symbol of a new America coincided with the rise of what came to be called the Sunbelt States and the preeminence of California. Only in the mid-1960s did California surpass New York as the most populous state, and only then did the inevitable consequence of unrivaled natural resources, abundant open space, benign climate, rapid growth, and phenomenal economic and educational expansion finally elevate California into the class for which it had been destined. It was much more than one of the fifty American states, more even than the nation's superstate. As Reagan often said, California would be the world's seventh-ranking economic power if it stood alone. It was the place where movements flourished in bewildering profusion and where experimentation in personal life-style, in sex and language, music and film and video image, architecture and apparel, was viewed with tolerance. It strongly influenced the rest of the nation.

Ideas now flowed in waves from west to east, it was said, reversing the old pattern of influence, so that what started on the public campus of Berkeley would in time be adopted as the new thinking even in the elite atmosphere of Harvard.

This was an oversimplification. Despite public fascination with frivolous California styles, and despite the far more serious way in which ideas and formulas produced on California campuses and in California laboratories genuinely shaped the future, considerable influence over the nation's destinies remained in the East.

The center of finance and commerce still stood, as it had since George Washington was inaugurated there, on Wall Street. From northeastern private colleges and universities came the next wave of recruits who would staff and ultimately lead the great law firms and publishing houses. From the television network news headquarters in New York City came the collective self-portrait of America drawn daily and telecast into the home of every American family. From the political capital in Washington came the political consensus that resulted in the dispersal of national treasure, laws and regulations that affected every citizen, and direction of the world's mightiest military and paramilitary forces.

For all the obvious new importance of California in American life, among eastern power bases of capitalism, communications, and politics there was a strong tendency to discount its real influence.

California was not to be taken seriously. It was flaky, mellow. California was Lotusland, dark glasses, Hollywood; all show and no substance. In eastern eyes especially, its principal players were seen as insubstantial, and none more so than Reagan, who was believed to be a perfect blend of illusory worlds of Hollywood make-believe and California-kooky politics. Even some who came to admire Reagan after serving him politically, confessed they initially viewed him from an eastern perspective and dismissed him as another California aberration.

One such was Norman ("Skip") Watts, an intent young political operative who spent hundreds and probably thousands of hours with Reagan during the 1967 to 1972 gubernatorial period. Watts, grandson of a conservative congressman from the San Fernando Valley, Edgar Hiestand, and a Richard Nixon advance man before joining Reagan's inner team, began to reassess Reagan after watching him debate Robert F. Kennedy in May 1967 over network television.

Kennedy was then the nation's most intensely publicized and romanticized political figure, perceived by many as the nation's potential leader. Like Scotland's Bonnie Prince Charlie, Robert Kennedy would signal his loyal legions to arise, reclaim the crown, and rekindle the flagging national spirit. Then in the Senate, Kennedy was viewed widely as a likely successful challenger to President Lyndon Johnson, who was trapped in the increasingly unpopular war in Vietnam and civil disruptions at home. To the extent that Reagan figured at all in national consciousness then, after having been governor only four months, he was seen as a passing California fad. So California voters had placed an actor in the governor's mansion? What else was new?

Skip Watts shared that view. "I think the network people just saw Reagan as somebody who was articulate and formidable to oppose Kennedy," he recalled. "They didn't want Nixon or Rockefeller. They wanted some fresh faces. I was disdainful of Reagan. . . . I guess the East Coast syndrome had hit. . . . Anyway, the point is that I remember watching that [debate] and being impressed with Reagan and his ability to stand in there with Bobby Kennedy. In fact, he really did Bobby in on that show."

Many who were "keeping watch" over such political encounters for signs of new forces and personalities failed to read that lesson, even though Reagan had clearly, as Watts said, outperformed Kennedy.*

Watts discovered that others held misconceptions about Reagan when they began working for him. "Some felt he was cardboard and prop cards and Hollywood," Watts said of some of those on Reagan's staff. "But most came to realize that wasn't the case. He was deeper than most people think."

The popular picture of Reagan, then and later, was of an amiable fellow in over his head—the actor who can't perform without his cue cards. Some of his associates contributed to an impression that Reagan was lazy and even stupid. But numerous observers of Reagan testify to his determination and personal ambition. Though many who worked with him say he seldom took charge of meetings he chaired, they learned not to mistake this trait for disinterest. Appearances aside, the evidence is that Reagan burned with desire to

*A notable exception was my colleague David S. Broder, who, with his coauthor, Stephen Hess, in *The Republican Establishment: The Present and Future of the GOP* (New York: Harper & Row, 1967), described how Reagan "easily dominated the program with his firm and well-documented defense of the American military involvement in Vietnam" and identified Reagan then as a strong presidential prospect who could well win and change the country's direction.

achieve his political goals. The end, not the means of governing, was what counted.

Once, in Sacramento, someone showed him a crude cartoon poking fun at the welfare state and supposed chiselers who lived off the public dole. Reagan loved it. He sent a copy to one of his cabinet secretaries, James Hall, and scrawled a note that Hall later framed as testimony to Reagan's real political thinking and as evidence that Reagan thought of himself as leading a political revolution:

> Dear Jim:
> You fellows should
> have this as a reminder
> of the good old days—
> B.U.B.—Before Us Bastards.
> Ron

So, too, the popular dismissal of Reagan as "only an actor" capable only of reading lines others prepared for him. Reagan spent endless hours perfecting his political speeches. He understood, if others didn't, that his training as an actor was a great asset for a politician, especially in the age of television.

His preoccupation with what he said, and how he said it, his constant employment of cue cards, for instance, did not deserve the scorn they received then and later. To Reagan, they were essentials in the art of political leadership. They were deliberately chosen tools of his new trade, and they reflected what *he* thought, the message *he* wished to deliver, not just the thoughts crafted by hired ghostwriters. "What he was happiest with was working over his four-by-six cards," Paul Haerle remembered of those Sacramento days, "and how he was going to communicate Cap [Caspar] Weinberger's latest ideas about tax policy, what fiscal reforms ought to be initiated, and how it would cut down waste in Sacramento, at his next speech, or in his next news conference, or in his next televised appearance of some sort or another."

The public also saw Reagan as a man given to telling innocent stories, certainly not the kind of person who relished dirty jokes. Yet the testimony is that among Reagan's apparent vast repertoire of stories were innumerable raunchy ones that he told with pleasure and at great length. Some were scatological and racially offensive, according to those who heard him, though his brand of humor tended to be more gentle than insulting. He seems to have had an insatiable appetite for the telling of them.*

That wasn't the side of Reagan the public saw. From the beginning his staff seems to have sheltered him. One remembered how staff members felt "we had to protect him and keep him away from the press and keeping him from putting his foot in his mouth."

An underlying vein of contempt, perhaps unintentional but nonetheless striking, runs through recollections of those who were instrumental in forging Ronald Reagan's political career. Their accounts, again perhaps unwittingly, give the impression they viewed Reagan as a malleable figurehead who would enable them to achieve what *they* wished politically.

Repeatedly they tell of lecturing Reagan, of educating him, in their view, as they attempted to transform his political opinions.

This was true of Moon Reagan, who testified that he continually argued politics with his brother and sought to persuade him to share Moon's staunchly anti-New Deal beliefs. This was true, too, of the man who accompanied Reagan throughout the country when Reagan became host of the "General Electric Theater" in 1954 and GE spokesman for eight years.

"His politics were in the process of change," remembered Earl B. Dunckel, a burly former newspaperman known to his friends as Dunk. As a GE public relations man Dunckel was responsible for developing the concepts of the "GE Theater" and for scheduling the national tours Reagan made for it. "He had been a New Deal Democrat," Dunckel said. "He didn't like the way things were going, the trend of things. I was, am, and always will be an arch conservative. Always. I was drumbeating this at him all the time. Whenever he tried to defend New Dealism, or what was passing for it at the time,

*In Sacramento people who saw Reagan regularly in his governorship days told me that in certain men-only social gatherings Reagan regaled lobbyists and political people with bawdy stories. Years later they could still recall word for word "Ronald Reagan's favorite dirty joke," a joke with a notably offensive racial punch line. In his memoir about his experiences as Reagan's White House chief of staff (*Donald T. Regan for the Record* [New York: Harcourt Brace Jovanovich, 1988]), Regan wrote: "The president knew more funny stories, ranging from jokes innocent enough for a Sunday-school class to the raunchiest locker-room humor, than anyone I had ever met."

we would have some rather spirited arguments. I think this helped him to realize, as he put it later, that he didn't desert the Democratic Party; the Democratic Party deserted him. They had turned the corner and gone a different direction, he felt."

Reagan's GE experience was critical in his development as a public figure. He had been suggested as TV host by the advertising agency Batten, Barton, Durstine & Osborne, which had good contacts at the Music Corporation of America, the influential manager of Hollywood talent, including Reagan. Reagan fitted what GE wanted. "We had been very, very definite as to the kind of person we wanted," Dunckel said. "Good moral character, intelligent. Not the kind of person with the reputation for the social ramble. . . . When Ron was suggested, it went through almost immediately."

GE sought something more than good character; it was also concerned with political beliefs. As Dunckel put it, GE was then "ultraconservative" and "ultra careful that no touch of anything 'negative' would attach to any of its people." This was at the peak of McCarthyism, when anti-Communist fervor seized the nation, and GE was in the forefront of corporate battles with what it perceived to be Communist leanings among electrical unions. It was also a leading business exponent of the belief that excessive liberalism dominated government and imperiled American society, a view reinforced inside the company by a massive conspiracy and restraint of trade antitrust suit brought against it and other major electrical companies by the federal government.*

For Reagan, opportunity to host a national television program came when his movie career was foundering and his divorce from Jane Wyman did not help his all-American boy-next-door image. Dunckel decided to have Reagan personally visit GE's seventy-five plants around the country, exposing him to many of the company's 250,000 employees. "One of the objectives of this, and I stated this in my plan," Dunckel explained, "was to have Ron meet and charm these GE vice presidents all over the country so they would stay off our backs long enough for us to get the program moving. . . . My theory was that this guy is so charming and so nice that if you met him, you couldn't dislike him. If you liked him, you weren't going to

*_U.S. v. General Electric Co.,_ 272 U.S. 476 (1926).

do anything to throw obstacles in the way of the program with which he was associated."

Those months on the road with Reagan, racing from plant to plant and then back to Hollywood for the shooting of "GE Theater" shows, made an indelible impression on Dunckel and, it appears, on Reagan, too. "I practically lived with the man," Dunckel remembered. "We ran for trains together. We walked plants together. We spent our spare time together. We had hotel suites together. We did everything together, almost."

And all the while "Dunk" continued to push his political views on Reagan: "I can't think of anything we didn't cover. . . . This was an era when the public was first starting to realize how far left government was bending and was starting to get concerned about it. So this was something . . . that we kept discussing."

Dunckel's brand of political conservatism found conspiracies rampant everywhere, even in the conservative company for which he worked. He believed that there were "left-leaning GE executives" fairly high up in the company. "Most of them, I don't think, were liberals by nature," he explained. "They were liberals out of fear, particularly those people who read the *New York Times.* It was the first thing they did every morning. All you read in the papers then was the liberal message. The liberals were very, very effective as far as propaganda was concerned. . . ."

Gradually Dunckel saw a change in Reagan: "During this time, through a juxtaposition of many things, he came to the realization that he was no longer a Democrat, that the gap had widened just too far to be bridged."

As Reagan toured GE plants scattered throughout thirty-eight states, plant managers, eager to capitalize on their hired celebrity, began asking him to make a few remarks as a community public relations device at local service clubs, Rotary, Kiwanis, and Optimists. These brief appearances were so successful that word quickly spread to other GE towns. Soon he was giving more and more short speeches (sometimes as many as fourteen a day) that became more and more political in content. Just as theater people perfected their plays and acts in road tours and summer tryouts, so Reagan's long travels for GE became political tryouts for greater public engagements.

Even before Dunckel and GE, Reagan had begun to perfect a definable political style and message in national appearances. By the early fifties, at least two years before he began working for GE, he had established his themes of flag-waving patriotism laced with warnings that America faced dangerous new ideological struggles. Two passages from his June 1952 commencement speech entitled "America the Beautiful" at small William Woods College for women at Fulton, Missouri, are especially interesting as evidence of how he employed fables to make political points:

> There is a legend about the group of fathers of this country meeting in a long debate in Independence Hall regarding the signing of the Declaration of Independence. As the hours wore on and the talk was filled with the sound of treason, traitors, heads rolling, we shall hang, at the very peak of this, there stood up a man and [*sic*] spoke out and with his voice all was stilled. He said, "Sign that document, sign it if tomorrow your heads roll from the headsman's axe. Sign that document because tomorrow and the days to come, your children and all the children of all the days to come will judge you for what you do this day." As he went on speaking his oratory was so great, his words so sincere and so moving that there was sudden movement to the front of the room, and the Declaration of Independence was signed. When the ceremony was completed and they turned to find the man that had swayed the issue, they could not find him. The doors were guarded, and they asked the guards and no one had seen anyone leave; and no one knows to this day, although his words are recorded, who the man was nor could they find anyone who had spoken the words that caused the Declaration to be signed.

Such an incident, of course, never happened. Nor, so far as it can be determined, has anything remotely resembling that story been written about, recorded, or passed on as "a legend" about the signing of the Declaration of Independence. Ronald Reagan seems to have made it up out of whole cloth. It was invented, an apparent product of his fanciful world of pretend.

Similarly, a second story he told that day was offered as refutation of what he called momism: the tendency, then fashionable, he claimed, to deplore "the influence of the American female on the men of this man's world and blaming them for the fact that a large number of the young men have been unable or unwilling to face the test of [the Korean] war in behalf of their country." If that were so, Reagan said, momism was equally responsible for the bravery of sixteen million young men who were willing to fight in Korea, just as momism had contributed to the bravery of young Americans in World War II. He then told a story about a U.S. B-17 bomber returning to England from a mission over Germany that he continued to repeat publicly for at least thirty years, always with powerful effect on audiences:

> Disabled by ground fire, losing altitude, they had taken a direct burst in the ball turret underneath the B-17, the ball turret gunner was wounded, and the turret was jammed so they could not get him out. Finally the pilot had to order, "Bail out," and as the men started to leave the plane, the trapped wounded kid in the ball turret knew he was being left behind and he cried out in terror. Even the dry words in the citation in military language for heroism cannot hide the drama and the nobility of what happened then. The last man to leave the plane saw the co-pilot sit down and take the boy's hand and he said, "Never mind, son, we'll ride it down together." Congressional Medal of Honor posthumously awarded. . . .*

Reagan's association with Dunckel and the speeches he made for GE enabled him to polish these and similar stories, many just as false. But the eight-year GE experience was not the first link in Reagan's break from his previous New Deal liberalism; long before he took to the field for GE, he had veered sharply away from his earlier views.

The first formative influence in his political evolution grew out of his experience as six-term president of the Screen Actors Guild. He came to believe that the guild, and most film industry unions, either had been taken over or were strongly influenced by the Communists after World War II. It was this belief that led him into secretly

*While traveling with Reagan early in his 1980 presidential campaign, I and other reporters heard him tell this story several times a day and saw him cry on cue each time that he delivered the kicker line, his voice breaking as he said, "Never mind, son, we'll ride this one down together." No such incident is known to have occurred in World War II, and no Medal of Honor was awarded for anything resembling this story. The story was either the product of Reagan's imagination or a scene he remembered from a World War II Hollywood movie.

assisting the FBI in its antisubversive activities and publicly testifying as a friendly witness before the House Un-American Activities Committee anti-Communist hearings in Washington.

Reagan's second marriage was another factor in his political change. Nancy Davis, like Jane Wyman and himself, was a child of early misfortune and bad family luck. Born Anne Francis Robbins, she, too, had been abandoned by her natural father and, like others involved in Reagan's personal life, was drawn to the stage and to a Hollywood film career. She came by it naturally; she was the daughter of an actress, Edith Luckett, who had performed as a trouper with George M. Cohan, and the niece of a theater stock company manager in Washington, D.C. Nancy Reagan's stepfather, Dr. Loyal Davis, whom she revered, enabled her to attend Smith College and was himself a strong-willed and outspoken ultraconservative Chicago neurosurgeon. Dr. Davis had a desert home in Arizona, where he became a close friend of Barry Goldwater. There Davis engaged his new son-in-law in many political conversations, including ones about a Reagan political career.

Some accounts of Reagan's evolution from liberal to conservative depict him as a man adrift, passively responding to events instead of trying to anticipate and turn them to his advantage. It is a romantic portrait of a man borne by fate toward a destiny he neither imagined nor sought, and one Reagan himself embellished, but it is untrue. Ronald Reagan was not a reluctant actor upon history's stage. Though he repeatedly denied having had political ambitions or even wanting to become a political candidate, his accounts are flatly contradicted by the testimony of those intimately involved in getting him to run. Even at small Eureka College, twenty miles from Peoria, Illinois, where he was an undistinguished student but a "big man on campus," Reagan was attracted to politics. A speech he delivered while leading a student strike in a move to oust the college president after a ban on campus dancing made a lasting impression on him: "I discovered that night that an audience had a feel to it and in the parlance of the theater, that audience and I were together. . . . They came to their feet with a roar. . . . It was heady wine. Hell, with two more lines I could have had them riding through 'every Middlesex village and farm'—without horses yet."

In fact, Reagan thought about politics, participated in it, and seems to have considered a political career often. As early as 1941 the actor Dick Powell suggested to him that Hollywood friends would raise funds to finance a congressional race if Reagan would switch parties and become a Republican. Interest in politics led him into union leadership in Hollywood. It was instrumental in the failure of his marriage to Jane Wyman, who complained that all Ronnie was interested in was politics.

The possibility of a Reagan political career had been looming for at least several years before the idea of becoming governor took hold. It was broached to him directly, and he took it seriously, not lightly. Politics was a motivating factor in his brother's mind when Moon was instrumental in getting Ron the starring role on the network television program "Death Valley Days" soon after Reagan's GE contract expired in 1962. "It kept him in the public eye for what I figured might be helpful if he ran for governor in a couple of years," Moon recalled.

Also in 1962, before a Goldwater Republican presidential candidacy, Reagan was approached about becoming a candidate for the U.S. Senate seat then held by a Republican, Thomas Kuchel. The offer of support came from some of the same wealthy conservative Southern Californians who were responsible for shaping Reagan's political career. And Reagan seriously entertained *that* idea before rejecting it.

"I went with a group of people, including Holmes Tuttle, to see Ronald Reagan at his home to see if we could get him to run for U.S. Senate back in . . . 1962," said Edward Mills, another self-made millionaire and major fund raiser for conservative Republican candidates in California. "He didn't give us an immediate answer, yes or no, but he said he'd like to have a week to think about it and [asked] if we'd come back. He made an appointment for us to return. We went back as a group, and he told us he didn't think he could make the financial sacrifice that would be necessary based on his family obligations and on his own financial situation and the salary that would be available as a U.S. Senator should he be successful. So he declined."

That same year of 1962, according to Lyn Nofziger, a group of Californians asked Reagan to run for governor. "Congressman H. Allen Smith from Glendale was a friend of mine," Nofziger recalled, "and he told me that a group of people had gone to Reagan. I said, 'What, that liberal?' Smith said, 'No, no, he's changed!' "

Two years later Reagan's involvement in the Goldwater campaign was much more than the casual giving of occasional speeches that he claimed. His brother, Moon, worked closely with Goldwater and helped polish Goldwater's television appearances. Reagan was brought into the Goldwater campaign early and became the Arizona senator's California cochairman. He spoke tirelessly on Goldwater's behalf throughout the state and around the country.

Before Goldwater was defeated in the Lyndon Johnson landslide, both Reagan and his wealthy political backers seem to have thought that he could become the ideological heir of the Republican right and its future leader. Reagan's nationally televised speech for Goldwater in the last month of the presidential campaign, which attracted such attention to him, appears to have been given with that in mind. Reagan's backers, and he himself, were already looking beyond Goldwater. Some say Reagan had his eye fixed on the presidency from that point and was already planning a presidential campaign four years away in 1968. Whether that is so cannot be entirely determined, but there is no doubt that Reagan was driven by political ambitions; all of his actions bespoke it.

Typical of Reagan's supporters was Rus Walton, a political operative who later worked for Reagan in Sacramento and helped recruit some of Reagan's political team.

Like many of those who became active in California Republican conservative circles, Walton was not a native Californian. He had made his way west from New Jersey, winding up in California courtesy of the U.S. Air Force. And like Earl Dunckel, Walton made his first contacts with Reagan through a business public relations background. Walton's ultraconservative political views motivated him to help form the United Republicans of California, whose acronym, UROC, symbolized a new conservative force that would launch a new national movement.

In Sinbad the Sailor's mythical adventures, a roc is a bird large enough to carry away an elephant. That, as Walton explained, was UROC's goal from the beginning: "to get the Republican Party where we thought it should go." UROC was a major factor in Goldwater's California presidential primary victory, a vital step toward his nomination and the end of eastern dominance over the Republican party.

After it was clear that Goldwater's was a losing cause, Reagan's wealthy Southern California backers prevailed in getting him, instead of Goldwater, to give a nationally televised address days before the campaign ended. "As we were raising more money than anybody else, we were entitled to have Goldwater speak in Los Angeles," recalled Henry Salvatori, another self-made millionaire from an immigrant background who worked his way west and made a fortune in the oil business. Salvatori was Goldwater's California finance chairman and the man responsible for Reagan's appointment as Goldwater's state cochairman. "I told the national [finance] chairman . . . whom I knew well: 'Look, we will have a very successful dinner here in Los Angeles. We don't need Goldwater. . . . Maybe you can use him where he can make more money.' So Goldwater didn't come and we had our own speaker, Ronald Reagan, speak at our dinner. And, of course, his speech electrified the nation."

It did no such thing. Lyndon Johnson's landslide proceeded as forecast; he swept the country, including California, which he carried with 59.2 percent of the votes. Nationally Johnson's percentage of the popular vote, 61.1, was the greatest ever, even exceeding Franklin Roosevelt's 60.8 percent of ballots cast in 1936.

Liberalism had triumphed resoundingly and appeared to be even more in the ascendancy.

CHAPTER 5

THE NEW CONSERVATISM

The small group of Californians who set out to make Ronald Reagan first governor of California and then president of the United States knew exactly how they intended to achieve their goals. They saw Reagan as the vehicle for first transforming progressive California into a bastion of political conservatism and then doing the same for the nation. Their eventual success rested on much more than ideology. Two watershed years of American life, unleashing a chain of events that plunged the nation into sudden violent disharmony after a period marked by unity of purpose, made possible their take-over. The process of change began with the political results of 1964, an election which seemed to make a mockery of forecasts that America was about to enter a conservative era.

By that year the national impulse to reform and perfect society had set the tone of American politics for most of the century. It had moved America through the Social Justice movement and the Progressive Era of the early twentieth century, producing the strong presidencies of Theodore Roosevelt and Woodrow Wilson, and continued through the burst of legislative activity that marked Franklin Roosevelt's New Deal and its successors, Harry Truman's Fair Deal and John Kennedy's New Frontier. These decades of continuing expansion of government's role in American life had represented a profound shift from the dominant nineteenth-century tradition of "the neutral, umpire state, which gave special favors to no class or interest," as Princeton's Arthur S. Link characterized it, to a twentieth-century one exemplified by Theodore Roosevelt's belief "that the federal government should play a dynamic, positive role by directly regulating business activities and giving special protection to labor and farmers."

It was this idea of increasing progressive governmental activism that a brilliant young historian at Columbia University, Richard Hofstadter, believed had run its course, leading him to predict in 1955 in *The Age of Reform:* "In our own day, perhaps for the first time since the 1890's this situation is changing, for there are some signs that liberals are beginning to find it both natural and expedient to explore the merits and employ the rhetoric of conservatism. . . . [T]hey feel that we can better serve ourselves in the calculable future by holding to what we have gained and learned, while trying to find some way out of the dreadful impasse of our polarized world. . . ."

Hofstadter accurately predicted emergence of what some writers and intellectuals of the mid-1950s already had described as a New Conservatism. Yet the greatest burst of governmental activity crested a decade later in 1964 with public ratification of what Lyndon Johnson called the continuation of a century-long effort to create a "Great Society." Johnson expanded the federal government's role in extending to previously uncovered groups of citizens concepts of "entitlements" and "rights" through new laws and regulations. As the writer Nicholas von Hoffman said, Johnson fought the nation's second Civil War and carried out its second Reconstruction. He launched a war on poverty and disease and secured passage of legislative acts that constituted something close to a social revolution in America through installation of Medicare and Medicaid programs and aid to education, cities, and mass transit systems. Passed were the Voting Rights Act, a fair immigration law, bills strengthening cancer and stroke research, and others tightening clean air and water pollution controls. Under Johnson, more mental health facilities were established, more medical libraries, more aid to the arts and humanities.

Against this backdrop of support for greater governmental activity, Reagan's televised speech for Goldwater in the final days of that campaign was viewed as so insignificant that when Theodore H. White wrote his masterly narrative history of the political process that year *The Making of the President 1964,* he not only failed to mention Reagan's speech but didn't include a single reference to Reagan.

Still, Reagan's speech was an extraordinary political debut, and it stirred ranks of conservatives reeling under the Goldwater debacle. By focusing their attention squarely on him, it represented a passing of the ideological baton.

For years his themes in that speech, the end product of all his political tryouts, had echoed on the ideological fringes of American life. Then, a generation later, they became the American political mainstream. They had three elements: antitax; anticommunism; antigovernment. Overlaying them, and giving them rhetorical force, was exposition of patriotism. Reagan evoked memories of heroic battles and flag and country, interlacing his remarks with mythological references culled over decades. He borrowed shamelessly and without attribution, directly appropriating material from great political addresses and weaving them into a seamless passage delivered as his own. In just two sentences, for example, he appropriated phrases and themes by Franklin Roosevelt, Abraham Lincoln, and Winston Churchill without crediting any of them: "You and I have a rendezvous with destiny [Roosevelt: "This generation of Americans has a rendezvous with destiny"]," he said. "We will preserve for our children, this the last best hope of man on earth [Lincoln: "the last, best hope of earth"], or we will sentence them to take the last step into a thousand years [Churchill: "if the British Empire and its Commonwealth last for a thousand years"] of darkness."

He began with a call to end the supposed crushing tax burden inflicted on American taxpayers, coupled with a warning about the peril America faced from growing national debt:

> No nation in history has ever survived a tax burden that reached a third of its national income. Today thirty-seven cents out of every dollar earned in this country is the tax collector's share, and yet our government continues to spend seventeen million dollars a day more than the government takes in. We haven't balanced our budget twenty-eight out of the last thirty-four years. We have raised our debt limit three times in the last twelve months, and now our national debt is one and half times bigger than all the combined debts of all the nations of the world.

He was wrong on a number of counts; to cite only one, that "no nation in history" had survived a tax burden that reached a third of its national income. At that time Germany, France, the United Kingdom, Canada, Belgium, Denmark, Finland, Iceland, Norway, Sweden, among others, derived nearly a third of their national revenues from tax sources.*

As for peace, it was illusory while the menace of communism was real and present: "There can be no real peace while one American is dying some place in the world for the rest of us. We are at war with the most dangerous enemy that has ever faced mankind in his long climb from the swamp to the stars, and it has been said that if we lose this war, and in so doing lose this way of freedom of ours, history will record with the greatest astonishment that those who had the most to lose did the least to prevent its happening."

Assault on government lay at the heart of his message. He lashed out at straw men targets fashioned from the bureaucracy, evoked memory of the Founding Fathers, and, mixing historical fact and fiction, said: "[T]hey knew that governments don't control things. . . . They also knew, those Founding Fathers, that outside of its legitimate functions, government does nothing as well or as economically as the private sector of the economy."

At that point Reagan's political positions were years ahead of his times. This was *fourteen years* before California voters passed Proposition 13, the voter initiative that rolled back state property tax assessments, ignited national tax revolts, and came to symbolize what the *New York Times* called "a Primal Scream by the People against Big Government." It was before California voters passed Proposition 14, an anti-fair-housing proposition that signaled public reaction against the civil rights movement. It was before California voters considered Proposition 16, an antipornography measure foreshadowing the rise of religious fundamentalists who later adopted such "social" issues as their cause. It was also before Vietnam polarized the country.

*Reagan's antitax theme and his attacks on Washington's "puzzle palaces on the Potomac" went back at least as far as 1961, when in a Phoenix speech he used a "stack of bills" metaphor to describe the rising national debt, changing the figurative height of those bills from 18 miles to 67 miles in his first economic message to Congress. By the time he left office, with the national debt nearly tripled, his metaphorical "stack of bills" would have risen to more than 170 miles.

Not only had Republicans lost the presidency overwhelmingly that year, but they had lost everywhere, at every level of government. Democrats swept the U.S. Senate and the House of Representatives, shrinking Republican numbers to only 140 in the House and 32 in the Senate. Not since the FDR landslide of 1936 had Democrats held such commanding congressional margins.

Republican losses at state and local levels were equally severe. They controlled only seven of the fifty state legislatures and seventeen governorships. In California the popular Edmund ("Pat") Brown had a solid grip on the governorship. Two years before, he had defeated Nixon in the gubernatorial contest by nearly three hundred thousand votes, dashing Nixon's comeback hopes in his home state. In 1964 Democrats strengthened their hold, winning both the California Assembly and the Senate. Everywhere Republican and conservative fortunes were at low ebb.

"We didn't want that to be the demise of the Republican Party," said Holmes Tuttle, a wealthy Beverly Hills car dealer (and another self-made man, who had moved to California from Oklahoma) who had been promoting Reagan's political career for years, "so we thought the best way to start rebuilding was here in California. I came up with the idea that, 'Here. Here's a man. Why should we look any further for a candidate? If the people of this country respond to him like they did in this speech and are concerned about the things that he enumerated, why shouldn't we consider him as our candidate here in the state of California, the largest state in the Union, to run for governor?' My associates at that time, Ed Mills, [A. C.] Cy Rubel and Henry Salvatori—there were only the four of us—talked about it, and I said, 'Why shouldn't we see if we can convince Ronald Reagan to give up his career and run for the office of governor of California?' Anyway, we thought that might be a good idea, so I went to see him. In fact, Mrs. Tuttle went with me and we spent the evening at Ron's home. At that time I presented the idea: What would he think of the idea of running for governor of the state of California? I said that I felt that we had to start rebuilding, and if he would, we were committed to see that he got the necessary funds and the organization to run. . . . We decided that night that he would talk to his family, talk to some of his friends, and we would discuss this with other people, and we would keep in touch with each other. After about thirty days—I never will forget—he called me and told me that he would run if we still felt the same way. He and Nancy had discussed it and decided we should try it. He suggested that instead of announcing that he was going to run, we should just kind of put feelers out. . . . So fine; we did. But not too surprisingly the response to it was overwhelming, and he kept getting stacks of mail at his home. That's when we acquired the services of Spencer-Roberts [a California political consulting firm that had handled, among others, Nelson Rockefeller's California presidential effort]. We made a deal with Spencer-Roberts—Mr. Salvatori, Mr. Rubel, Mr. Mills, and myself—that they would manage the effort if we decided to announce that he would be a candidate in the primary [election campaign]. We then formed what we called the Friends of Ronald Reagan."

From the beginning Reagan pressed aggressively for the political effort to begin. William E. ("Bill") Roberts of Spencer-Roberts & Associates, then forty years old, a habitually disheveled, balding, overweight, energetic man, remembered that it was Reagan who pressed Spencer-Roberts early in 1965 to accept the Tuttle group's offer to manage his campaign after they had only one or two get-acquainted sessions at Reagan's home on San Onofre in Pacific Palisades.* "Well, are you or aren't you?" he said Reagan demanded of them.

His partner, Stuart K. Spencer, then thirty-eight, an aggressive man with a heavily lined face and closely cropped brown hair, remembered Reagan pushing them to handle his campaign after only one or two preliminary telephone conversations *before* they met at his house. "Ron called us from Scottsdale or Phoenix [where he was] over there with his [Nancy Reagan] in-laws, and said, 'Well, are you going to run the campaign or not?' "

From that small beginning, and that small circle, came the political structure that captured first the California governorship and later the presidency. Tuttle and his group formed what became known as

*Roberts died in the summer of 1988, Reagan's last year as president, at the age of sixty-three. He had lost both his legs and his eyesight to diabetes. Spencer continued his Reagan association and that same summer was brought in to manage Dan Quayle's troubled vice presidential campaign.

the kitchen cabinet, resurrecting the term used to describe first Andrew Jackson's private advisers in Washington and later those of Theodore Roosevelt's and other presidents.

They began planning political moves in the business offices of Cy Rubel, recently retired as board chairman and chief executive officer of the Union Oil Company and leader of California's antiunion right to work forces. Gradually they expanded their circle to include men of similar wealth and ultraconservative political views. They raised much of the early money and recruited the political operatives, personally overseeing the hiring of key people. They took charge of Reagan's personal finances, made investments for him, and arranged for him to have a personal legal adviser, recruiting from a prestigious Los Angeles firm William French Smith, who became Reagan's personal attorney, and, ultimately, his first U.S. attorney general. They helped devise strategy and met with Reagan, his wife, and the Spencer-Roberts team at his home every Monday morning to discuss tactics; later, in Sacramento, they met and dined often with Reagan and had instantaneous access to him. The boast of one, Justin Dart, was as revealing as it was accurate: "I could get Ronald Reagan on the telephone any time of the day or night." In time they played crucial roles in staffing the Reagan governorship team in Sacramento—and then in Washington.

That was the key, though they, and Reagan himself, claimed only one purpose motivated them: the cause of good government guided by "right" principles. Once Reagan won, they wanted nothing from him; furthering the interests of citizenship was reward enough. This is a fanciful tale but, again, one that Reagan often told publicly, once in a tape-recorded interview with Sarah Sharp of the University of California, San Diego, a year before he became president.

Sharp: "And these people who supported you early on, like Holmes Tuttle and Henry Salvatori—they supported you for ideological reasons?"

Reagan: "Yes."

Sharp: "Because they thought that you would be the governor, the kind of governor that they wanted? The speeches that you made and the ideas that you put forth were their kinds of ideas?"

Reagan: "Yes. As a matter of fact, the night that I was sworn in, at midnight—that is a whole other story, as to why I was sworn in at midnight*—we went back to the governor's office. Holmes Tuttle told me to sit down in the governor's chair there, at the desk, and I did. Then he said, 'I don't know whether anyone has ever been able to say this to a governor of California. But now you are sitting in that chair. And you don't owe any of us anything.' He said, 'All we wanted was good government. We believed that you could do that. You have no commitment, no promise to keep to anyone at all. You just do what you believe should be done.' "

If Reagan believed that, he was indeed naive, for there is no doubt that these men knew what they wanted and how to get it. As Salvatori said, "We feel that the kitchen cabinet's primary function has been to insure that the top people in the government were conservative-minded people." Reagan knew this, too, for he worked closely with and deferred to their wishes in selection of the key personnel to staff his gubernatorial administration. He did more than defer: He turned over the personnel selection process to them.

The Reagan people called themselves conservatives, but they were not conservatives in the tradition of Locke or Burke or John Adams, individuals concerned about preserving what they believed to be best traditions of governance and immutable religious and ethical standards. Nor were they philosophical allies of the new conservative types exemplified by William Buckley and his group at the *National Review,* which had been founded in 1957 and attracted serious attention among intellectuals.

These men around Reagan were a familiar American type, self-made men who espoused rugged individualism, free (that is, unfettered and unregulated) enterprise, and a belief in the survival of the fittest. They were Social Darwinists who had made it out of poverty. So could others, if they were worthy. If not, well, then, to each his own and to each his own fate. Their maxims were simple ones—for example, the Lord helps those who help themselves. Protestations about good government notwithstanding, essentially they believed in

*Years later, when Donald T. Regan disclosed that for years Nancy Reagan relied extensively on an astrologer to set times for Reagan's presidential appearances, it was suggested that her astrologer was also responsible for the strange hour of Reagan's gubernatorial oath-taking ceremony in California. Reagan denied it.

no government—or none that would impede their interests. In their minds, *their* interests were the best American interests. Sink or swim, rise or fall, prosper as Horatio Alger had done through pluck and perseverance, just keep government out of my way and my business: this was the glory and the genius of America. To the extent they had a philosophy of government, that was its essence.

A bedrock belief in a laissez-faire approach to society's problems was shared by virtually all those who initially formed behind Reagan. It bound them together; it led them to seek others who believed exactly as they. Over and over they articulated the same viewpoints. "The Roosevelt administration was the beginning of what we have increasingly had since, [which] is that the government's responsibility is more or less cradle-to-grave," said Winfred M. Adams, another who moved west to California (from Arkansas) in the depths of the depression to become Reagan's cabinet secretary in 1967. "I don't think most of us in my generation agree with that philosophy or with that approach. I think probably in this country we have basically two viewpoints of government. . . . One would be liberal and one would be conservative. I think it is difficult for people like myself to think in terms of the common man. . . . Reagan or I or most of us really [can't] think in terms of the common man. We don't think that way. We think more in terms of the individual."

Henry Salvatori expressed the creed this way: "We are more realistic than liberals are. We don't think that human nature is that pure and that simple; therefore, we don't want to give in to the temptation to help those who are not truly needy and thus destroy the incentive to go to work. That's a problem that is generally recognized now. Even some black leaders now are saying that by giving the poor these handouts we have created an underclass who have lost their initiative and incentive to seek work. Now, you say, 'You would make them all starve?' No, of course not."

Reagan's ability as political communicator and public celebrity was what attracted them, including Reagan's own brother. "Well, he might have a lot to learn," Moon Reagan said, "but he does have the most important thing: there isn't a better communicator in the business."

His speech-making ability was also one of the factors that motivated Spencer-Roberts to manage Reagan's campaign. "Another reason that we decided to go with him is that he was a master of the electronic media," Stu Spencer said. "He is the first master of the electronic media the state of California ever had and has had to date. It's his medium, he understands it, he knows how to use it, and he's good at it."

To Mills, it was Reagan's star quality and name recognition that counted. Reagan was a salable commodity; that was his political value. "It's very difficult and expensive to reach a large segment of the public," he said. "One of the things that we looked at in the early days relative to Reagan was his prominence. If you wanted to measure it in money [chuckle] compared to, say, a product being known, you would have had to spend millions of dollars to have the position that Reagan occupied in 1965 and 1966. His radio situation, the G.E. *Theater of the Air* ["General Electric Theater"], his baseball broadcasting, which wasn't major, but his *Death Valley Days* and his political efforts *were.* All of this and his movies contributed to name value, so to speak."

When asked why he was for Reagan for governor, Justin Dart, another who had made it on his own and became a millionaire in the drug business, quickly answered: "He's a commonsense guy, and that's the essence of being capable and being responsible. More than that, he communicated so well and was a great leader. I mean, communicating had been his business in motion pictures, and then he was the head communicator for GE for a long time. It isn't just enough to be a governor or a president, you have to be a leader as well."

Dart added: "All I gave a damn about was that he was philosophically oriented in the right direction, doing as near as he knew how the right thing for the most people in California all the time. Look, for instance [at such issues as] abortion, NAACP, equal rights, and all those. Those are all, forgive me, trivial issues as far as I'm concerned. There are two basic issues that are overriding as far as I'm concerned: that is our economic health, economic leadership, or economic dominance: and our military defense ability. . . . The minor issues, like the Watts riots,* they come and go. When I was a kid in

*Racial riots in the Watts section of Los Angeles began on August 11, 1965, and lasted for five days, setting a pattern in succeeding summers that plunged race relations to a new low, raising fears that America was becoming two societies in conflict with each other.

Chicago, we had riots on the south side of Chicago. That didn't bother me. They go away. They were symptoms of some disturbance in the society, but they were minor as far as I was concerned."

Therein was a perfect exposition of Social Darwinism as it had survived in the America of the mid-1960s, perhaps the most liberal period of public life in the twentieth century. It bespoke something more than insensitivity toward others less fortunate and a renouncing of public responsibility to ameliorate social distress. What was being expressed here was an old American strain born of strong counterreaction to disturbing events. Hofstadter described it perfectly. "No doubt the precise line between useful and valid criticism of any society and a destructive alienation from its essential values is not always easy to draw," he wrote. "Some men, and indeed some political movements, seem to live close to that line and to swing back and forth across it more than once in their lives. The impulses behind yesterday's reform may be put in the service of reform today, but they may also be enlisted in the service of reaction."

CHAPTER 6

THE GREAT REACTION

In electing Ronald Reagan as governor in 1966, California voters signaled the end of the progressive period that had set their state's course since 1910.

For more than half a century California had produced such strong progressive Republican governors as Hiram W. Johnson, a reformer who earned a national reputation for prosecuting corporations and dishonest public officials and was Theodore Roosevelt's Progressive party vice presidential running mate in 1912, and Earl Warren, the Republican vice presidential nominee in 1944. At that very point in 1966 Warren was nearing the end of his tenure as chief justice of the United States after presiding over the most liberal Supreme Court in American history. Decisions of the "Warren Court," rendered over a fifteen-year span, marked the final flowering of the Age of Reform and political progressivism.*

With the emergence of Reagan, many disaffected political groups found a force of counterreaction around which to rally. Not only California voters but citizens everywhere had reason to react against the tide of events that had dramatically worsened in the two-year period from Goldwater's defeat to Reagan's election as governor.

In Vietnam the trickle of bloodshed had turned into a torrent as

*Chief Justice Earl Warren submitted his resignation to President Lyndon B. Johnson before the 1968 presidential election. Johnson's nominee to succeed him, the liberal Abe Fortas, was rejected by the Senate. The conservative Warren E. Burger was appointed by President Richard M. Nixon and confirmed the next year.

the dispatch of American troops increased. From fewer than 4,000 U.S. military personnel in South Vietnam at the end of 1962, the number rose to 16,000 by the time of John Kennedy's assassination. By the spring of 1965, 53,000 Americans had been assigned to what was described officially as defensive noncombat duty in "strategic hamlets" and coastal enclaves, and B-52 bombers had begun their daily runs over targets in North Vietnam. By early summer of that year American forces had doubled to 125,000, their mission changed from a limited one of protecting U.S. installations to engaging directly in combat.

By January 1966 the number of troops stood at 185,000. Within a year the figure had risen to 385,000, and with their increasing ranks came a corresponding rise in casualty lists. Death came to 1,369 Americans in Vietnam in 1965; to 5,008 in 1966; to 9,378 in 1967; to 14,869 in 1968. Higher and higher the toll mounted, proceeding in deadly lockstep with the increasing commitment of troops.

In the United States civil disobedience was in the air. Students took to the streets and rioted on campuses, holding rallies to burn draft cards and American flags. From a thousand campuses came the cry "Hey, hey, LBJ! How many kids did you kill today?" Political consensus was replaced by embittered dissent. A resurgence of old American strains began to appear: ideological certitude; patriotism; nationalism; America's God-given mission in the world. These were Reagan's themes. He did not create them; they resurfaced strongly in periods of reaction, such as in the great Red Scare of the early 1920s and the hunt for subversives in the early 1950s, but their reappearance in the sixties made Reagan's themes more acceptable, nowhere more so than in California.

California campuses, especially the one at Berkeley, were the symbolic center of national protest. At Berkeley the impulses of the sixties found their most flagrant expression and attracted the most intense media attention. They formed the backdrop against which Reagan ran.

In other times, such protest and experimentation with personal life-styles might have been dismissed as an inevitable (and invaluable) need for each generation of Americans to define its identities and establish its values by breaking with past manners and mores. This was no mere passing phenomenon, though. Reaction on the campuses was based on grim realities. The war in Vietnam was real and growing more deadly with each passing day. It was dividing the nation, sapping its spiritual and economic strength, and leading to a political and psychological crisis unparalleled since the American Civil War. The toll was measured in more than human lives lost. Cost of feeding new troops, planes, and ships into the war machine and maintaining supply lines across the Pacific to Southeast Asia reached thirty-three billion dollars a year and continued to rise. With it came an inflationary spiral, placing new strains on the U.S. economy.

Nor was the war the only divisive new factor threatening national stability. The nonviolent civil rights movement that brought together blacks and whites in marches across the segregated South had turned violent. In northern cities U.S. military force was required to quell riots, and new racial polarization developed. Fear of disintegration of American society was widely expressed.

All this, too, produced reaction on campuses and led to savage denunciations of all authority, especially the authority of the president of the United States.

Nowhere in the nation was Johnson as reviled as on the campus at Berkeley. It was a Berkeley graduate, Barbara Garson, who wrote a poisonous parody of *Macbeth,* called *MacBird!,* which perhaps best captures the embittered political climate of that time. MacBird/Johnson was depicted thus:

Messenger: Beatniks burning draft cards.
MacBird: Jail 'em.
Messenger: Negroes starting sit-ins.
MacBird: Gas 'em.
Messenger: Latin rebels rising.
MacBird: Shoot 'em.
Messenger: Asian peasants arming.
MacBird: Bomb 'em.
Messenger: Congressmen complaining.
MacBird: Fuck 'em.
Flush out this filthy
scum; destroy dissent.
It's treason to defy your

President.
You heard me! Get on,
get your ass in gear.
Get rid of all this protest
stuff, y'hear.

Such outrageousness, taking place amid the shattering of consensus, led to the greatest national reaction of all: a strong counterreaction against these events. This was as inevitable as it was powerful; it was a reaction created in equal measure by disgust, fear, and desire for bringing order out of disorder. Through Reagan the public had a vehicle to express resentment at both national disorder and political leadership.

Reagan used the campus protests, particularly at Berkeley, as examples of what was wrong in California and the nation. He called student protesters "bums" and likened them to monsters who "devoured their young," played up their supposed immorality, and titillated audiences by saying in shocked tones that Berkeley students conducted "sexual orgies so vile I cannot describe them to you." He opposed student protesters on Vietnam and adopted the motto of Douglas MacArthur after the Korean War had ended in stalemate: "There is no substitute for victory." That became Reagan's theme for Vietnam. It was ridiculous, he said, "that our young men are dying in a war with a country whose whole gross national product is less than the industrial output of Cleveland, Ohio." His solution: Use American power "to level Vietnam, pave it, paint stripes on it, and make a parking lot out of it."

Two years before, Goldwater had taken similar positions and been rejected as an extremist. Reagan was rewarded politically for expressing the same views because he had the ability to make extreme stands sound mild—"nonharsh," as one of his operatives said admiringly. This was his political, or actor's, talent, his capacity to "express conservative ideas in a moderate way."

Reagan prepared for his campaign the way an actor prepares for a performance. Spencer-Roberts provided him with experts, consultants, and voluminous briefing papers. They became pioneers in a multibillion-dollar political consultant campaign industry. In this, too, California was a trendsetter, and Spencer-Roberts forerunner of the future. From an amateur back room business, managed for the most part by familiar "old pol" types, Spencer-Roberts transformed political campaigns into a slick, high-powered profession that merchandised candidates as effectively as advertising agencies sold brands of soap, toothpaste, tobacco, and deodorant. They were political entrepreneurs; the products they sold were candidates, and their money was made by devising winning strategies and fashioning politically popular electronic media "messages."

Spencer-Roberts conducted extensive market research analysis, with continuous polls and surveys, to determine public attitudes. What was then a new technique, widely suspect among traditional political people, became commonplace campaign practice.

Reagan was packaged as a candidate, just as his critics later charged. But political manipulation aside, Reagan himself had an instinctive feel for political mood. Both Roberts and Spencer were struck with Reagan's intuitive sense for picking an issue and turning it into a matter of public concern. In this, he was often far ahead of them and at odds with what their sophisticated survey data suggested to be effective issues. Campus unrest was a classic example.

"Campus unrest did not show up in our research as a major issue in '65," Spencer said. Nonetheless, Reagan continued to raise it aggressively in his speeches. As he did, his repeated critical references to campus radicalism and unrest generated more and more emotion from audiences. "So Bill and I kept saying, 'It doesn't show up in the research, but the question keeps coming up. It's got to be a sub rosa emotional issue with people.' "

After closely observing Reagan deliver his attacks, they concluded that a strong undercurrent of public opposition to campus protests existed even though their own surveys gave no evidence of it. "We jumped on it as an issue." Reagan intensified his assault on California's great public university system, previously regarded as a political untouchable, comparing it with a breeding ground for civil disobedience. He hammered hard at campus unrest until it took hold as a major issue. "I think Reagan escalated it into an issue," Spencer said, "and it started moving up in the polls."

It was one of the reasons for his victory. Another was that he seemed too warm and friendly to be dangerous. It was inconceivable to the public and a generally favorable press that he would engage in deception and outright lies. The evidence, however, is that at times he did.

Lyn Nofziger remembered a campaign incident when Reagan deliberately dissembled in public, to his advantage politically.

They were in San Francisco, where Reagan was about to address the influential Commonwealth Club. Reporters covering the event suddenly surrounded Nofziger. Had Nofziger heard that Reagan's opponent, Governor Pat Brown, was being quoted as saying on TV that it was an actor who had shot Lincoln? Smelling blood, the reporters pressed Nofziger for immediate reaction from Reagan. He hadn't heard about it, Nofziger told them.

"So I went and found him at the head table," Nofziger recalled. "I went up and got him aside, and I said, 'Brown apparently has said something to the effect that it was an actor who shot Lincoln. I think you ought to play it very cool. Don't get mad or be shocked about it.' "

"Don't worry, don't worry," he says Reagan replied.

Reagan delivered his speech without mentioning the Brown statement. Immediately after, the reporters pressed forward. Had he heard that Governor Brown had just said that it was an actor who shot Lincoln? they shouted. What did he think about that?

Reagan looked startled. "Pat said that?" he finally said. "Why, I can't believe that. Pat wouldn't say anything like that. I wouldn't want to comment on that until I hear further."

He left with Nofziger at his side. As they walked off, Nofziger told him: "Well, you at last won an Academy Award."

"Shush," he says Reagan replied. "Reporters may be listening."

Those are the things you remember about a campaign, Nofziger said later.

On November 8, 1966, two years after Goldwater had lost California by 1.3 million votes, Reagan carried it with a plurality of 1 million votes and defeated the Pat Brown who had crushed Nixon four years before.

This extraordinary reversal of political fortune was no California aberration. Republicans picked up eight governorships that day, putting them on equal terms with Democrats in control of the number of statehouses. Most important, they controlled seven of the ten most populous states, tripled their number of state legislatures, regained forty-seven seats in the U.S. House of Representatives, and won unheard-of victories in Democratic strongholds across the South and West. After predictions of their demise as a political party just two years earlier, they were in position to reclaim the presidency and had a new star in the West to lead them.

CHAPTER 7

THE TAKE-OVER

Holmes Tuttle oversaw the effort to replace California's progressive approach to government with a conservatism presided over by Ronald Reagan. Executive personnel "headhunters" were instructed to find potential Reagan appointees among California corporations, and those selected came to office strongly disposed toward corporate interests or conservative politics. The two goals were synonymous and were achieved by careful screening.

Kitchen cabinet members personally were involved in the selection process. As he later did in Washington, Tuttle, for one, "went over the qualifications [of prospective Reagan appointees] individual by individual." Task forces were formed to screen everything from judicial appointments (they sought young judges, preferably about forty years of age, who would render "correct" conservative decisions over long years on the bench) to the staffing of executive agencies with similar ideologically "correct" appointees. "We met down at the California Club," Tuttle explained. "There were about ten or twelve of us. We started by taking each department of government: The Department of Education, the Department of Motor Vehicles. . . . To these, I don't like to call them headhunters, executive hunters, we'd say, 'We want you to look through the state's corporations and maybe go to some corporations.' We'd say, 'Who is the head transportation person in their organization and throughout the state?' We'd get that and we'd go through all these people. We would sit there, with ten or twelve of us around this big table, and we'd go through all these people or anybody else that we would want to recommend, you understand. Maybe I had somebody I knew, or others had somebody, and we'd discuss it and discuss it. Finally, we reduced it down to never less than three, and maybe, sometimes, we would give him [Reagan] five names. After we decided that those were the top five names, we'd send those to him with all the résumés and all the backgrounds."

An ideological litmus test was imposed. If someone was perceived as liberal, he wasn't considered for a Reagan post. They all understood what was meant by "good government." In practice, "good government" meant turning over the government to private interests on a scale unmatched anywhere in the nation since the twenties, with the possible exception of Louisiana and Texas. Ed Mills described the way that early effort at privatizing government functions worked: "It wasn't very long after he was in office when we organized a non-profit corporation, the Committee for Efficiency and Cost Control [actually the Task Force on Efficiency and Economy in Government]. Ultimately, that involved raising three hundred fifty thousand dollars, and I think about two hundred fifty people from business and the professions went to Sacramento—we did hire some professional leadership—to study government and its activities to find a way to operate more efficiently. This was a noble effort."

This turnover of public functions to private operators, a pattern first established at state level, later was applied to national government in Washington. Reagan's wealthy friends also raised money to pay for his inauguration in Sacramento. They even saw to it, once the governorship was won, that Reagan lived in what they regarded as a more fitting and comfortable style than that provided by the people of California in the governor's mansion. Typically they arranged the deal so that they themselves would profit personally from it. ("I headed the group of individuals who purchased a house which we rented to the governor," Henry Salvatori said. "This group consisted of fifteen individuals who invested five thousand dollars each to purchase the house. After Reagan left Sacramento we sold the house and everyone made a small profit on the transaction.") Later they established a private account in the Republican State Central Committee, designated as GOP Number One ("Governor's Political Account Number One") through which "political money would be sent to the governor's office."

No sooner had the governorship been won than Reagan's influential advisers, operating in great secrecy, began making plans for him to run for president in 1968. The first strategy session for a Reagan presidential campaign took place privately at Reagan's Pacific Palisades home ten days after the election and more than two months before his inauguration as governor.

In this effort, too, Reagan was a willing and active participant, albeit one who played the role of a silent partner. Operationally the incipient Reagan presidential campaign was run in a more or less secret office on Kearny Street in San Francisco under the supervision of Reagan's patronage secretary, a wealthy young San Franciscan named Thomas C. Reed. Besides Reed, those staffing the office included Norman ("Skip") Watts and his wife, Jill Watts, who had done congressional staff work in Washington.

Paul Haerle, Reagan's appointments secretary then, remembered the secrecy surrounding that presidential operation. "If you went to the office you found on the door some other name," he said. "You walked into the anteroom and there were pictures of mining equipment or oil wells or something like that on the wall because it was not to be known as the Reagan campaign office. . . . The process by which the funds were brought aboard and banked and paid out, I never got involved in. But I knew that the actual operations office scheduling Reagan to make speeches in all the states where there were going to be primaries, such as Oregon, was handled by Reed and various people scattered around the country and plugged into him."

Haerle was certain that this operation was known to Reagan and represented a "classic political process." By that he meant: "Tom was deniable. He was expendable. If the operation got blown or Reagan decided to totally abandon the thing for personal or fiscal or other reasons, he could do so and Tom would be left, as John Ehrlichman would say, twisting slowly, slowly in the wind. But Tom understood that and understood the way the game was played."*

*This incident is revealing for several reasons. It comes from someone who had served Reagan closely, who later in 1968 was detached from Reagan's gubernatorial staff and went on salary for that year's Reagan presidential nomination effort, who helped organize the Reagan effort at the Republican National Convention in Miami Beach that summer, and who assisted Clifton White in Reagan's convention delegate-hunting operation out of the top floor of the Deauville Hotel there. All this occurred nearly twenty years before a much more serious covert

By the spring of 1968, after a year and a half of Reagan's term as governor and after Reagan had delivered numerous well-publicized speeches around the nation before carefully selected influential political groups, it became clear to prominent Republicans that a Reagan presidential campaign was being prepared in earnest. In an attempt to determine what sort of political figure the actor turned governor really was, the progressive Republican group the Ripon Society prepared an extensive study of Reagan's public record as candidate and governor.

Relatively brief though the Reagan public record then was, the report prepared for distribution to Republicans that June 1968 was remarkably prescient.*

The Ripon report's first conclusion dealt with Reagan's administrative ability as governor. While he had spoken frequently "on the dangers of big government, the need for lowering taxes, the desirability of cutting budgets, and the importance of private initiative," illustrating his points forcefully "with engaging anecdotes and well-turned phrases," Reagan's actual performance did not match his words. The report said:

> Instead of using his first year of office to lay the ground for better management, for more efficient provision of public services, and for the gradual transfer of some governmental activities to the private sector, Governor Reagan has wielded a crude meat cleaver. He has attempted dramatic budget cuts and drastic cutbacks in existing programs. But foolish economies have often produced greater expenditures and many of the cutbacks have been untenable. While

---

operation, raising questions about giving Reagan deniability, made Lieutenant Colonel Oliver L. North and Admiral John M. Poindexter household names during the so-called Iran-contra affair. Also, the oral history interview from which this account is drawn was conducted on May 26, 1982, in Haerle's San Francisco law firm office, sixteen months into Reagan's presidency and years before anyone ever heard about Iran-contra, North, Poindexter & Co. The Tom Reed referred to became secretary of the air force in the Ford administration and returned to Washington with Reagan as special assistant to the president for national security, operating out of the White House. He was subsequently indicted for lying in sworn depositions and for falsifying documents in a stock-trading case. Those charges were dismissed in 1985.

*The twenty-four-page report, *Ronald Reagan: Here's the Rest of Him,* was written and researched for the Ripon Society Governing Board by Michael C. Smith and reviewed by members of the Ripon Society's Los Angeles chapter. Throughout the Reagan presidency I often referred to it and always found it eerily descriptive of Reagan presidential administration events nearly twenty years after it was written.

> the attention of the Reagan Administration has been focused on these token issues, California has had the biggest budget in its history. The Governor, after taking well-publicized but short-sighted stands on such issues as taxes, mental health, poverty programs, open housing, and education, has been forced to back-pedal to issue contradictory public statements that have compromised his credibility within the state.

This led to a harsh judgment: "We are forced to conclude that at this early stage in his public career Ronald Reagan has not developed the managerial skills to control, guide, and effectively limit a large governmental bureaucracy."

Its second conclusion dealt with Reagan's views on international affairs. It noted:

> [F]oreign policy was an area in which the Governor's better instincts as a public speaker often desert him. Usually he has a healthy skepticism of "expert advice," but when the "experts" happen to be right-wing military men he endorses their every word. Usually he shuns labels and strives for an approach which sounds both "moderate" and full of "common sense." Not so on Vietnam, where, alone among the [1968 presidential] candidates, he labels himself a "hawk" and where his approach is shrill and uncompromising. Reagan on Vietnam sounds like "common sense" only to those who think that conducting a foreign policy is like winning a football game.

Ripon's final judgment was strongly critical: "We conclude that Governor Reagan is today unsuited for major responsibility in any area bearing on diplomacy or the conduct of foreign policy. . . ."

Many of those attracted to Reagan's service in California were young and shared similar backgrounds. "We thought we were the new broom," said Paul Haerle. "We had the arrogance to think that we were cleaning out the Augean stables, as we looked at our job up there. It was almost a messianic attitude of superiority to the existing Republican establishment in Sacramento." Many of them had either experienced lay preacher work or otherwise been more than casually involved in religion, especially fundamentalism, and many had military backgrounds. A striking number came from the fields of public relations and advertising.

Reagan's California team also enlisted people without prior political or governmental background, and such lack of experience was viewed as an asset. An attitude of contempt for government, and for the public sector and public institutions in general, was common.

Verne Orr, for instance. With a chuckle he recalled proudly how he had once argued with the University of California president that "Hell, the president of any good pickle factory can run a university."

Orr and others like him held the same sort of contemptuous attitude about government. "It doesn't matter how you get the experience," he said; "your experience is to teach you how to do business with people. . . ."

They had already taken to calling themselves the Alumni, these people who had been with Reagan in Sacramento and made the journey from West to East Coast with him. During the 1980 presidential campaign some had attracted much public attention; many others, like Orr, who was to be the new secretary of the air force, and Tom Reed, were less well known, but they were to be as important in Washington as they had been in Sacramento.

Among the best known was the jovial Edwin Meese III. Meese had been Reagan's personal executive assistant in Sacramento, the man who ran the governor's office and who was first among equals there. He was to become presidential counselor in the White House after the inaugural ceremony.

Coming to Washington with Meese was his personal secretary, Florence ("Flo") Randolph Procunier, trim, blond, intense, totally loyal. Her close professional association with Meese in Sacramento had left her with two strong impressions about her longtime boss: his superb memory and his desire to help his personal friends.

Ed Meese was never too busy to see and assist those friends, she remembered. While others seeking appointments with him in Sacramento were turned away during the crush of official business, he issued clear instructions to her to make certain that his friends would always have access to him. "You knew certain people that wouldn't get in," she recalled, in describing how she would handle Meese's personal appointments schedule. "But one thing I liked about . . . Mr. Meese is that no matter who they are, or who they were, if they are his friends, he would try to work them in, even if it was just for a few minutes. If they had problems, he would try to listen to them first and then funnel them to where they would go. I would work it out with the other departments, and we managed for them to see whoever it was necessary for them to see."

The second quality that struck her most about Meese was his memory: "He has a fantastic memory. I have never seen anybody with a memory like Mr. Meese's. . . . I wish I had the capacity for remembering names like he does. He is remarkable, absolutely. . . . Mr. Meese was fantastic with his recall. . . . He also wanted to be on top of everything. . . . He likes to know everything that's going on."

Another prominent Reaganite making the shift from state to national governance was the somewhat owlish-appearing Michael K. Deaver. Rus Walton, then cochairman of the Santa Clara County Republican Central Committee, first spotted and hired Deaver and brought him into local politics and then to Reagan's service. "I do remember that Mike," he recalled, "who had studied for the priesthood and then had taken a trip around the world, was playing the piano in a bar when we interviewed and hired him."

Deaver was a PR man, whose expertise was image, the Reagan image, and he was especially attentive to Mrs. Reagan's wishes.

Lyn Nofziger, a strong conservative who had been Reagan's gubernatorial campaign press secretary, was another who came to Reagan through the kitchen cabinet. Nofziger was a reporter for the conservative Copley newspaper chain in San Diego when recruited to come to Sacramento. "Eventually what the Ronald Reagan people did," Nofziger remembered, "was go down to [newspaper owner] Jim Copley. Henry Salvatori and, I think, Holmes Tuttle went down and asked him to give me a leave of absence, which he agreed to do. Then Spencer-Roberts came and frankly offered me twice what I was making."

He took the money, and the job, and became a regular in Reagan's service. Now he, too, was headed for the White House.

There was Caspar W. Weinberger, a Harvard-trained San Francisco lawyer who walked with a habitual slump, making him appear even shorter than he was. Congenial, hatchet-faced, with a tendency to mumble, Weinberger had been considered for Reagan's first finance director in Sacramento when the kitchen cabinet was forming that original team. He was eliminated because he was thought to be too liberal. Three months later, when the original appointee didn't work out, Weinberger succeeded him. Subsequently he served as budget director in Richard Nixon's cabinet, where he earned a reputation as a sharp pencil man and tenacious budget slasher known as Cap the Knife.

Now Weinberger was returning to Washington with Reagan to apply his budget management expertise to the Pentagon. He was to be the new secretary of defense.

Of course, there was Nancy Reagan herself. Wide-eyed and petite, she appeared high-strung and sensitive and most vulnerable to criticism. She had not been a popular figure in Sacramento; she was regarded as aloof and superior, more concerned with the doings of fashionable Rodeo Drive and the celebrities of Hollywood than with the governmental groupings of Sacramento. This belief was not limited to legislators, their wives, and the lobbyists and political operatives who worked out of Sacramento. It was the private belief, too, of a number of loyal Reagan administration officials. No one doubted, though, the closeness of Nancy and Ronald Reagan. They were indispensable to each other.

Nor was there any question about her toughness or the major role she played in his public life—so major, in fact, that she was widely, if privately, feared. She was seen as a real power, perhaps *the* power, behind Reagan. What Nancy wanted, Nancy got, a fact of life that Reagan aides quickly learned. Verne Orr was one of them.

When Orr headed the Motor Vehicles Department, a new series of state license plates was being issued. Someone on his staff suggested creating a personalized license for Nancy Reagan that would bear her initials, N. D. R. "So I put through the order and Mike Deaver called me," Orr said later. "He was horrified and he said, 'We've been thinking this over, and Nancy Reagan has threats, like all executives' wives, and if you give her license plates 000-NDR, everybody in the world will know that it's Nancy Reagan's car, so I want you to stop it."

Orr concurred. Fine. He would see to it. A month later he got a phone call. It was Mrs. Reagan.

"Hello, Verne, this is Nancy."

"Yes, Mrs. Reagan." (He remembered he didn't know her well enough to call her by first name then.)

"How is my license plate coming?"

Orr said, "Mrs. Reagan, I am sorry, but I was told to stop it."

Silence, then: "Verne, whose car is it?"

"It's yours, Mrs. Reagan."

Years later Orr remembered clearly how that incident ended. "She said, 'I want that license plate,' and she hung up the phone." Laughing, he added: "So she got NDR!"

Of them all, the foremost figure was Ronald Reagan himself riding in that limousine down Pennsylvania Avenue toward the Capitol for the inaugural ceremonies.

This was no world of pretend. This was a moment of reality that made all prior dreams of imaginary triumphs seem wildly improbable. So many times before it appeared as if his chances for the presidency had passed. There had been many missed opportunities, many of what Churchill called the "terrible Ifs":

What if Reagan had won the Republican nomination at Miami Beach in 1968? What if he had won the presidency that year? What if there had been no Nixon presidency, no Watergate, no resignation under threat of impeachment, no Ford and Carter presidencies? What if, as was more likely, he had gained the nomination and lost the presidency to Hubert Humphrey that year, in all probability ending his chances for the presidency and his political career?

What if Nixon had appointed him, instead of Ford, vice president after Spiro Agnew's forced resignation in 1973? Reagan's key advisers had lobbied hard on his behalf then, Tuttle remembering: "I took quite an active part in that, and I think that President Nixon made a very bad mistake when he didn't appoint him. I did my best, and so did Mr. Dart, to convince Nixon that he should. You bet I did."

What if he had defeated Ford for the Republican nomination in 1976? That race, too, had been close, extremely so. And what if Ford, having won, had offered him the vice presidency then? Despite denials of Reagan's interest in that position, he would have accepted, so at least Tuttle said authoritatively: "He wasn't asked. He would have accepted. No question about it. He was not asked. He was never asked. . . . I want to get it straight. Ronald Reagan never turned down the vice presidency. He was not asked."

And what if he had gained that vice presidential nomination in 1976 or the presidential one that year for that matter? Would he have defeated Carter? Probably not. That, at least, was the measured opinion of many of his advisers and political experts. Conditions were not yet right for him. It took four years of Carter and inflation and gas lines and, above all else, the hostages, always the hostages, to create his opportunity for victory.

Even the hostages could have become the agent of his defeat instead of his victory. For he knew, as did all his political people, that had Carter succeeded in freeing them before election day, the resulting national glow almost certainly would have guaranteed his reelection. Even now, as the clock inched toward noon, Carter still had an opportunity to claim some of the credit and share in some of the ensuing goodwill.

CHAPTER 8

A NEW ERA

Delay and more delay. Now the split-screen televised drama intensified as images beamed back from orbiting satellites flashed dizzying scenes from Washington to Algiers and into TV sets in tens of millions of American homes. It was clear that the ayatollah was deliberately adding one final insult. He was holding back release of the hostages until the new president was inaugurated.

Walter Cronkite, whose television presence had reassured America in times of crisis, reflected the nation's fury. "I try to remain the cool correspondent, impartial and unaffected by events," he sputtered over network television just as the inaugural ceremony was about to begin, "but it seems like the most uncivilized touch to an uncivilized performance that I can imagine. . . . They seem to dangle this in front of us, deliberately making it as difficult as possible." He called the Iranians "diabolical."

Inside the White House small groups of Secret Service agents, secretaries, and other permanent personnel gathered around the television sets and watched as Ronald Reagan stepped to the podium to take the oath of office. The hostages were still in Iran; the first plane carrying them to freedom would not take off until 12:35 P.M. Reagan, not Carter, would be given the opportunity to make public the announcement of their freedom.

Precisely at high noon, as Reagan became president, his newly appointed presidential assistant for management, John Rogers, and four assistants briskly moved into the Oval Office and began rearranging the furniture. They had already finished changing the president's private study off the Oval Office. Bookcases containing biographies of Carter's favorite presidents, Jefferson, Lincoln, and Truman, had been emptied and the books packed in cases for shipment back to Georgia.

Clement E. Conger, curator of the White House, an affable man who had demonstrated bipartisan eagerness to please during four previous presidencies, poked his head into the Oval Office just as the inaugural ceremonies were being concluded. Over the television sets came the booming sounds of the traditional cannon salute echoing over the Capitol grounds.

"Oh, I see you've rearranged the furniture," he said. "I'm glad. I didn't like the president's—that is, the past arrangement. This is much better."

Conger surveyed the three busts—Washington, Franklin, Truman—standing in the Oval Office and volunteered a suggestion.

"If you don't like Mr. Truman, you can move Mr. Truman out."

He walked across to the Cabinet Room, where other changes were being made. Down came the presidential portraits of Jefferson and Truman. Lincoln remained in place. A new presidential portrait was hung: Calvin Coolidge. "It's a new era," Conger explained.

BOOK TWO

AMERICA
JAN. 20, 1981

CHAPTER 9

THE CABAL

They called themselves supply-siders and were apostles of a new economic creed. Nothing like them had appeared on the national scene since the early New Dealers, filled with ideas for remaking the American system, came to power with Roosevelt. No less imbued with ideas than their predecessors of the thirties, the conservative theorists of the eighties were determined to undo the modern American social welfare state created by the New Deal and replace it with a new model. As the writer John Brooks observed, their economic theory was "diametrically opposed to the way the economy has been managed in the United States most of the time over the past half century" and "is, by common consent, the biggest new or quasi-new idea to come along in its field since 'the Keynesian revolution' of the nineteen-thirties."*

All this was no small achievement for such an unlikely band of young ideologues and self-promoters, but the circumstances that created their opportunity for influence in the Reagan era were not surprising. The conjunction of cumulative national disenchantment with Washington policies, disapproval of economic conditions, arrival of Ronald Reagan as America's leader, and reemergence of laissez-faire as the operative philosophy of the eighties all contrib-

*Of books and articles on this subject, Brooks's "The Supply Side," published on April 19, 1982, in the *New Yorker,* provides the best single account of supply-side theory and theorists I have read. Essential to understanding of the subject is William Greider's celebrated article "The Education of David Stockman," published December 1981 in the *Atlantic* and later in book form.

uted to the climate in which they thrived. The surprise was that a radical, untested theory (an unprecedented example of "a relatively pure theory coming first and application afterward," as Brooks said) would be implemented despite warnings about its risks.

Supply-siders were the intellectual handmaidens of the tax-cut revolution that flowered in California with passage of Proposition 13 in 1978 and the natural heirs of Reagan's get-government-off-our-backs themes. By his inaugural day their supply-side doctrine had assumed dimensions of a new economic religion.

Cut taxes, they proclaimed, and miracles would occur: Economic growth would soar, tax revenues would actually *increase,* inflation would decline, savings rates would rise, and all this would be achieved without having to go through the painful process of slashing federal spending and experiencing recession. Theirs was a fail-safe, pain-free formula for economic success, and it was all so simple. Cutting oppressive top tax rates meant people would have more money to spend. Higher tax rates discouraged investment; lowering them encouraged it. Also, lower taxes created incentive for people to work harder because they would keep more of their earnings. By freeing pools of capital through lowered tax rates, investments would be stimulated, jobs and wealth be created, spending for consumer goods and manufactured products rise, and new tax revenues flow into government treasuries. Furthermore, the more taxes were cut, the more economic activity would be generated. The greater the general prosperity, the greater the tax revenues for the general good. Utopia.

For too long, they argued, Washington policy makers had been dominated by the "demand model," the idea that consumer purchasing power drives the economy. For too long Washington had followed the theories of John Maynard Keynes and the Keynesians, who managed "demand" and sought to control the up-and-down swings of the economic cycle by priming the pump of government spending when consumer purchasing lagged and by using the tax system as a lever of control over the economy. That path produced stagnation and lowered productivity. For too long had their opposing mainstream economic philosophers—the monetarists—attempted to manage the same demand by manipulating Federal Reserve and exchange rate policies to control the quantity of money.

That path led to inflation and decline in the dollar's value. All that was past. Keynesians and monetarists alike, representing the majority opinion of liberal *and* conservative economists, would be discredited. The old demand model was being shed, the new theorists proclaimed, like "a tattered snake skin."

Supply-side economics would also work a political miracle. By stimulating economic growth, it would permit both Republicans and Democrats to enjoy the best of political worlds—a prosperous, productive, recession and inflationproof America. As one of the theorists said enthusiastically, Republicans could then "argue for a reduction in the national debt and an increase in the defense budget while the Democrats [could] push national health insurance."

The seductive supply-side myth took tangible form, its acolytes claimed, in Washington early in December 1974 during the Ford administration, when three men met for cocktails at the Two Continents restaurant, a block from the White House. There, in a moment of frustration over his inability to explain to Richard Cheney, Ford's chief of staff, the benefits that would ensue if his tax-cutting theories were adopted, a bubbly young economist named Arthur B. Laffer seized a cocktail napkin and drew on it what became known as the Laffer Curve.

It showed, in graph form, a line of tax rates between zero and 100 percent. Neither produced any revenues, Laffer explained while scribbling on his napkin, the zero rate for obvious reasons—it collected no taxes to begin with—and the 100 percent rate none because confiscating all income through taxation removed incentives to work. He described how revenues would rise on the left side of his curve as tax rates were lowered in descending order toward the zero mark and would diminish on the right side as rates rose toward the 100 percent mark. On the lowered end of the tax rate collection scale, he demonstrated with his pencil, was the optimum point that would produce the greatest revenues. "I had never seen it before, and I was immediately excited by it," said Jude Wanniski, an editorial-page writer for the *Wall Street Journal* and the man who had set up the meeting. "What I saw, mind you, was not some new piece of information. I already understood the basic principle. . . . But I saw the curve as something useful as a teaching device. From then on I talked and wrote constantly about the Laffer Curve."

Wanniski's life had prepared him to be a polemicist. Though he had no training as an economist, he boasted of having become "a true revolutionary, a fanatic," in the service of supply-side economics, a term that he himself coined. Such fervor was typical of someone who believed he could change the course of history. "Over and over again he kept repeating it," David A. Stockman later said of Wanniski. "It was his mantra: 'Overturning an existing order starts with one person and an idea. An idea persuades a second person, then a third, then a fourth. . . .' "

Garrulous, emotional, argumentative, with black hair, a swarthy complexion, and bushy eyebrows, Wanniski was the son and grandson of Pennsylvania coal miners who were given to political causes. His grandfather was a self-avowed Marxist. After studying for the priesthood, his father became a strong supporter and member of John L. Lewis's United Mine Workers union. In Brooklyn, to which his family moved in the late 1930s, Wanniski grew up thinking of himself as a Fabian Socialist. By the early 1970s he was a journalist working in Washington for the *National Observer,* a sister publication of the *Wall Street Journal.* It was there that he met Arthur Laffer, then thirty years old and working as an economist for the Nixon administration.

Laffer was already a controversial figure professionally as well as a somewhat unusual one personally. Short, plump, with a sunny countenance and demeanor, Laffer hardly matched the popular portrait of the sober economics professor or government bureaucrat. John Brooks, for one, upon first meeting Laffer was struck by his "pixie air of youth and mischief which makes him seem, at first glance, more like a clever advertising man than like an economic guru."* He also had an alarming tendency to balloon in weight, dramatically altering his appearance, a problem he resolved by severe and unusual crash diets (fighting fat by spending long periods in cool water to drain off body heat, for example). Laffer used the weight loss results to demonstrate his willpower, proudly boasting to

*My own impression, upon first meeting him about the same time when we appeared as speakers on a business program at an Arizona resort, was of a smooth-talking, jovial door-to-door salesman.

interviewers how he had lost, depending on his version, fifty pounds in forty days or seventy-five pounds in ninety days.

He was the son of a beer dealer in Youngstown, Ohio, and followed his father to Yale. There he was a poor student. Before taking a year's leave and returning to complete his senior year, he ranked near the bottom of his class. Laffer said he then was graduated with high honors in economics.* At Stanford he earned a master's in business administration, but not a doctorate, a fact that created controversy after he joined the University of Chicago faculty and was charged there (falsely, he maintained) with concealing from university authorities his lack of a Ph.D. Later he completed his Ph.D. requirements and obtained his Stanford doctorate.

At the Office of Management and Budget in Washington, Laffer became controversial for having devised an economic projection for the Nixon administration that predicted a considerably higher gross national product for the United States in 1971 than nearly every economist anticipated. Laffer's forecast created more controversy when it was reported that he based it on an unproven computer-based econometric forecasting model that he claimed was simpler than most models. Eminent economists, ranging from the conservative "monetarist" Milton Friedman to the liberal "Keynesian" Walter Heller, called Laffer's model "crude" and his forecast embarrassing. Later his methods and conclusions were strongly criticized by a Federal Reserve Board staff report released by Congress. Laffer was unabashed. "I've never done an econometric model before but I'll match this against anything else," he told syndicated economics columnist Joseph Slevin early in 1971.

It was then that Laffer met Wanniski, who interviewed him on his controversial economic forecast. Wanniski was impressed. These confident young men (Wanniski, at thirty-three, was three years older than Laffer) began meeting regularly, and when, in 1974, Wanniski heard Laffer's intellectual idol and mentor, the conservative Canadian economist and Columbia University professor Robert Alexander Mundell, expound *his* tax-cutting theories at a world economics conference in Washington at which Laffer also appeared,

*The Office of the Registrar at Yale University reports that one Arthur B. Laffer was graduated in 1963 with a regular B.A. without honors.

Wanniski's enthusiasm grew boundless.* "Now I kept thinking, *that's* what Art meant," he recalled. "I was so excited I could hardly contain myself."

Brimming with this newly revealed truth, Wanniski hastened to impart it to his boss, Robert L. Bartley, son of an Iowa veterinarian and editor of the editorial page of the *Wall Street Journal,* for whom Wanniski had begun writing editorials two years earlier. "I ran to New York," he said, "grabbed Bob Bartley by the lapels, and began explaining the Mundell-Laffer hypothesis. He couldn't get it at all. Like just about everyone else, he was living in a demand-oriented, Keynes-conditioned world. All the economic metaphors were geared to that, all the economists were trained to it. I saw then that my task as educator in this new economics was cut out for me."

Wanniski proceeded to proselytize Bartley, a conversion process that proved not to be difficult. Despite Bartley's initial doubts about the miraculous tax-cutting theory ("I thought it was a little wacky myself"), he was himself in the process of intellectual change even as he was beginning to exercise major influence over national political and economic opinions.

Two years before, at the age of thirty-five, Bartley had taken control of the *Wall Street Journal*'s editorial page. The *Journal,* with a daily circulation approaching two million and through new satellite production techniques published simultaneously in twelve cities across the country, was then the nation's only national newspaper and on the rise to new journalistic excellence and influence. Bartley remade the *Journal*'s editorial and opposite editorial pages into the near-official voice of the new conservatism. It was Bartley who recruited a stable of bright, young economic conservatives to proclaim the new wisdom, Bartley who opened his pages to other conservatives and so-called neoconservatives whose writings had been largely

*Mundell, who strongly influenced Laffer when they both were on the University of Chicago faculty in 1968, had been suggesting the value of tax cuts to stimulate the economy since 1961. Over the next ten years he formulated virtually all the principal "supply-side" ideas, including a ringing rejection of the concern expressed by leading economists and financiers that such policies would lead to large federal budget deficits and/or a recession. When a distinguished colleague said, "Ah, but that means a budget deficit," after listening to Mundell during an international economics conference in Bologna, Italy, in 1971, a transcript of the session shows Mundell replying: "Suppose it does mean a budget deficit in the United States—who cares?"

confined to ideological journals of limited circulation. Bartley provided them with a mass audience. He introduced their ideas to people of power and influence across the nation. By editorially sanctioning their beliefs, he lent them credibility and cloaked them with the respectability of the *Wall Street Journal.* He set the tone of combative ideological discourse that came to mark the *Journal*'s pages, and as Bartley acknowledged, Wanniski was a powerful factor in that evolution. "Jude had a tremendous influence over the tone and direction of the page," Bartley later told the *Washington Post*'s Dan Morgan. "He taught me the power of the outrageous."

Bartley's *Journal* provided more than an ideological platform for influencing opinion; it became a training ground for producing active political players. A number of those who worked for Bartley or were widely published by him became key members of the Reagan administration. Among them were supply-side economists Paul Craig Roberts III and Norman B. Ture, respectively Reagan's assistant secretary of the treasury and assistant secretary of the treasury for tax policy, and the young Washington political operative and later congressman David A. Stockman, Reagan's budget director.

The young conservatives who exercised power in the eighties were not members of the establishment, nor were they seeking entry to it. If anything, they had a contempt for traditional politics, for big business and big government (and big labor) alike, and for the workings of the two political parties. Theirs was a rejection of the old ways of doing political and economic business in America. They saw themselves as bearers of new ideas who intended to create their new order by returning to old principles. Free-market forces would again determine events.

While they were antigovernment, anti-Washington, antiregulation, and anti-Communist, the supply-siders were not necessarily antiliberal as such. They had shared some of the liberal views of their peers in the sixties but concluded, not incorrectly, that liberalism and its leaders had failed to fulfill their promises. Their reaction was not only against the failed policies and personalities of liberalism but also against the personal excesses of the sixties. In no small part, therefore, they were waging war within their own generation—or at least against the part of their generation that had taken to the streets in political protest and continued to cling to the discredited (by them) liberal belief that government intervention was an answer to problems instead (as they believed) of being the problem itself. They also possessed the true believer conviction of being absolutely right. Ideologically they were purists.

By the mid-seventies Wanniski, Laffer, and Mundell had begun meeting with other converts to discuss political moves and strategy. "We called the group the cabal," Wanniski said. "We were plotting and scheming how to take over economic policy."

At the suggestion of Bartley, Wanniski sought out a young conservative congressman (and former pro football quarterback) from Buffalo named Jack Kemp, who became another supply-side convert and sponsor of supply-side tax cut legislation on Capitol Hill that attracted Ronald Reagan's attention. Eventually Wanniski became a Kemp adviser and "policy coordinator."

As the circle of supply-siders grew, Wanniski contributed his own book to the public debate in 1978. Modestly titled *The Way the World Works,* Wanniski's book extolled the supply-side thesis and praised the efficacy of the Laffer Curve, claiming to discover in it applicable historical analogies of success dating from the Roman Empire, fourteenth-century Muslim experience, the American and French revolutions (both of which, he said, represented "rebellions against the upper reaches of the Laffer Curve"), and even the historical events surrounding the birth of Christ when Caesar Augustus pronounced his unpopular decree that all the world should be taxed. Laffer, in turn, reciprocated by providing a book jacket blurb for Wanniski. "In all honesty, I believe it is the best book on economics ever written," the creator of the Laffer Curve said of the propagandist who praised it.

By 1978, thanks largely to the *Journal* and its polemicists, "supply-side economics" had entered the political policy debates that preceded Reagan's election. Even then it was already intensely controversial. Converts hailed it, in the words of columnists Rowland Evans and Robert Novak, as "an economic doctrine that is radically transforming Republican theory and possibly American politics" and Laffer, to quote Evans and Novak again, as the "most politically explosive theorizer since John Maynard Keynes." Critics, such as economics Professor Robert M. Dunn, Jr., of George Washington

University, derided Laffer and his theory as the "new Moses" attempting to "sell old snake oil in a new bottle" and warned of dangers that would occur if supply-side economics were implemented. "The conclusion of this theory is that a large reduction in U.S. taxes would actually raise government revenues," Professor Dunn wrote on July 9, 1978, in the *Washington Post.* "Rep. Jack Kemp (R-N.Y.) has embraced this argument to advance his proposal to reduce federal taxes by thirty percent. Unfortunately, like all other perpetual motion machines, it will not work. It is a lovely vision, but it is actually a mirage—and a dangerous mirage at that."

Similar judgments were made repeatedly during the 1980 presidential campaign, the most famous being the characterization of supply-side economics as "voodoo economics" by Reagan's opponent George Bush, a former Republican congressman and Central Intelligence Agency director.

Ronald Reagan was the most important supply-side convert. Since 1978, Reagan had been meeting with Kemp, whose tax cut ideas he often quoted, and receiving supply-side memorandums from Wanniski, among others. Before the presidential campaign he was briefed extensively by Kemp, Laffer, and Wanniski, who "thoroughly hosed him down with supply-side doctrine."

What Reagan heard about less government, less regulation, slashing personal and corporate tax rates, encouraging entrepreneurship and the acquisition of wealth had long been articles of faith with him. He was also introduced to the Laffer Curve, with positive results. "It set off a symphony in his ears," according to Wanniski. "He knew instantly that it was true and would never have a doubt thereafter." Typically, Wanniski claimed that Reagan's improved 1980 presidential prospects were attributable to the Laffer Curve.

"The Reagan of 1976 did not have the concept of the Laffer Curve," Wanniski explained in a lengthy interview with Alexander Cockburn and James Ridgeway in the *Village Voice* that April, months before Reagan won the Republican nomination in Detroit.

> So . . . we have Laffer coming along and saying it's not demand that moves the economy, it's supply. Every individual on the face of the earth will demand as much as he or she can possibly consume. We

> all want to live like Frank Sinatra, to move from place to place in our own private jets. What limits us is our ability to supply our talents in the marketplace in order to exchange for the jet planes and everything else we want. So that's why we are called supply siders. We want to maximize the individual's ability to fulfill his potential.

Did Reagan believe in supply-side economics? Wanniski was asked. "Yes, Reagan loves the stuff," he replied. How could Reagan achieve his stated aim of balancing the budget while slashing taxes, dramatically increasing defense spending, and not proposing cuts for such "entitlements" as Social Security payments? Simple. "Out of the bigger economy." Would not welfare and social programs have to be cut? "No," Wanniski declared. "Social programs are left in place. 'The safety net,' we call it."

Doesn't the emphasis on individualism and far less government regulation and oversight inevitably mean a return to the dog-eat-dog, survival-of-the-fittest nineteenth-century days, when "you had children dragging coal carts along in the mines"? Not at all, Wanniski maintained. The spirit of the marketplace would see that such a retrogressive step did not occur.

> The only thing the government does is to provide for the security of the marketplace. It keeps the bandits out. . . . In an expanding economy the individual expects more. He will move from the entrepreneur who is not cutting corners. In an expansion, you have less need for regulation. If you provide an environment that is conducive to opportunity and growth, then competition will result in more safety and health and more concerns for the environment, but not without vigilance of the collective maintaining watchdogs.

He did not identify those vigilant watchdogs or describe how they would perform in a new atmosphere of reduced federal personnel and a climate that valued private profit over public functions. Nor did he address whether there might be a need for someone to watch the watchmen in the new antigovernment, deregulated era aborning. Was there any proof for these claims of wonders to be produced by adopting supply-side dogma in a Reagan administration? "This is all theory," Wanniski conceded, but "one of the first insights I had was when I asked Laffer, 'How can these incentives be instantaneous?

Won't we have to wait three years for them to occur?' Laffer said, 'How long does it take you to reach over and pick up a fifty dollar bill in a crowd?' That's how quick it is. If the incentive is there, the production is there."

Not everyone inside the Reagan camp was as bullish about supply-side economics, but the one who mattered most, Reagan, was. Whether he understood the implications of supply-side philosophy, or whether anyone at the top of his team did, was another matter.

Curious strains of idealism and cynicism seem to have motivated the admittedly zealous young men who conspired to force upon the new American president their newly discovered tablets of economic truth. They seemed torn between a sincere belief that they were heralds of a better way and a simultaneous conscious pursuit of self-interest and personal ambitions. No one exhibited these conflicting drives more than David Stockman.

Like Laffer and Bartley, Stockman was a midwesterner. Son of a fruit farmer, pale, bespectacled, intense, Stockman had traveled a circuitous ideological journey before coming to Washington in 1970 as aide to Republican Congressman John B. Anderson of Illinois. At Michigan State, where he was the first member of his family to attend college, Stockman participated in student antiwar protests and was a member of the far left national organization Students for a Democratic Society. Upon graduation in 1968, he enrolled in Harvard's Divinity School (thus obtaining a student draft deferment from Vietnam War service) and made a significant political contact as a live-in baby-sitter for Daniel Patrick Moynihan, who had himself traveled an interesting ideological journey from Harvard liberal to Kennedy activist to neoconservative presidential domestic adviser in the Nixon White House. (Later Moynihan became a prominent Democratic senator from New York and perhaps the nation's most effective spokesman for the liberal/progressive tradition.) Stockman left an indelible impression on Moynihan. Moynihan recalled in 1981, in half-teasing, half-serious vein:

> Back at Harvard, Liz [Moynihan's wife] and I were assigned David Stockman. Fresh from Michigan State and the Students for a Democratic Society and Vietnam summer, Dave was everything you could dream of in a mole. Cornfed and cowlicked, he was the best

> boob bait for conservatives ever to come out of the Middle West. The only trouble was he couldn't stop talking about the Viet Cong and American imperialism and the immorality of the Vietnam War. So we installed him in the top floor of our house and got him into the Harvard Divinity School. There he was taught, of course, that there *is* no such thing as morality. Now, if there is no morality, it follows that there is no immorality. *Tertium non datur.* . . . Dave caught on right away and started to think about *numero uno.*

Moynihan added of Stockman: "I have never known a man capable of such sustained self-hypnotic ideological fervor. One day he arrives at Harvard preaching the infallibility of Ho Chi Minh. Next thing you know, he turns up in Washington proclaiming the immutability of the Laffer Curve."*

In Washington, cashing in on contacts and demonstrating high intelligence and capacity for hard work, Stockman rose quickly. By the time he himself became a member of Congress from Michigan in 1976, Stockman was part of the Kemp/Wanniski/Laffer cabal and had shed his Vietnam era radicalism for a different ideological brand. Now he was a supply-sider, a believer in "minimalist government—a spare and stingy creature," and determined to play a leading role in "a frontal assault on the American welfare state."

His opportunity came when he helped prepare Reagan for the presidential debates in September 1980 at the Virginia estate of Senator John Warner and Elizabeth Taylor, which the Reagans were using as their East Coast retreat. Stockman was nervous as he arrived, but also imbued with opportunism, which he exemplified, wittingly or not, in his memoir, *The Triumph of Politics:* "I was about to meet the big-time players who, if their candidate won, would be running the country. This always happened—every time I took a step up the ladder. You always thought the people up on the next rung were going to be supermen. Few of them actually were."

*From Moynihan's off-the-record speech at the Gridiron Club, in Washington, March 28, 1981, before an audience that included President Reagan and Stockman. I was among hundreds present. His speech was later reprinted in Moynihan's *Came the Revolution: Argument in the Reagan Era* (New York: Harcourt Brace Jovanovich, 1988).

William Casey, the campaign chairman, former intelligence operative, and wealthy Wall Street lawyer, "mumbled much of the time." James A. Baker III, the debonair campaign manager and smooth Texas lawyer, a former Ford White House official who "cussed a blue streak and told off-color jokes," impressed Stockman "as the one who really knew what he was doing." Not so Reagan's closest adviser, the portly Edwin Meese III, who had been Reagan's chief aide and counselor in California and obviously, to Stockman, the one who best understood Reagan's mind. "Meese seemed to have two or three short points on every topic. Some of them didn't make much sense, but I figured that was due to the wear and tear of the campaign." Off to the side was Michael K. Deaver, Reagan's "image" adviser, "saying very little, as was his wont whenever substance was involved." Finally, there was the candidate himself, the new convert to supply-side economics.

Stockman's description of the supply side's leader was withering. "Reagan's performance was, well, miserable," he wrote. "I was shocked. He couldn't fill up the time. His answers just weren't long enough. And what time he could fill, he filled with wooly platitudes." He felt sorry for Reagan, the amiable man in the plaid shirt and cowboy boots, but was disturbed by what he saw. Still, Stockman was a believer himself; he would play the loyal soldier and keep silent. Besides, as he said, "By then it was too late for second thoughts. I'd already converted . . . so for better or worse, Reagan now *was* the voice of the revolution. It was just a matter of getting him up to speed for the debates. I was there as an actor, so it wasn't for me to take the lead in the follow-up critique. But nobody seemed to want that role. The campaign staff handled him with kid gloves. No one would tell him, 'That was a lousy answer.' "

The session left Stockman deeply disquieted. "By now two things were clear," he said. "One, that the candidate had only the foggiest idea of what supply side was all about; and two, that no one close to him had any more idea."

However that may have troubled him then, Stockman didn't show it. He was on the way up, and his close association with the big players helped him ascend even faster. Stockman also didn't disclose another aspect of the supply-side theory then. That was his own dirty little secret, one he finally revealed in his famous confession to William Greider: that supply-side doctrine "was always a Trojan Horse." Its high-sounding philosophy notwithstanding, Stockman had come to understand that in reality supply side was nothing more than the old trickle-down theory of economics favoring the rich over the poor. As Greider put it, after he and Stockman had met weekly for extensive tape-recorded conversations, Stockman "was conceding what the liberal Keynesian critics had argued from the outset—that supply-side theory was . . . only new language to conceal a hoary old Republican doctrine: give the tax cuts to the top brackets, the wealthiest individuals and largest enterprises, and let the good effects 'trickle down' through the economy to reach everyone else." As Stockman himself explained to Greider, "It's kind of hard to sell 'trickle down,' so the supply side formula was the only way to get a tax policy that was really 'trickle down.' Supply side is 'trickle down' theory."

Stockman had come to another conclusion that he also kept to himself: that the huge supply-side tax cuts that were endorsed by the Republican National Convention as a party plank that summer, and that Reagan aggressively campaigned on (along with his oft-stated promises to balance the federal budget within three years after taking office), could not possibly achieve their goals. Despite supply-side assurances to the contrary, Draconian budget cuts amounting to *one hundred billion dollars a year* would be required to offset new Reagan proposals for massive defense spending increases and drastically reduced tax revenues. Stockman therefore devised a deliberate strategy of deceit for what he later described as "a blueprint for sweeping, wrenching change in national economic governance." His solution, which he knew would "hurt millions of people in the short run," required "abruptly severing the umbilical cords of dependency that ran from Washington to every nook and cranny of the nation." It meant implementing "the ruthless dispensation of short-run pain in the name of long-run gain."

In this, Stockman saw the implicit failure of supply-side theory as an opportunity, not a problem. It provided a chance to have gigantic tax cuts *and* military increases—yet also dismantle despised social welfare programs that had accumulated since the New Deal. His secret solution was to let the federal budget deficits rise, thus leaving

Congress no alternative but to cut domestic programs.*

Whether Reagan was aware of this cynical strategy of public deception will long be a matter of debate, but certainly the goals Stockman sought to achieve were Reagan's, too. Nor was there ever any question about the essential premise of supply-side economics.

From the beginning, the creators and propagandists of supply-side economics acknowledged that it represented regressive tax policies that would benefit the rich more than the poor and inevitably widen the gap between the two. They made no apologies for the results they expected. Their repeatedly invoked incantation "A rising tide lifts all boats" was explicit utterance of their belief in the overall good that would result. By rewarding the wealthy, by redistributing wealth, by encouraging risk takers through tax breaks and incentives, they would in the end benefit everyone in society. So they argued.

Long before Reagan was inaugurated, critics repeatedly warned about economic and social inequities that would result if the supply-side Kemp-Roth tax cut bill were passed. As Yale economist and Nobel Prizewinner James Tobin said, adoption of supply-side economics would send a clear message: that "inequality of opportunity is no longer a concern of the federal government." To such as Tobin, it was highly doubtful that the supply-side theory would work as advertised. "What it is sure to do," he predicted, "is to redistribute wealth, power, and opportunity to the wealthy and powerful and their heirs."

Supply-siders did not quarrel with that analysis. In their view, rewards of entrepreneurship had been stifled by the heavy hand of government. Finally they had a chance to change that situation.

Stripped of slogans and magic economic curves, supply-side theorems were nothing more than the old selfishness dressed up in new garb for the 1980s.

It was a familiar pattern. Twice before, America had entered

*His former mentor Moynihan was the first to charge that the Reagan administration "consciously and deliberately brought about" higher deficits to force congressional domestic cuts. Moynihan was denounced and then proven correct—except that cuts to achieve balanced budgets were never made, and deficits ballooned ever higher.

periods that were characterized by a national climate of selfishness. Each came after periods of great national exertion, strain, and disillusionment, and in each the greed of the times was rationalized by the nation's leaders as being driven by nobler motives.

In the Gilded Age of rampant materialism and corruption after the Civil War, the Gospel of Wealth took form. It held that robber barons amassed fortunes only out of service to a higher deity. In 1877, amid hard times in his city, the popular Brooklyn preacher Henry Ward Beecher, who himself lived handsomely on the then vast annual income of twenty thousand dollars, dismissed the notion of inequality by declaring that "God has intended the great to be great and the little to be little. . . . [T]he man who cannot live on bread and water is not fit to live." Acquisitiveness was invested with theological blessing. In a popular textbook of the time, *Christian Ethics,* Daniel S. Gregory wrote: "The Moral Governor has placed the power of acquisitiveness in many for good and noble purposes." In a celebrated public address entitled "Acres of Diamonds," a Baptist clergyman from Philadelphia, Russell Conwell, argued that Christians had a duty to make money. Money was power, and not to seek it was to say, "I do not wish to do any good to my fellowmen."

After citing these tenets of the times in his monumental *The Growth of American Thought,* historian Merle Curti observed wryly that "the inequality of riches in American society was justified by the argument that riches rested on natural laws no less than on God's revelation."

In the Roaring Twenties, when acquisition of wealth again became a national obsession and was again bestowed with theological favor, business leaders were as venerated as religious figures. As Frederick Lewis Allen noted, "so frequent was the use of the Bible to point the lessons of business and business to point the lessons of the Bible that it was sometimes difficult to determine which was supposed to gain the most from the association."

A New York realtor, Fred F. French, quoted to his salesmen the commandment laid down by Matthew ("the greatest human-nature expert that ever lived"): Knock, and it shall be opened to you. Follow that as a business guide, he advised them, and Fred F. French salesmen will strengthen their characters and powers and be enabled "to serve our stockholders at a lower commission rate, and yet each one earn more money for himself than in nineteen twenty-five."

The Metropolitan Casualty Insurance Company issued a pamphlet declaring Moses to have been "one of the greatest salesmen and real-estate promoters that ever lived."

An advertising executive, Bruce Barton, author of *The Man Nobody Knows,* for two years the nation's best-selling nonfiction book, celebrated Jesus as the "founder of modern business" and termed His parables the "most powerful advertisements of all time." Jesus, he said, was a great executive who "picked up twelve men from the bottom ranks of business and forged them into an organization that conquered the world. . . . Nowhere is there such a startling example of executive success as the way in which that organization was brought together."

When Reagan's admired presidential model, Calvin Coolidge ("The chief business of the American people is business"), took office in the twenties, he embarked on an economic program that historian Charles Beard described as "transparent in its simplicity," adding: "Taxes were to be reduced—not indeed on goods consumed by the masses but certainly on the incomes of those who sat highest at the American feast. This was to be done, he urged, with a view to leaving more money in the hands of the rich for investment, so that the opportunities of the poor to gain profitable employment might be multiplied. Correlatively, there was to be less interference with business through administrative orders and through the prosecution of trusts before the courts. . . ."

The pattern repeated itself in the eighties. Not only were the conditions ripe for a new era of greed through reemergence of trickle-down economics under a new name and under sponsorship of the highest office, but once more acquisition of wealth had been given a moral rationale. "Search and you shall find, give and you will be given unto, supply creates its own demand," wrote perhaps the most fascinating of the supply-siders, a best-selling economics writer named George Gilder. "It is this cosmology, this sequential logic, that essentially distinguishes the free from the Socialist economy."

A visionary and another indefatigable promoter, a person of both casual charm and intellectual certitude, Gilder was the scion of an old New England family. Like other supply-siders, he flirted with liberalism before adopting another ideological approach. Gilder had an unusual childhood. His father died in World War II, when Gilder was three, and his mother then converted her husband's New York home into a rooming house. While she taught music, young Gilder was raised by the staff, all of whom were followers of the black religious leader Father Divine, who claimed to be God and whose disciples, or angels, as they were called, went by such names as Celestial Kindness and Gratifying Love.

Gilder attended prominent schools and did poorly scholastically, finishing last in his class at Exeter, then flunking out of Harvard after his freshman year. After Marine Corps reserve service, he returned and was graduated from Harvard a year late. He drifted into freelance journalism, wrote for the leftist *New Leader,* dabbled in presidential campaign politics, was a congressional speech writer and legislative assistant in Washington, and gradually attracted attention with publication of books that stirred controversy.

In *Sexual Suicide,* published in 1974, he inveighed against a perceived "feminist menace" that was "undermining civilized society." Writing in tones of moral absolutism, he denounced homosexuality and marijuana and concluded that "woman's place is in the home." The God-given mission of women was not to compete with men (and if they did, they should be paid less) but to marry and have children.

Gilder celebrated monogamy, excoriated sexual permissiveness and the sexual revolution. Not surprisingly, his thesis was both praised (by William Buckley) and denounced (one reviewer called it permeated with "shrill moral exhortations and febrile cross-mongering" and "weak in logic and appallingly weak on facts"). But it was noticed. By the Reagan inaugural Gilder's best seller *Wealth and Poverty* had become a bible of the supply-siders. (Stockman, for one, praised it as "promethean in its intellectual power and insight.")

It was Gilder who provided what supply-side religion had lacked: a new theology of capitalism. He came by it naturally. First and foremost, Gilder was a believer—a believer in belief itself, for, as he said, "belief precedes knowledge." He was also a believer in extrasensory perception. "ESP is important to me," he said. "I learned that it absolutely exists . . . the trick is that you have to have faith." Faith he had, in abundance, coupled with energy, flash, and a missionary talent for selling himself and his ideas. "Faith in man, faith in the future, faith in the rising returns of giving, faith in the mutual benefits of trade, faith in the providence of God are all essential to successful capitalism," he declared.

The Gilder message, also disseminated through the *Wall Street Journal,* was unfailingly positive. Capitalism was not selfish; it was noble, selfless. "Capitalism begins with giving . . . thus the contest of gifts leads to an expansion of human sympathies." He beat the drum for entrepreneurship, for risk taking, for free markets, new ideas, new approaches, new wealth, a new order, and always in tones of high moral principles.

If Bartley was the drum major, Laffer the economics high priest, Wanniski the proclaimer of dogma, Kemp the political practitioner, and Stockman the plotter, Gilder was the public troubadour, the good preacher of the new Gospel of Wealth. His homilies on poverty were right out of Horatio Alger: "The only dependable route from poverty is always work, family, and faith. The first principle is that in order to move up, the poor must not only work, they must work harder than the classes above them. Every previous generation of the lower class has made such efforts. But the current poor, white even more than black, are refusing to work hard."

Discrimination? Inequity? Favoritism? Excuses only, fake crutches for the unsuccessful to cover their own lack of drive and willingness to work. About the "myths of discrimination" Gilder said: "It is now virtually impossible to find in a position of power a serious racist. . . . Problems remain, but it would seem genuinely difficult to sustain the idea that America is still oppressive and discriminatory."

In speeches and editorial page articles Gilder proclaimed the coming of the new way. With adoption of tax cuts and business breaks, he predicted that the Reagan era would sweep out "the claims of the obsolescent past" and produce an economic boom unmatched since the twenties. Even as he privately drafted the introduction to Reagan's economic report that the new president was soon to deliver to Congress, Gilder planned a forum to celebrate the "surge of growth and wealth creation" that was about to come. It would be held at the Century Club in Manhattan, and he would speak. His title: "The 1980's. Era of Success."

CHAPTER 10

RUSTBELT

Far from Wall Street's visions of new supply-side riches, a feeling of failure gripped the region that produced the nation's steel, ore, cars, trucks, and machine tools. Across Pennsylvania, Ohio, and Indiana, along the Great Lakes and up into Michigan, through Minnesota's Mesabi Iron Range and foundry towns of Wisconsin and Illinois, factories were shuttered, their smokestacks stilled. They had been symbols of industrial might. Now, gray and ghostlike, they were remnants of an empire that had fallen.

Physical signs of collapse were everywhere throughout this new Rustbelt. In Youngstown, Ohio, in the nation's "Steel Valley," bridges were closed because cement had cracked and fallen from them. Funds for repairs were not available. "It's been total devastation," said a union local president. "It's just like an earthquake. When an earthquake hits, you can't believe the destruction that takes place."

In Aurora, Minnesota, among pine and birch woods of the iron range, stores along Main Street were boarded up and others were closing. For Sale signs were posted on cars, campers, trucks, and motorcycles standing on lawns before houses that were also on the selling block. There were no takers.

In Danville, Illinois, a foundry town of forty thousand near the Indiana border where Lincoln once practiced law, the unemployment rate had been stuck in double-digit figures for more than a year. The *Saturday Evening Post,* that bible of small-town middle-class American values, once described Danville as a quintessential midwestern community where "You Could Still Do It." The "It" meant the ability to start on a shoestring and amass a fortune, proving, as the magazine said, how great "are the little man's chances for success in a free society." Now an ominous sense of despair had settled over the community.

All these were surface signs of deeper trouble and of a greater story, that of American industrial decline and loss of technological leadership. It was a complicated story, and by the eighties it had begun to affect basic attitudes and behavior. No longer did people of the Rustbelt assume they would always have more. Personnel executives there encountered job applicants who falsified their academic credentials—downward—as college graduates, some with postgraduate degrees, said they had only completed high school. They did not want to be considered overqualified for scarce factory work.

In industrial community after community, a familiar pathology of poverty emerged. Social agencies reported increases in family abuse cases, in drinking and drug use, acts of violence, and divorce. Older people on retirement became increasingly fearful of losing their Social Security benefits after hearing horror stories of others being cut from rolls. Family separations became commonplace as unemployed men beat a path to the South and West, where boom times were occurring even as the Rustbelt had gone bust. Too often the result was the same: They returned with intensified feelings of failure after being unable to find work at wages that enabled them to pay their debts and relocate their families. They also were bewildered by the suddenness with which their way of life had ended.

"I remember when the steel mills caused so much soot in this valley that the Mahoning River never froze over," said Bill Jones, whose family had helped shape Youngstown's economic development for generations, "and my father used to say to me, approvingly, 'See that silt on the windowsill? That's a sign of prosperity.' Now we have the clearest valley around. Remember the story, *How Green Was My Valley*? Well, our valley is now green, and you're going to have wheat fields down along the banks of the Mahoning River. Maybe we'll become an agricultural community, recycling industrial prosperity back to an agrarian society."

Workers shared his views and exhibited new strains of isolationism and xenophobia. Management and labor blamed each other for outmoded union work rules and for placing desire for profits over welfare of employees, and both blamed the government. Everyone blamed foreigners.

In the collapse of steel lay the story, and the lesson, of post-World War II industrial America. Steel, the most basic of basic industries, had produced fortunes for capitalists, created economic security for workers, and forged the modern American industrial state. Steel built America's cities, bridges, railroads, provided its tools and implements, heavy manufactured goods and war matériel. Without steel the United States would not have won the Second World War. Pittsburgh alone produced more steel during the war than Japan and Germany combined. At war's end, with Japanese and German mills in ruins, the United States stood supreme in its steel productive capacity. Nearly two out of every three tons of steel produced in the world was made in the United States.

Less than forty years later the United States accounted for under 15 percent of global steel production. Nationally the steel industry operated at only three-quarters of capacity, and the industry was even outclassed by such once-inconsequential producers as South Korea and Spain.

Reasons for the demise were many. The United States had rebuilt the industrial base of its former enemies and neglected to modernize its own. Steel executives, conditioned to nearly a century of profits and accustomed to controlling their industry through a few blocks of concentrated power that also controlled market territories and raw material supplies, had grown comfortable and less inclined to be rigorously competitive. They also had become hidebound. "I think we declined because we weren't hungry anymore," said William Sullivan, a lawyer working as a consultant to the Jones & Laughlin Steel Corporation with responsibility for making redevelopment plans for closed mills. "The industrialists got too fat and sassy and spent too much time at the country club instead of scratching and the employees too much time striking because they could afford to do it."

To meet new safety requirements, steel owners cut costs. They depreciated equipment and permitted condition of mills to deteriorate until they were in danger of becoming obsolete, opening the way for foreign competitors and for domestic manufacturers using smaller minimills to make such steel substitutes as aluminum and plastics. They opted for short-term profits at the expense of long-term gains. Perhaps most damagingly, they stubbornly refused to reinvest adequately for research and development.

By the mid-1960s steelmakers were putting back into research and development only sixty cents of every hundred dollars of revenue earned. Competing industries were spending five and six times more for aluminum, concrete, plastics, and other steel substitutes.

While foreign competition increased, the U.S. portion of the world market declined. By 1967 steel had become Japan's top export and the U.S. import figure had risen from 31,466 tons to 4.5 million tons. Steel shipped from Japan was as good as or better than American steel produced at mills within a two-hundred-mile radius of the Port of New York—and it was 15 percent cheaper. Finally, another factor afflicted top steel management: greed. As their companies declined or were taken over, senior executives exited with "golden parachutes" guaranteeing them severance packages in the millions of dollars.

These conditions had long been developing. By the time the mills began shutting, the cumulative effects were felt in the Youngstowns and Danvilles, in the Rockfords and Garys, and on the iron range. Just a few years before, one huge iron range mining operation alone, Erie Mining, shipped nearly eleven million tons of iron ore pellets a year by Lake Superior to the lower Great Lakes and directly into the mills of Cleveland and Gary. They formed the steel that went into automobile assembly lines. Since then Erie's production had virtually ceased; unemployment and economic hardship were the inevitable result. The decline was also felt in Detroit, where automobile production had fallen and foreign imports were rising.

If steel, as John Gunther once said, was the backbone of industrial America, the car was the product that expressed what America thought of itself and that enabled it to change so rapidly. Nothing better typified the American ideal of individual freedom and mobility, size and speed than ownership of the most luxurious car—the bigger and more powerful, the better. And by the eighties nothing symbolized the industrial decline of the United States more than its automobile industry.

Over the decades Detroit had become more than a great industrial city; it was the heart and soul of the American dream of success.

Year after year Americans labored and competed so they could boast of owning the latest model Detroit produced. The sales volume of Detroit's auto industry was greater than the national income of most of the countries in the world, and Detroit had long been the U.S. government's leading indicator of the economic health of the rest of the nation.

Detroit auto executives were even more arrogant than the big steel executives, and as wrong about the changing competitive environment. They contemptuously dismissed forecasts that small European and Japanese imports could seriously affect the American market. Even more impossible to accept was the notion that these foreign products could capture it. "I can assure you that most executives and most salespeople and dealers in luxury cars back in the early seventies had never sat in a small car or a European car—or even seriously considered that they were transportation," said Cadillac's chief engineer, Robert Templin, the person who after much internal struggle designed the first so-called baby Cadillac, the Seville. "They were just not interested."*

Even the Arab oil embargo in the mid-seventies failed to change attitudes about relationship between size and design of cars and fuel. Detroit had long heard, and long discounted, warnings about depletion or disruption of the world's finite supply of oil.

Such smugness was dissipated during the economic battering that Detroit, and the nation, experienced as the oil crisis ignited a rising spiral of inflation that formed the economic backdrop for Reagan's election.

For the auto industry, the eighties began amid a climate of fear. Inventories were up, sales down, layoffs increasing. Uncertainty plagued the marketplace, while inflation ate away at everyone's purchasing power and standard of living. As the big-car market declined, Detroit for the first time was forced to consider whether the deeply ingrained American attitude that big was best, and biggest better yet, had disappeared. "If you could sit in one of our planning

*Several years before, while I was preparing an article on the auto industry in Detroit, a top executive for one of the Big Three manufacturers asked what kind of car I drove. He was aghast when I said a Toyota. That was "unpatriotic." When I replied I'd be happy to buy a small U.S. model of comparable quality if Detroit produced it, he suggested I was "un-American" and added that Americans did not want small cars.

meetings, like the one we had yesterday, you'd swear you were at the ayatollah's staff meeting," said Cadillac's Templin. "We end up shouting and screaming and pounding the table because we can't arrive at a clear consensus on a lot of these controversial issues. We see the future as being one where all the traditional givens are going to be much more difficult to obtain. The cheap oil, of course, is gone. The readily available materials are far more expensive, and of course, the capacity of the world to produce materials has not grown nearly as fast. Ten years ago, for instance, we didn't have to worry about how much steel we used. Now you no longer can say you're going to use all the steel there is, or all the glass, or all the aluminum. These have to be looked at as critical materials."

By the eighties Detroit, where market research and salesmanship were king, had evolved a term for this apparent switch in national attitudes: "downsizing." It was a term that equally applied to the country at large in a time of difficult transition. The question, as a new president took office, was, Downsizing to what?

Evidence had long been accumulating that America's technological preeminence was eroding, and in areas other than production of steel and autos. As only one of many indications, in 1971 the number of U.S. patents issued to American inventors was roughly sixty thousand. By 1980 it had dropped by half to thirty thousand. During the same period the number of patents issued to Japanese inventors nearly tripled, while patents issued to other foreigners doubled. American companies, some inventors and patent holders claimed, were more interested in short-term profits than in innovative products that involved risk and required greater time for development.

"Companies these days are run by business school graduates who are profit-oriented, not product-oriented," said Howard I. Podell, a registered patent agent and successful inventor from Tucson, Arizona. "They don't want to take the risks involved in investing in money to patent inventors for new products. Therefore, U.S. inventors have had to go abroad [as he had done] to patent their products." One result was increasing penetration of U.S. markets by foreign companies. "There's hardly a thing I own anymore that comes from the U.S.," Podell said, "my camera, my car, my TV—you name it. My grandchildren will have to learn

Japanese if they're going to do any kind of technical work."

For most of its history America's belief in its spirit of innovation was a principal reason for Americans to think their country superior. The idea of a nation of tinkerers and inventors—of Edisons, Bells, Fords, and Wright brothers—laboring creatively in their basements and garages to produce the electric light, the telephone, the self-starter, and the airplane was a national source of pride. Those who achieved practical creations were rewarded with riches and became national heroes. For a host of reasons, by the eighties true creativity appeared to be less appreciated and national heroes came from the worlds of Hollywood, sports, television, and music instead of science and invention. America, a nation of creators, had become a nation of consumers.

And increasingly, the scientists, inventors, engineers, and technicians who created the products of mass consumption were not native-born Americans. They were products of educational systems that set higher standards than those required of American schoolchildren. At the same time the number of Ph.D.'s in physics produced nationally each year was only about two-thirds what it had been in 1972. Nor was the nation committing sufficient resources to reverse the situation. "The investment in our research and graduate education enterprise, when measured in constant dollars, began to fall about 1968," observed William R. Corson, president emeritus of Cornell University, from a perspective of the eighties. Since then, he added, "the research and graduate education infrastructure has deteriorated. Modern instruments of research are unavailable in adequate numbers. Slowly, but surely, our base for international competition is eroding."

Pessimism was not limited to the industrial sector of the Rustbelt. It also enveloped the region's colleges and universities, and perhaps nowhere in the country was the change in behavior that came to characterize the eighties more starkly displayed than on the campus of Kent State University in northeastern Ohio.

A decade earlier Kent State became a symbol of violent divisions spawned by the Vietnam War after four students were shot dead and nine others wounded when a National Guard volley was fired directly into a milling crowd of antiwar protesters. Within days nearly a thousand U.S. colleges and universities had either shut down or come close to it and serious people spoke about revolution. To revisit that campus a decade later was to enter a different America, with startlingly different attitudes about the nation and its future.

Kent State still grappled with aftereffects of the late sixties and the new industrial ruin of the late seventies. Administrators looked back nostalgically on the time, not long before, when they were flush with federal funds and believed in growth as an article of faith. In the eighties, as one of them said, they faced the process of leading a retreat. "All we did was turn on the spigot and the dollars poured out," said Gordon W. Keller, associate vice-president of academic and student affairs. "We were thinking big, and a lot of our students were, too. They were blue-collar kids from Akron and Youngstown, first-generation college students, and they got involved in political ideology and took it very seriously. The same kinds of currents sweeping the country were sweeping Kent, too. What happened in Kent was a historical accident; it could have happened anywhere. If you were a political scientist like me, you couldn't have been in a better place. Kent was the U.S. in a kind of microcosm, with all its good and its potential and all its bad at the same time. Then the roof fell in, and we went through the fires of the damned. We were thinking big. Now we're thinking of a diminution of resources, of how to do with less. Now we're consumed with managing change and decline."

On the surface, a state of normality had returned to the campus. Fraternities and sororities were again popular; clothing and hairstyles were more conservative, and grades and careers, not dialectics and political protests, were again student preoccupations. Neither was it fashionable to criticize the U.S. government or condemn its support of corrupt dictators. Anti-Americanism, if it ever really had been that, was replaced by patriotism, flag burning by flag-waving. During the hostage crisis American flags hung from Kent State dormitory windows and students talked about "nuking" Iran. Instead of campus talk about righting wrongs—social justice, feminism, racism—jobs were the common concern.

But the greatest change lay in the students' views of themselves. At the student center, during a midmorning coffee break, three students were seated around a table piled high with books, talking animatedly: a coed, who turned out to be that year's Homecoming Queen, and two young men, one of them a fraternity president wearing a green Sigma Chi T-shirt.

"I think our generation's a little bit different in that it's kind of scary graduating and not thinking that things are going to get better," the coed remarked. "I mean, maybe in the fifties and sixties you had something to work for. You could afford that car, you could afford that house. Now it's like everyone's got a degree, and am I going to have enough money even to put down a down payment? Things aren't getting better, you know. We look to the future, and we wonder even if we should attempt to have children. I want to develop my own career, and I don't want to have to mesh it with someone else's and find out when we mesh our careers, we end up being different people. I want to channel all my efforts into just being successful. That's where it's going to be. That's what's going to satisfy me most. That's why I'm here."

The fraternity president agreed. "I'm hardheaded," he said. "I'm a very stubborn person, and there's no one, as far as I'm concerned, who is going to get in my way on the road to success. That's something I've *got* to do. Back in the sixties, I think they could have a more lackadaisical attitude. Now that things are tougher and the economy's tightening up, the people who are graduating have a better attitude toward a career. They realize how hard it's going to be to accomplish that goal."

The second male student spoke up: "My personal goal I know I'm going to get. I'm not worried about what my down payments are going to be, I'm going to be working my butt off. That's all that really matters to me. Really the attitudes have changed. More and more people are saying the same thing."

In time a term was coined to characterize them: "yuppies."*

*Precise origin of "yuppies"—young urban professionals—is unclear, but the American penchant for pop-culture definitions to characterize groups of citizens became a feature of the eighties. Other terms used were "grumpies" (grim, ruthless, upwardly mobile, young professionals, especially on Wall Street), "buppies" (black urban professionals), and "dinks" (dual-income couples with no kids commuting from suburbs to high-income professional jobs). The best exposition of this subject is Paul C. Light's *The Baby Boomers* (New York: W. W. Norton & Company, 1988), an assessment of the seventy-five million members of the baby boom generation born over the nineteen-year span from 1946 to 1964 who either came of maturity or assumed American leadership roles in the eighties.

CHAPTER 11

SUNBELT

In the Sunbelt people knew they were in the ascendancy. "Our best-case scenario for Houston is a worst-case scenario for the United States," a banker there said, and economic statistics proved his point. While national profit figures were declining, while unemployment was rising, and growth slowing, in Houston and the Sunbelt the opposite was so. Ads in the papers pointed to the connection that produced this new prosperity. "Are you involved in ARAB BUSINESS?" one read. "Then you can't afford not to have our books on your office shelf." Titles listed were: *Leading Merchant Families of Saudi Arabia, A Selected Directory of Business Contacts in the Arab World, Arab Markets, 1980–81, The Arab Travel Guide, A Practical Guide to Living and Travel in the Arab World.*

"As a result of all the activity down here, why, the rest of the country can be having a depression, but hell, you don't know it down here," said J. Hugh Liedtke, chairman of the board of Pennzoil and former business partner of the new vice president of the United States, George Bush. "I used to live in Pittsburgh, and God, we went through some of those recessions up there. People in the alleys, you know. Burning stuff in the barrel. You came down here to Houston—hell, they didn't know it was happening."

Houston was destined to be a boomtown, but the shock from the Arab oil embargo of the mid-seventies accelerated its growth. Twenty-four oil and energy companies moved to Houston after the embargo, and Houston became Growth Center, USA, as new freeways, supermarkets, and apartment complexes sprang up everywhere. Skyscrapers rose from the prairies with the greatest of all, the Texas Tower, still under construction. When completed, Houston people proudly said, the tower would be seen from fifty miles away, thereby testifying to the belief that, in the Sunbelt at least, big was still best.

No zoning regulations made order of this explosion of steel and concrete, and no mass transit system, not even a good bus line, prepared for the possible day when gas lines might grip that area, sending motorists into panic. Already motorists experienced massive traffic jams while driving into the city from the new airport some twenty-five miles away.

The movement of Americans westward accelerated. Out of the northeastern and north-central states flowed a steady stream of people. From 1975 to 1978 each of those regions lost nearly seven hundred thousand people. The Sunbelt states were the beneficiaries, growing, as Census Director Vincent P. Barraba said, "at a phenomenal rate." In those three years alone a million people moved into the South, and another four hundred thousand into the West. As mills of the Rustbelt closed, the pace of migration intensified.

The entire Sunbelt was growing, but it was Texas, the land with the golden touch, that led the way. An amazing boom, spawned by development of the "oil patch" to the west of Houston and centered on Abilene, Midland, and Odessa, transformed the Sunbelt, producing new wealth, real estate developments with new half-million-dollar houses, and seemingly limitless opportunities. New banks and savings and loans began to lend heavily to speculators and to invest aggressively in rapidly expanding oil and realty markets.

Month after month the flow of immigrants to Texas increased, with Houston alone recording nearly six thousand new people a month. Though Texas businesses and communities had launched national radio and TV campaigns to recruit workers, many Texans viewed the migrants with a contempt born of regional pride and a belief that Texas was immune from cyclical swings of the national economy. Texans were winners; the others were losers. Bumper stickers belittling Rustbelt migrants sprouted across the state. "Freeze a Yankee in the Dark," one read.

At the private Abilene Club, atop the Abilene National Bank building at 1 Petroleum Plaza, where the lobby contained an oil portrait of John Wayne, three businessmen were talking over lunch. "To tell you the truth, I don't give a damn what happens to those people," one man said, referring to unemployed workers in the Rustbelt. "They got themselves into their mess, and they can dig themselves out of it." Others around the table agreed. Too many of the jobless were not willing to work, they said. The unions brought it on themselves; they were unproductive, their wage scales way out of line. What good were people from Michigan whose only skill was welding?

Not everyone took such a provincial view, of course. Even amid the boom, private expressions of concern about the future were heard, often from some who profited from the expansion. Pennzoil's Hugh Liedtke was one. Outspoken and thoughtful, Liedtke had warned of impending energy problems for years. In his boardroom he showed visitors a tape of an Edward R. Murrow broadcast from 1954 in which Murrow warned that never had a nation "consumed so much coal and steel and oil and copper and lumber and water and strange minerals that came out of the earth, and at the same time [given] so little thought to where it came from." Murrow's message, which Liedtke emphasized to all who would listen, was that "although America is the land of the plenty, the plenty is giving out." As Liedtke would say, "Anybody in the business could see this shortage coming. The question was, What are you going to do about it? And the facts of life are that we've done remarkably little."

As a member of the president's National Commission on Materials Policy Liedtke had raised these warnings throughout the seventies and failed to stir a response from officials in Washington. "Oil and gas shortages are only the tip of the iceberg—well, that tip's pretty much out now; it's a whole continent maybe—but what is not being realized is that this nation is short of virtually every natural resource on which its industry depends," he said. "I'm talking now of high-grade copper and high-grade iron ores, on and on and on. It's going to get worse and worse for raw materials as time goes by. I do not think it realistic to suppose that this country is going to be self-sufficient in probably any area."

Liedtke's was a centuries-old theme—the notion of limits, the idea that eventually raw materials run out—but in the American experience this was an unpopular attitude. Until the oil shock Americans had never faced the idea that their society, like others, might have limits. All our history and experience taught otherwise. America was a nation that gloried in endless frontiers.

The late sixties and seventies had begun to force painful reexamination of the old faith, and the energy crisis was only a symptom of deeper concerns. In that same period Americans became aware of environmental degradation, of new health problems caused by smog and pollution. Environmental and "quality of life" constituency groups were formed, leading to passage of new laws and regulations. Spurred by these concerns, a new group of theorists, popularly called futurists, had arisen to promulgate what sounded like an old theme, that of the exhaustion of natural resources leading perhaps to decline.

By the eighties the ideas of the futurists about America's facing a "limits to growth" problem had become increasingly influential. America was at a turning point, they argued, and the time to make national choices to minimize dislocations was critically short.

Their ideas sprang from scientific and technological research, not theology or philosophy. Through the computer they developed models of social and economic behavior of the United States that enabled them to forecast not only the condition of Americans then living but the lives of their children and children's children. Since the early seventies the center of their work was on the banks of the Charles River in Cambridge, Massachusetts. There a spare, unassuming man named Jay W. Forrester led a group of doctoral students and professors at the Massachusetts Institute of Technology in developing the computer model and presenting preliminary findings.

Forrester was an unlikely candidate for a philosopher king of the future. He had grown up on a cattle ranch in Nebraska, son of one of the last homesteaders, and came to his MIT position by applying principles of a World War II engineering background, in which his work with fire-control devices and radar systems led him into early digital computer work and then to develop computers for defense systems. Since 1956 he had led development of what he called systems dynamics at MIT, a process that relied upon computer models to analyze how social systems behave and interact. His first computer models examined corporate behavior and attempted to pinpoint factors that caused a company first to grow and then to stagnate. Next he turned to the behavior of cities, examining factors that caused cities to grow over a 150- to 200-year period and then exhibit signs of decay as unemployment, poverty, crime, slums, and urban abandonment appeared. From there he carried his work into world structures. Eventually his research led him to promulgate a thesis about inevitable limits to growth, which brought him worldwide recognition and also made him the subject of controversy.

At MIT Forrester attracted a cadre of bright young believers. Unlike the supply-side theorists then predicting an explosion of growth that would result from adoption of their formula, Forrester's group approached its task with a modest sense that it might be wrong. Nor was Forrester given to sweeping pronouncements of infallibility as he and his group began to develop computer models with a 250-year time span, covering the U.S. period from 1850 to the year 2100.

Forrester's preliminary findings about growth limits struck familiar chords in American and world history. They evoked Frederick Jackson Turner's thesis of the passing of the American frontier; of Henry and Brooks Adams's fears that the industrial age would produce colliding forces and set loose unimaginable destructive energy, leading to eventual degradation and decline; of Malthus and the threat of rising population creating shortages and famine; of Charlie Chaplin portraying human frustrations with work on the assembly line.

However abstract, in focusing attention on new forces that he believed threatened traditional American assumptions, Forrester raised many of the questions people in the Rustbelt and other sections had begun to express. His basic thesis about growth was provocative:

> Growth is a temporary process. Physical growth of a person ceases with maturity. Growth of an explosion ends with destruction. Past civilizations have grown into overshoot and decline. In every growth situation, growth runs its course, be it in seconds or centuries. . . . In the United States the use of energy has been doubling each ten years. For the world, population has been doubling every thirty years. A twenty-year doubling time is typical of modern industrial society. Any growth that repeatedly doubles will, in time,

> overwhelm its host environment. At some time, growth produces its own termination.

Critics of Forrester and his advocates argued that they were modern-day Jeremiahs preaching a philosophy of pessimism. Americans in the main tended to agree. Many were convinced energy shortages were artificial, either products of a conspiracy (the Arab oil cartel and its Western capitalist collaborators) or a preoccupation of gloom-and-doomers. Besides, they had heard those warnings about shortages before, had always ignored them, and had been conditioned by experience to believe, like Mr. Micawber, that something would always turn up. While Forrester and his associates considered themselves neither pessimists nor optimists but realists confronting difficult new conditions, that wasn't what a majority wanted to believe.

Americans did not want to accept the idea that their country was in decline, and they looked to Ronald Reagan for a restoration of national power and prosperity. They wanted a successful America like the Sunbelt, not a depressing one like the Rustbelt, and the promise that appealed to them was a supply-side one of new abundance and wealth, not of a limits on growth and need for sacrifice.

On his inaugural day Reagan gave them what they wanted to hear. Like Franklin Roosevelt's, his creed was optimism. America was not, he said, "as some would have us believe, doomed to an inevitable decline." The way to resolve a momentary crisis was not through government, he said, because "government is the problem." He would fight terrorists and conquer them. He would cut taxes and liberate the citizens. He would rearm America and restore its strength. Most specifically, he would reduce the deficit:

> For decades we have piled deficit upon deficit, mortgaging our future and our children's future for the temporary convenience of the present. To continue this long trend is to guarantee tremendous social, cultural, political, and economic upheavals. You and I, as individuals, can, by borrowing, live beyond our means, but only for a limited period of time. Why, then, should we think that collectively, as a nation, we're not bound by that same limitation? We must act today in order to preserve tomorrow. And let there be no misunderstanding: We are going to begin to act, beginning today.

A month later, on February 18, 1981, Reagan presented Congress with what proved to be the most wildly inaccurate economic forecast in American history, a program that called for cutting taxes by 30 percent, increasing defense spending by three-quarters of a trillion dollars (a sum that over five years would amount to an increase of $1.46 trillion), and achievement of a balanced budget after three years. The national debt then was just under $1 trillion. Reagan said his plan would cut that deficit to $45 billion after one year, to $23 billion after the second, be *balanced* at the end of the third, and produce a surplus after that.

That's what Americans wanted to hear. They wanted to believe it in the Rustbelt, and they certainly believed it in the Sunbelt. In Midland, Texas, entrepreneurs in the nation's oil production capital gathered at the Holiday Inn to celebrate Reagan's inaugural. On a buffet table, surrounded by nachos and barbecued smoky links, they placed a cutout of the Capitol dome in Washington. On it was one word: "Ours."

CHAPTER 12

CAPITAL OF SUCCESS

Bright and articulate, Mayor Lawrence ("Larry") Stone was that American rarity at the beginning of the eighties, a political success in a time of political failure. Stone presided over a city that resembled a real-life political model for Ronald Reagan's political rhetoric. Sunnyvale, California, in the heart of the fabled Silicon Valley, then had a seven-million-dollar surplus and was thinking of giving money back to taxpayers as a rebate. Nationally Sunnyvale was known for the quality of its public services, for its parks and recreational system, and for providing better city services with far fewer workers than communities of comparable size. It also rewarded its employees with a merit system of pay and benefit incentives, generating high esprit. Mayor Stone was also unconventional. He was a liberal Democrat who had voted for Carter without enthusiasm ("I don't think any of them is qualified to be president; the system is designed to produce mediocrity") but who came to politics from an investment background and himself remained a successful entrepreneur.

He had been a Wall Street stockbroker before moving to Silicon Valley, and he operated a real estate business that owned shopping centers there. "When I became mayor, Harvard selected thirteen of us from around the country to take an intensive weeklong government program on how to become a better mayor," he recalled. "The mayor of Youngstown, Ohio, was in our group and I explained to him how we had too many jobs, how we were strangling on our success. As one wag said, we had made a mess of success. He couldn't understand how that was a problem. He couldn't focus on why the hell too many jobs and too many people and not enough housing units could be considered problems in this day and age. So I guess this is the American dream being enacted out here more than any place else."

On January 20, 1981, no area of the United States held greater promise as model for a more prosperous, successful America than Silicon Valley. Forty miles south of San Francisco, at land's end of the western continental frontier, it was the place where dreams still came true, and Sunnyvale, just above San Jose, was its capital.

Here was the wave of the future, a land of new technology that created new fortunes and new communities, and all out of valued American ingredients: hard work; enterprise; innovation. In the past these traits had led to development of the cotton gin, steam power, railroads, electricity, telephones, sewing and weaving machines, and the mass-production techniques upon which modern American industry rested. Silicon Valley was proof that American technology was still capable of developing an industry for the future that was, its creators believed, recession proof and pollution free.

As Mayor Stone boasted, its industry produced no decaying cities, its products did not foul the water or air or rely upon finite natural resources, like the oil that fueled the prosperity of the Southwest. It was both new and lasting, infinite in its possibilities, "the spearhead of evolution," as one of its promoters boasted.

Already the influence of Silicon Valley was being felt around the world, and it was destined to have even greater impact. It had come about with remarkable rapidity, and it was all, literally, a culture built on sand. "Do you know what silicon really is?" an engineer asked a visitor to this place of new wonders. "Sand. It's symbolic that this whole thing is built on sand. A basic industry that creates a basic way of life. It almost seems like an unreal sort of bubble."

In 1959 invention of the silicon chip had touched off an electronics revolution that contained unlimited possibilities. On a crystal made of silicon, about the size of a fingernail, were placed tens of thousands of transistors, diodes, capacitors, and other electronic material that formed the so-called integrated circuits, or semiconductors, of the space age technology that has reshaped modern life. Silicon chips were the brains of computers and the building blocks of everything electronic. They performed a range of tasks from controlling the path of unmanned missiles and operating household appliances to providing digital watches. They converted sunlight into electricity, opening up the prospect that someday they would fuel the machines of the future just as petroleum had powered the engines of the nineteenth and twentieth centuries.

A boom rivaling gold rush days transformed Sunnyvale and surrounding Santa Clara County. From the benign agricultural community of the recent past, that San Francisco Bay Area had become a succession of affluent suburban houses and low-lying structures that housed the new high technology electronics companies. By the 1980 presidential election, Sunnyvale alone boasted of having six hundred companies recognized around the world. There were seventeen hundred high tech firms in Silicon Valley. They brought prosperity—and more and more people. In 1950 the city numbered fewer than 10,000 people; by the end of that decade the population had risen to 53,000. Another ten years saw an almost doubling of the population. By 1980 the population was 106,000 and still rising, but approaching saturation point. Another 100,000 people commuted there daily.

In a time when other American industries were declining, or dying, by the eighties Silicon Valley was the vanguard for an industry that made millionaires overnight and that appeared to have no limits on its growth. By the year 2000 it was expected to be the third-largest industry in the world.

To Sunnyvale and the valley came some of the nation's brightest young engineers. Lured by stories of new success, others came from around the globe. They were risk takers, pioneers, venture capitalists, creators of economic legends of the eighties.

"What we have here is a culture of inventiveness mixed with a great deal of entrepreneurship," said Regis McKenna, who with his wife, Dianne, Sunnyvale's vice-mayor, had relocated from their native Pittsburgh in 1963, witnessed the valley's expansion, and, in a way, helped create it. McKenna formed his own company and shared in the high tech boom. "But growth industries in this country tend to be inhibited by our government," he said. "Look at the biomedical industries moving to Europe. That's because our government acts more as an inhibitor than as a traffic light. In most other countries today, say, Japan, France, and Germany, governments try to encourage growth industries. They see it as a base for future jobs. Our government still invests in Chrysler and the steel industries and shoe factories—the dying industries, not the growth ones. The steel industry or the textile industry or the chemical industry, they're gone, we'll never get them back. Why is Youngstown, Ohio, depressed? I'll bet their comparable cities in Japan and Germany are doing well today."

Sunnyvale and Silicon Valley demonstrated that supply-side theorists were right in one respect. Entrepreneurship and risk taking still created new wealth and produced economic success. At the same time Silicon Valley's experience seemed to underscore the warnings of Jay Forrester that growth had its own limits and extracted its own price—that, in time, uncontrolled growth would overwhelm its environment.

Now, some people in Silicon Valley were saying, they were in danger of being strangled by their success. "This was the land of opportunity, but what we learned is that the 1990s got here in 1980," said William Powers, Sunnyvale's community development director. "We're beginning to destroy the very things people came here for." During the presidential election year, in a move that attracted national attention and business consternation, Sunnyvale's city council proposed a four-month moratorium on industrial growth in order to assess its future development. Sunnyvale was saying it couldn't handle more jobs. It needed more breathing room.

These were problems that other sections of America wished they had to endure, and a certain smug satisfaction accompanied Silicon Valley statements of concern about experiencing too much success.

On Ronald Reagan's inaugural day, millions of Americans were in a hopeful mood as they awaited the new president's leadership. "My own feeling is hope that Reagan will bring in good people," Regis McKenna said in Sunnyvale. "I want to see a change of people advising on economic policy in Washington. I don't believe that the Carter administration understood economics. I don't like Carter, and I don't particularly like the morality and the leadership of Reagan; but I also think we've got to get our economy back in shape or we're going to lose everything."

Elsewhere Americans might think that the country had lost its way or that the government had broken down, or fear the country was in decline, or despair of the future. For the people of Silicon Valley, there was no such pessimism. Their vision was Reagan's vision, and the country hungered for it. It was a vision of success.

BOOK THREE

THE TEFLON YEARS

CHAPTER 13

ELECTRONIC CULTURE

In the eighties Ronald Reagan and television fitted into American society like a plug into a socket. Together they produced a parade of pleasing images that glowed in more and more living rooms and affected the country like little that had gone before. Reagan did not create the television age, as he had invented himself, but his sports and entertainment background was rooted in it. He governed through the eye of the camera and by using devices of the entertainer. His, quite naturally, was a presidency of pictures, symbols, and staging. Every public act of his presidency was planned by his media experts for its maximum impact through television. Every word he uttered, either to welcome a visitor or to address a group, was scripted for him. Although to the press he was the least accessible president since the twenties, to the public his daily media event and photo opportunity made him the most familiar chief executive.

As Donald T. Regan later wrote, key members of Reagan's inner circle "designed each presidential action as a one-minute or two-minute spot on the evening news" and "conceived every presidential appearance in terms of camera angles." They regarded the president "not as the powerful and utterly original leader that he was, but as a sort of supreme anchorman whose public persona was the most important element of his presidency."

Reagan was perfectly suited for the role of master entertainer and for fulfilling a public need for reassurance. Unfailingly he sent forth the message that people wanted to hear: Better days were ahead; national pride had been rekindled, faith in the future restored. News was no longer bad; it was something to celebrate. It was "morning again in America."

He was the Sun King, presiding electronically over the new national celebration from the White House. Under his reign, all lines blurred: news and entertainment, politics and advertising.

In the television age Reagan was right for America, and America was ready for him. Through television he offered simplicities and slogans. By accentuating the positive, by preaching success, he encouraged Americans to believe that all was well; their troubles were behind them. They could enjoy the fruits of the present without worrying about the problems of tomorrow. Like the media itself, with its quick and fleeting images and its emphasis on simplicities, Reagan personified a short-term approach. Living for today was what counted. He and his media managers were experts in manipulating television for their political purposes. But then television itself was inherently an instrument of mass manipulation—by advertisers, entertainers, preachers, politicians, athletes. It was there to be used, for better or worse, by those who best understood its power and had the most access to it. Television, too, dealt in slogans, myths, happy endings, and fragmentary images, and like the country, it had a short attention span. It was not that all its news was good or that it failed to inform Americans, as some Reagan critics charged, but it was true that Americans, with Reagan leading them, were in no mood for being bothered by problems. Reagan, and television, gave them what they most wanted: a chance to feel good again.

Television had long been the nation's common theater and common market, and the pictures it presented reflected, and reinforced, America's image of itself. Television entertained and informed, trivialized and made more sophisticated, bound together and further fragmented American life. All these tendencies were strengthened in the eighties. Through the new mass products produced for the electronic culture, and through the more individualistic political climate that Reagan helped create, it became increasingly easier for Americans to disconnect from unwelcome intrusions and search for new rituals to fill their daily lives. They could momentarily escape from problems and amuse themselves, if they wished, and the evidence was that many so wished.

In the eighties the symbiosis between Reagan and television

raised new questions. Was it possible the predominant values of success, winning, fame, and fortune that television transmitted into American homes had begun to manifest themselves in the character of the country? Were Americans becoming what they saw? Were they being held hostage by the miracles of their own technological inventions? Did their repeated exposure to fictional happy endings create an appetite for more of them in real life and make it more difficult for them to face life's realities?

Reagan affected television and the viewing public in two significant ways. First, and most important, was the power of his own soothing personality. Both he and television offered new opportunity for diversion and helped breed a new passivity in public life. Under Reagan's lulling spell and the television trance, increasing numbers of Americans became spectators instead of participants. Politically and personally they were "couch potatoes." Second, he changed the way that television itself functioned.

To head the Federal Communications Commission (FCC), he appointed a strong proponent of deregulation. "Television is just another appliance," said Mark S. Fowler, a former lawyer for broadcasters. "It's a toaster with pictures." As FCC chairman Fowler took the position that "It was time to move away from thinking about broadcasters as trustees. It was time to treat them the way almost everyone else in society does—that is, as business."

Under Fowler, laws and regulations that governed programming were changed, affecting everything from advertising to public service programming. His FCC scrapped the system of public licensing of the airwaves that had been in effect since 1934. Also abandoned were FCC regulations requiring broadcasters to devote a minimum portion of their airtime to news and public service programs, a requirement that affected religious, children's, and public affairs programming.* This greatly expanded the potential for profitability. The FCC raised the ceiling on the amount of advertising a station could run in each hour, resulting in a sharp increase in the number of spot

*This drastically affected programming devoted to children. An FCC study for the years 1979 to 1983 showed that actual commercial TV program time for children dropped from 11.3 to 4.4 hours per week.

commercials aired and a drastic shortening in their minimum; the fifteen-second spot became a new standard, one that further shortened the nation's time span and led to snappier, simplistic political and commercial slogans. It also abolished a log-keeping requirement that had enabled groups promising better public service to evaluate and challenge programming offered by television license holders.

In addition, Fowler got Congress to raise the limit on the number of TV stations a company could own from five to twelve. This ignited a flurry of take-over attempts. Between 1982 and 1984 the average price of a television station doubled from twelve to twenty-four million dollars, and the total price for all stations sold in 1983 and 1984 reached five billion dollars, or 60 percent more than the corresponding figures for the first two years of the Reagan presidency. Network ownership itself was affected. Capital Cities Communications acquired ABC; General Electric, NBC; and the Loews Corporation interests, headed by Laurence A. Tisch, CBS. A network like CBS was forced to fight a take-over by raising capital and substantially increasing its debt; one result was deep cuts in its news department.

The Reagan FCC was the first to vote to abolish the agency's long-standing fairness doctrine, which required broadcasters to air controversial issues by providing a balanced presentation of public issues. Congress refused to go along and voted new legislation to reinstate it. Reagan vetoed it. When Reagan threatened a second veto after the same legislation had been attached to a major spending bill, Congress capitulated. The fairness doctrine was abolished, and television operated in an atmosphere of even fewer constraints.

There was no doubt about the overall effect. Driven by bottom-line profits, the networks and their new corporate managers eagerly responded to the new climate of deregulation. They gave the public what they thought it wanted—and whatever led to greater audience ratings and higher profits. Increasingly even the news divisions were dragged into the ratings battle and pressured to produce greater profits.

American television, that "cultural wasteland" of conformity, had long been losing its internal battle between providing "quality" programming and mass entertainment. As far back as 1958 Edward R. Murrow, in a celebrated speech, had warned against the growing trivialization of television. He urged the networks to "get up off our fat surpluses and recognize that television . . . is being used to distract, delude, amuse and insulate us." By the eighties all this was more pronounced.*

In the wake of the success of CBS's "60 Minutes," entertainment programs with a news patina were introduced. "Economics is behind the rash of newsmagazine shows," "60 Minutes" executive producer Don Hewitt observed, commenting on the introduction of such entertainment network programs as ABC's "That's Incredible" and NBC's "Real People." While factual, these new programs relied upon bizarre examples to achieve high audience ratings: a man who catches a bullet in his teeth; a woman who runs an "adopt-a-ghost" agency; a farmer who has rolled the world's largest ball of string.

At the time Hewitt spoke, in mid-1980, his program boasted the largest network television audience. At decade's end the lines separating news and entertainment had merged as shows selling entertainment in the guise of news became among the hottest of the decade and spawned a new television form: "reality-based" television programming.

This pattern accelerated as ever more abusive programming (Geraldo Rivera, Morton Downey, Jr.) competed for attention and introduced "trash TV" or "tabloid television." The docudrama, entertainment in the guise of history, also came more into vogue. Prime-time docudrama miniseries productions costing millions to produce purported to depict what historical figures (Roosevelt, Truman, Kennedy, Churchill) actually did and said even if they didn't do or any say any such things. The public became conditioned not to notice, not to care, or not to be concerned about distortion of the historical record.

Serious television journalists worried that they were losing the battle to provide information of substance to the presentation of froth. In the face of competing television offerings, network news audiences began to drop. Networks responded by turning more and more to entertainment techniques to win higher ratings. They promoted their news anchors, celebrities in their own right, and rewarded them with star-level multimillion-dollar contracts. In the

*Todd Gitlin's *Watching Television* (New York: Pantheon Books, 1986), a collection of essays about television in the Reagan era, offers an excellent overview of the subject.

news business, pleasing personalities—and looks—were even more valued commodities. There were notable exceptions of journalistic substance and distinction: Ted Koppel's "Nightline" on ABC, the "MacNeil/Lehrer NewsHour" on PBS, the special productions by Bill Moyers, and individual examples of reporting, often at personal risk, by network correspondents. Television news, at its best, could still inform as well as entertain.

But increasingly television gave people an opportunity to substitute TV fare for real-life experience. Audiences were drawn into a new participatory role—in "talk" shows, where argument, accusation, and ideological posturing were more valued than serious discussion of issues; in game and catch-a-thief dial-in shows. With sex channels and late-night evangelist broadcasting, television charted new territory and became a direct hookup to the libido or the soul. Little thought was given to the long-term effect of these programs. No matter how outrageous or offensive, as long as they made money, television produced them.

Television's role in the Reagan era also benefited from the coming of age of innovations such as cable television, a proliferation of new channels through satellite dish offerings, and videocassette recorders. By the end of the eighties Americans spent an average of six hours and fifty-nine minutes per person per day (up from five hours and eleven minutes thirty years earlier) watching TV. Videocassette recorders became one of the fastest-selling appliances ever; more than 60 percent of American homes had at least one VCR, and 21 percent of households more than one (only 10 percent of the homes had *any* in 1982). Americans rented two billion tapes for their VCRs annually and purchased another sixty-five million a year at a combined annual cost of $6.4 billion.

The VCR alone had greater impact on individual and family leisure habits than anything since the electronic culture began to form after World War II. It induced people to spend even more time before their TV sets, playing rented or purchased tapes that offered movies, music, sports of all kinds, exercise programs, culinary and homemaking arts, and business lessons. One new television gadget created a new national pastime. With three-fourths of American homes equipped with remote-control devices for their sets, a viewer's ability to hop from channel to channel and follow several programs in the same time period became known as grazing. In the eighties the entire country was grazing.

The programs Americans watched throughout the Reagan years suggest that people had become more obsessed with individual success, the acquiring of wealth, and happy endings.

On "Dallas," the level of consumption caught the world's eye like a jewel in the sun. "Dallas" was the number one show not only in America but in Britain and other countries as well.* To millions who watched, "Dallas" portrayed a life-style absurdly unrealistic and unattainable, thus all the more desirable. With its great wealth, outrageous behavior, and dubious morality, the Texas-based Ewing family that appeared each Friday night in tens of millions of American homes became a national obsession. (When Miss Ellie underwent a mastectomy, 50 percent of all television viewers were watching "Dallas," an audience size achieved only by great sports events.) Never had television presented such a diabolically greedy man as J. R. Ewing. He was a heartless monster driven by his libido and his lust for money. Never had viewers seen such a procession of wealth and possessions and desirable women. In the cattle- and oil-rich fields of Texas, J.R. was the American dream gone haywire, but it was, on the viewing evidence, an American dream millions wished to experience.

Americans appeared inordinately curious—or perhaps confused—about the reality of the stars playing the heroes and villains who occupied their time and filled their minds. Was Joan Collins really Alexis? Was Alexis really Joan Collins? Was Larry Hagman really J.R., or J.R. really Larry Hagman? Resolving these riddles was made more difficult as the lines between fantasy and reality became as blurred as those between news and entertainment and between politics and advertising.

America's love affair with fame and fortune developed a new dimension. If one goal (wealth) was out of reach for most people, the

*Its impact was great overseas, too. As a young Jamaican journalist said: "Because of what they see on television, everyone in Jamaica thinks that our country is poor and underprivileged, and that everything in America is wonderful. Shows like 'Dallas' make it look like the land of milk and honey. It makes people think that money and material wealth are the only ways to be rich in this world."

other (fame) was more readily achievable. In the media and television culture, people could become "famous" for just about anything that attracted mass attention—from slashing a model's face in New York to shooting John Lennon or spinning the "Wheel of Fortune" and playing "Jeopardy" on TV. Often, transitory "fame" (or infamy) could translate into riches thanks to the appetite for obtaining exclusive TV rights to the new, the obscure, the bizarre, and the tragic personal life story. Now fame, and perhaps power, too, could be achieved merely by attaining wide public recognition.

"Dallas" and its prime-time imitators were not the only avenue to escape problems by entering a fictional world where, as historian Ruth Rosen put it, a yearning "for perfect love in a mythic community" could be fulfilled. By decade's end the daytime TV soap opera audience had risen to about eighty million each week, 80 percent of them women between the ages of eighteen and forty-nine (male students and older men also began watching the soaps in increasing numbers). These "soap addicts" fitted into every social and economic category: unemployed mothers; socialites; high school and college students; secretaries and professional women who watched on lunch-hour breaks or after work on their home recorders.

For the networks the soaps were a source of handsome profits and relatively inexpensive to produce. They allotted twice as much commercial time to daytime drama as to prime-time fare. Huge revenues were generated, producing, as Ruth Rosen reported, a gross of more than $253 million from advertising alone for "General Hospital" in the 1981 season and commanding $60,000 per minute of commercial time. Two years later ABC was reported to have cleared $1 million a week from the revenues from "General Hospital." In 1984 advertising revenues from the soaps yielded the three networks more than $1 billion.

In the eighties alone, television advertising revenue increased two and a half fold and accounted for $26.3 billion annually by 1990. Advertising people, of course, were sensitive about criticism of their influence and power and resented being thought of as hucksters and hidden persuaders. Their industry, they insisted, policed itself as much as or better than others, and their standards were no lower, and perhaps were higher, than those of others in business. "If you're really going to believe that the basics of this capitalistic society exist by the very fact of competition," a senior New York advertising account executive said, "then you have to believe in advertising. How else do you tell people what you have to sell so that they can make the choice? At least advertising gives the public an option. That's probably the best thing it does. And I guess that's how we justify ourselves."

This executive had trouble justifying one area of TV advertising, however. She had worked on a major politician's TV ad campaign just before Reagan became president and was disturbed by the experience: "If you can convince the world to buy a certain brand of toilet tissue by the amount of spending, you can convince them by the weight of your advertising to elect a president. That's the frightening thing. You create an image and an aura about him that doesn't exist. It's not in the selling of products that it's scary. It's in the selling of people." By the end of the eighties her fear had become fact.

Nowhere was the connection between television and the mass culture more striking than in the impact of televised sports events on American life. In the seventies, in his provocative *Sports in America,* James Michener had decried "the cross-fertilization of sports and industry" that resulted in TV's glorification of excessive violence, commercialization, and competitiveness and in the increasing use of religion as a sports metaphor. This led Michener to wonder if America had not completed a circle of civilization: from the Age of the Pyramids, to the Age of Temples, to the Age of the Stadia, to the Age of Cathedrals, to the Age of the Skyscraper, and back to the Age of the Super Bowls, Super Domes, and Super Bucks. The analogy was even more pertinent in the eighties.

By the time Reagan left office, eight of the top ten shows in television history were sports events—all of them Super Bowl football games. (The two exceptions, ranking third and eighth respectively in total viewers, were a special production of the Korean War drama "M*A*S*H" and the final episode for the racial saga "Roots.") The astounding rise in the cost of commercial spots for those Super Bowls reflects the hold of sports on television. In 1967, for Super Bowl I, each sixty-second commercial spot cost $80,000. By 1989, the cost of commercials had risen to $675,000—*for each* *thirty seconds,* or $22,500 a second! The networks had no difficulty selling commercials at such prices. With an audience approaching 130 million, they reached 40 million more Americans than the number who voted for president of the United States in 1988.

Because of television, multimillion-dollar contracts for sports stars became commonplace. An average professional football player's salary was two hundred thousand dollars. Professional baseball players on average earned nearly three times that amount. These costs were passed on to the public in the form of higher prices for products advertised on TV and higher prices for tickets. Television money forced professional and collegiate teams to accede to its scheduling needs, whatever the hour or place, and dictated breaks in an athletic contest for the airing of more TV commercials. "We think TV exposure is important to our program and so important to this university that we will schedule ourselves to fit the medium," said the late Paul ("Bear") Bryant, head coach of the University of Alabama. "I'll play at midnight, if that's what TV wants."

It was a system made for corruption. With such financial rewards* to be won by schools, franchises, and individuals, athletic scandals were widespread. These ranged from recruitment violations to individual athletes relying upon illegal drugs and steroids (and even "blooddoping," or illegal blood transfusions) to enhance performance. Distinction between amateur and professional athletics virtually disappeared. In the Olympics "amateur" athletes were paid to wear athletic apparel furnished by sponsors—and then were paid again to appear on television commercials and promote those products.

Increasing public cynicism, and a further diminution of national heroes, were an inevitable result. It was obvious that "amateur" athletics were not so. It was obvious, too, that for the right price everything was for sale. Identities of venerable college bowl games became those of their commercial sponsors. It was now the Mobil Cotton

*NBC paid a record three hundred million dollars in rights and another one hundred million dollars in expenses to cover the 1988 Summer Olympic Games in Seoul, Korea. Similar rights had cost eighty-seven million in 1980. The same kinds of increases were recorded in TV advertising dollars committed to all sports.

Bowl, the USF&G Sugar Bowl, the Sunkist Fiesta Bowl. These were part of the price of sponsorship, and the sponsor's price was high indeed.*

The public response to these conditions was, in large measure, to turn the other way.

A case in point: In the fall of 1985, during a cocktail hour at a midwestern country club, a group of business executives were casually discussing the latest sports news. A stranger, listening, noticed that no one brought up a big-league players and drugs story then being played prominently on network news. What did they think about it? they were asked. One person shrugged. The others were silent. Were people talking about it? Did they hear expressions of outrage or disappointment? Again, silent shrugs. And why was that? How did they account for the absence of public reaction?

"Look," one of them finally said, "it's just not surprising to anyone. It's a hell of a note, but everyone knows it goes on. I guess we have come to expect the worst."

That remark triggered a flood of conversation. They launched into a denunciation of professional athletes and what they regarded as obscene salaries, grandiose life-styles, out-for-number-one philosophies, and lack of commitment to the teams that employed them or the cities in which they performed. Their bitter response was typical of other reactions encountered around the country and suggested an undercurrent of disgust over scandals plaguing sports.

But the athletes and networks weren't the only ones who bore responsibility for the sad condition of American sports. To each sports scandal, whether it involved recruiting, cheating, or drug use, public response was the same: a collective yawn and a figurative wink. If ingesting drugs, injecting steroids, bribing officials, or skirting collegiate rules helped make one's team win, so be it.

The greater problem involved national values. By elevating sports over scholastics, by encouraging a win-at-any-cost, by-any-means mentality, and by furthering a climate in which people know-

*By 1989 TV commercial advertising rates for top college bowl games had risen to $275,000 for a half minute of the Rose Bowl broadcast, $225,000 for the Orange Bowl, and down to $100,000 for the Fiesta Bowl.

ingly ignored evidence of corruption, the nation only created more problems for itself.

Of all the mass communications devices of the eighties, the creation of MTV, or music television, was the best example of a true TV innovation that created an audience and a public taste and the one that seemed best to offer clues to future public behavior. MTV took sleaze and made it respectable, or at least acceptable.

Music television, or music with pictures, existed only as an idea in 1980, and the concept, put into practice a year later by Warner, was initially viewed with skepticism. Its demographic target was the teenager, the generation that had grown up with television and had TV as its main reference.* Within three years MTV had gained 24.2 million viewers. The bursts of rock music fantasy fitted easily with the psyche of a young America. Presented in three- to five-minute videos were elements that fulfilled a need for fantasy and escape. Whatever was done on MTV was generally considered "cool" or totally acceptable. From sex to drugs and violence, there were virtually no limits to the territory MTV explored.† Images it could offer twenty-four hours a day, seven days a week became symbols for the rock music culture. Price for membership in this ever-growing club was relatively low: the time in front of the screen and the price of an occasional album. Largely because of MTV, record sales soared in the early eighties. By the decade's halfway point MTV had turned on the nation's youth, and music videos appeared everywhere there was time to kill or something to sell: in clothing stores and malls, fast-food restaurants and bars, Laundromats and ski resorts.

The landscapes, the people, their outfits, their relationships re-

*Television's impact on children has been the source of much study, but more needs to be done. Studies show children are particularly receptive to visual stimuli and are more likely to remember images than sounds. Thus, they base their perceptions on what they see rather than what they hear. A study on the effect of TV commercials on children published in 1981 for the *Journal of Advertising* concluded that children tended to treat repetitive TV ads "as information sources and perceive no need to question their recommendation. . . ."

†"Negative" effects of rock music videos on teenagers sparked growing debate. In 1988 an American Academy of Pediatrics study said too many music videos promoted "sexism, violence, substance abuse, suicides, and sexual behavior." It found that teenagers spent an average of two hours daily watching rock videos. Of those with a theme, 75 percent contained sexually suggestive material, and 56 percent featured violence.

sembled nothing in everyday life. Their obscurity, their phantasmagoric quality were a large part of their appeal. MTV ignited emotions; it played to the heart and the ego, not to the mind. And always the videos were trying to sell something: an image; an identity; a hairstyle; a life-style. Often the sales pitch came in a convenient package deal. By purchasing the record, you could possess the sounds that were part of the image. Then you could practice the scenes played out by the musicians; you could simulate their "look" and their relationship to the world, be angry or violent, dress in leather or chains, be a melancholy beach walker at sunset contemplating your lost love or your painful new solitude. In MTV isolation was part of the appeal.

MTV reflected the times in other ways. Its message was strongly individualistic. Leather jackets and spiked hair could be shared, but the experience itself was personal and private. All that was needed to escape into a world of fantasy was cable television and free time. For millions of its inhabitants, that world often was more entrancing than any real world could possibly be. It was a world of illusions, in a time when America itself was in a mood for escape.

Despite the new world of electronic marvels, something was missing. Amid personal and technological changes that were nothing short of radical, Americans experienced new strains and pressures. The family, already in a state of fundamental change, experienced even more stress. Single-parent homes had become common, and existing families were rarely together in the extended form; even in the nuclear form they were often apart. In the modern world there seemed little room for them. The glue of custom and convention that once held couples together was gone. Under the pressure of separate careers husbands and wives had less time for each other. Women, if not actually liberated, were less bound to the traditional role of homemaker. Full-time working women represented the greatest American demographic change and by decade's end constituted 42 percent of households.

Both men and women played new roles. For many men this meant adapting to the new position of house husband and adjusting to a different status in the workplace. For some it bred a sense of desertion at home. For women greater opportunities to enter the previously closed male world of work brought new rewards and independence but also new demands and stresses. The value of marriage itself was depreciated. A new national state of individualism, and a new national loneliness, were being born. Thanks to the pleasure-providing machines created by high technology, means to fill those voids were easily at hand: the personal computer and its nationwide network of electronic "bulletin board" electronic messages; the Walkman; the VCR; the latest video or compact disk. These touched people at basic levels of existence and, by changing the way people lived, potentially changed the structure of society.

Machines themselves affected lives in numerous ways and made it possible to do things never done before, but they also contributed to intensified feelings of being alone. They facilitated the work of everyday life; enabled expeditious communications; permitted access to money with plastic banking cards; opened global markets; made possible bicoastal living, express mail, fax machines, portable telephones, advanced electronic networks linking homes and offices; and provided multiple forms of home entertainment.

The machines were ubiquitous. They spoke when Americans dialed 411 for information or when doors to new automobiles were opened. They delivered telephone weather forecasts and told time to the precise second. They relayed recorded messages from business associates, family, friends, lovers. Perhaps most important, they shifted attention from what people once did for each other to what machines could now do for them. People were approaching a time, if it had not already arrived, when they were spending more time relating to machines than they did to each other. Many even saw their machines more than they saw each other. Their machines held more possibilities than could be fathomed, and yet by lessening human contact, they left many feeling controlled or plundered by them.

CHAPTER 14

MYTHS AND REALITIES

Two events transformed Ronald Reagan from a politician of dubious credentials and public achievements into a mythic figure in American life. Those two events influenced all that was to come in the decade over which he presided. First and incomparably foremost was the assassination attempt just nine weeks after his inauguration. The circumstances of that attempt, the manner in which he responded to them, and, most of all, the fact that he survived combined to elevate Reagan into a place in the affections of his fellow citizens that he never lost during his years as president. His survival from a bullet wound lodged an inch from his heart was taken as an augury of a national turn for the better; it signaled the breaking of the skein of bad luck that had plagued the nation and its leaders for nearly twenty years. It led to a surge in his personal popularity, strongly affected his ability to dominate Congress and win passage of his military and economic legislative programs, and produced a strange yet not surprising suspension of public judgment on his presidential actions and policies that continued until the day he left the White House eight years later.

The other, perhaps less obvious event was his action four months later in breaking a strike of the nation's air traffic controllers. His response to the walkout of 11,600 air controllers was to fire them all. It was a move of such boldness and decisiveness that he was henceforth seen not as an engaging actor playing a president but as the kind of leader the country longed for and thought it had lost: a strong president, willing to take unpopular risks to achieve what he believed to be in the best public interest. That action strengthened his standing not only among Americans but among foreigners as well. "I've asked so many leading European financiers when and why they started pumping money into this country," a British friend in Washington with impressive contacts in the international economic community remarked years later, "and they all said the same thing: when Reagan broke the controllers' strike."

Timing of these events was crucial to Reagan's subsequent ability to dominate the political agenda by appealing through television over the heads of politicians and press in Washington to the general American public beyond the capital. In so doing, he succeeded in achieving what the philosopher Joseph Campbell had described as the ability to reacquaint Americans with "the literature of the spirit" and to rekindle a powerful national mythology. Had the assassination attempt and controllers' strike come late in his term, he would never have been able to forge the commanding national presence that gave his presidency such power and force, for better or worse. That they occurred in the very infancy of his term, with historical story lines yet to be assigned and chapters still unwritten, was fortunate and taken by many as a sign of fate.

He had made a strong beginning. Capitalizing on the public euphoria and new state of goodwill and national celebration that resulted from the release of American hostages minutes after he took his inaugural oath, he moved aggressively in his first weeks in office to present the boldest assault on the working of government since the coming to power of Franklin D. Roosevelt in 1933. Its approach was sweeping; its spirit, sternly ideological. At its heart was an attempt to unravel, if not dismantle, basic functions of the federal government established over the last half century. Day after day in those early weeks of his administration, front-page newspaper headlines simply and starkly told the story:

JOB, FOOD, SCHOOL PROGRAMS
NEW REAGAN BUDGET TARGETS

and:

TASK FORCE ON INTELLIGENCE
TO EASE RESTRICTIONS ON DOMESTIC SPYING

and:

AX POISED FOR POVERTY AGENCY
AND ANTI-SMOKING PROGRAM

and:

EL SALVADOR:
WHERE REAGAN
DRAWS THE LINE

and:

WATT TARGETS STRIP MINE LAW

and:

REAGAN ASKS 16% BOOST
IN SPENDING FOR DEFENSE

and:

REAGAN SENDS BUDGET TO HILL
AS "MANDATE FOR CHANGE"

All these had appeared within the first six weeks of his administration. By March 15 the full thrust of the all-encompassing economic and political program, presenting its fundamental grand assault on government functions, had taken form publicly. His great supply-side tax cuts had been proposed to Congress. So had his $1.3 trillion defense increase proposal. Plans for dramatic changes in ways of doing public business, affecting everything from abortion and hitherto illegal CIA operations at home to greater military involvement abroad, had been set forth. Elimination of basic health and social service grants on a vast scale was recommended.

Perhaps even more critical to his intent to reverse the role of government was the strong effort he immediately launched to deregulate governmental powers and policies. As with so much else that he set in motion, Reagan was not the first to seek aggressive action on this front. His immediate predecessors, Carter, Ford, and Nixon, all had attempted to loosen the bonds of governmental rules and regulations, and with some success. Nor was the issue of the proper amount and degree of regulation new to the closing decades of the century. It had formed a central source of political and economic tension and conflict since Congress passed the Interstate Commerce Act in 1887. That landmark legislation established the legal principle that the federal government had the right to intervene and regulate private interests when they were deemed to present a threat to the public interest.

Implicit in that law, and all subsequent federal regulatory actions that followed, was the recognition that the "invisible hand" of the free enterprise marketplace was not always adequate to maintain public standards of safety, equity, and corporate responsibility. Creation of such federal regulatory agencies as the Interstate Commerce Commission in the nineteenth century and the Food and Drug Administration in the depression era to oversee and police, if necessary, the nation's economic interests was followed in succeeding decades by an ever-expanding range of governmental regulations and agencies that moved inexorably into social and personal quality-of-life areas.*

By the time Reagan came to power, the federal government's regulatory hand had extended into virtually every area of increasingly complex American life. It affected air, water, banking, communications, transportation, nuclear plants, the workplace environment, product safety, and consumer goods content. Under Jimmy Carter, whose presidential campaign promises—cutting the bureaucracy, reforming the tax and welfare system, removing onerous governmental restrictions—foreshadowed those of Reagan, the process of deregulation of such areas as the nation's air system had already begun. Reagan accelerated it. Once in office, he moved quickly to eliminate or repeal long-established regulatory processes in U.S. industry, financial markets, and lending institutions. He had promised American business "regulatory relief" during his presidential campaign. Through his appointment power, he immediately began naming officials who would attempt to achieve the most massive rollback of regulatory functions ever either through change of statute or sim-

*An excellent scholarly overview of this subject, with attention to the effects of the Reagan years, is Larry N. Gerston, Cynthia Fraleigh, and Robert Schwab's *The Deregulated Society* (Pacific Grove, Calif.: Brooks/Cole Publishing Co., 1988).

ply by taking a permissive position toward enforcement of existing regulations. This was as central to his political appraoch as his promise to achieve a massive defense buildup.

Under the rubric of a plan for "rearming America," he advocated a profound shift in national priorities in the allocation and distribution of national treasure and resources. The Pentagon was named the beneficiary of an enormous infusion of funds, the domestic ledger the target for deep cuts in programs and spending. So munificent was the defense buildup plan Reagan endorsed that as part of attaining a six hundred combat ship navy, he even sought to bring back into active service from "mothballs" that old symbol of American military prowess the battleship, at a cost of additional billions. Many military strategists thought the notion foolish. In their view, battleships were dinosaurs of the seas, obsolete in the missile and nuclear age, when atomic-powered submarines carrying enough power to destroy the world patrolled the depths virtually undetected and when intelligence earth-orbiting satellites continuously circling the oceans left no place for battleships to hide. They were, besides, hopelessly limited in their capacity for modern warfare, their sixteen-inch guns woefully out of range and no match for missiles against which they would be forced to defend.

Retrieving battleships from the cobwebs of the past, analysts argued, was a signal that Reagan did not understand the military lessons taught by America's painful recent experiences. In the eighties America and the world had entered an era of limited wars, of guerrilla operations and organized bands of terrorists. In that world big bombers and big battleships blasting away with massive amounts of conventional firepower did not assure victory against peasant forces in Vietnam or guarantee rescue of Americans held hostage by Muslim fundamentalists. Smaller, leaner, more diversified, less conventional forces would seem to be the way of the future. Yet those battleships were precisely the symbol of strength that Reagan sought and that he most understood. They evoked the time, only a few short decades before, when America stood supreme militarily and economically, when the United States had the greatest naval and merchant armada the world had ever seen, some fourteen thousand seagoing ships at the end of World War II. It was to that era, to that mythical period of American life, if you will, that Reagan sought to return by reversing direction and leading America back into its past.

It was not at all clear that the Americans who elected him supported the kinds of fundamental changes he proposed. On the contrary, the evidence suggested otherwise. At that point there was nothing to indicate that a majority of Americans agreed with his ideological pronouncements. One month after he took office, a CBS/*New York Times* poll found that the public favored a balanced budget over more military spending. It opposed large tax cuts. It opposed cuts in Social Security, mass transit, pollution control, and aid to students.

Similarly, a Gallup poll taken after the election found that the American public and the president did not agree on two key campaign issues, the Equal Rights Amendment and abortion. While Reagan opposed the ERA, the public favored it by an overwhelming two to one margin. Reagan favored a ban on abortions except when the life of the mother was at stake; the public took the opposite view. It strongly was against banning any abortions. Gallup also found that a large majority differed from Reagan's views on other public questions: It wanted stricter handgun controls and favored keeping the fifty-five-mile-per-hour national speed limit; by a narrower margin, the public opposed construction of more nuclear plants. In all these, and in others, the public was not then supportive of Reagan's views and approaches.

Later it was claimed by some of his critics that he had misled the nation by hiding the nature of the changes he proposed. Or, in a corollary argument, it was charged that the press failed to do its job and disclose the severity of the changes he sought or explain their potential impact on people.

Part of the reason for the subsequent search for scapegoats was attributable to David Stockman. Later Stockman admitted that he and Reagan officials had deliberately kept hidden from Congress, press, and public their knowledge that the Reagan economic plan could never work as advertised and their belief that when forced to make difficult budget choices between defense and domestic spending, Congress would have to choose military over social needs.* Part was attributable to the stunning success Reagan achieved, in contrast

*For fuller exposition of this subject, see pages 107–11.

with his immediate predecessors, in securing passage of his political agenda. Still, while some duplicity was surely involved, neither Reagan nor the press was guilty of the larger charges of a deliberate conspiracy to deceive the public. As those page one headlines culled from the first weeks of his administration demonstrate, the Reagan proposals were fully and immediately aired; they formed the material for instant public debate. Reagan had practiced no deceit, nor was there any hidden agenda on his part. Americans had every opportunity to become fully informed about the scope of the political revolution being proposed.

Two months into his term there existed a clear and growing conflict between public desires and presidential wishes. Reagan had clearly defined his interpretation of his mandate. He had plunged ahead aggressively in an effort to turn back the political clock, but there was no assurance he would succeed and considerable reason to believe he might fail. His proposals were already stirring intense controversy, with the promise of more to come. Then, suddenly, all equations, political and personal, were altered with the assassination attempt on March 30, 1981, in Washington, sixty-nine days after he became president.

The attempt on Ronald Reagan's life followed a familiar pattern. Once again the would-be assassin was a pathetically disturbed young man acting out a fantasy formed by the illusory world of Hollywood, in his case repeatedly watching the film *Taxi Driver* and becoming fixated on its young actress, Jodie Foster.* John W. Hinckley, Jr., was a familiar type in other respects. He was a child of wealth and privilege who became one of the nation's lonely drifters, living in a constant state of illusions as he wandered from place to place, until he sought to "prove" his love for Foster by killing the most famous person in the world. The Devastator bullets containing explosive tips that he fired from an easily purchased, cheap handgun marked the fourth time in less than twenty years that gunshots had been fired at a

*In *Taxi Driver* Foster plays a young runaway who ends up as a New York prostitute and befriends a lonely, mentally unstable cabdriver (played by Robert De Niro) who stalks a political candidate and is prepared to assassinate him before being frightened off by a security agent. In a life-imitates-art-imitates-life aspect, the screenplay was inspired by the life of Arthur Bremer, a Milwaukee busboy who attempted to assassinate George Wallace with a handgun.

president of the United States from streets of a large American city.

Moments after the crackle of gunfire echoed off the stone wall outside the Washington Hilton Hotel shortly after two-thirty in the afternoon on a sodden spring day, an eyewitness said, "I knew it was more than just firecrackers." Within minutes Americans everywhere knew it had happened again: another president shot, another political promise interrupted by violence. For hour after hour that day there was no way for Americans to escape the replaying of an old national horror. Over and over, from daylight into dark, in slow motion, in stop action, and in all the other techniques of electronic communications, television brought home the latest installment of an all-too-familiar American tragedy. The sudden pap-pap of gunfire, the bodies hurtling to the ground, the hoarse shouts, the presidential limousine speeding off to the hospital emergency room, the gathering of the silent crowds standing outside in a driving rain, the ominous news bulletins reporting on the president's condition coming furiously throughout the day, the clusters of people gathered before their TV sets all forced people once again to think the unthinkable.

Those television scenes formed inseparable parts of an unending spasm of violence that had struck the nation with blow after blow. For a generation, violent acts had disrupted the political process, torn at the nation's leadership, left citizens numbed by a cycle of terror.

No one could say with certainty what the cumulative impact of these acts had been on individual Americans or on the country as a whole. Obviously it had been great, and made more so by the age of instant video communications. As Americans once more sat before their television sets anxiously awaiting news bulletins and wondering what was happening to their country, this time there was a different ending. Reagan survived, and did so in a manner that won American hearts.

The bullet had entered his body below the left armpit, struck the seventh rib, glanced off the bone, punctured the lung, and lodged near his heart. Despite repeated reassurances given then and later by officials that the wound was not serious—"not all that serious," as one newspaper report typically put it—he had been gravely injured. His blood pressure was alarmingly low, his left pleural cavity was filling with blood, he was laboring for breath, and he was approaching a state of incipient shock as he was placed inside a trauma unit at George Washington University Hospital.

He displayed genuine courage and humor in adversity. When he saw the panic-stricken look on his wife's face as she watched the doctors begin examining him, he quipped: "Honey, I forgot to duck."

In a time when so many direct quotations said to have been spoken by a president and put out publicly in his name were false, to anyone who knew anything about Ronald Reagan this one was authentic. They were the identical words Jack Dempsey had spoken into the radio microphones after losing his heavyweight crown to Gene Tunney in the twenties. Reagan, the sports buff, radio fan, and budding sports announcer, must have heard them as a college student and remembered. Similarly, his joking remark to the doctors who were about to operate on him—"I hope you're all Republicans"—had the ring of the authentic Reagan.

These remarks, when instantly relayed to the press, understandably had a powerful and positive effect on the American public. The subsequent cheerfulness and grace Reagan displayed during his long recovery in hospital and White House, his ritual waves and smiles given during the daily long-range photo opportunities, also contributed strongly in reassuring the public. They all conveyed a sense to the public that Reagan possessed larger-than-life qualities. That his recovery itself was a far more difficult process than let on by his political and public relations advisers was not in itself significant.* Reagan's survival alone was proof enough that the country's luck had turned for the better.

Reagan had entered a new phase of public popularity and acceptance; his political team effectively capitalized on them. As pollsters reported a wave of admiration for Reagan from around the country,

*The reality of Reagan's recovery, like the seriousness of his wound, was carefully kept from the public. At the time I, and surely others, heard numerous accounts from people in the administration who maintained that Reagan had been left far more debilitated than the public knew. This was in contrast with the cheering demeanor and jaunty waves he delivered for the cameras in the brief appearances staged for the media by his public relations people. The best published account of this period appears in Bob Woodward's *Veil: The Secret Wars of the CIA, 1981–1987* (New York: Simon and Schuster, 1987). In it, Woodward described the shock and concern the few key aides felt when they saw Reagan's "pale and disoriented" appearance, his faltering manner, and his ability to concentrate "for only a few minutes at a time."

White House officials moved to push for passage of the president's legislative program.

Typical of the media blitz instituted out of the White House was the appearance of Treasury Secretary Donald T. Regan on ABC's "Good Morning America" television program the day after the shooting. The president's temporary incapacitation, Regan said, had made his cabinet members "determined, even more, to push his program and 'win one for the Gipper.' " Similar remarks were made by the rest of the Reagan team. "We have to formulate another political campaign in which we're selling a product, not a candidate," said Reagan's closest friend in Congress, Senator Paul Laxalt of Nevada, in describing the political strategy Republicans would employ to gain passage of Reagan's tax cuts, defense increases, and domestic spending reductions.

Others immediately foresaw that the assassination attempt could have lasting political implications. Robert Teeter, a leading Republican pollster who later became a chief adviser to George Bush in the 1988 presidential campaign, shrewdly summed up what he correctly understood to be the new political realities. "It certainly makes people feel more personally sympathetic to him," Teeter told David S. Broder of the *Washington Post* hours after the assassination attempt, "and makes it harder for the Democrats to criticize him directly. A lot of his support was soft and the fact that he handled his first crisis well . . . will firm up that support. I think at the minimum it buys him more time and makes opposition harder."

Leading Democrats and Reagan opponents shared the sense that something of great political importance had happened. Comments of two other politicians whom Broder interviewed immediately after the shooting reflected that feeling. "I think he will remain popular throughout his term now, whether or not his program works," said William R. Hamilton, who took political polls for many Democratic members of Congress. "When he showed the ability to go through this with a quip, it was something the average man can understand. It probably makes him immune from ever dropping to the low level of personal popularity Carter reached." Morris Udall of Arizona, one of the most respected Democratic members of Congress, who himself had sought the presidency in 1976, said: "This is a long-term plus for

Reagan. He has been through the fire and escaped. There is an aura there that wasn't there before."

Within three months, as Democrats broke ranks by the scores, Congress overwhelmingly voted for the Reagan tax cuts and the big defense buildup. Reagan then stood, like Roosevelt before him, as king of Congress and legislative master of all he surveyed. On the day the tax cut legislation passed, a Texas Democratic member of Congress amused reporters in the House press gallery by paying rueful tribute to Reagan's gifts of political salesmanship by remarking, "I sure hope he doesn't go on television to promote the elimination of fucking."*

In the glow of that triumph, and only days after he celebrated passage of the supply-side tax cuts, Reagan took the second step that further solidified his hold on the public and transformed his presidency.

On August 3 the Professional Air Traffic Controllers Organization (PATCO), whose 11,600 members were responsible for directing, routing, and controlling landings and takeoffs of all commercial air traffic in the nation, began a nationwide walkout. It was a disastrously conceived strike, born of internal feuding and political jockeying within the union and a great miscalculation on the part of union officials about Ronald Reagan. PATCO had been one of the few national labor unions that supported Reagan in his presidential election campaign of 1980 (the teamsters' union was another). Its leaders counted on that fact and on Reagan's own oft-stated union background when, as head of the Screen Actors Guild, he had led a strike of actors in Hollywood.

The union had legitimate grievances. Airport facilities badly needed technological modernizing. Air traffic had increased steadily nationwide, leading to greater congestion and delays. The work load of controllers had also increased, placing heavier strain on people whose jobs already subjected them to tremendous pressures. Still, the decision to strike could not have been more destructive for the union.

*Reported by Laurence I. Barrett of *Time* magazine in his detailed account of the early White House years, *Gambling with History: Reagan in the White House* (New York: Doubleday & Company, Inc., 1983), p. 170.

It played directly into Reagan's hands and presented him with the trump cards if he chose to use them. The strike was illegal. It violated public trust and the public oath taken by the air controllers.

Reagan seized the opportunity by demonstrating to the public that he could deal as effectively with confrontational union politics as he had with the Congress. In the process he showed an instinctive understanding that the public always backs presidents when they take a strong stand on clear-cut public interest issues. Harry Truman had set an example when, at the low point of his presidency in the wave of strikes following the end of World War II, he faced simultaneously a walkout of the nation's coal miners and a national rail strike that together threatened to bring America to a standstill. As William Manchester wrote, in his brilliant narrative history *The Glory and the Dream:*

> The leaders of the two unions had long been allies of the Democratic Party, and when Truman called them into the White House three days before the strike deadline and offered generous arbitration awards, he expected them to accept. Instead they shook their heads stubbornly.
>
> "If you think I'm going to sit here and let you tie up this whole country," he said, "you're crazy as hell."
>
> "We've got to go through with it, Mr. President," one of them replied, "our men are demanding it."
>
> Truman rose. "All right," he said. "I'm going to give you the gun. You've got just forty-eight hours—until Friday at this time—to reach a settlement. If you don't, I'm going to take over the railroads in the name of government."

The deadline passed without compliance. Truman seized the railroads, went before Congress, asked for and got authority to draft into the Army all railroad workers, regardless of their personal situation. The unions caved. The rail strike never occurred. Leonine old John L. Lewis, the miners' union leader, who had loudly boasted, "You can't mine coal with bayonets," was forced to capitulate. He ordered his men back to work. Truman's popularity soared, and his political power increased.

Reagan's action was not so melodramatic, and he did not take Truman as his model for presidential action; but he was every bit as decisive, and the effects were the same. He fired the union air controllers, placed members of the armed forces into the air control towers, and ensured that air traffic continued to move without interruption. His action not only broke the strike but destroyed the union. PATCO lost its union certification and went bankrupt.

Even some of Reagan's supporters thought he had overreacted. It had not been necessary to eliminate the union and fire all its federal employees, they thought. They also believed him wrong in thinking that such a demanding and intensely pressurized job could be performed with fewer workers. More controllers, not fewer, would be needed. Concerns were expressed, too, that his action might endanger the long-term safety of air travel. Nonetheless, public response to his move was immediate and strongly supportive. Many who traveled by air in the days immediately after he fired the controllers were struck by the vehemence of public comments. "They ought to shoot them," one person told another at Washington's National Airport. "They" were the government; "them," the controllers.*

Interestingly, Reagan's model for action was the president he said he admired most, Calvin Coolidge. It proved that Coolidge's most famous political action (there were not many) still stirred a deep response among Americans. Coolidge, in the statement that lifted him from relative obscurity as governor of Massachusetts and made him a national hero after World War I, had called out the National Guard and told striking Boston policemen: "There is no right to strike against the public safety by anybody, anywhere, any time."

Reagan's emulation of Coolidge was not accidental. On the day he entered the White House, on his orders, Coolidge's oil portrait

*Three years later 20 percent fewer controllers were handling 6 percent more air traffic, and serious questions about air safety and deregulation were being expressed nationally. Newly hired controllers were less experienced than those who had been fired and, ironically, they began voicing the same job concerns that had helped precipitate the PATCO walkout: that controllers were being required to work overtime hours in an already stressful position and also forced to do more with less. In that same period the Reagan administration cut the number of Federal Aviation Administration field inspectors by 23 percent while seventeen hundred more commercial planes were brought into service. Gradually the number of air controllers was increased until there were more on the job by 1988 than at the time of the PATCO strike although the given figure can be misleading. The FAA now included traffic management coordinators in the air traffic controller definition, even though they do not control traffic. Questions about the connection between safety and stress of the job continued.

had been dusted off and brought down from the attic and hung in a place of honor near him in his Cabinet Room. In public, in those early months, Reagan began comparing himself with Coolidge. "Now you hear a lot of jokes about Silent Cal Coolidge," he said admiringly one day that spring while still recuperating from being shot, "but I think that the joke is on the people that make jokes because if you look at his record, he cut the taxes four times. We had probably the greatest growth and prosperity that we've ever known. And I have taken heed of that because if he did nothing, maybe that's the answer [for] the federal government."

The comparison was well taken. Though they differed in personality and temperament, intellectually and philosophically they had much in common. The most original thing about Reagan, like Coolidge, was his uncompromising unoriginality. They embraced the same governmental approaches: tax cuts; get government off the backs of citizens; prime the pump; help the rich first; let benefits trickle down; laissez-faire.

More important, Reagan, like Coolidge, perfectly matched the temper of his times. In some ways, like his predecessor, he helped create them. Coolidge had been canonized as the patron saint of business, and the views he expressed had struck a deep chord with Americans. As Frederick Lewis Allen wrote:

> Calvin Coolidge still believed in the old American copy-book maxims when almost everybody else had forgotten them or was beginning to doubt them. . . . This philosophy of hard work and frugal living and piety crowned with success might have been brought down from some Vermont attic where *McGuffey's Reader* gathered dust. But it was so old that it looked new; it was so exactly what uncounted Americans had been taught at their mother's knee that it touched what remained of the pioneer spirit in their hearts; and Coolidge set it forth with refreshing brevity.

The same was so of Reagan. Critics might rail against his simplicities, his evoking of nostalgia for a national past supposedly simpler and more pleasant, for presenting illusions that easy solutions to complicated problems existed. Americans in the eighties felt otherwise. Never mind hard realities and challenges of a far more competitive world. They were in a mood for the resurrection of old myths. In the survival and good luck of Ronald Reagan, they found what they were seeking. "The era of self-doubt is over," Reagan had said in his inaugural address, and the nation cheered. In believing in him, they were reaffirming a belief in their nation and in themselves. It was an irresistibly powerful combination.

CHAPTER 15

PRIVATIZING

In the summer of 1983, after learning that he was about to be fired for "abuse of office," Emanuel S. Savas resigned as assistant secretary of the U.S. Department of Housing and Urban Development (HUD) in Washington. It was a momentary embarrassment to the Reagan administration, barely attracting attention and worth noting in the larger context of Washington in the eighties only because it so perfectly captured the irony surrounding many of the ethical misconduct cases involving Reagan's political appointees.

Savas was unknown to the general public, but the nation's mayors knew him well as the Reagan political appointee who had written an urban policy report criticizing them as "wily stalkers of federal funds." He was also chief architect of the administration's effort to reduce federal aid to cities. Seven months before resigning he was put on paid government leave, an action prompted by press reports that he had directed several HUD employees to spend government business hours typing and proofreading the manuscript for a book he was writing for private publication. The title of his book was: *Privatizing the Public Sector: How to Shrink Government.*

Subsequent investigation revealed that Savas had adopted other standards for "privatizing" government. Before entering federal service, he had received $33,000 in consulting fees from a firm that later was awarded a $495,000 HUD contract. Savas himself selected the panel that awarded the contract, and it was granted even though two competing firms submitted bids at least $190,000 lower. In 1982, while working to shrink government and publicly lambasting mayors for trying to garner federal funds, and at a time when his own agency was raising rents for indigent public housing clients, Savas charged the federal government $14,000 for transportation expenses. Included in his government expense vouchers were four "official" trips to Europe and twenty weekend trips to New York. On each of those trips he stayed with his family at his home in nearby New Jersey. When questioned about those trips and expenses, he explained it was cheaper to combine weekend family visits with official speaking engagements there.

The Savas case was symptomatic of problems involving Reagan officials in a wide range of federal agencies, departments, bureaus, and commissions. Similar incidents occurred at the Postal Service, the Environmental Protection Agency, the Federal Aviation Administration, the Agriculture Department, the Health and Human Services Department, the Federal Home Loan Bank Board, the Veterans Administration, the Federal Emergency Management Agency (FEMA), the Legal Services Corporation, the U.S. Commission on Civil Rights, the Transportation Department, the Consumer Product Safety Commission, the Economic Development Administration, the government-sponsored Synthetic Fuels Corporation, the Social Security Agency, the Bureau of Land Management, the Occupational Safety and Health Administration (OSHA), and the Pentagon.

At their heart were insensitivity to appearances of conflicts of interest and desire to take advantage of the very federal offices and programs that the officials said they sought to diminish. "If they're going to shower all this money around, we're going to get some of it," Reagan's former secretary of agriculture John Block told the *Wall Street Journal* when questioned about why he had applied for federal aid for his own farm in Illinois. As secretary Block had been a strong advocate of slashing farm subsidies.

Even allowing for tighter ethical rules and guidelines in effect during his presidency, which made acts once acceptable, or only questionable, now subject to official sanction, the Reagan years were marked by numerous instances of officials cashing in on their public positions for personal profit. Some of the cases resulted in reprimands and ethical or criminal investigations. Others were briefly reported (or not all) in the daily press and led to a quiet departure of an official. In many instances, no action was taken; the official remained on the job. The greatest examples of corruption, at a cost of hundreds of billions of dollars to the taxpayers, did not come to light until the Reagan administration itself had passed into history.

Two types of problems typified the ethical misconduct cases of the Reagan years, and both had heavy consequences to citizens everywhere. One stemmed from ideology and deregulatory impulses run amok; the other, from classic corruption on a grand scale.

The first example involved Environmental Protection Agency actions and oversight. In Reagan's first term accusations of favoritism toward industries that the EPA was supposed to regulate led to congressional investigations and criminal prosecutions. By the end of his third year in office more than twenty senior EPA employees had been removed from office and several key agency officials had resigned under pressure. The assistant administrator resigned amid charges that he had been unduly influenced by chemical industry lobbyists. The acting agency administrator resigned after accusations had been made that he had pressured employees to tone down a critical report on a chemical company accused of illegal pollution in Michigan. The agency's general counsel was investigated for possible perjury for statements made to Congress about his involvement in the cleanup of a hazardous waste dump used by a former employer. The deputy chief of federal activities was accused of compiling an interagency "hit" or "enemies" list, like those kept in the Nixon Watergate period, singling out career employees to be hired, fired, or promoted according to their political beliefs. A political candidate for the agency's third-ranking position withdrew from consideration after suggestions were made that he had simultaneously represented private companies regulated by the EPA while serving as part-time consultant to the agency's chief executive.

The most intensely publicized cases involved the official Reagan had first named to head the agency, Anne Gorsuch Burford, and an Edwin Meese political protégée appointed to be in charge of hazardous waste matters, Rita Lavelle. Controversy centered on the way the agency was administering the so-called Superfund, a program created by Congress to assist in cleaning up hazardous waste sites nationally. Congressional committees and energy and environmental public interest groups accused the EPA of favoritism toward polluters and mismanagement. Eventually Burford resigned in the midst of congressional accusations that she had politically manipulated Superfund money. Lavelle was fired after an internal memorandum she had written to the White House was "leaked" and became public. In it she accused a senior EPA official of "systematically alienating the business community." She was later indicted, tried, and convicted of lying to Congress and served three months of a six-month prison sentence.

After extensive investigations and hearings into the EPA situation, at the end of August 1984 a U.S. House of Representatives Energy and Commerce Oversight Subcommittee concluded: "During 1981, 1982 and 1983, top-level officials of the Environmental Protection Agency violated their public trust by disregarding the public health and the environment, manipulating the Superfund program for political purposes, engaging in unethical conduct, and participating in other abuses."

Another health and safety regulatory situation that surfaced publicly toward the end of Reagan's presidency involved the Nuclear Regulatory Commission (NRC), with its obviously critical role in providing oversight of the nuclear industry. In April 1987 a Senate committee learned that the NRC's chief investigator had discovered sensitive internal commission documents in the private files of a nuclear power company in Louisiana. The investigator testified that the documents contained allegations of safety defects at the nuclear plant. In a sensational piece of testimony he said he had also found with the documents a note requesting that company officials keep them confidential to "protect the source with the NRC." Subsequent investigation strongly suggested that they had come from Thomas M. Roberts, whom Reagan had appointed one of the NRC's commissioners. Roberts initially testified that he had determined that no one in his office had been responsible for making the documents available to the private company. They had therefore been destroyed, along with all commission notes on the matter. When a criminal investigation was launched by the Justice Department, Roberts said he had located the documents in question and forwarded them to the committee. After he was called to testify before the Senate Governmental Affairs Committee, Roberts cited his constitutional rights and declined to answer pertinent questions.

In the closing weeks of the Reagan administration and the early months of the new Bush administration, it became evident that a critical situation involving nuclear safety had been allowed to develop in the eighties. Immense sums, estimated at two hundred billion dollars or more, would be required over the next decade to replace and make safe America's aging, deteriorating, and dangerous nuclear facilities. Similar heavy bills were then coming due on another long-festering national problem. Hundreds of billions of dollars would be needed to bail out savings and loan institutions that either had failed during the eighties or were in danger of bankruptcy. At the same time, renewed concern about the effect of deregulation on commercial air safety and travel had intensified. A blue-ribbon presidential commission on aviation safety assessed the changes wrought as airline deregulation replaced economic regulations that had shaped the industry since the 1920s. The commission concluded, guardedly, that the national air system was safe "for now" but added that "the present governmental structure is not working effectively enough to ensure its safety in the future."*

All these problems were part of the price the country would have to pay for excessive deregulation, official inattentiveness, or indifference to functions of government that involved fundamental questions of national economic security and safety. The scandal here was not one of political corruption. It was of public negligence.

Three great scandals stained the Reagan record, and they all involved the age-old form of corruption formed by the connection between money and politics. What distinguished them in the Reagan

*This was a disturbing report. In it the Aviation Safety Commission concluded "that the present safety regulatory structure designed to ensure aviation safety is inadequate to deal with future growth and technological change. Now is the time to equip the regulatory system to accommodate changes in the numbers and kinds of aircraft, to take advantage of new technology in aircraft design and manufacture, to respond to heightened sensitivity on the part of the public to aviation safety, and to act on the backlog of potentially worthwhile safety improvements that have been languishing because of defused authority and accountability. In short, *now* is the time for decisive action by Congress and the Executive Branch." The words were strong, but decisive action was not forthcoming.

years was the number of buyers and sellers involved and the amount of money there was to be made. The sheer volume of both had multiplied beyond any previous measure. Nothing better illustrated the problem than a case that connected some of Reagan's closest associates, a score of top government officials in several departments and agencies, and the kind of political corruption that extended back to the Washington of Grant and Harding: influence peddling, government contracts, cash, bribes, kickbacks, fraud, and conspiracy. Before it was ended, it had dragged Meese, Lyn Nofziger, and many others into its net; led to indictments, trials, and convictions; and besmirched the reputation of the Reagan administration. It became known, popularly, as the Wedtech case.

In 1981 the Welbilt Electronic Die Corporation was a struggling machine shop in the South Bronx that had been founded a decade before by the son of Puerto Rican immigrants. It had ended that year with a net loss of $1 million and was trying, unsuccessfully, to win a five-year defense contract to produce small gasoline engines for the Army. Its record on winning minority contracts from the government was poor. Only a few small such contracts had come its way. Welbilt's latest attempt to win gasoline engine contracts had failed when the Army deemed its bid ($39 million) to be twice as high as it wanted to pay ($19.5 million).

Within five years all that had changed. Welbilt had been transformed from a failing firm into the renamed Wedtech Corporation and was a phenomenal success, a hundred-million-dollar-a-year military contractor showered with new government contracts, grants, and loans.

How Welbilt/Wedtech became a success provides a textbook example of the way the world of Washington influence dealing works, with its high-level revolving door between government and industry. In an elemental sense, Wedtech's success was simple. It became a great moneymaking enterprise almost entirely by winning the same kinds of no-bid federal contracts established to assist minority-owned companies that it had lost previously. The way it won them was through having friends in high places who were willing to exert heavy pressure on its behalf.

The story deriving from sworn testimony properly begins in 1981, when Wedtech hired a close friend and personal lawyer of Edwin

Meese's named E. Bob Wallach, of San Francisco. In the next year Wallach sent Meese at least sixteen memos about Wedtech. Wallach was amply repaid for his efforts. Testimony later revealed that he received more than $1.3 million in cash and stock from Wedtech. The second phase in Wedtech's sudden rise to prosperity began in January 1982, when Nofziger left the White House as Reagan's political director. Like Michael Deaver after him, he became a public relations consultant in Washington. One of his new clients was Wedtech. Nofziger and his public relations partner also profited handsomely from their Wedtech connection. They received Wedtech stock and fees ultimately worth $1 million.

Inside the White House a former aide to Nofziger pressed the Army to negotiate its contract with Wedtech. He and another White House aide attended contract negotiating sessions between Wedtech, the Army, and the Small Business Administration (SBA). The SBA officials subsequently described the two White House aides as having been "advocates for Wedtech." Nonetheless, the head of SBA at the time declined to award the contract, agreeing with the Army that it was overpriced. He and his deputy were fired a month after their meeting on the contract. They claimed they were dismissed because they had failed to approve the contract.

The next critical phase came several months later in April 1982, when Nofziger met with Meese and asked his help in securing the Army contract for Wedtech. Three days after their meeting, Nofziger sent the attorney general a follow-up memo about Wedtech. Meese said that he "probably saw" it, but he could not recall whether it prompted him to take any action. The next month, in May, Meese's top deputy, James Jenkins, convened inside the White House itself an unusual meeting with representatives of Wedtech, the Army, and the new SBA head. Jenkins later testified that Meese personally ordered the review that led to the White House meeting and that he arranged the session despite warnings about possible ethical problems from the White House counsel and the Reagan cabinet secretary. In the meetings, Jenkins testified, he warned those present that he would not stand any "foot dragging" on awarding the Wedtech contract.

There was none. The Army agreed to pay Wedtech $27.7 million for the engines. Wedtech also received a $2 million loan and a $3 million grant from the SBA, an amount that represented a third of *all* such grants awarded that year by the agency. When later urged by a congressman to investigate whether Wedtech had received undeserved preferential treatment, the new SBA administrator, James Sanders, reported that he had found nothing improper. Later he testified that he had treated Wedtech as an "exception" to the SBA's policy of limiting grants to $100,000 after he got a phone call from Meese aide Jenkins asking him to approve a full $3 million grant.

The next phase saw the revolving door in action. Sanders left the government as head of the Small Business Administration and rented office space from his old friend Nofziger. He then became president of the Beer Institute. Jenkins left the Justice Department and became a consultant to Wedtech. Later he became its full-time Washington representative. A friend of Wallach's, Meese's lawyer, W. Franklin Chinn, also became a Wedtech consultant in the spring of 1985. In his consulting arrangement with Wedtech, Chinn agreed to "introduce the company to sources of potential financing." One month later Meese invested $60,000 in a "limited blind partnership" with Chinn.

In the meantime, Wedtech had taken off. It was a smash. During the 1984 election campaign, Ronald Reagan called Wedtech's founder, John Mariotta, "a hero for the eighties" at a Republican fund-raising dinner in New York.* Over a four-year period Wedtech won Pentagon no-bid minority contracts totaling $250 million. Wedtech's profits from Pentagon deals were not limited to the Army. It was awarded $135 million to build pontoons for the Navy. The pontoons were delivered two years late.

Wedtech's success was enjoyed by those who helped create it. In the four-year period from 1982 to 1986, Wedtech paid "insiders" and consultants nearly $11.6 million in salaries, fees, bonuses, and other incentives. Eventually seven of Wedtech's officers and advisers (among them Nofziger and his public relations partner) sold their Wedtech shares for $10 million. This transaction was referred to the

*Mariotta, it later was shown, had become an instant millionaire by continuing to use the Small Business Administration's minority contracts program even though Wedtech should not have been eligible for federal aid after it became a publicly traded company. The SBA regional official in New York who approved a three-year extension of Wedtech's minority status was later indicted and convicted on federal racketeering charges in connection with the Wedtech investigation.

Securities and Exchange Commission for investigation of possible insider trading because it came before the Small Business Administration had dropped Wedtech from its minority business program in 1986, an action that caused the stock to drop sharply.

The balloon burst late that same year, when Wedtech declared bankruptcy in federal court after negative publicity about criminal investigations into its operations had left its financial position weakened. E. Bob Wallach, the original point of reference, and Chinn, who by then had risen from consultant to member of Wedtech's board of directors, were indicted on racketeering, fraud, and conspiracy charges in connection with the Wedtech investigation. Wallach was accused of taking $525,000 in cash from Wedtech in return for influencing Meese and other government officials. Chinn and financier R. Kent London were charged with helping Wallach conceal the real purpose of the payments and of receiving more than $1.3 million from Wedtech in kickbacks, bribes, and fraudulent consulting fees. Wedtech's short but spectacular rise and fall and its tangled web of relationships continued to be highlighted in stories about progress of the various investigations, special prosecutor proceedings and findings, and criminal trials well into the Bush administration.

A footnote served to close the circle on the Wedtech story. In September 1988, when the country was focusing on the next presidential election campaign, the former director of the Navy's Office of Small and Disadvantaged Business Utilization, Richard D. Ramirez, pleaded guilty to charges that he had conspired to receive $60,000 in bribes from Wedtech and $120,000 from United Chem Con. In exchange for the money, Ramirez kept Wedtech informed of "everything that was taking place inside the Navy" and "setting out qualifications that really apply only to Wedtech." It turned out that even though criminal proceedings against him were pending, two months before he pleaded guilty, his business, R. D. Ran, Inc., had won a multimillion-dollar Navy contract. Ramirez had also been granted a "secret" security clearance.

The Ramirez case, with its Wedtech connections and overlapping charges involving Pentagon contracting, was part of a greater scandal that began to unfold in the final months of the Reagan administration and continued long into the next administration of George Bush. Public awareness of the new scandal began on June 14, 1988, when it was disclosed that homes and offices of Pentagon officials and defense contractors in twelve states had been searched by Federal Bureau of Investigation agents and that electronic surveillance of those suspected of involvement had been conducted secretly for months. That initiated what became the biggest government procurement scandal in American history.

It also began to lay bare the connection among defense contractors, defense consultants, and Pentagon employees. Together they formed a U.S. defense industry that was spending $160 million a *day* on military procurement. Favors, gifts, rigged contracts, trading of inside information, smuggling of classified documents out of Pentagon offices to be passed to military contractors all were part of the story. The greater story was the subterranean world of Washington that it exposed.

Appearing on ABC's "This Week with David Brinkley" after the scandal began, Arkansas Senator David Pryor described it this way: "A few yards from here is Connecticut Avenue, and we see all the beautiful hotels and office buildings and grand shops, but underneath there's a subway system that is running day and night where people are getting on and they're getting off. . . . Some of the people that are getting off of that subway . . . have either been with the Department of Defense or with a private consulting firm. They go to a contractor. They're in the Pentagon private consulting firms or their own contractors, and they're all sloshing around in the subway system with all of this money and we're in trouble because of it. There is an interconnection there and it is an incestuous relationship, and now we're feeling the real impact of it. . . . We have extended an open invitation in the last . . . eight years I would say to a totally regimented society that is a delegated government, a shadow government, a government by contract, and it has been an eight-year feeding frenzy at the Department of Defense. . . ."

A major factor in the scandal was the enormous infusion of money that poured into the Pentagon year after year. It was money that came in a sudden burst after the lean Carter years and that provided an open invitation: Plunder in the name of patriotism.

Perhaps the most disturbing aspect of the Pentagon procurement scandal was that it occurred despite repeated warnings that grave problems and potentially widespread criminality existed. Exactly two years before it began, Reagan had received a blunt report from a blue-ribbon commission that he himself had appointed to examine the defense contract situation. It came after increasing evidence of misconduct had accumulated. By May 1985 there were 131 separate investigations pending against forty-five of the Defense Department's one hundred largest contractors. These cases involved such issues as defective pricing, cost and labor mischarging, substitution of products, subcontractor kickbacks, and false claims.

From June 1983 to April 1985 twelve separate official investigations were instituted against one major defense contractor alone. The report submitted to Reagan by the so-called Packard Commission, headed by industrialist David Packard, in June 1986 added more disturbing evidence. It described "the increasingly troubled relationship between the defense industry and the government" and warned that the Defense Department's proper reliance on private industry had now been "clouded by repeated allegations of fraudulent industry activity." Investigations had established "a dysfunctional and adversarial relationship between DoD [Department of Defense] and its contractors." After similar kinds of stern warnings, the commission made specific recommendations to the president about the need to implement stricter standards of conduct for contractors and better policing of federal contracting processes. Like so many high-level reports, it had little, if any, effect. Two years later the greatest of all defense scandals was exposed.

All the elements at work during the Reagan years combined to create an inevitable result in the Pentagon procurement case. It had money, politics, power, ambition, profits. It had consultants and contractors working hand in hand with procurement officers inside. It had power concentrated in a few hands. There were only two major manufacturers of rocket fuel, for example, and two shipbuilders to build submarines. It had the revolving door out of control as today's procurement officers of the government became tomorrow's weapons contract consultants. Some worked not just for one company but for several, bartering among them for the best deal. It had secrecy and the cloak of national security; many of the weapons systems were in the so-called black operations area. They were thus shielded from ordinary public scrutiny and normal congressional oversight by being placed on a secret, or "black," budget beyond regular accountability.

Congressmen and senators battled for defense contracts for their cities and states. Defense contracts meant jobs, jobs meant votes, and votes meant perpetuation of political power. In some instances the Pentagon was forced by congressional pressure to buy weapons systems—a plane, a tank, an armored vehicle—it didn't want or need. Congressional oversight was gravely flawed. Furthermore, members of Congress themselves were shown to race through the revolving door and become immensely paid defense consultants upon leaving office.* Finally, the Pentagon procurement scandal was abetted by the public itself. The Pentagon enjoyed public blessing. Everybody was for defense.

Under the best of conditions, all these presented obvious potential problems. They should have dictated greater vigilance, oversight, attention to standards, and scrupulous adherence to legal contract requirements. In the prevailing climate of Washington, they did not. The result was a scandal waiting to happen, one that squandered national resources. Instead of making the nation stronger militarily, it left it weaker.

A different kind of "feeding frenzy" formed the most cynical of the Reagan era scandals, the one that most closely resembled those of the Harding years. The essence of this scandal at the Department of Housing and Urban Development was familiar. It was of fixers and influence peddlers profiting from high political connections and the awarding of lucrative government contracts. What elevated it above others in the Reagan years was the utter betrayal of public trust that it represented. The money made through the connection between the fixers and political friends was at the expense of the poor—the very people HUD and the federal government were pledged to assist through low-income housing grants.

*President Bush's nominee to become secretary of defense provided a perfect example. As a U.S. senator John G. Tower of Texas had been chairman of the powerful Armed Services Committee, which oversaw defense systems. Upon leaving the Senate, he earned between three-quarters of a million and a million dollars in two years as consultant to some of the same defense contractors he had dealt with as a senator—and would be overseeing again as defense secretary. Significantly Tower was brought down not by his potential conflict of interest but by his personal (and private) behavior.

Though massive fraud and mismanagement had plagued the twenty-billion-dollar federal agency throughout the eight years of Reagan's presidency, none of this was known publicly until the spring of 1989. Then, months into the Bush presidency, congressional investigators began documenting abuses at HUD that would cost the taxpayers billions of dollars in losses. Worse, the scandal that unfolded was shown to have been one in which all the normal processes of accountability and oversight within the executive branch, HUD, the Congress, and the press had broken down. In the vacuum that resulted, HUD became the personal vehicle for the rich and politically well connected to exploit low-income housing programs designed to help the poor.

Long before the investigations were concluded, the public was given an inside look at the way Reagan HUD officials, former high Reagan government appointees, and Republican officials and former officeholders operated for their mutual self-interest through the awarding and receiving of government contracts. They knowingly profited from poverty. Dozens of former officials, many from HUD and others with close ties to the Reagan White House, earned millions of dollars in consulting fees in return for their efforts in winning HUD housing subsidies and grants for their clients.

Many of these people had no background or expertise in housing; their reward was based solely on high political connections. Thus, James G. Watt, the former Reagan interior secretary who had been a symbol of the administration's desire to privatize the federal government by turning over federal lands to private developers, earned $420,000 by making a few phone calls on behalf of clients that resulted in HUD backing for three housing projects. When called to testify about his role before a congressional subcommittee, Watt acknowledged that he had no housing expertise. The "system was flawed," he said with a smile during his testimony, but that did not stop him from profiting from the kinds of government programs he himself had condemned as a Reagan cabinet official.

John N. Mitchell, Nixon's attorney general during the Watergate scandal, earned $75,000 for work on one HUD project. Richard D. Shelby, a Reagan White House personnel officer, was paid $445,000 for himself and for the consulting firm that employed him for his work on two HUD projects. Gerald Carmen, a political appointee who headed the government's General Services Administration during the first three Reagan years, and a partner earned $2.3 million in the sale of tax credits for a subsidized HUD project. Carla Hills, Gerald Ford's housing secretary and later George Bush's special trade representative, received more than $138,000 for her HUD contacts that helped win subsidies for two housing projects. Paul Manafort, a top political consultant to both the Reagan and Bush political campaigns and an associate of the Reagan-Bush political operative Lee Atwater, received $348,000 for client efforts that obtained HUD subsidies for housing projects. Many more examples were uncovered.

As more details of the HUD operations were disclosed during Bush's first year in office, the scandal provided a classic example of both political hypocrisy and profiteering by those with favored connections. It was also an example of the costs of privatizing government functions. A result was a demoralized bureaucracy that felt compelled by self-interest and survival to do the bidding of political superiors, even when career federal employees knew their programs were being cynically abused. "You could hear it all over the place," one senior HUD career executive told the *Washington Post* of the climate that developed inside the agency as internal knowledge of the abuses became more widespread. "People would throw up their hands and say, 'Why worry? I may not have a job next week.' "

From the president down, HUD had been singled out as the kind of domestic government agency the Reagan administration wanted to eliminate through severe budget cuts in funds and personnel. Those goals were accomplished with devastating effect. Between 1981 and 1987 HUD's budget was slashed from nearly $33.5 billion to just over $14 billion, a cut of 57 percent. At the same time the number of HUD employees was reduced by 30 percent. Year by year the personnel ax fell. From 16,323 employees in 1981, HUD's ranks dropped steadily each budget cycle to 11,470 in 1987. Whatever esprit and sense of mission HUD had was destroyed. Its career employees, fearful of being the next to go, adopted a don't-rock-the-boat attitude. As government rules and procedures were cynically flouted, the career employees looked the other way. Entire HUD divisions were abolished by administration cuts, further intensifying fears of employees for their security. Many senior executive positions remained unfilled for months, adding strongly to the internal sense of drift and uncertainty. Other key positions were subjected to constant turnover. For instance, the assistant secretary for housing, the post responsible for overseeing the department's main programs, changed seven times in eight years.

Making a bad situation infinitely worse was the way in which HUD was politicized during those same years. HUD became a dumping ground for Reagan political appointees. Many of these appointees were young, with little or no housing experience background, and sternly ideological. The "brat pack," they were called sneeringly by career employees.* They ran the department, and ran it with ideological and political fervor. They dispensed the available government funds. They ensured that political insiders reaped rewards. They saw to it that tens of millions of dollars in contracts went to developers who had hired prominent Republicans with HUD political connections as consultants.

Reagan's choice as HUD's cabinet secretary, Samuel R. Pierce, Jr., a former Wall Street lawyer and the administration's ranking black appointee, proved to be an ineffectual manager and a man who allowed his friends to put their hands in the government cookie jar. According to sworn testimony about his performance from agency associates, Pierce was happy to delegate authority to younger aides. Key among them was a twenty-eight-year-old woman who became, through political contacts, Pierce's executive assistant.

This was Deborah Gore Dean. Her previous main work experience had been as a bartender in Georgetown during the eight years she spent earning a college degree, but she had other attributes that assisted her in gaining a powerful position inside HUD. Dean's wealthy family had important Republican connections. Key among them was former Attorney General Mitchell, whom she referred to as her "stepfather" because of his close relationship with her widowed mother.

As "Debbie" Dean acknowledged in a *Wall Street Journal* interview, she assumed authority over a housing program that was "set up and designed to be a political program." Thousands of pages of HUD

*Of many articles about the HUD situation, perhaps the most revealing was one by Bill McAllister and Chris Spolar in the *Washington Post* of August 6, 1989, under the page one headline THE TRANSFORMATION OF HUD: "BRAT PACK" FILLED VACUUM AT AGENCY.

documents made available to reporters in response to Freedom of Information requests showed that Dean had sponsored receptions, solicited donations, and interceded for politically influential people who profited from HUD projects. In addition, federal investigators uncovered evidence that outright theft had occurred. They alleged that private escrow agents working for HUD may have taken more than twenty million dollars due the federal Treasury from sale of government-owned homes. At least three of those agents were charged with crimes in Justice Department suits, and at least a dozen around the country were under investigation. "There's not a program within HUD that doesn't have a problem," a young Republican congressman from Connecticut, Christopher Shays, said in disgust while serving on a House subcommittee investigating HUD abuse and mismanagement.

Month after month, during Bush's first year in office, daily news reports about long-standing problems at HUD, from both congressional investigation and belated news media inquiry into operations of the department, added greater evidence of internal mismanagement. The revelations led even some of Reagan's staunchest supporters to turn on him. Among them was the columnist James J. Kilpatrick, who wrote:

> For conservative pro-Reagan Republicans (I count myself among them), these have been disheartening times. Since the first of the year, it has been one damned thing after another. In my bailiwick we hunger for some really good news.
>
> The scandals within the S&L [savings and loan] industry were bad enough, but at least these scandals were more private scandals than public—though heaven knows the public will have to pay most of the bailout bill. What is more deeply distressing is the unfolding story of scandals within the Department of Housing and Urban Development. The more one hears of this rotten affair, the worse it gets.
>
> It now appears that the taxpayers will take a loss of at least $2 billion [later raised to at least eight] on the cozy little, sleazy little, greedy little deals that were made. Let it be said up top: the primary responsibility for this debacle lies squarely in the lap of Ronald Reagan. The buck stopped there. For the eight years of his administration, it now seems evident, the president paid virtually no attention to this huge, costly department. . . . We voted Reagan into office

on a pledge to bring honesty and efficiency into government.

The boys and girls at HUD, and on the Hill, looked at that pledge and snickered.

Months later, with the investigations still producing more evidence of fraud and abuse at HUD, an event took place that further elevated the HUD scandal in history's rank. For months the House Government Operations Subcommittee investigating HUD had sought the testimony of former Secretary Samuel Pierce. Three times he failed to appear on dates set by the subcommittee. When he finally appeared, Pierce invoked his Fifth Amendment privilege against self-incrimination and refused to testify. Not since Albert B. Fall had a U.S. cabinet officer pleaded the Fifth before a congressional investigating committee. That was in the early twenties in the Teapot Dome scandal that forever stained the reputation of Warren G. Harding's administration.

A president, James Madison said in the First Congress, is "responsible for the conduct of the person he has nominated and appointed." Measured by that standard, Ronald Reagan's actions in office made him ultimately responsible for the ethical improprieties in his administration. By the end of his term 138 administration officials had been convicted, had been indicted, or had been the subject of official investigations for official misconduct and/or criminal violations. In terms of numbers of officials involved, the record of his administration was the worst ever.

Reagan's customary response to instances of wrongdoing by aides was to criticize those who brought the charges or to blame the media that reported them. This was most pronounced in his habitual defense of trusted senior aides when they became involved in ethical misconduct cases, including three of his most valued associates: Michael Deaver, Edwin Meese III, and Lyn Nofziger.

Deaver was given a three-year suspended jail sentence, ordered to perform community service work, and fined one hundred thousand dollars for lying under oath to Congress and a federal grand jury about his lobbying activities upon leaving the White House. Nofziger was found guilty on three counts for violating the 1978 Ethics in Government Act, sentenced to ninety days in jail, and fined thirty-thousand dollars. His sentence was later overturned on appeal. Meese's tenure as attorney general was marked by repeated official inquiries into his own ethical conduct, including a fourteen-month-long special prosecutor and federal grand jury investigation for alleged criminal activities while serving as the nation's chief law officer. Meese had to excuse himself from so many major federal inquiries because of association with Reagan officials or friends being questioned that morale among career law enforcement officials dropped to its lowest point in many years. Inside the Justice Department, Meese became an object of scorn and derision, causing graffiti about his misadventures and continuing ethical problems to appear upon department corridor walls, something never before seen in the memory of career employees. Ultimately the special prosecutor found that Meese had filed a false income tax return while attorney general, understating the amount of taxes he owed by more than three thousand dollars. The prosecutor also concluded that Meese had probably violated federal conflict of interest laws by reviewing telecommunications policy at the Justice Department while owning thousands of dollars' worth of phone company stock. Despite these findings, he declined to recommend that Meese be indicted because he had not found reason to think that the attorney general was motivated by desire for personal gain. On the most serious matter under investigation by the special prosecutor—that Meese had taken bribes or illegal gratuities—the prosecutor said ambiguously that there was "insufficient evidence" to indict the attorney general.

Reagan's defense of members of his administration involved in ethical misconduct cases could be interpreted as laudatory, if misplaced, examples of loyalty to friends and subordinates. But it signaled something more serious about the ethical standard Ronald Reagan set as president of the United States. He never bothered to establish stricter standards of conduct. Nor did he ensure that existing ones were properly enforced. In eight years in office he never made a single formal address on the question of government ethics, never issued a single call for adherence to higher standards. The standard that he set and that was followed by many whom he appointed to serve him was not to police or regulate the system; rather, it was to disband and deregulate it. The idea was to let private market forces work in the public sector. They did.

Reagan contributed strongly to the climate in which the various scandals occurred. He came to Washington with a basic contempt for the processes of government and the institutional rules that governed it. His was a grandee approach, distant from the daily process of governance. Others followed his lead. Too often the result was an every-man-for-himself pattern of political operation. Besides, Reagan believed in dismantling government and advocated selling off major public assets, such as naval petroleum reserves and parkland, federal power marketing operations like the TVA, and the National Technical Information Service. His mission was to privatize government's functions and turn them over to market-oriented entrepreneurs who would operate them as private concerns. Even before taking office, he had clearly spelled out his criterion for the kinds of people he wanted in government. "I want people who are already so successful that they would regard a government as a step down, not up," he told James Reston, in an interview published on November 12, 1980, in the *New York Times.* It was a remarkably revealing statement expressing the lack of value the fortieth president placed upon public service. By background and belief, Reagan's appointees were chosen to tilt the governmental balance from public to private interests.

This was a supply-side approach carried beyond taxes to the structure of government itself, and the people he brought into government strongly shared his beliefs.

Lax enforcement and a hands-off approach to regulation became a pattern that extended from the Securities and Exchange Commission overseeing Wall Street trading practices to regulators responsible for ensuring proper practices at banks and savings and loan institutions. It was more than a passive approach. Speculation and risk taking on Wall Street and in S&Ls were actually sanctioned and encouraged by new top officials who were supposed to regulate and police the system. Deregulatory fervor also seized Reagan officials appointed to oversee agencies charged with protecting public health and safety.

For the most part, these areas of benign oversight attracted little public attention. When they did surface through press accounts or congressional investigations, it was only after a problem had reached critical state. That's what subsequently happened with the most costly of all the scandals in the Reagan years: the foundering savings and loan institutions, which accumulated hundreds of billions of dollars of debt throughout the eighties until their economic plight became critical after Reagan left office. The same was so for regulatory oversight practices on Wall Street and in commodities markets. They received intense public scrutiny and official investigation only after economic wreckage nationally had resulted at the end of the Reagan years.

Reagan could not be blamed for all the problems, of course. Cashing in had become a way of life in Washington. Over the years the reasons for coming to Washington had changed. No longer was a career in government a principal motivation. Increasing numbers saw government service as a means of attaining credentials and contacts that would be more salable when they changed from public to private sector and then sought to profit by dealing with the government they had just served. As the savings and loan, HUD, and Pentagon scandals showed, the opportunity for corruption was greater because the financial stakes and amounts to be made were higher. The entire ethical climate was more permissive.

One reason for all this was that the cost of running for office had risen astronomically. Some candidates for U.S. Senate seats were raising as much as ten million dollars for their campaigns. It was money that came from many of the companies and lobbyists that would be seeking favors later. Bolder, less reticent behavior became more characteristic. As Clark M. Clifford, former secretary of defense and counselor to presidents going back to Truman, said of Washington influence peddlers in the late Reagan years, "I think they are bolder now than in the past. It is considered to be perfectly appropriate to be working at a high level in the White House when the B-1 bomber was being considered and then to leave the White House and lobby to try and get them to build more B-1s. I am concerned over the fact there seem to be so many lobbyists coming out of the administration. They are so active. They are so bold. There seems to be no reticence about them."

A greater scandal was at work in Washington, and it did not begin or end with the administration of Ronald Reagan. For years the ranks of the federal government had been increasingly demoralized as the antigovernment climate in the country, stirred by political attacks on Washington and its federal bureaucracy, extracted a heavy toll. During the Reagan years this situation was compounded by new strains placed on the federal service.

While the Reagan administration repeatedly sought large reductions in personnel, as at HUD, it ordered the remaining workers to do "more with less." Consequently, the work force was stretched so thin it could not possibly perform all its missions. The only two federal agencies whose purpose was to make money for the United States—the Customs Service and the Internal Revenue Service—were prime examples of the kind of damage that resulted.

Though assigned more and more drug enforcement and commercial fraud programs to oversee, Customs operated with fewer inspectors checking ever-rising amounts of material entering the country. More and more contraband went undetected. So stripped of resources and personnel was Customs that it was able to inspect only about *2 percent* of *all* shipments entering the United States. Thus, the penny-wise, pound-foolish cutbacks actually resulted in lost revenues that would have been collected. During the Reagan years the IRS experienced a chaotic breakdown caused in part by severe personnel problems stemming from budget cuts, increasing work loads, problems with new computer technology that did not always work as advertised, and sinking morale.

Despite such conditions, the Reagan administration continued to cut employees from agencies providing essential public services. In the first five years of his presidency, Reagan succeeded in reducing the nondefense federal work force by one hundred thousand people. Ninety percent of that was done through attrition—that is, by not filling jobs as people retired or quit. His greater goal of turning over to the private sector half a million of the approximately three million federal work force proved unattainable.* But the knowledge that someone's department, or one's own job, might be the next to be abolished obviously did not contribute to a sense of stability or increased efficiency throughout the federal government.

In 1986 a General Accounting Office report found that lack of

*This was the goal outlined by Reagan's Private Sector Survey on Cost Control, popularly known as the Grace Commission after its chairman, the industrialist Peter Grace.

staff resources because of budget cuts had hampered the Securities and Exchange Commission's enforcement of legal violations on Wall Street. Despite a sharp increase in stock registrations and financial reports filed with them, the report found, the SEC had a backlog of 15,551 unprocessed company annual reports in just the first six months of that year—three times what it had been three years earlier. Similarly, investigators concluded that a contributing factor to the *Challenger* space shuttle tragedy, in which American astronauts were killed, was overworked space agency employees operating under greater pressure to do more.

Increasing job stress was not the only problem. Workers were also subjected to the most extensive use of lie detector tests in the history of the U.S. federal service and became the subject of further controversy as Reagan sought to impose government-wide drug tests.

The value of public service was further lowered. Not only were the burdens of the job greater, but the rewards were diminishing. By Reagan's last year in office, rank-and-file pay had fallen 24 percent behind the private sector. It was even more severe at the highest ranks of the career service, where pay lagged 40 percent behind comparable private remuneration. Young lawyers and business school graduates with Master of Business Administration degrees—summer interns, even—were earning through salaries and bonuses in their *first* year as much as or more than federal judges and heads of agencies and bureaus overseeing billions upon billions of dollars and charged with major public health, safety, and national security responsibilities.

Congressional pay, when measured with inflation and rising wages in the private sector, had not kept pace either. But Congress was able to take care of itself, and did. In the last five years of the Reagan term, members of the House and Senate accepted an estimated ten million dollars in outside fees and honoraria from the very lobbyists and interest groups that petitioned them for legislative favors and raised money for their election campaigns. Some members kept, solely for their own use, hundreds of thousands of dollars from political campaign contributions. And while congressional pay, like that of the federal workers, managers, and judges, dropped farther behind, Congress enjoyed many privileges and perquisites of office—and continued to pocket outside honoraria from private interest groups. ("Dishonoraria," the Washington lawyer and former presidential counselor Lloyd Cutler put it when he chaired a presidential pay commission that unsuccessfully sought to raise federal pay early in 1989.)

Within federal ranks the turnover rate increased rapidly. Of the Senior Executive Service (SES), which comprises the highest-ranking federal managers, 40 percent ended their government careers between 1979 and 1983. In four more years those numbers had nearly doubled. The civil service Merit Systems Protection Board, concerned over the numbers of top people leaving the federal government, surveyed 1,500 members of SES who had resigned rather than retire in that first four-year period. Of these, 90 percent said they had left federal service for higher-paying private sector jobs. Of those responding to another survey, 80 percent were concerned to a "great" or "considerable" extent about morale among career employees. Toward the end of the Reagan administration a survey of 1,364 senior federal managers still working in the government, conducted by the Federal Executive Alumni Association, found that 61 percent would not recommend a federal career for young people. That negative figure had increased by 10 percent from a similar survey taken a year earlier by the same group.

Less scholarly, and more emotional, was the testimony of twenty-nine senior federal executives who attended a private Brookings Institution seminar on executive leadership in Charlottesville, Virginia, about that same time.* All held top civil service positions and represented a cross section of key U.S. agencies, including the Defense Department, Central Intelligence Agency, Defense Intelligence Agency, Tennessee Valley Authority, and National Aeronautics and Space Administration. These were people who performed some of the nation's most demanding, and difficult, jobs. Their comments about conditions inside government were strong and tinged with bitterness: "I believe we have destroyed the purpose of working in government. . . . I think the greatest thing we have lost is not pay or

*I addressed that seminar, in June 1986, and then conducted an open discussion about government service. The quotes cited here are from that session.

pension benefits for the future. What we're being robbed of is a sense of idealism and purpose. . . . I worry about the future and what this work force is going to become. . . . I think Ronald Reagan's lasting contribution to government in the next decade or so will be that he completely illegitimatized government service. Whatever the Kennedy period did to make government attractive to people of talent has been absolutely undone and reversed. 'What! Your kid is working for the federal government! What's the matter with him?' "

Within federal ranks there was also growing resentment of the riches being distributed around them. It was perhaps inevitable that many of the corruption cases in the Reagan years involved mid-level civil servants selling inside information (often for a small price) to contractors and consultants or the selling of secrets to foreign governments in espionage cases of the times.

All this formed a public issue that grew more complicated during the eighties, one that Paul Volcker called "a quiet crisis" facing the nation, but it was a crisis that few knew existed or cared about. Upon leaving his position as chairman of the Federal Reserve Board at the end of the Reagan administration, Volcker attempted to call public attention to this problem through a bipartisan Commission on the Public Service that he headed.

There existed, he said, "unmistakable evidence that the government in general, and the federal government in particular, is increasingly unable to attract, retain, and motivate the kinds of people it will need to do the essential work of the Republic in the years and decades ahead." He warned of a weakened government and a demoralized civil service, legacies of years of antigovernment rhetoric from politicians and citizens. He cited a recent study of 365 seniors at Yale showing that only 1 expressed interest in a civil service career. At Harvard's Kennedy School of Government, he said, figures showed that only 16 percent of those who completed the two-year master's program in public policy over the last ten years were in the federal career service, and only another 3 percent of those graduates worked on Capitol Hill. "If that's the pattern at a graduate professional school which has as its very *raison d'être* training for the public service," Volcker commented, "we shouldn't expect much enthusiasm to be evident in schools and colleges across the country. And it's not." He cited surveys taken since the early eighties showing that an increasing majority of the federal government's Senior Executive Service and the next level below—"essentially the people we count on to manage the machinery of government"—said they would not recommend that their own children or other young people emulate their careers and go into government service.* Volcker warned that America ran the risk of the "worst of all possible worlds—mediocre civil servants and mediocre subordinate political appointees as well" and observed:

> The plain fact is that the federal government today does so many things in total, and so many things that require a high level of professional skill and understanding, that the idea that we can settle for mediocrity in our public services would, in time, become an invitation to mediocrity as a nation. . . . Amid all the complexities and complications of the late Twentieth Century, the wishful thinkers are those that think we can make do with the mediocre. There is less room for error in our foreign relations, not more. Technology demands faster responses, not slower, to problems as widely removed as air safety and financial regulation. National security demands that we know how to build military equipment that works and that we can afford. Our very survival may literally depend on how we respond to complex threats to our environment and to our health.

*This was the single most disturbing finding of a three-month journalistic investigation of the operation of the U.S. Customs Service I conducted in 1986, later published as a lengthy series of articles in the *Washington Post,* from which I have drawn material for this chapter. Virtually everyone interviewed would not recommend that his or her children seek a federal career. The point was made with special force when the wife of a highly regarded Customs inspector in Newark, New Jersey, listened as her husband spoke about his job frustrations. Asked if she would want her son to work for the government, she said sharply: "No, never! I would discourage it." She wished her husband would leave because "in private enterprise he would be much farther ahead than he is with the government." She added: "And as far as how John feels about the government and the flag and what all that means, that's sad, because we're definitely losing that."

CHAPTER 16

GOD AND MAMMON

Susan Gutfreund went to great pains, and not inconsiderable expense, it was reported, to have a small refrigerator installed in her Manhattan apartment bathroom because she liked her perfume chilled after her bath. For the wife of the head of Wall Street's largest investment house, money was not a factor when it came to satisfying such personal desires. She and other privileged people had more than ample reserves and in the eighties spent accordingly.

In Washington guests paid five thousand dollars a ticket to attend a fund raiser for the Princess Grace Foundation and to meet the princess herself, the former movie actress Grace Kelly. Among the touches provided, according to a *Washington Post* reporter who covered the event at a hotel, were toilet bowls filled with chopped carnations. "After they were flushed," she wrote, "a hotel maid sprinkled more fresh flowers in them."

That same weekend notables from the president and First Lady down—or up, depending on the rank accorded royalty present—gathered for a gala tribute to Princess Grace ("a glitz blitz of spectacular proportions," as one reporter described it). A Secret Service agent watched guests as they passed through a metal detector. "It takes a heavy chunk of gold to set off this machine," he said amid sounds of buzzing from the detector. Gold there was, and diamonds, pearls, and other precious stones in what was the most conspicuous display of wealth since Ronald Reagan's inaugural festivities.

And in Charlotte, North Carolina, after the "televangelist" Jim Bakker finished his regular PTL (for Praise the Lord) TV ministry program that helped generate more than four million dollars a month for his electronic religious empire, he retired to his luxurious dressing room. There the professed disciple of Jesus, who had knelt to wash the feet of His followers, took off his shoes and socks and placed his feet on a glass table. Bakker then demanded a foot rub from aides and staff members gathered before him.

It was the commonality of these displays, the very boldness and unashamed nature of them, that gave the eighties their singular cast. Not in decades, perhaps not in the century, had acquisition and flaunting of wealth been celebrated so publicly by so many. The signals sent from Wall Street, from Washington, and from the electronic pulpits into tens of millions of homes was that selfishness was in and "greed was good." Upon the evidence, those signals were avidly received as worthy of emulation by the public.

In the eighties, also, the art of self-promotion was elevated into a new category. The most successful exemplar of the form was also the brashest and the one who perhaps gave the age its most deserved name. It was the Age of the Art of the Deal, and no one received more attention as the premier deal maker of the times than Donald Trump of New York.

As a self-promoter Trump was without peer. Young, tall, well dressed, habitually striking a swaggering stance with thumbs linked inside his belt, he breathed arrogance and profited from it by assiduously courting publicity that made his name even better known—and no matter if the publicity was often negative, as in the daily playing out of the wreckage of his marriage. Even notoriety seemed to sell. "No one has done more in New York than me," he said, adding: "I love to have enemies. . . . I like beating my enemies to the ground." Trump had not arrived as a self-made man; his father had put together good real estate deals in other New York boroughs, and Trump built his empire with money already acquired. On his own, he stamped his name on a succession of properties—the Trump Tower (a Fifth Avenue condominium with pink marble walls and an eighty-foot waterfall splashing in its atrium), Trump's Castle (an Atlantic City gambling casino), the *Trump Princess* (a twenty-nine-million-dollar yacht once owned by the international arms dealer Adnan Khashoggi that came with gold-plated bathroom fixtures, another waterfall, and a rotating sun bed), the Trump Shuttle (formerly the

Eastern Airlines Shuttle). He gloried in his possessions and showed them off: six helicopters, a Boeing 727 jetliner, a 47-room "weekend cottage" in Greenwich, Connecticut, a 117-room Palm Beach estate with private golf course and four hundred feet of beach that had been owned by the grain and cereal heiress Marjorie Merriweather Post. Perhaps his ultimate piece of self-promotion was his ghostwritten book *Trump: The Art of the Deal,* which became a hard-cover best seller for nearly a year (and later the number one best seller in paperback), partly, as *Time* noted, "because of Trump's own purchases" of it.

Absurd or pathetic though all this posturing was, Trump was important to the eighties only because there were so many types like him and so many others who wanted to be like them. They all exemplified an era in which "making it" and "showing it" were styles that suited both society and business. In the last of the Reagan years a slick magazine, appropriately titled *Success,* devoted an entire issue to the theme proclaimed on its cover. The "Selling Issue" it was called, and its message was: "The New Heroes. How Salespeople Can Save American Business." Explaining the special issue, the editors noted: "The techniques of selling are an art form unto themselves. *Success* went into the field to report on selling in the Eighties; we came back with the conviction that when everybody sells, America wins."

Among the titles to articles written to explain the creed were: "Fire in the Belly," offering tips from a "super seller" of computers; "Closing Tactics," with descriptions of "four hot closes for entrepreneurs"; "Selling at the Top," detailed winning tactics from Trump and Lee Iacocca of Chrysler; "Bulletin Board," an exposition of how to "make rejection a delight"; "He Sounds Great, But Can He Sell?," a guide to spotting sales talent; and "Rich Rewards."

Left unsaid was the difference between salesmanship and creativity. While Americans demonstrated that they preferred the quality of goods produced in Japan and Europe by buying them in ever-greater quantity, American manufacturers clung to the belief that merely *claiming* to be best would be sufficient to motivate consumers. Emphasis on selling rather than creating something new and better was not coincidental. In the eighties impression counted.

Nor was it coincidental that the Reagan years saw the reemergence of luxury as a national goal. On the first Labor Day of the Reagan presidency, the *New York Times Magazine,* in its widely followed annual "Fashions of the Times," previewed the new styles and proclaimed in 280 pages of golden ads and breathless text that "at long last" luxury was back. As the *Times* said, "Thank goodness it's back—that froth in the confection of language, that lovely whipped cream of a word—luxury. At this very moment, it is returning to its rightful place in the scheme of things, rescued from years of undeserved disrepute, restored from ignominious exile, refurbished, refreshed and ready to wallow in, wrapped around fabulous furs, buttery leathers, wonderful wools, gossamer chiffons and whispery silks. All courtesy of the fashion industry."

Here was a perfect blending of the appeal to materialism and the the assurance that self-gratification was not only acceptable but desirable. Throughout the decade acquiring of wealth was invested with a noble, if not godly, purpose. Lives of the rich and famous were catalogued weekly on television, with the implication being that wealth *was* fame and that wealth alone constituted a virtue. The most absorbing soap opera of the decade was not a daytime or prime-time TV drama; it was the morality play chronicle of the fallen angels of "televangelism" with their real-life stories of temptation, seduction, and golden temples turned to dross. In the eighties God and Mammon had merged and become inseparable.

In 1978, 25 Christian ministries regularly broadcast over television in the United States. By 1989 the number of TV ministries had grown to 336. Of them, 36 were being audited by the Internal Revenue Service. The electronic church formed a multibillion-dollar televangelist empire serving what the Christian evangelical movement claimed to be sixty million Americans. "Almost without our recognizing it, the communications revolution is reshaping American religion," wrote sociologists Jeffrey K. Hadden (credited with coining the term "televangelism") and Anson Shupe in *Televangelism: Power and Politics on God's Frontier.* "And American religion, in turn, is using this same electronic communications technology to reshape the country—and beginning to reach out to reshape the world. How could this be? The answer is simple. Evangelical Christians have developed the most sophisticated communications system on this planet. They did so in full view of the American public, but nobody was paying attention."

It is not true that no one had paid attention. The rise of televangelists to a new position of power and influence, political as well as religious, was one of the most widely reported stories of the eighties, including their direct access to Reagan and the Oval Office. But Hadden and Shupe were correct in ascribing to Ronald Reagan a singular contributing influence to the new success of the electronic preachers.

> One cannot possibly understand or account for the rapid movement of religious broadcasters into the political arena during the 1980's without examining the role of Ronald Reagan in legitimizing both their causes and their involvement in politics. Largely unnoticed by the media and, hence, the general public, Reagan's first term in office saw evangelicals enjoying unprecedented access to the presidency and the White House, with theological liberals and moderates virtually locked out. Reverend Jerry Falwell replaced the more establishment evangelical Billy Graham as the White House's unofficial chaplain. No president during this century has so completely snubbed the established religious leadership of this nation as has Ronald Reagan. His embrace of the New Christian Right has, in effect, rewritten the book on who is "The Establishment."

Televangelists flourished because they combined all the elements that most characterized the Reagan era: money, morality, conservatism, entertainment, and religious and patriotic symbolism. In the electronic entertainment age they provided one of the best acts going, acts that claimed to be divinely sanctioned and thus above temporal criticism. Their constant televised appeals for money were accompanied by warnings that their ministries would end unless the faithful immediately gave more. The complex fund-raising network they employed through the public airwaves was made possible by the permissive, deregulated environment of the eighties. Televangelists also capitalized on the prevailing cultural political conservatism of the time, expressed compellingly by Reagan himself. His message reflected theirs, or theirs his. It made no matter, this chicken-and-egg question, which came first and which one most directly influenced the other; they went together, with powerful political and religious effect. Then, too, because of their religious standing, televangelists were given tax-exempt status. Thereby they were able to keep the revenues their TV ministries generated through cash contributions and sale of cassettes, videos, books, special editions of the Bible, enrollment in home biblical studies, and religious memorabilia.

Televangelists operated in the newly fashionable intellectual climate that equated moneymaking with the purest strands of Christianity. George Gilder, the popular promoter of supply-side dogma, wrote that capitalism succeeds in fulfilling human needs because it "is founded on giving."

The scholar A. James Reichley wryly observed in his well-received Brookings Institution study *Religion in American Public Life* that Gilder "seems to suggest that what free-enterprise capitalism mainly unleashes is a religiously inspired spirit of benevolence." As Reichley noted, Michael Novak went even farther in equating free-market capitalism with the noblest strains of Christian idealism. Novak, a Catholic theologian who had moved from sixties liberal political activist and onetime speech writer for George McGovern to eighties "neoconservative" commentator at the American Enterprise Institute, was a diplomatic emissary for the Reagan administration. It was in the eighties that Novak found in the operations of modern business corporations "metaphors for grace, a kind of insight into God's ways in history."

For the electronic preachers, God's grace also meant being showered with worldly possessions and wealth. They espoused what came to be called the Gospel of Prosperity and were aggressive advocates of laissez-faire enterprise. "The free enterprise system is clearly outlined in the Book of Proverbs," Jerry Falwell proclaimed. The preachers kept that biblical sanction in mind and acted upon it.

In the process they, their ministries, and their numerous expanding commercial enterprises all prospered magnificently. Starting with the electronic ministry itself, one enterprise begat another, and then another and another. The preachers branched into real estate, records, amusement parks, books, lectures, and personal appearances. They traveled by private jets and expensive automobiles, lived in luxurious mansions, and enjoyed life-styles filled with comfort.

Jim and Tammy Faye Bakker had six homes, at least one with

gold-plated fixtures and a celebrated air-conditioned doghouse. Bakker received interest-free loans and, at his peak in 1986, annual compensation of at least $1.6 million, a figure that did not include cash advances and bonuses. In Fort Mills, South Carolina, the headquarters of his empire, stood the biggest of all spin-offs from his electronic ministry: Heritage Park USA, a twenty-three-hundred-acre "theme park" modeled in the Disneyland manner, with a water park, rides, swimming, a five-hundred-room Heritage Grand Hotel and plans for a $100 million replication of London's Crystal Palace.

The other leading televangelists also enjoyed affluence. In Baton Rouge, Louisiana, Jimmy Swaggart sang, pranced, shouted, sweated, and cried his way before cameras that broadcast his weekly sermons into thirty-two hundred stations in 145 countries. He also led a Bible college, a major printing and mailing operation, a TV production center, and a studio for recording music. In 1985 Swaggart borrowed two million dollars from his ministry to build three luxurious houses in a wealthy Baton Rouge subdivision and had the use of a quarter-million-dollar ministry "retreat" in California.

In Lynchburg, Virginia, Jerry Falwell's electronic evangelical empire included his Thomas Road Liberty Baptist Church, Liberty University, and a cable television system that broadcast his "Old Time Gospel Hour" over the Liberty Broadcasting Network and reached 1.5 million subscribers weekly. He lived in a handsome 150-year-old house provided by the church and traveled in an Israeli-built corporate jet also furnished by his ministry.

In Virginia Beach, Virginia, Marion G. ("Pat") Robertson, the son of a Democratic U.S. senator, presided over a daily TV talk show, "The 700 Club," broadcast over his Christian Broadcasting Network (CBN). CBN was the nation's largest TV cable system, with thirty-three million subscribers. Among other enterprises that formed part of his ministry's estimated annual income of $183 million was a graduate school. Robertson lived in a $400,000 "chancellory" owned by his CBN and made available to him without charge, stabled his horse in a CBN University stable, and had use of a CBN country home in Hot Springs, Virginia.

In Tulsa, Oklahoma, Oral Roberts was the head of a $500 million empire that included the Oral Roberts University, with its two-hundred-foot-tall Tulsa Prayer Tower, made of glass and steel that depicted massive hands clasped in prayer, and the City of Faith Hospital, which was both medical research center and clinic. He had the use of two houses worth approximately $3 million and owned another house estimated in value at more than $550,000.

These evangelical Christians differed in terms of their faith. Robertson, a Southern Baptist, was the most traditional, just as his denomination was the largest among the evangelicals. Falwell was a fundamentalist, a direct descendant of the southern group whose literal interpretations of the Bible led to the famous Scopes evolution trial in the twenties. Bakker and Swaggart were Pentecostalists, a discipline that believed in faith healing and speaking in tongues. Roberts was a "Charismatic" Christian, closely allied theologically to Pentecostals but, stylistically, a movement that has cut across denominations to include Catholics. It was the fastest-growing movement among evangelicals. Despite any theological differences, they all shared three characteristics: They all were electronic evangelists, they all preached a conservative message, and they all generated immense sums of money.

The rise of the television ministries to such power and prominence involved a considerable religious and political paradox. Among American religious denominations, evangelical Christians traditionally had been the least likely to be involved in active politics. They were not even inclined to vote; voting registration statistics showed them to be near the bottom of demographic groups in registering to vote and actually going to the polls.

Yet by the early eighties evangelicals had become *the* religious group most likely to be involved actively in politics, and according to a Gallup survey then, they had become more likely to register and vote than nonevangelicals. This dramatic shift was the result of two factors.

First, and most important, was a basic change in Federal Communications Commission policies governing the public airwaves. For years, under the rubric of public service programming, FCC regulations required television stations to provide a specified amount of time each week to religious broadcasting. Because of television broadcast policies, many of the local TV network affiliates throughout the country were not permitted to accept paid religious broadcasting. To satisfy both FCC and network policies, stations for many years made airtime available free to local churches or to such well-known evangelists as Billy Graham and Rex Humbard, whose sermons were broadcast nationally.

By the early 1970s the FCC had ruled that it would consider paid religious broadcasts as satisfying its public service requirements. At the same time it permitted local stations to charge for the time they set aside for religious broadcasting. Local affiliates, which were becoming increasingly independent of network control, immediately began selling off their Sunday morning time—traditionally, the "Sunday ghetto" hours that attracted relatively few viewers and thus could be purchased cheaply. It was into this new territory that the evangelical preachers moved. They saw an opportunity that the mainline churches shunned, and they seized it aggressively.

The nationally syndicated religious broadcasters, now vying with one another for a new and expanding market, in turn began financing their programs through public fund-raising appeals over the airwaves. Traditional churches had avoided this kind of fund raising and continued to refuse to be a part of it in the eighties. To help generate more money, televangelists employed new technologies: the national 800 telephone numbers, telephone banks, and computerized files as well as elaborate feedback loops that enabled them to provide "personalized" direct mail letters and solicitations to callers.

All this produced an enormous expansion in the national audience for religious broadcasting. Reichley cited a 1963 study showing that only 12 percent of American Protestants watched or listened to religious broadcasts then. By the late seventies that figure, as measured by Gallup, had more than doubled. In Reagan's first year as president, it was estimated that 27 percent of the public had watched at least one religious program in the month preceding the taking of a national poll. Three years later more than thirteen million Americans were estimated to be regular watchers of religious broadcasts. Audiences and the amount of money involved were increasing. Annual expenditure of TV ministries had gone from fifty million to six hundred million dollars in the seventies; by the end of the eighties it had climbed into the billions.

In a relatively short period a remarkable change had taken place in American life, and one with major consequences. As Frances FitzGerald noted in *Cities on a Hill:*

> The local stations, by selling off their Sunday-morning airtime, had permitted those evangelicals with no scruples about commercializing religion to drive much of the other clergy—Protestant, Catholic, and Jewish [who would not solicit contributions by TV appeals]—off the air. In 1980, 90 percent of all religion on television was commercial, and almost all of that was controlled by conservative evangelicals. In the view of the mainstream clergy, this represented a distortion of the medium and a great injustice to the majority of Americans.

However that may be, significant change had occurred. The next step into national politics was inevitable.

Separation of church and state notwithstanding, the connection between religion and politics had always been a central factor in the American experience as well as a source of tension. In the first volume of *Democracy in America,* published in 1835, Alexis de Tocqueville had set out the historical context, and provided his own acute observations:

> The greatest part of British America was peopled by men who, after having shaken off the authority of the Pope, acknowledged no other religious supremacy; they brought with them into the New World a form of Christianity which I cannot better describe than by styling it a democratic and republican religion. This sect contributed powerfully to the establishment of a democracy and a republic, and from the earliest settlement of the emigrants politics and religion contracted an alliance which has never been dissolved. . . .

At the same time, as Tocqueville shrewdly observed, while Americans regarded religion as the foremost of the political institutions of their country, they uniformly and strongly ("to every rank of society") held the opinion that religion should take *no* direct part in the government. Religious freedom meant religious diversity and tolerance of differing beliefs, including the absence of any theistic belief, if one chose. Thus, as Tocqueville said, the very importance of religion in the democratic experiment was that it "facilitates the use of free institutions." No sect would therefore be able to dictate its views to another, and any that tried would meet with public condemnation from all the others.

It was here, nearly a century and a half later in the 1980s, through the conjunction of the televangelists and the presidency of Ronald Reagan, that religion and politics combined into a new and disturbing phenomenon in American life.

The surprise was not over the conservative political ideology held by Christian evangelicals who had branched into television and then into national politics. Conservatism, nativism, suspicion of outsiders, and a strain of outright racism and religious bigotry had always been present in some evangelical sects, especially in the Deep South. Some of the TV preachers had been segregationists and shared a strong strain of anti-Semitism, however veiled. ("God Almighty does not hear the prayers of a Jew," one prominent southern minister said in 1980.*) Nor should there have been any question that the national climate was ripe for the rise of a new morality and a new intolerance. It was the same climate that helped create Reagan's opportunity for national leadership. The surprise was in the nature of the transition—in how successful and swift the conservative evangelists were in entering politics and becoming a national political force. It was a transition made possible by television.

The classic example involved the case of an Alabama congressman named John Buchanan. In 1980 Buchanan became one of the early targets of the recently formed Moral Majority† movement, as it was self-styled with impressive immodesty and led by the Virginia fundamentalist Jerry Falwell. Buchanan's case also set a chilling example for other politicans in the Reagan years because it illustrated how far the political pendulum already had swung.

When he came to Washington in 1964, John Buchanan was a rarity—a minister in politics, a cleric in Congress. He brought with

*This was said by the Reverend Bailey Smith, who was then president of the Southern Baptist Convention. Falwell stirred national controversy during the 1980 presidential campaign when he was quoted as saying, "I believe God does not hear the prayers of unredeemed Gentiles or Jews." Asked about that on an NBC-TV "Meet the Press" program on October 12, 1980, on which I was a panelist, he conceded making that statement but insisted under questioning, "I believe that God hears the prayers of all persons, black, white, red, yellow, Jew, Gentile, God hears everything."

†The Moral Majority, Inc., was founded in June 1979. Its name was a derivation of Richard Nixon's "Silent Majority," a political slogan Nixon and his operatives used successfully in 1968 to appeal mainly to the George Wallace constituency of white ethnic blue-collar voters alienated by liberalism, crime, racial quotas, and affirmative action policies.

him into national public life special credentials that made his election then notable. He had been elected as part of the supposed conservative "emerging new Republican majority" sweeping the Old South in the mid-1960s.

In that 1964 presidential year, when conservatives said they finally offered American voters a genuine choice, not a liberal echo of policies past, Buchanan had run as a member of the Goldwater GOP faction. Although Goldwater lost nationally, Buchanan won a congressional seat in the Alabama district that includes Birmingham and its surrounding area. Only the year before, Birmingham had been the scene of bloody violence unleashed by church bombings and use of police dogs to quell civil rights protesters. Buchanan, white and conservative, was elected as part of the backlash *against* the civil rights movement.

His background could have qualified him for inclusion in one of Sinclair Lewis's tales of small-town American life. He had been a Mason, Kiwanian, World War II Navy veteran, county GOP chairman, director of finance and public relations of the Republican party in Alabama, and long active in church work. For ten years he had been a Baptist minister, a graduate of the Southern Baptist Theological Seminary. Once in Washington, he continued his church work as interim minister and Sunday school teacher at a small Baptist congregation.

And he voted "right." No one had better conservative credentials.

When the Vietnam War was at its peak, he was one of those who called for greater military efforts and use of force. He favored removing limitations from restricted bombing targets in North Vietnam. Later, when Richard Nixon began to be engulfed by Watergate, Buchanan was one of Nixon's strongest supporters. He also supported the National Rifle Association and opposed legislative efforts to limit the sale of firearms. He was the author of a constitutional amendment to permit voluntary prayers in public schools and led what was believed to be the first attempt to put Congress on record against persecution of Christians in the Soviet Union. Repeatedly in his public addresses he spoke about the menace of atheistic communism.

To those who worried about ministers in politics, Buchanan had a ready answer. Once when that question arose in his congressional office, Buchanan got up from his desk, walked over to a cabinet, and pulled out a large, worn Bible. "See here," he said, after opening the Bible to a certain passage. "It says the magistrate is 'God's minister.' That's me."

Still, Buchanan was no mossback, and gradually he changed with the times. But no one could ever accuse him accurately of being anything other than what he was: a conservative white Republican representative from conservative northern Alabama. For nearly sixteen years after he came to Congress, he had run, and won, every time.

Until, that is, September 1980. Then John Buchanan lost the Republican primary in Alabama. He was overwhelmed by the forces of the Moral Majority, which had vigorously backed a far more conservative candidate. They succeeded in persuading a majority of voters that Buchanan, the ex-Baptist minister and Sunday school teacher, was too liberal. He was attacked for his support of the Equal Rights Amendment and for his moderate position on blacks, who constituted a third of his congressional district. He was also portrayed—inaccurately—as being against prayer in schools and not being "pro-family" enough.

By wedding the basic hard right-wing political issues to religious fundamentalism, the Moral Majority forces had made it seem that a vote against their candidate was close to being immoral. As one of Buchanan's campaign aides said later, "For them it was a holy crusade to dump John." When the election was over, the Alabama papers reported, the anti-Buchanan Moral Majority forces held a prayer meeting. They thanked the Lord for the victory, terming it the "will of God."

"How do you fight that?" the same aide said.

Buchanan's people were stunned. Their private polls had not picked up the move against them. They had been confident that by getting out their normal vote, they would again be victorious. Get out their vote they did, and in even greater numbers than previously. It was not enough. They were outorganized, outworked, and outvoted. "They caught us completely by surprise," Buchanan's political operative said. "We were probably beaten early on and never realized it."

The rise of the Moral Majority had been foreseen nearly thirty years earlier by a California longshoreman named Eric Hoffer. His small book *The True Believer* became one of the most important and provocative of a generation. In examining "the true believer" mentality and its impact on mass movements, Hoffer said:

> All mass movements . . . irrespective of the doctrines they teach and the programs they project, breed fanaticism, enthusiasm, fervent hope, hatred, and intolerance; all of them are capable of releasing a powerful flow of activity in certain departments of life; all of them demand blind faith and singlehearted allegiance. All movements, however different in doctrine and aspiration, draw their early adherents from the same types of humanity; they all appeal to the same types of minds.
>
> Though there are obvious differences between the fanatical Christian, the fanatical Mohammedan, the fanatical nationalist, the fanatical Communist, and the fanatical Nazi, it is yet true that the fanaticism which animates them may be viewed and treated as one.

Without realizing it, Hoffer had described the elements that made up the Moral Majority, or Christian Right, thirty years later. They were America's new old-fashioned zealots. And they were a misnomer. In reality, they were not the Moral Majority. They were more accurately the Militant Minority, and they were created by the same kinds of true believer frustrations that Hoffer spoke of in general: "Faith in a holy cause is to a considerable extent a substitute for the lost faith in ourselves." In the eighties the Moral Majority demonstrated how such a militant and intolerant minority can take control when zealously motivated.

Its move into national politics was not limited to areas in the South, where evangelicalism and fundamentalism had long been a factor politically. During the 1980 election the Moral Majority expanded into other carefully selected regions of the country. It worked ceaselessly to elect Reagan and oust prominent liberals with national reputations, such as Senators George McGovern of South Dakota, Birch Bayh of Indiana, Gaylord Nelson of Wisconsin, John Culver of Iowa, Warren Magnuson of Washington, and Frank Church of Idaho. Moral Majority campaign literature, including issuance of moral "report cards" that attacked Senator Church and were distributed throughout Idaho, typified other races in which they played a crucial role. Church, the chairman of the Senate Foreign Relations Committee and an influential, popular Democratic senator for nearly twenty-four years, was called "one of the most radical, liberal members of the U.S. Senate." He was accused of supporting "anti-taxpayer, anti-defense, anti-family votes."

How the Moral Majority forces operated was illustrated by that Idaho race and the involvement of their statewide leader, the Reverend Buddy Hoffman, a fundamentalist Baptist minister.

Hoffman was an outsider. A slim, pale man of twenty-seven, who kept his black hair cropped short and who dressed in a black three-piece pin-striped suit set off by somber tie and white shirt, he had come to Idaho four years before from Atlanta, by way of Hammond, Indiana. He didn't know a soul at first, he recalled that fall during a long conversation in his Idaho home several weeks before the presidential election. After knocking on doors, passing out brochures, and proselytizing the people, he became head of the Treasure Valley Baptist Church, which then boasted of having the largest single-day attendance of any Baptist congregation in the state.

He described his deep involvement in the effort to defeat Senator Church and replace him with the Moral Majority-backed candidate, Steven Symms, in quiet, matter-of-fact tones that became more intense as he spoke. Here was the voice of the modern true believer:*

"Frank Church represents the trouble we're in today. I see ourselves in very near a critical condition as far as making an impact on the nation because of the Church-Symms race. It'll show that we're serious. My grandfather's a preacher. I've got uncles that are preachers. None of them has ever been politically active, although I'm sure that long before that my great-grandfather was. He worked with Billy Sunday on prohibition. I see what we're doing in much the same light. We're beginning to see the pendulum swing back. . . .

"We've drawn from some of the political savvy of individuals who have been in this sort of thing before. It doesn't take a lot of effort from one person; it takes a lot of effort from a lot of people. We've been working through the local pastors, encouraging their

*From a 1980 tape-recorded interview with me in Idaho.

people to go out and register to vote and then go to the ballot boxes and put their two cents in. Nobody's telling anybody who to vote for; we're just defining issues. . . .

"Traditionally people that are church-oriented people don't vote. The more often a person goes to church, the less likely he is to vote. I think that's immoral. But now they've pushed us into a corner in many places in the country, and the worst thing you can do is push a coward in the corner. He'll kill you trying to get out. That's what they've done. They've pushed us and pushed us and pushed us in different areas. People are beginning to stir. . . . You know, the Moral Majority has taken a lot of flak from the press. You tend to say, 'Okay, I don't care what you think.' See, the truth is there's nothing the press or the media or anyone else in the world can do to stop it. See, we're not after any press. I could care less. We're not after influence. We're after impact, and if nobody even knows we exist, it doesn't matter to me."

Frank Church's political career ended when he was defeated by Steve Symms. The margin was fewer than four thousand votes, or less than one percentage point of all ballots cast. George McGovern, Birch Bayh, Gaylord Nelson, John Culver, and Warren Magnuson were also defeated. Of all the liberal Democratic senators targeted by the Moral Majority that year, only Alan Cranston of California survived.

The defeat of such prominent national figures demonstrated the new power of the religious right in America and sent a tremor throughout the entire liberal establishment. Before the election Democrats held a comfortable eighteen-seat margin, fifty-nine to forty-one, in the U.S. Senate. When it was over, their Senate control had been broken for the first time in nearly thirty years. Republicans controlled the Senate by a four-seat margin, fifty-two to forty-eight. As Buddy Hoffman had predicted in Idaho, 1980 marked a major change in voting behavior and suggested that the role of religion in politics had been altered.

Four years later, by the next presidential cycle, the influence of the religious right and the televangelists had increased to such an extent that they came close to capturing the Republican party. The most lasting impression of the 1984 convention in Dallas that renominated Reagan was the manner in which the so-called Christian conservatives exhibited their penetration, if not control, of the party of Lincoln. The evidence was everywhere.

At breakfast one morning in the convention headquarters hotel, a middle-aged delegate publicly displayed what was a popular political message there in the form of two large campaign buttons pinned side by side. One read, "Christians for Reagan," with the words superimposed on a cross. The other read, "Cut Out All Non-Defense Spending Now!" It was a curious Christian point of view, especially since out of that "non-defense spending" came funds to help the poor and sick and those less able to help themselves, but it did express attitudes that prevailed among many delegates, especially those of the religious right.

Reagan in Dallas gave them a powerful boost, making it clear he wanted to strengthen ties between politics and religion instead of maintaining the traditional separation between church and state. His remarks at a prayer breakfast attended by seventeen thousand people in Dallas's Reunion Arena were virtually unprecedented for an American president addressing the role of religion in politics. He drew his greatest applause, and was interrupted repeatedly, when he said: "The truth is, politics and morality are inseparable. And as morality's foundation is religion, religion and politics are necessarily related. We need religion as a guide. We need it because we are imperfect, and our government needs the church because only those humble enough to admit they're sinners can bring to democracy the tolerance it requires in order to survive."

His prayer breakfast audience roared out the chant: "Four more years. Four more years."

Something more than rhetoric about religion was involved with Reagan and the Republicans in Dallas, and something more significant than the normal desire of politicians to invoke God and morality was at stake. What was striking about that Republican convention was the way in which the agenda of the religious right—on school prayer, abortion, godless communism—dominated the public political discourse from opening session to final fundamentalist benediction. Even more noteworthy was the way those issues also dominated private conversations among Republican officeholders, whether senators, members of the House, or governors. The sense they expressed, always privately, was of how powerful the representatives of the religious right had become. No longer were conservative Christians on the fringes of Republican deliberations; they were seated in the center of the hall, and they set the agenda.

How powerful they had become was evidenced in the reaction of a Republican delegate from Virginia. Flying back to Washington, on the day the convention ended, she talked about her impressions. She was a lifelong Republican, wealthy, active in church and volunteer groups, conservative, and had been a supporter of Goldwater in 1964; she was also a believer in Reagan. Dallas and the convention had been splendid, she said, but something about it had troubled her deeply. She wondered "if the press had picked up on the fundamentalists at the convention." Then she proceeded to express her concern about the strength of those in the religious right: They had begun to control entire state delegations, including her own; they were taking over, forcing others to submit to their will; and they weren't like the kinds of conservatives with whom she identified. They were "scary." She repeated the word several times. Scary, scary, scary. She just wanted to know if the press had "picked up on it," she said again. The display in Dallas of religious evangelism sweeping through a great political party was prelude to Reagan's reelection victory that fall. He carried forty-nine of the fifty states and had a virtual tie in the fiftieth state, winning almost half the votes cast there. No presidential candidate had ever come so close to carrying every state. Walter Mondale won his own state of Minnesota by the extraordinarily narrow margin of only 3,761 out of 2,680,967 votes cast. Judged by those election returns and their efforts on Reagan's behalf, the members of the religious right possessed even greater political potential nationally.

That they did not prevail in reshaping the political future was not from lack of effort or backing from the president. The issue of school pryaer was a perfect example. As defined by the religious right and repeatedly endorsed by Reagan in the eighties, it was argued constantly that lack of public school prayer was contributing to America's supposed declining standards of morality. On numerous occasions Reagan maintained that God had been "expelled from the classroom." He, the religious right, and their supporters were determined to get God "back in the classroom."

On the face of it, this point of view was riddled with political and theological absurdities. Why would God, being all-powerful, permit Himself to be expelled from public classrooms? A second puzzle was which God did they—meaning the ungodly—throw out of America's public school classrooms? The God of the Greeks, Zeus? Or of Israel, Jehovah? Or of Buddha, Confucius, Muhammad? And what did that God look like anyway? Did He have cold blue eyes and a stern white face and a long, flowing beard? Or was His (Hers, Its) skin yellow, black, brown, or red? Another baffling question: How was that in the Land of the Free, Americans had fallen so far from grace that they had willfully stopped their children from standing up publicly for God?

Then there was the purely political contradiction implicit in this and other church and state issues. Reagan and the members of the religious right, who wanted to get government off the people's back and God back in the classroom, proposed to achieve that goal by changing the laws and putting government deeper into the thicket of church and state; they would place the hated federal government more squarely in control of dictating behavior involving religious observances. The government would be central to the business of God. This was not a conservative view; it was a radical approach to church and state.

Early in 1984, for example, the Office of Policy Information at the White House put out an eight-page document giving its official version of the school prayer controversy. It was a political document, tailored to reach a political audience in that presidential election year and as such formed an important part of the Reagan White House's attempt to energize what his political operatives called the Christian community, typified by the Moral Majority. It was also packaged patriotically: Alongside the seal of the President of the United States, emblazoned in red and printed in large uppercase letters, were the words "Issue Alert."

Here is how the White House described what were among "many ways" public school officials could arrange time for students to offer their "voluntary and neutral"—whatever that meant—prayers at the beginning of each school day:

> A teacher could call on a student voluntarily to offer a prayer at the beginning of the day, and rotate each day to a different volunteer.

> Schools could ask for student volunteers to offer a prayer over the public address system at the beginning of the day. Teachers could ask students, especially younger students, to volunteer a day ahead of time, so they have a chance to discuss with their parents what prayer they will offer. Students who object to prayer can be allowed to leave the room. Or students who want to pray can be provided an empty room.

It is unlikely than any such document has ever been put forth by the Office of the President of the United States. At the core of this issue was not whether Americans were praying less often, or less well, or less loudly, or at all. It was about a cast of mind that felt impelled to make others trumpet their religious beliefs publicly and to make those who did not wish to pray—or believe in prayer, or anything—feel pressured either to conform or to be singled out as "different" from their peers. In so doing, it made a mockery of prayer itself, something that in the American notion of democracy and freedom of choice was, and should be, deeply personal and private.

The compulsion to want others to pray publicly was hardly new. Jesus, for one, had spoken about it no uncertain terms. He likened it to hypocrisy. His feelings about the virtues of private versus public prayer could not have been more clearly expressed:

> And when thou prayest, thou
> shalt not be as the hypocrites are:
> for they love to pray standing in
> the synagogues and in the corners
> of the streets, that they may
> be seen of men. Verily I say unto
> you, They have their reward.
>
> But thou, when thou prayest,
> enter into thy closet, and when
> thou hast shut thy door, pray to
> thy Father which is in secret;
> and thy Father which seeth in
> secret shall reward thee openly.

It was not the conservative political message of the televangelists and the "moral majority" that failed. Nor, in the end, was it vigilance from the official regulators of the public airwaves or an aggressive press* that brought down the televangelists and their multibillion-dollar electronic church. They fell because their empire had become too large and tempting a target and because they began fighting among themselves to possess its rewards and spoils. Like many others before them, they had become too careless in their exercise of power and too convinced of their own invincibility. They did not practice what they preached.

When the story broke in the spring of 1987, at first it involved only the oldest of fall-from-grace kinds of tales. Jim Bakker of PTL had confessed to having an affair with a young church volunteer named Jessica Hahn who was paid $265,000 in "hush money" to keep the incident quiet. Then it became a nationally televised soap opera as Bakker, weeping while his wife's heavy mascara was running from *her* tears, went on TV to announce his resignation from PTL—not, he said, because of the affair but because of a "diabolical plot" by televangelist Jimmy Swaggart to take over the PTL network and its Heritage USA park. Swaggart, in turn, denied any interest in "stealing" PTL but denounced the Bakker sex scandal as "a cancer that needed to be excised from the body of Christ."

The Bakker-Swaggart exchange of charges came at the same time that the Oklahoma faith healer Oral Roberts was taking to *his* television network to say that God would "call him home" unless the faithful contributed $4.5 million within weeks to save his missionary work. In succeeding months the televangelist story became even more lurid. Falwell had taken over PTL, in an attempt, he said, to save it; Swaggart, in an unexcelled moment of bathos, had sobbingly confessed on national television to having been involved with a New Orleans prostitute; Jessica Hahn had sold her story to *Penthouse* (and, naturally, posed nude) and described how Bakker had forced her to have sex while telling her during the act itself, "When you help the shepherd, you're helping the sheep." Lawsuits, charges, countercharges, more sensational disclosures, and confessions followed.

By 1988, Falwell was out of PTL—and out of the Moral Majority, too. His resignation as head of the Moral Majority, which itself had

*The Pulitzer Prize reporting and commentary of the *Charlotte Observer* on the PTL financial operations were a notable exception. In general, the press paid little attention to economic dealings of the televangelists, just as the government failed to exercise oversight.

been renamed the Liberty Foundation, was prompted, he said, by his desire to devote more time to his church in Lynchburg.

Televangelists fell on hard times. In the wake of the scandals, audience ratings dropped. So did revenues. As donations to the ministries declined, layoffs were imposed and broadcast airtime was cut back. Public opinion polls registered sharp shifts from favorable to unfavorable. The great electronic tent show of the eighties, if not struck, was collapsing. The religious empire of televangelism, like temporal ones in American boardrooms and corporate headquarters, was riven with dissent and locked in territorial take-over and acquisition battles. It was not over, however. The causes that created it, and the forces that gave it such political shape and power, remained.

CHAPTER 17

THE INSIDERS

When the Wall Street financier Ivan Boesky spoke before an open campus audience at Berkeley on September 12, 1985, he was cheered as he said, "Greed is all right . . ." adding, to more cheers and laughter: "Everybody should be a little bit greedy. . . . You shouldn't feel guilty."

Boesky, a lean, intense man, was said to thrive on twenty-one-hour workdays and live like a feudal lord. He was then forty-eight years old and the foremost stock dealer of the era, as well as a prominent philanthropist. His was one of those legendary American success stories given continual rebirth: the driven man, consumed with a vision, whose life embodied those familiar traits of pluck and perseverance that generations of business leaders had celebrated as quintessential American values. Just a year earlier Boesky had made more than $100 million in two big deals alone. His public image, though, was not of consuming greed but that of a public benefactor. His good deeds included numerous gifts to charitable groups, participation in fund-raising drives for public institutions and worthy causes, and service on the boards of distinguished universities and foundations, as well as speaking often before student groups.

He had come to Dwinelle Hall at Berkeley under sponsorship of the students' M.B.A. Finance Club and the business school. In part, he was there to promote his new book *Merger Mania,* in which he modestly explained that his phenomenal financial success was rooted in old-fashioned hard work and good sense. "There are no easy ways to make money in the securities market," he wrote. But Boesky was also there on a mission that he often undertook publicly: to impart a message to the next generation of American business leaders.

To judge by the public response to his remarks that day about "Risk Arbitrage: Wall Street's Best Money Making Secret," the business students and faculty members in his audience liked what they heard. So much, in fact, that Boesky was invited back to Berkeley that next spring to deliver the business school commencement address.

When he spoke at Berkeley on May 18, 1986, Boesky again recited the verities as the path to success. Once more, it was rags to riches: "I am pleased to stand here before you and tell you that I am working class," he began. "My father was a Russian immigrant Jew, and I am here to tell you, dear students, you will be running this nation's enterprises. I urge you to do so in a manner that will enhance the mantle *businessman** with dignity and honor." Boesky's message was to be aggressive. Be restless; be impatient, he said. "Dare to stretch, imagine, create, and then market your skills. Be entrepreneurial in spirit." Then, reinforcing his earlier themes, he told the future business leaders:

> I urge you, as a part of your mission—to seek wealth. It's all right. Does anyone disagree with that? No! But do it in a virtuous and honest way, the purer the process gathering in that way, [*sic*] it is one of the surest ways to having a voice in the system. Having wealth, if you aim high, can allow you to be what you want to become in this great land. You could be more of a person who could make a difference. As you accumulate wealth and power, you must remain God-fearing and responsible to the system that has given you this opportunity. Be respectful of the history of your people and your nation. Give back to the system with humility, and don't take yourself too seriously.

Six days before Boesky delivered that commencement address, Wall Street and the nation's financial community had been stunned when the Securities and Exchange Commission announced the arrest of a young investment banker named Dennis Levine. Boesky made

*This word was not underscored in the copy of Boesky's Berkeley commencement address that university officials later made available to me. I have done so because textually the emphasis seems clearly implied. Otherwise, I have quoted the text as written and punctuated.

no mention of it, though he and Levine were already fatefully linked in ways that were to have great impact upon Wall Street and the American corporate world. Levine was one of the rising young stars in the hot new financial field of corporate mergers and acquisitions. At thirty-three he already earned a million dollars a year and had an affluent life-style to match, complete with Park Avenue apartment, Long Island beach house, and bright red Ferrari. Levine was charged with concocting elaborate illegal schemes to use advance knowledge of fifty-four impending mergers or other similarly big hostile take-over deals to make more than $12.6 million in personal profits.

That was the beginning of the great insider stock scandal of the eighties—or, as *Newsweek* put it in a cover story published several days later, "a spectacular insider-trading case scandalizes the investment community," one that highlighted "Greed on Wall Street." The magazine summed up the news:

> Perhaps most troubling, about thirty of Levine's alleged fifty-four trades—including the first one—involved stocks of companies that first became enmeshed in takeovers or other deals, but in which neither Levine nor the firms he worked for were involved. That suggests Levine may have plugged into a network of financial-community tipsters, possibly stock arbitrageurs—traders who seek to make legal profits on the shares of companies involved in mergers or other deals—or other sources with access to material nonpublic information.

Six months later, on November 14, 1986, the Securities and Exchange Commission made an announcement that set off an even greater tremor. At a Friday afternoon press conference held just after the New York Stock Exchange had closed for the weekend (and thus scheduled to avoid a panic on the Street), the SEC and the New York prosecuting attorney announced that the greatest arbitrageur of them all, the biggest professional stock speculator of the corporate take-over dealers, Ivan Boesky, had copped a plea and was cooperating with authorities in the expanding insider stock trading scandal.

Boesky had been fingered by Dennis Levine, an act that led to the subpoena of Boesky's own records and his subsequent plea bargaining and indictment. As Levine had implicated him, now it appeared that Boesky was about to implicate others.

According to the SEC announcement, Boesky had agreed to pay the U.S. government one hundred million dollars to settle civil charges that he had used confidential information about upcoming take-overs to trade stocks illegally. He had also agreed to plead guilty to one criminal charge. Boesky faced up to five years in prison. News accounts made clear that Boesky had cut a deal for himself. In exchange for lesser charges and possibly a lighter criminal sentence, Boesky would help the prosecutors and government investigators. As Eric Lewis, a Washington attorney who taught criminal law at the Georgetown University Law Center, later said, "Boesky agreed to tell all and wear a wire. The great white shark would implicate the tuna in exchange for concessions." Rumors that Boesky had been secretly tape-recording conversations with businessmen with whom he dealt further increased the fear in the financial community that weekend. When the stock exchange reopened for trading on Monday, frightened traders dumped stocks of companies that were involved in take-over bids.

During his Berkeley commencement address Ivan Boesky had made a passing reference to "a Berkeley alumnus by the name of Michael Milken." The name was as unknown to the general public then as Boesky's was prominent, and Boesky's mention of Milken was entirely tangential. Milken, he said, had been one of those who helped provide "a lot of corporate debt securities" then being written about. As such, Milken deserved credit for realizing "that in a corporate democracy the young and the middle-sized have the right to financing in order to grow and assume a rightful place in corporate America just as those who are established and who have been here a long time and who are already wealthy."

On the surface, Boesky and Milken could not have been more dissimilar. Boesky lived flamboyantly. He courted attention, lived in lavish style, and was given to the *beau geste.*

Michael Milken, by contrast, was a recluse. He lived simply, almost monastically, and was oblivious of material comforts, possessions, and dress. He wore an ill-fitting toupee and appeared to have no interest in social gatherings or standing. At Berkeley, in the mid-sixties, he had seemingly been untouched by the disturbances around him. He was then a straight arrow and later a business major who remained a fraternity member and who shunned stimulants of any kind, including coffee and carbonated beverages.

He was also a fairly familiar type: the brilliant, arrogant, impatient, obsessive loner. When he was graduated Phi Beta Kappa from Berkeley in 1968, as violence and dissent reached its apogee in America, he went east for his M.B.A. to the Wharton School of Business. Then, while others of his generation were caught up in the conflicts produced by the Vietnam War and the racial and political turmoil of that period, he entered the world of Wall Street. There he created a singular impression.* Early each morning, long before daybreak, commuters making the two-hour bus trip from Cherry Hill, New Jersey, to Manhattan, became accustomed to seeing a strange passenger intently studying a mass of papers he extracted from a bulging bag.

Milken's appearance was unforgettable. Strapped over a leather aviator's cap that he habitually wore was a miner's headlamp. Once seated, he turned on the single large light and leaned forward to shine its bright beam onto the papers before him.

In the early seventies Milken traded low-rated bonds for a firm then known as Drexel Firestone. He became an expert in identifying troubled or bankrupt firms whose assets were undervalued by the public markets. These were companies who had not previously been able to raise capital by selling bonds to finance their growth because of a combination of poor credit ratings and the obligation to pay prohibitive short-term interest rates charged by prospective lenders. They were unable to get traditional long-term financing from banks at more favorable interest rates. Thus, for many, the cost of borrowing was so high that it did not seem worth the effort even to apply for loans.

Milken discovered otherwise. He learned that enormous profits could be made from seemingly failing firms that were nonetheless tempting targets for take-overs and mergers. Their debts could be used as tax write-offs, their less efficient individual corporate parts could be sold off piecemeal and further depreciated, while their most

*I have relied here on Connie Bruck's brilliant description of Milken, whom she interviewed and studied for her book centering on him, *The Predators' Ball: The Junk-Bond Raiders and the Man Who Staked Them* (New York: American Lawyer/Simon & Schuster, 1988).

profitable units were retained, merged, or sold again to form a new profitable entity for investors who got in early. Instead of borrowing from the banks, funds could be raised for these failing or undervalued firms much more cheaply by using brokerage firms as financial intermediaries. By underwriting so-called high-yield—or "junk"—bonds for companies rated below investment grade because of the debts they carried, sometimes at only twenty cents on the dollar, investors could in turn parlay these investments into big profits by selling interests in them to the hostile take-over dealers. As a result, a number produced enormous profits for investors.

Thus a new form of American business had been created, though not necessarily business that would have lasting substance and value. The worth tended to stem more from immediate paper profits for the dealers than from long-term rewards produced by better products and stronger companies.

From his early dabbling in low-yield bonds, Milken had risen to become the high-yield (because of greater risk involved) "junk bond king" for the newly renamed and increasingly prominent Wall Street powerhouse Drexel Burnham Lambert of the eighties. And by underwriting junk bonds alone, Milken and his Drexel investment bankers had financed billions of dollars for a new breed of American entrepreneurs. They were the bold "raiders" who led an assault on corporate America that reshaped the U.S. financial world, introducing the greatest wave of buying and selling of major businesses in the history of the United States. Hundreds of major companies were subjected to leveraged buyout or merger and acquisition deals. In the three-year period from 1984 to 1987 alone, there had been twenty-one such deals for a billion or more dollars each.*

What came to be called the leveraging of America, or the restructuring of the nation's corporations, meant that many of these businesses were left with more debt and less equity. It also contributed to a sharp increase in national debt. Until 1982, for nearly thirty years the overall debt rate had risen in line with the nation's gross national product. Then it suddenly skyrocketed. The result was greater earn-

*During the Reagan years the wave of corporate mergers, take-overs, and restructuring resulted in more than twenty-five *thousand* deals, cumulatively valued at more than two *trillion* dollars.

ings and economic activity for the short term, but economic problems with long-term consequences. Both in order to fend off hostile take-overs and to boost earnings and company stock prices, American businessmen were issuing debt and buying in stock at the greatest rate since the twenties. Investors, wary or bold, watched to see which weak company would become the next target for assault by the raiders. "So the problem becomes," one Wall Street stock analyst advised clients at the end of 1986, "which dog do we buy, and when?"

By then it was no longer only corporate "dogs" that were being attacked by Wall Street "wolves." Take-over dealers were targeting some of the biggest, most venerable, and seemingly invulnerable corporate giants like the Gulf Corporation, Walt Disney, Conoco, the Federated Department Stores, R. H. Macy to hostile take-over bids. Now few corporations were immune from attack by the raiders.

Milken was their Svengali, a man able to raise vast sums of money—a hundred million or more for a single deal—for them to finance their take-over attempts. Along with deal maker Ivan Boesky, whose arbitrage business managed enormous pools of money available to speculate on take-over deals, he formed one of the most fabulous business success stories of any era. The key to their success was debt: the ability to manipulate, manage, finance, and profit from it. Along with this was a willingness to take great risks to win high rewards. As Boesky had told the Berkeley students six months before his indictment, "Commercial buyers are not just looking for commercial loans these days. They want ever more complex, new kinds of debt." As he also said, in his casual reference then, it was Michael Milken who had provided much of the new corporate debt securities of the eighties.

Like Boesky, Milken thrived on work around the clock. After he had transformed the junk bond and deal-making business, he moved back to the San Fernando Valley neighborhood of his Southern California youth. There he ran his Drexel Burnham Lambert junk bond operation from a Beverly Hills office, arriving at work between four and four-thirty in the morning. Often he conducted business until midnight or later. During the course of a single workday, he later said in sworn depositions, he regularly and personally handled five hundred telephone calls and as many as a thousand business transactions.

Again like Boesky, he earned immense sums annually—in the year 1987 alone he was paid *$550 million,* more than the annual gross national product of many small nations—and had become a billionaire before he reached the age of forty.* Between them Boesky and Milken made perhaps more money than any comparable pair in the nation's history.

So dazzling was their success, so stunning were the financial returns and rewards, that they began to gather annually to celebrate their achievements and make future plans. The occasion was Drexel Burnham Lambert's annual High Yield Bond Conference held in Los Angeles and staged each year by Milken. This was the so-called annual Predators' Ball, a bringing together of leading players in the new hundred-billion-dollar take-over market. All were dedicated, as Connie Bruck wrote, to the proposition that "any predator, no matter how small, was capable of swallowing any prey, no matter how large." The trick was in knowing how to employ the best technique and method and in selecting the best target.

To the Predators' Ball came some fifteen hundred clients, many of them arriving in chauffeured limousines from Boesky's Beverly Hills Hotel, where they were staying. They were money managers for savings and loan institutions and other institutional investors, portfolio managers for private and public pension funds, college endowments, insurance companies and trusts, mutual funds, and offshore banks.

Also present were those who, unlike Milken, had achieved such high public visibility they had become household words: T. Boone Pickens, Jr., Carl Icahn, Oscar Wyatt, Carl Lindler, Saul Steinberg, Irwin Jacobs, Sir James Goldsmith, Ronald Pearlman, Nelson Peltz. These were the new raiders, the take-over kings.†

*According to calculations by the *Wall Street Journal,* based upon the federal government's disclosure of Milken's Drexel compensation for that year, that amount far exceeded any ever paid an American, placing him ahead of John D. Rockefeller's peak earnings of $400 million a year in comparable dollar figures during the 1910 to 1913 period. The *New York Times* figured Milken's pay came to $1,046 a minute. Nor do these figures include earnings Milken made that year from trading stocks and bonds from his personal account or returns from his other investments and partnership deals. A Milken client was quoted as saying Milken probably made as much or more on his personal deals as he had received in annual compensation from Drexel. If so, he earned more than $1 billion that year alone.

†A decade before, there had been a different kind of raider—a public raider led by Ralph Nader and the Public Citizen movement that challenged American corporate practices and

Where men like Milken and Boesky most resembled each other was in a conviction of their own infallibility. Each had a sense of destiny. Each expressed a new form of the old Gospel of Wealth and intellectually ascribed noble purposes to their business activities. Boesky had preached that good news in his Berkeley commencement address. "As businessmen and women," he told the students, "we must be missionaries with financial clout. To enter business to create goods and services, the successful are given money as a reward."

Milken was also a missionary in the art of making money. He espoused, as Connie Bruck wrote, "The gospel according to Milken—a gospel which taught that these corporate behemoths deserved to be taken over because they were being run inefficiently, so it was not only profitable to do so, but right." He alone would save corporate America from itself. As one of his business associates said of Milken, "He only cared for bringing the truth. If Mike hadn't gone into the securities business, he could have led a religious revival movement."

Like all true believers, Milken and Boesky adopted an end-justifies-the-means mentality. The end was making money, by whatever means it took to achieve it. These included junk bonds; "poison pills," or complex anti-take-over plans adopted by corporations to protect themselves against assaults by raiders; greenmail, the practice by which a raider who threatened a company with a hostile take-over profited when management bought back his stock at a premium not offered other shareholders; LBOs (leveraged buyouts); and REITs (near-bankrupt real estate investment trusts that as investments were gambles that often yielded extraordinarily high returns). Also used was the technique of "parking" stock (one investor holding stock for another to conceal the true ownership of the stock, with the holder being guaranteed against losses).

Boesky himself is credited with inventing the practice of stock loans (buying stock, "lending" it to other firms in exchange for cash, taking that money and buying more stock, then again "lending" the shares for still more cash). Even more seductive was a new scheme

---

produced change through new legislation and public pressure. In the eighties "Nader's Raiders" were eclipsed in power, if not favor, by the private raiders.

that seemed to be the perfect fail-safe financial device: insurance against future stock market declines through something called stock-index futures. These were new speculative financial instruments, commonly traded in the commodity exchanges of Chicago, that in effect enabled buyers to place bets on the future up-or-down movements of the stock market as a whole without, wonder of wonders, having to buy the stocks themselves. Under this device, when stock prices started to fall, large portfolio managers could hold on to their stocks and sell stock-index futures they had purchased instead. Sale of the futures would defray losses in the underlying stock values. Then, when the prices began to rise again, they would stand to profit by holding shares that were now higher in value than when the decline started. By the late eighties billions upon billions of dollars had been invested in these stock-index futures that seemed to guarantee the ultimate assured return with minimal or no risk.

Much more than an insider scandal was at work on Wall Street. The nature of the markets as well as the people entering them had changed radically in just a decade. Computerized trading had transformed the ability of the markets to perform. Now global communications linked capital markets worldwide as never before. As Ivan Boesky liked to say, the financial world had become a global village, "truly a global bazaar in which a dazzling array of financial instruments are bought and sold." Yet no longer was the U.S. position so overwhelmingly dominant. It was still the largest player by far in the global stock market, but increasingly it faced tougher foreign competition.

The dollar continued to decline when measured against other currencies, and the U.S. trade and debt situation continued to worsen. By 1986 U.S. brokerage firms were operating 250 branch offices in thirty foreign countries. At the same time, nearly 100 foreign firms had established offices in the United States. The link between the U.S. and foreign markets was growing ever closer and more complex. Some experts were even predicting that the rapidly developing new international trading environment would lead to the death of the trading floor and the end of the New York Stock Exchange.

The closed, comfortable world of Wall Street had changed in

other ways. Gone were the days of the ten-to-three-o'clock gentlemen bankers and brokers, that privileged clique with ample time for clubs and boating. The great old financial institutions with their elaborate unwritten business codes and the social customs formed over generations were disappearing along with the "old school" people who inhabited them. On Wall Street and in the financial world, past practices had been discarded.

More than anything else, deregulation had altered the functioning of the financial industry. Safeguards that had been in place since the stock market crash of '29 and the Great Depression of the thirties either were gone or were being modified by the Reagan administration. The Securities and Exchange Commission, created in the early New Deal to serve as police officer and regulator of Wall Street and discourage speculation, operated in a new, more passive environment in the eighties. Its enforcement activities were officially de-emphasized. Letting market forces work their will was now the operative philosophy. In the new deregulated financial climate, nothing seemed the same. Everything was up for grabs.

One thing was obvious. A major shift in preferred career choices of those planning to enter American business had taken place. In that same year of 1986, when initial details about the insider trading scandals began to emerge, the Harvard Business School produced a survey of its graduates that contained striking findings.

Ten years before, the leading career choice by far had been manufacturing. More than 30 percent of Harvard's M.B.A. graduates then chose it for their life's work. That was three times as many as the next favored careers of consulting, investment banking, and high technology and electronics, which were all clustered together statistically in a group. Now investment banking was the overwhelming career choice of Harvard M.B.A.'s. Twice as many said they planned to enter that field as manufacturing or consulting. A preference for high tech and electronic work had fallen far back.

Investment banking not only was hot but created a style that contrasted with the older, more circumspect Wall Street manner and was perfectly in harmony with the hyperactive big deal environment of the eighties. Here was where the money was, literally and figuratively, present and future. Young M.B.A.'s were typically *starting* at eighty thousand dollars a year as new investment bankers in big Wall

Street firms. Within three to ten years the really hot investment banker like Dennis Levine could expect to earn more than a million dollars a year—and have the life-style to go with it. The Manhattan condo or co-op, the beach house, the BMW, the health, tennis, or racquet club membership, the red suspenders and the "dress for success" look, even the lunch-hour cocaine break—all were there for the superperformer, the young man or woman with the top M.B.A. degree who entered the "fast track" on Wall Street.

Of course, other fields paid remarkably well on Wall Street. Next to investment bankers in average starting compensation were money managers at seventy-five thousand dollars, followed by beginning Wall Street lawyers at sixty-five thousand and venture capitalists at fifty-five thousand. Advertising, the hot career for gray flannel suits in the fifties, trailed far behind. Average entry pay for advertising junior account executives was forty-five thousand.

Whether all that expenditure for talent, energy, and drive actually produced something that made America stronger and more competitive was, even then, a highly debatable question. After the insider trading scandal broke, *Newsweek* quoted a recent Harvard M.B.A. bitterly critical of his Wall Street-bound peers: "We have created two big myths in the 1980s. One is that you need to be smart to be an investment banker. That's wrong. Finance is easy. Myth number two is that investment bakers somehow create value. They don't. They shuffle around value other people have created. It's a parasitical industry. The flight to Wall Street now is a brain drain from the rest of American industry." Brain drain or not, the flight to Wall Street continued.

CHAPTER 18

DEREGULATION

Speaking privately in Washington in the spring of 1986, a month before the Dennis Levine case triggered awareness of the insider trading scandal, the criminal lawyer Edward Bennett Williams was much more troubled about ethics on Wall Street than about Reagan administration ethical misconduct cases in Washington. As someone whose clients had ranged from Mafia don Frank Costello and Teamsters hoodlum Jimmy Hoffa to Senator Joseph R. McCarthy, Williams knew intimately about ethical misconduct and how it worked. What bothered him most about the eighties were the take-over tactics used by investment bankers. "The worst charlatans I've found in my old age, absolutely nadir to the morality of economics, are those investment bankers," he said. "Those fuckers, they are the worst. They go out there and sell glass insurance to greenhouses while they break windows. You know, they'll say, 'You're ripe for a take-over.' That's the way the gangsters used to do it: 'You're ripe for a take-over.' . . . They don't give a shit for the shareholders. So you have to have a whole defense against a take-over. A whole defense. And then these guys will charge ten million dollars for being on your side, or ten million dollars if they come in work the other side. Wow! You read those stories? Deadly!"*

In the weeks and months that followed, more and more people

*From a tape-recorded conversation with me that spring two years before his death from cancer on August 13, 1988.

representing major financial institutions became involved in the expanding insider trading criminal investigations. Each new indictment naming employees at Drexel or Shearson Lehman or Kidder, Peabody or Goldman, Sachs, or E. F. Hutton, among others, touched off even wilder rumors about where the trail led next on Wall Street. Not only employees of financial firms were shown to have been involved in the insider deals; a young *Wall Street Journal* reporter, R. Foster Winans, was convicted of securities fraud after he acknowledged that he had been paid secretly to pass on tips about market items that the *Journal* planned to publish in its widely read "Heard on the Street" column.

By early 1987, barely four months after Boesky's plea, rumors of impending indictments had reached epic proportions. Increasingly, published speculation centered on the activities of Drexel's junk bond office in Beverly Hills as a prime target for investigators. These rumors, *Newsweek* declared, "seem out of hand." But if true, the magazine continued, it could result in the shutting down of the office headed by Michael Milken and imposition of as much as a half-billion-dollar fine. And such a settlement would probably mean that Drexel would be forced to sell its assets and go out of business. It all seemed unlikely.

News reports about the insider scandals assisted prosecutors by placing greater pressure on suspects to cooperate with investigators and, in exchange for information about others involved, receive more lenient sentences or be granted immunity from prosecution. The intense publicity also contributed to a public sense that Wall Street activities were undergoing vigilant scrutiny from federal investigatory and regulatory authorities. This was misleading, especially as it applied to oversight functions being exercised by regulatory agencies.

Most notable was the functioning of the Securities and Exchange Commission under the chairmanship of John Shad, whom Reagan had appointed in 1981. For the first time in its history the SEC's policing of Wall Street was led by someone who had left a senior executive position on Wall Street to take up federal regulatory responsibilities in Washington.

Shad's tenure was notable in other respects. As among the first Wall Street businessmen to support Reagan publicly in the 1980 presidential campaign, Shad shared the strong belief in deregulation that motivated many who came to power with Reagan. He assumed his new SEC post determined to press aggressively for changes that would substantially reduce or eliminate long-established governmental regulatory functions affecting Wall Street.

Philosophically Shad was a believer in easing the old adversarial relationship that had long existed between Wall Street and the SEC. Like others high in the Reagan administration, Shad generally favored a return to laissez-faire. Once in power, he announced plans to cut the SEC's staff and to reorder its operational patterns and priorities. During his seven years as chairman he succeeded in keeping total SEC employment either below its 1981 level or about the same number. In that same period the number of stockbrokers over whom the SEC had regulatory authority nearly doubled. He shifted emphasis for policing Wall Street from the federal government back to Wall Street itself.

Historically the SEC's enforcement division had been one of the strongest and most effective in the federal service. Shad changed its top priority from overseeing corporate practices to pursuing cheating by individuals. He also succeeded in reducing governmental restraints on stock trading, including in those new speculative stock-index futures. Shad actually believed that a certain amount of speculation was good for the markets: It helped the flow of capital; it made it easier for companies to obtain funds for growth.

Individually and collectively these changes all had major impact on the workings of Wall Street and the functioning of the stock market. The cumulative effect was best expressed in a carefully documented series of articles about Shad's reign at the SEC by two *Washington Post* reporters, David A. Vise and Steve Coll, which were based upon more than two hundred interviews with present and former SEC officials and Wall Street executives and upon examination of commission documents, court files, and congressional testimony.* Vise and Coll concluded:

> Shad's policies contributed to fundamental changes in the nation's stock markets that cannot feasibly be reversed. . . . He threw out

*They were published February 5–8, 1989, two weeks after Reagan left office, and later won the 1990 Pulitzer Prize for explanatory journalism.

> SEC regulations that he considered duplicative and expensive for companies, freeing billions of dollars for other uses. Without the SEC peering as closely over their shoulders, some of the biggest investment firms witnessed a breakdown in discipline among their stockbrokers, especially in the area of fraudulent sales practices. Many institutional investors evaded federal rules designed to control speculation in the new financial products. . . .

Shad's approach was not as radical as some of the ideologues who advocated even more dramatic changes. Vise and Coll reported that he rejected, for instance, a Reagan transition team report recommending that the SEC's enforcement division staff be dismantled and its members dispersed to regional offices throughout the nation. He also dismissed the even more radical theories advanced by some magic-of-the-marketplace economists who argued that insider trading should be made *legal* because it would help the stock market. Nor was Shad insensitive to the long-term economic and social consequences of the use of heavy borrowing to finance corporate takeovers.

Near the end of Reagan's first term, as the take-overs continued to multiply and corporate debt levels increased, Shad became so concerned that he issued a public warning. "In today's corporate world, Darwin's survival of the fittest has become 'Acquire or be acquired,' " he said in a June 1984 speech to the New York Financial Writers Association. "The more leveraged takeovers and buyouts today, the more bankruptcies tomorrow." He expressed his concern that companies burdened by take-over debt would not be able to invest in plant, equipment, research, and development of new products. In a time of recession, many would be unable to survive. Their debts would sink them.

Nor did Shad accept the view about the unlimited benefits of mergers and buyouts then popularly articulated by take-over dealers and conservative free-market theorists. These people argued that the nation's corporate structure was being strengthened because it was the inefficient, poorly managed businesses that were targeted for take-over and merger or elimination. Shad believed otherwise. A number of firms taken over had strong, effective managements, not weak ones. His "Leveraging of America" speech was a signal that he was considering leading a move to crack down on corporate takeovers. Vise and Coll suggested persuasively why that never happened: "At a key moment when some in the Reagan administration feared Shad was about to push for takeover restrictions, officials and economists privately told him that he was deviating from the free-market philosophy of the administration. Although the SEC is an independent agency, and not part of the administration's economic policymaking apparatus, several conservative economists in the administration lobbied Shad steadily to make sure he did not intervene."* Whatever the reasons, the record shows that Shad did not.

The SEC was not the only example of zealous deregulatory fervor that affected Wall Street and major financial institutions. The same kind of climate prevailed at three other federal agencies responsible for policing the marketplace, the Federal Trade Commission, the Antitrust Division of the Justice Department, and the Federal Home Loan Bank Board, charged with overseeing regulation of the nation's savings and loan industry.

At the Justice Department the problem was one of attitude and ideology. The Reagan Justice Department simply did not wish to exercise its regulatory powers aggressively. The spirit of laissez-faire reigned, and nowhere with greater impact than in the antitrust field. During the Reagan administration corporate mergers received their most favorable official blessings since the antitrust laws had been created. "Most of these massive combinations—in oil, steel, airlines, and other basic industries—would never have passed muster under any other administration, be it Democrat or Republican," Attorney General Robert Abrams of New York commented in explaining why he and colleagues from the other forty-nine states had joined in criticizing the administration's antitrust policies in Reagan's last year. At the Federal Trade Commission a combination of severe budget cuts and the more permissive regulatory climate had left that agency "gaunt and bloodied" by that same time, according to the testimony of its commissioner, Andrew J. Sternio, Jr., a Democrat. "Since fiscal

*Vise and Coll also reported the revealing reaction to Shad's "Leveraging of America" speech by the SEC's recently hired chief economist, a young conservative named Gregg Jarrell, who believed that "the best of worlds is the termination of federal regulation." When Shad gave him a copy of his speech, Jarrell wrote "B.S.!" in the margin and "made so many marks on the page that he turned his copy red."

year 1980," Sternio also noted, "there had been a drop of more than 40 percent in the work years allocated to antitrust enforcement. In the same period, merger filings skyrocketed to more than 320 percent of their fiscal 1980 level."

The impact of deregulation was even greater on the savings and loan institutions. Until the early 1980s the S&Ls had played a quiet but important role in the nation's growth and prosperity. They were created to accommodate the small investor, as opposed to the large institutions with accounts insured by the federal government. Such loans enabled millions of Americans to buy homes.

Deregulation of the industry in the early eighties dramatically affected the way the thrifts performed. They were given greater investment power than even banks enjoyed and were free to engage in a wide range of high-risk speculative investments and to make equally high-risk loans: in real estate development projects, gambling casinos, windmill farms, and the like. New high rollers entered the field and, driven by greed that at least equaled that on Wall Street, proceeded to use their institutions to profit personally. Some of the new S&L entrepreneurs seemed to want to emulate a Donald Trump-like life-style through the purchase of yachts, airplanes, desert and beach vacation homes. Though gross mismanagement and corruption occurred within these institutions, federal regulators as well as their patrons in Congress failed to step in and assert control. As loans turned sour and losses rose during 1986 and into 1987, the number of S&L insolvencies reached record proportions. Still, there was no remedial action, and still, the regulators and their political allies in Congress and White House chose to look the other way.

During that same period another scandal that directly bore on the operation of the nation's financial markets was developing. This time, though, federal investigators moved quietly and effectively (if perhaps belatedly) to accumulate massive evidence of fraud.

For at least a decade federal investigators had known of allegations of corruption in the nation's largest commodity markets based in Chicago. These were the Chicago Board of Trade, the world's largest futures market, and the Chicago Mercantile Exchange, the second largest. The so-called futures pits had evolved over the decades into a frenzied arena for speculation, where, as the *New York Times* reported, "brash young traders bent on getting rich quickly could bet on the future value of everything from Douglas fir to the Japanese yen to stock and bonds." In that world of cliques and traders and instant fortunes, the temptation to cash in on inside information was inevitable. Many did, according to evidence gathered over a two-year period by Federal Bureau of Investigation agents who posed as traders and secretly recorded hundreds of conversations with genuine commodities traders. It was a spectacularly successful sting operation that produced evidence of widespread cheating of customers by brokers.

What the futures traders of Chicago did resembled the insider trading on Wall Street. An insider trader on Wall Street with knowledge could tip off investors to a large stock purchase order about to be placed so that they and he could buy that same stock before the sale went through and its value increased. Futures traders in effect could do the same thing by a practice called dual trading, which permitted them to trade for themselves while at the same time handling orders for customers. Thus, the futures broker who received a big order to buy soybeans could place an order for himself *before* completing his customer's purchase.

It was this practice of dual trading, illegal but difficult to detect, that FBI agents sought to document when they began working the futures trading floor. Through an elaborate series of false fronts and identifications—leased office space, bogus company trading names, mail deliveries, telephone answering services—they gradually built up relationships with the illegal futures dealers. With membership under assumed names in health clubs and occupancy of luxury apartments overlooking Lake Michigan, they socialized with other young traders after hours, on weekends, during workouts, and at parties and dinners—all the while secretly recording the conversations. "Some of the agents had a device about the size of a cigarette case strapped to the small of their backs," the *New York Times* reported. "Others hid recorders that resembled wallets in their breast pockets. What appeared to be rings and pens were, in fact, wireless microphones. When the agents began trading in 1987, the tapes were rolling." The insider scandals rolled on with them.

As he left the chairmanship of the Securities and Exchange Commission in June 1987 to become Ronald Reagan's ambassador to the

Netherlands, John Shad gave a final public defense of the financial industry. "Wall Street has long been a favorite target, and yet Wall Street's ethics compare favorably with other professions and occupations," he told graduating business school students at the University of Rochester, where he accepted an honorary degree. ". . . By the highest conjecture, securities fraud is a tiny fraction of one percent of the enormous volume of securities transactions. . . . The few Robber Barons who existed were born a century ago, and were buried in the debris of the 1929 crash. Today, the bulk of American industry and finance are managed by a generation of giants."

Shad was certainly correct about the relatively small numbers involved in outright fraud. Yet he implicitly revealed his own concerns about the ethical climate that had operated on Wall Street during his tenure when he made a personal announcement shortly after leaving the SEC post. He said he was donating most of his twenty-million-dollar personal fortune to establish an ethics program at the Harvard Business School.

CHAPTER 19

THE LEDGER

It is easier to describe what happened in the eighties than to explain why it happened. The multiple scandals on Wall Street, in Washington, the Chicago futures markets, the savings and loans across the country, the evangelical empires, and the amateur and professional athletic franchises all differed in degree and manner. But they contained common threads.

Institutional standards had broken down, and loyalties toward the institutions themselves had been displaced. At least three elements contributed to this breakdown. First, and obvious, was simply the great amount of money to be made from the boom of the decade, coupled with the knowledge that so many were making so much. The wave of take-overs and mergers that characterized the times eliminated mainline industries and firms and left executives and employees feeling less secure and more inclined to put their own interests first. Part of the problem stemmed from a more general climate of cynicism and disaffection.

People no longer felt as bound to their companies or law firms; they didn't even feel as much allegiance toward their professional sports teams. Nor did they believe that their companies were as loyal to them. Defection of partners and senior executives to competing firms became as common as athletes selling their talents to the highest bidder or Washington officials rushing to profit from dealing with the same people they had been overseeing. Furthermore, employees, even senior executives, knew that top management took care of itself through golden parachutes that guaranteed *its* financial comfort even if its firms collapsed. Knowledge of illicit financial transactions spurred a sense that it was an insider's world; doing whatever was necessary became a protective, and perhaps operative, philosophy.

All this contributed to creating a new individualism that elevated personal success above institutional success. At the same time the status and treatment of ethics in large corporations had undergone significant changes, and some with apparent ironic results. In the wake of the Watergate scandal and national preoccupation with ethical standards then, many large corporations reacted by setting what they believed to be new and stronger ethical standards. Some seem to have produced the opposite of what had been intended.

Between 1974 and 1979, for instance, 73 of the Fortune 500 companies responding to a special survey by the Ethics Resource Center and the Opinion Research Corporation reported that their firms had established ethical guidelines or codes of conduct in that period, and half the companies said their new codes had been promulgated for the first time. But their implementation appears to have had surprising and unfortunate effects.

First, their creation was placed in the hands of lawyers, who specifically designed the codes to protect the companies from the employees, not vice versa. Second, top management did not deal with the delicate and often subjective issue of ethics; it absented its responsibility by letting counsel deal with ethics implementation.

"The base on which these corporations are running is fundamentally flawed," said Gary Edwards, director of the Ethics Resource Center in Washington, an organization that includes top corporate officials on its board of directors and conducts independent surveys for major businesses, trade associations, and the federal government, during a long interview for this book in 1987. "The primary problem of every major corporation we've seen is that all the incentives are in the wrong place. Those in charge of evaluation have no idea of the shortcuts taken by their employees . . . and the shift from corporate ethics to corporate counsel made everyone think that ethical issues were taken care of. Of course, when they were surveyed, ninety-three percent of heads of corporations said that ethically, everything was fine. But less than one percent could cite a single example of why. There was little or no contact between top and lower levels of the same company."

In Edwards's expert view, it was intense pressure in the workplace, not criminal conspiracy, that contributed to many potential cases of conflict of interest and ethical misunderstandings. "They were usually nice people who did something the wrong way primarily because there was pressure from the company to get things done," he said.

Company incentives were based on statistical results achieved by individuals, too often with little or no attention paid to methods employed. Employees were thus under further pressure to produce no matter what the cost—a condition that favored younger, more energetic employees, often without family obligations, who could work the necessary long hours. These tended to be employees who were either professionally inexperienced or ambitious enough to sacrifice procedure and standards for desired results. Older employees and those who either couldn't "make the cut" or wouldn't cut corners were edged out of the company.

The situation on Wall Street, as contrasted with the nation's corporate world, was especially in flux in the eighties. As Wall Street firms expanded dramatically, in a new deregulation environment, the character of the institutions changed. Not long before, a well-ordered and carefully structured tradition had governed the investment and trading world there. A young employee labored years under the watchful eyes of "gray-haired men" before being given major responsibility for critical dealings. Informal codes of conduct fashioned over many years were imparted. Ethics were absorbed; they were naturally assimilated over years. But in the eighties, many of these traditions were cast aside. In the new environment management too often failed to address the question of how best to educate employees to agreed-upon standards of ethics.

More disturbing to people like Edwards was the ignorance of top management. As the insider trading scandals began to be exposed, starting with Ivan Boesky's indictment and plea bargaining, many senior executives tended to play down the notion that Wall Street was afflicted with fundamental ethical problems. There were no real problems on Wall Street, these executives said. Any problems that existed stemmed from behavior of "just a few greedy kids," as one high executive put it.

Such an attitude ignored the fact that trust in the system was being eroded. "What we have happening is suicidal," Gary Edwards remarked. "Politics and economics rely on public trust and confidence. If it erodes, nothing gets done. The key—the only code now—is do what you can get away with. And at this point the public is too jaded to care. It's the good ordinary working people who are broken by this. On some level they are ashamed of themselves and what they've done [cutting corners or breaking rules]. They become morally schizophrenic."

As serious problems on Wall Street and among defense contractors came to light, ethics training and development programs were instituted. Moves were made to shift treatment of ethics away from counsel back to managers. Devices like corporate ethics hot lines and ombudsmen to monitor and report on ethical questions were established internally. Too many of these moves, however, were superficial or ineffectual. They were both too little and too late.

Nor were these the only problem areas. By 1980 few graduate schools of business—only 16 percent—offered a specific, separate course in ethics. When such a course was offered, it was generally not required. While ethics courses at best represented only a Band-Aid on the problem, it was significant that fewer than 10 percent of business students were being exposed to the kinds of ethical questions raised in case studies discussed in those classes. As Edwards observed caustically of business school deans, "They were just like the CEOs—just as out of it.

"I must say," he added, "I am deeply concerned. I expect we'll see much worse than what we're seeing now in a year or two. . . . There is no one way to fix all this erosion. No one wants regulation; it makes us uncompetitive internationally and less efficient nationally. The Congress won't regulate itself. Take a look at their 'Code of Official Conduct' book. The white piece of paper clipped to the outside is all they read, which tells them what they can be busted for for a crime like bribery. Freedom is expendable; stability is not."

Beyond all this was an attitude that seemed to characterize much of the big-deal, high-risk, speculative spirit of the times. Making it personally had become an end unto itself. Even popular board games reflected a celebration of private gain. As people sat around the parlor, it was now possible to practice becoming a financier, merger and acquisition king, real estate magnate, stock manager, or manipulator. The new business practices could be learned by playing games sold under such titles as Acquire, Stocks & Bonds, The Bottom Line, Your Money, Arbitrage, Business Strategy. There was even one called Trump, created by none other than Trump himself. Another was called Greed.

They were seductive times for the favored few on Wall Street. Among many people there interviewed for this book, the comments of two are reflective of those young Americans who entered Wall Street to profit from and be affected by what they saw.* After achieving distinguished academic records, both entered the financial world when the great Reagan boom was just igniting in 1983 and when Wall Street was being remade by new players and practices, some of them illegal.

First, an excerpt from a tape-recorded conversation with Peter F. Schweinfurth, Harvard class of 1983, cum laude graduate in economics, Dean's List, Harvard College Scholar. Two years later, after apprenticeship on Wall Street, he earned an M.B.A. from Dartmouth and returned to New York to enter the intoxicating world of mergers and acquisitions (M&As). In a few years Schweinfurth worked for Dean Witter Reynolds, Inc., as a financial analyst, Morgan Stanley, Merrill Lynch Capital Markets, E. F. Hutton's mergers and acquisition group, finally Kelso & Company, specializing in "friendly management buyouts with an emphasis on the use of employee stock ownership plans."

"*When I first got to New York, being an investment banker was still kind of a cool thing to do. Not everybody wanted to do it. By the time I left to go back to business school two years later* [for a Dartmouth M.B.A.], *everybody was beating down the door. The environment had changed greatly from being one where corporate America had their relationship with each investment bank to becoming very transactional-oriented, where the biggest dealer was going to be the winner because he had the most money and got the deals done because he could throw the most resources at them. You also had Mike Milken financing all these guys like Boone Pickens that were just going after*

*For a different view of a young, successful Wall Street insider during these years, see Michael Lewis's *Liar's Poker* (New York: W. W. Norton & Company, 1989).

everything. That was the heyday of greenmailing, where these guys just roamed around, accumulated a stake in a company, made some noise about wanting to take it over, and then they'd sell their shares back and make huge amounts of money. That was the beginning of huge amounts of wealth for a lot of these people. Everybody started building up their capital, hiring a ton of people. Everybody had to have more money; everybody had to write bigger checks; everybody had to do bigger deals. . . . In a number of situations we saw huge run-ups in price that we knew were Ivan Boesky and that were ahead of the announcement of the deal. Apparently a lot of those were based on the type of tips that he got. But everybody at the time was awed. They thought, 'God, this guy is so smart.' We didn't know it was illegitimate inside information; we just figured it was inside tips. I think everybody was aware that it went on but thought it was a scratch-my-back, I'll-scratch-your-back kind of thing rather than taking cash in brown paper bags under the Brooklyn Bridge, which is what was actually going on.

"Over an eight-month stretch I averaged eighty hours a week. I had one day off. We all wore beepers, and it really sucked. We were on call twenty-four hours a day. Your whole world is at that firm. Still, you're willing to pay that price. You're right at the center of things. You get exposure in everything, as much as you want, as much as you can handle and take. You sacrifice so much. A lot of failed marriages and whatnot. That's one large reason why they have the younger people, people before they've made attachments. They lure people in and promise them a lot for blood, sweat, and tears. It's the whole eclipse."

Julie Katzman, also still in her twenties at the time of the conversation excerpted here, was graduated with honors from Georgetown University's School of Foreign Service in 1983, then went immediately into a management fast-track program at a Chicago bank, where she worked days and studied for her M.B.A. nights. Within a year she was doing international corporate financing assignments for United States and United Kingdom corporations in Kenya. A year later she returned to Chicago to become an investment banker with a group of fellow workers, dealing among other things with international computer financial models. They were, as she said, "young, aggressive, smart, and bored. If they didn't find something exciting to do, they were going to leave and go to real investment banks." Upon earning her M.B.A. in June 1986, she left for London. "Basically I'd decided that Chicago was on the periphery," she explained. "The guys I respected and worked with weren't going to stay there long because they weren't being challenged and they weren't being compensated and the world of corporate finance and mergers and acquisitions and high tech fund deals was exploding all around us." She also said: "I wasn't willing to come into the industry on a basis that wasn't advantageous to me."

In Europe she found herself dealing with worldwide markets and living "a bizarre life-style. Up at seven o'clock in the morning to talk to Australia to find out where the Australian market is that morning. Then you work till nine o'clock at night because the guys in Chicago need your help on something else. So you're sitting in this middle time zone that connects you all over the world, which is a fascinating feeling as well. The last thing you do before you go home is fax to Chicago whatever market positions you have that you're monitoring, and the last thing Chicago does is they fax to Tokyo. You have a trading book, and you hand the book across the time zones so that you're always trading the same positions." Next, she came to New York and joined Shearson Lehman Hutton.

"I constantly spend my time at the firm. I mean, all the time. I worked probably eighty hours a week. At the end of the summer, that Labor Day weekend, I got involved in another huge acquisition. That weekend I worked two and a half days without sleeping, and from that point until early December I didn't work a single week less than a hundred hours. You spend all your time working. You're kind of wiped out, but there's a lot of fulfillment. There's an incredible adrenaline rush. This is what you live on. You live on the highs. Someone once said to me, 'The highs are great, but the lows are really bad.' You just go from one high to the next really. But then you find you have cut yourself off from people and things. You tend to cancel all the time. The people that you know, and the circle of friends who are your friends, get narrower and narrower and narrower. That's really a dangerous thing because then when you do have free time, you don't know

who to call. Or it's so last minute that you don't want to call because you think, 'Oh, well, it looks like I had nothing to do.'

"I think people outside Wall Street have a sense that everything you do is just to enrich yourself. But in fact, if you can run a company more efficiently, it enriches the world. It enriches the country; it frees up money for airplanes to jet around the country and to do R and D. You can still save money even when you do that. That's what the best of these deals are all about. You hope you're connected with the best of the deals. I mean, the appeal of the industry, the reason people graduated from college in the eighties and went into investment banks, is because you're surrounded by incredibly intelligent, aggressive people. It's a self-selecting process because it's all people who were willing to work eighty or a hundred hours a week. Willing to kill themselves because they find it fun.

"It's funny, most of the guys who went to jail, I mean, they probably joined the business in the late seventies or early eighties. By the time they did what they were doing, by the time they had access to all the knowledge, they were vice-presidents, they were senior vice-presidents. They were people who knew very clearly what they were doing.

"People got more materialistic in the eighties. There was a greed factor, and Ivan Boesky stood up at Harvard [Berkeley] *and said, 'Greed is good.' You know, he's not a hundred percent wrong. I mean greed is good if everybody in pursuit of money for money's sake tries to make things more efficient, works harder, and gets things to work better. I mean, the Japanese work hard because they want to obtain other things. It's not spiritually any different. I think it's cyclical. You go through periods of time in which the spirit seems to be more important and periods of time when material things are more important. For every action there's a reaction. This craziness of Boesky and Milken and people bending the rules and going to jail shows what happens when you let the greed factor take over."*

The other side of the social and economic ledger in the eighties portrayed a starkly different picture of American society. For all the prosperity, new wealth, and affluent living achieved by many, abundant official statistical evidence showed that the number of Americans living in poverty had increased sharply during the Reagan years;* that class lines were lengthening; that more children were suffering from malnutrition; that one out of every four American children was living in poverty; and that more than 30 percent were living in or near poverty; that the nation's infant mortality rate was higher than that of seventeen other industrial nations; that the number of homeless people had multiplied across the nation; that after decades of moving up the economic ladder, American workers found themselves forced to accept lower standards of living. They were now moving down the economic scale.

These were manifestations of what the journalist and author Thomas Byrne Edsall called the new inequality. Edsall and others compiled statistical evidence that illustrated not only the widening chasm between rich and poor but the shrinking of the middle class. This occurred after a decade in which a majority of the American population experienced either a stagnating income or a net loss in after-tax income and the work force was diminished by loss of 1.6 million manufacturing jobs. At the same time those at the top of the economic pyramid were growing farther apart from those in the middle-income groups.

Average income of the top twentieth of the population increased by $33,895 during the years 1977 to 1988. While those in the top hundredth position economically saw their average incomes rise by nearly $130,000, Edsall wrote, "economic and political power are flowing from the middle class to the affluent. . . ."

After decades of progress this was the situation that had produced what he called the rise—or return—of a new inequality in America: "Inequality won't make today's headlines or lead to tomorrow's riots. Its manifestations are subtle: marginally frustrated hopes, a mocking disparity between the good life available to the few and the life that the many settle for—resignation, guilt, social helplessness."

*Average family income of the poorest fifth of the population *declined* by 6.1 percent from 1979 to 1987, according to U.S. government figures made public in March 1989, while family income for highest-paid Americans *rose* by 11.1 percent during that same period. As usual in virtually all such studies of individual and family income, blacks trailed far behind every other demographic population group, with black teenagers continuing to fall farther behind economically. See also documentation in Kevin Phillips, *The Politics of Rich and Poor: Wealth and the American Electorate in the Reagan Aftermath* (New York: Random House, 1990), published after this manuscript was completed.

It was one more sign that instead of reducing class and racial conflicts, the nation stood in danger of generating them. It was also a reminder that people at the top were growing ever more remote from those at the bottom.

CHAPTER 20

SECRETS

When they arrived at the secret airstrip called El Tamarindo on the Pacific coast of Costa Rica early that Saturday morning, the weapons had already been loaded onto their two small planes, the Piper Seneca and the Piper Navajo Aerocommander. This was unusual. They liked to supervise the loading themselves.

It proved to be costly, for the planes were dangerously overloaded. Part of the fault lay with César Rodríguez. In order to be with his family that Sunday, Father's Day, his plane carried an extra fifty-five-gallon fuel tank. It would permit him and his partner, Floyd Carlton, a fellow Panamanian national, to refuel after making their weapons drop in El Salvador and fly directly home to Panama without having to land for servicing at El Tamarindo.

Neither thought more of it as they climbed aboard their planes before daybreak and began taxiing down the small airstrip carved out of the Central American jungle.

By now these missions were routine. For two years they had made what they called their special charter flights into Nicaragua to supply weapons for the Sandinista forces fighting the regime of Anastasio Somoza. Now, in June 1980, with Somoza overthrown and the Sandinistas victorious, their charter business had shifted into new territory. Now they were making regular secret flights to supply arms for the Sandinista-backed Salvadoran rebels fighting the administration of José Napoleón Duarte. This flight was no different. Again, they carried Soviet-made AK-47 semiautomatic infantry assault weapons, grenades, and what they called Vietnamese bombs, a description they thought apt because the bombs were so powerful.

Ideology didn't motivate Rodríguez and Carlton, or the man for whom they had been working for fourteen years, Colonel Manuel Antonio Noriega, then chief of intelligence and security for the armed forces of Panama and head of its Guardia Nacional. They were in the business of gunrunning and smuggling—for profit, not politics—and they sold arms impartially to the highest bidder on the many jobs they did for Noriega. The planes they were flying were Panama Air National Guard aircraft, supplied for their clandestine arms flights by Noriega without the knowledge of the highest Panamanian officials.

Noriega had many such sidelines that he kept hidden from his superiors. Over the years he had engaged in numerous secret deals and, as those who worked for him knew, not a few double or even triple deals within deals. The black-market sale of arms was only one of them. He was on the payroll of the U.S. Central Intelligence Agency but also had close connections with Cuba's Fidel Castro. Typically Noriega played one side against the other, or many sides against many other sides, for enormous profit. Now, as the Central American battle scene moved from Nicaragua to El Salvador, the revolutionary National Liberation Front (or FMLN) Salvadoran guerrillas had ample money to spend. Another big secret arms market had opened. Noriega, through his private commercial pilots, moved with the game. Though he was being paid by the U.S. CIA, and the United States was backing the Duarte regime against the Salvadoran rebels, he had no hesitancy about selling arms to the rebels, so long as there was money to be made and the deals could be kept secret.

Carlton took off uneventfully and flew on, low, across the jungle toward El Salvador. As Rodríguez's plane lumbered into the air behind him and struggled for altitude, it struck a fence, snapping the plane's hydraulic fuel lines and brakes. He maintained control and flew slowly on, trailing far behind his partner in the other Piper. By the time his plane wobbled over the coffee plantation that was their destination, Carlton had already landed and finished unloading his weapons for the Salvadoran guerrillas awaiting them.

Rodríguez veered his Piper down toward the rough field below, landed safely, but was unable to stop. He aimed the Aerocommander toward a tree and crashed into it. Both doors on the left side and the wing were crushed. Rodríguez lay inside, immobilized and in shock, both legs broken.

Carlton smashed the windshield with the butt of a rifle and pulled out Rodríguez. He felt panic. If anything went wrong, their orders from Noriega were to burn their planes with incriminating Panamanian Guard markings. But to do so with the reserve fuel tank and all weapons still aboard would surely kill them all, Carlton decided. He quickly gathered up any papers he could find that might identify them and the origin of their flight, implored the guerrillas to burn the plane as soon as he took off, and dragged Rodríguez toward his own aircraft. Already he could hear the sound of the Salvadoran Air Force helicopters approaching. He strapped Rodríguez into the seat beside him and took off.

He flew even lower than before, skimming the fields and treetops, and was able to evade the slower helicopters and return to El Tamarindo for refueling. Then he immediately took off again and flew back to Panama. He landed near the Costa Rican boarder in Chiriquí Province, where both he and his severely injured partner had relatives. After taking Rodríguez to a clinic for treatment, Carlton called Noriega. "The first thing he asked me," Carlton later recalled in sworn testimony,* "was if I had destroyed the airplane, and I said yes. I lied to him at the time. And then he asked me how César was. So I said that he was fairly badly off, but that he was alive. And then he ordered me to hide in the province of Chiriquí until he contacted me again through the G-2 [the Panamanian intelligence forces that Noriega controlled]."

Minutes after Carlton entered a relative's home, where he intended to remain hidden, two carloads carrying Noriega security guards drove up to the house. Noriega had ordered them to find

*Carlton, under around-the-clock protection of U.S. marshals as part of the U.S. Witness Protection Program, testified, wearing a hood to shield his features from public view on February 10, 1988, before a Terrorism and Narcotics Subcommittee of the U.S. Senate Foreign Relations Committee investigating Noriega's involvement in the organized international drug trade. He described his role as Noriega's personal pilot flying many drug missions for Noriega between Panama and the international drug cartel headquartered in Medellín, Colombia, and his many gunrunning flights for Noriega, such as the one recounted here. By then his partner, Rodríguez, had been murdered in Colombia in what U.S. investigators believed was a plot to keep him from telling what he knew about Noriega's extensive drugs and arms dealings.

Carlton and have him call the colonel immediately. "When he answered," Carlton remembered, "he was furious, and he said that I had not destroyed the airplane, that no one had burned the airplane. And that they had already had news on international telexes announcing that a Panamanian aircraft had been captured in El Salvador. And he was very, very angry."

Alarms were going off elsewhere in Panama. About the same time Panama's "strong man" leader General Omar Torrijos received an urgent and angry call from the commander in chief of the Salvadoran Army, with whom he had close personal relations. He informed Torrijos that his forces had captured a Panamanian Air National Guard plane carrying weapons for their enemies. The Salvadorans wanted an immediate explanation. They demanded a meeting to discuss the situation.

Torrijos was furious and concerned. He knew nothing about the flight. The problem could not have come at a more awkward and sensitive moment, personally and politically.

The background is essential. At that point, with less than five months to go before the 1980 presidential election, Torrijos and the administration of President Jimmy Carter were working closely and privately to achieve a Central American peace plan aimed at ending the spreading warfare that was destabilizing the region. Carter and Torrijos had established good relations during the negotiations that led to adoption of the 1978 treaty ceding the Panama Canal back to Panama. Torrijos had also come to Carter's personal assistance when he granted Carter's personal plea to permit the dying shah of Iran sanctuary in Panama during the long U.S.-Iranian hostage crisis that year. Now Torrijos had initiated a plan with the Carter administration that, if successful, could create peace and stability in Central America—a region of desperate poverty, rising unemployment, soaring population, rigid class lines, and economic exploitation. These were the underlying conditions that historically had bred successive waves of revolution and repression pitting agrarian leftist reformers in the Castro Marxist mold against right-wing generals who ruled through force and employment of death squads. There seemed no middle ground. Nor did ideology seem to matter in mitigating the kinds of intractable problems that produced more impulses toward revolution and then repression. "What we see in Central America today would not be much different if Fidel Castro and the Soviet Union did not exist," the U.S. ambassador to Panama Ambler Moss remarked in 1980.

For generations U.S. response to festering economic, social, and political problems of Central America had basically been to align itself with the ruling class while attempting to encourage democratic governments through such publicly enunciated slogans as Franklin Roosevelt's Good Neighbor Policy and John Kennedy's Alliance for Progress.

While it talked democratic principles, the United States practiced gunboat or banana diplomacy. When direct intervention—send in the Marines—no longer was viable politically or diplomatically in a world of rapidly changing nations, the United States in the mid-twentieth-century cold war period had increasingly turned to covert military intervention to achieve its policy ends. The overthrow of the leftist Arbenz regime in Guatemala by a U.S. Central Intelligence Agency operation in 1954, and the similar failed attempt to oust Cuba's Fidel Castro through the CIA-planned and -equipped Bay of Pigs invasion of 1961 both flowed from the same policy motivations. They were attempts to achieve in private what the United States was not willing to attempt to achieve in public. In the process the United States had long since fundamentally departed from its original founding principles. From defending revolutions, it had become a defender of oligarchs.

In those final months before the American election the central trouble spot in Central America was not Nicaragua but El Salvador. The Sandinista regime, having triumphed in its decades-long struggle against the Somoza dictatorship in Nicaragua,* was poised between consolidating its power and deciding its next course.

While the Sandinistas were assisting their fellow revolutionaries in El Salvador with arms and other aid provided through Castro and

*A superb overview of U.S. relations and intervention in Central America is Cornell University historian Walter LaFeber's *Inevitable Revolutions: The United States in Central America* (New York: W. W. Norton & Company, 1983). Particularly helpful is his account of the counterrevolution led by the Nicaraguan patriot and guerrilla leader Augusto Sandino against U.S. occupation of Nicaragua by Marine Corps forces beginning in 1927 and lasting until 1934, when he was shot and killed, making him a martyr and the Sandinista namesake.

the Soviet bloc, and the United States trained and supplied the Salvadoran military forces fighting the FMLN, there was still hope that diplomatic efforts might contain the spreading violence in El Salvador.

Perhaps this was naive, but positive elements were present. The new Sandinista regime in Nicaragua was not openly hostile to the Carter administration. On the contrary, it was well aware that in the two years preceding the Sandinista victory Carter had attempted privately to ease Somoza from power. Furthermore, the Sandinistas desperately needed assistance. The long war with the Somoza forces had cost fifty thousand lives and left forty thousand children orphaned. A fifth of the country's population was homeless. Nicaragua's treasury was depleted, its credit destroyed. The Sandinistas took over a small nation saddled with a crushing $1.5 billion debt. Against that background, Carter had succeeded in obtaining congressional approval for more than $100 million in U.S. aid to the new Nicaraguan Sandinista regime.

At the same time both U.S. and experienced Central American diplomats believed that conditions in El Salvador were favorable to new diplomatic initiatives. Despite death squads that had terrorized the Salvadoran countryside, the new Salvadoran leader, José Napoleón Duarte, was a Christian Democrat (and graduate of the University of Notre Dame) who promised democratic land reforms. U.S. policy makers encouraged him in the hope that Duarte would be able to lead El Salvador down a centrist path. Thus, he could avoid the old perils of being caught and destroyed between the forces of left-wing revolution and right-wing repression. Furthermore, the American ambassador to El Salvador in those closing months of the Carter presidency was the liberal Robert White. He was a diplomat respected by leftists and moderates alike for his progressive views and sense of history of the region and especially for his understanding of the long-held resentment that people of Central America felt about U.S. intervention in their affairs.

It was in this context that Panama's Torrijos sought to play a major mediating role in El Salvador. He had reason to think he was in a special position to do so because of his good relations with both Jimmy Carter and Cuba's Fidel Castro and because of his standing among Central American leaders. Personal ambition, of course, was another factor motivating him. If successful in playing the part of peacemaker in Central America, Torrijos would unquestionably emerge as its leading figure. The idea that Torrijos and key Panamanian aides had been exploring with American and Salvadoran officials was the creation of a coalition government in El Salvador. If it were instituted, the revolutionary FMLN would become part of the country's militia operating under civilian leadership.

For these reasons, Torrijos instantly reacted with anger and alarm when the Salvadoran commander told him one of his own planes had been captured carrying arms for the rebels there. If true, that could destroy all hopes for peaceful resolution in El Salvador. Torrijos's assigned role of peacemaker would be ended, and with it his opportunity to play a larger part in Central America.

Immediately he phoned Noriega. What the hell was going on? he demanded to know. Noriega professed to know nothing. Torrijos then called in his closest political aide, José Blandón, whose responsibilities then and later included directing a special intelligence office that functioned exclusively for the commander in chief of Panama's armed forces, a position that gave Blandón access to all foreign and domestic intelligence sources operating in the country. Torrijos ordered Blandón to leave for El Salvador and meet with the military head of Duarte's regime. "It was a very tough meeting for me," Blandón said of that meeting with the Salvadoran military commander,* "because he was angry. He showed me the plane they had captured. I told him that Torrijos had nothing to do with this. He told me it was Noriega's people. He knew very well."

Before returning to report to Torrijos, Blandón interviewed César Rodríguez in the clinic where he was recovering from his injuries. Rodríguez said his flight had been authorized by Noriega. With

*This is from an extensive interview I had with Blandón lasting many hours over two days early in 1989. Blandón was then under threat of death and living under an assumed name under protection of U.S. marshals as part of the U.S. Witness Protection Program because of information he provided U.S. investigative authorities about Noriega's drug dealings with the Colombian cartel. Blandón's last official Panamanian position was as his country's counsel general in New York, a post he held until early in 1988, when he broke with Noriega and offered evidence against him, an act that led Noriega to accuse him of being the "Benedict Arnold of Panama." Blandón's account cited here is from my interview and his sworn testimony before the same Senate narcotics subcommittee at which Carlton and others who are quoted in this chapter appeared.

that final confirmation, Blandón flew back to brief Torrijos, who immediately summoned Noriega for an urgent meeting at which Blandón also was present.

"The meeting was a very harsh meeting," he remembered, "because at the time that Noriega was dealing weapons, we were also discussing with the Salvadorans—with the military *and* the guerrillas—trying to provide a peace project that we had initiated with the Carter administration and which we had discussed with Robert Pastor [a White House aide on Latin America to National Security Adviser Zbigniew Brzezinski] and William Bowdler [a highly respected career Foreign Service officer who was assistant secretary of state for inter-American affairs and active in negotiations with the Nicaraguans]. So this posed a problem for Torrijos. There was a very violent and heated discussion. As of then, General Torrijos launched an investigation of Colonel Noriega."

Blandón was assigned the task of monitoring Noriega's activities for Torrijos and traveling with Noriega wherever he went.

Torrijos was increasingly troubled at the prospect of failure in El Salvador. Unless an accommodation was reached, he believed that Central America would be racked by further violence and war, with the Sandinista type of revolution spreading throughout the countries and provoking a direct conflict with the United States. His concern was not altruistic: He feared that further conflict in Central America would provoke the United States to intervene militarily to protect its sphere of influence. That, in turn, could lead the United States to use the new war as an excuse not to honor the Panama Canal Treaty granting Panama what it had hungered for so long and only recently had achieved: sovereignty over its own territory.

With these concerns in mind, at the end of December 1980 he dispatched Blandón on a mission to meet with Castro in Havana and then with Sandinista leaders in Managua. Cuba, after all, represented the model for the Sandinista Revolution as well as being the principal source of its weapons. "It was clear to Torrijos," Blandón explained, "that the only way to have an arrangement with Salvador and Nicaragua was also to have an arrangement with Castro. So I went to Cuba and discussed this problem with Castro."

Castro was not interested in helping the United States. Neither were the Sandinistas when Blandón met with them. "The Sandinistas were so radical, so impressed by their power, that they didn't want to deal," he said.

The Sandinista answer was to expedite an enormous shipment of arms to the Salvadoran rebels, many of them U.S. weapons that had been captured by Vietnamese forces in the war against the United States and transported through the Soviet bloc to Cuba and then to Nicaragua and El Salvador. On January 8, 1981, twelve days before Ronald Reagan's inauguration, the Salvadoran rebels announced the launching of "a final offensive" with military assaults and a public summons to peasants to join the revolution in mass uprisings. Their offensive would result in swift victory, they asserted, and present the new president of the United States, Ronald Reagan, with an "irreversible situation in El Salvador" when he entered the White House.

"So war started boiling underneath," Blandón said. "We lost all momentum." And Torrijos lost his dream of being the Central American peacemaker.

In his last days in office Carter canceled aid to Nicaragua. The military offensive in El Salvador, coming on the eve of a shift in power in Washington, triggered a new version of the old domino theory debate in the United States: One by one the Central American states would fall until the entire area was under the control of Marxist-Leninist regimes backed by the Soviet Union and its Caribbean proxy, Cuba.

This was the situation that greeted a new president who had promised to stop communism, to restore U.S. military might and prestige, and who had run on a Republican platform that singled out as a special danger to U.S. interests "the Marxist Sandinista takeover of Nicaragua and the Marxist attempts to destabilize El Salvador, Guatemala, and Honduras." The Republican platform plank had condemned Jimmy Carter's offer of aid to the Sandinistas. It had also pledged to "support the efforts of the Nicaraguan people to establish a free and independent government." These were more than presidential campaign rhetorical pledges. Ronald Reagan believed them. He intended to act.

Fear that Central America could become another Vietnam and a more menacing base to spread Marxism throughout the hemisphere coincided with the ideological imperatives of the Reagan administration. However else Reagan would ultimately be judged for the wisdom of his presidential decisions, there was no doubt that he came to office holding sincere and strong convictions about the dangers of communism—and of the use of force to combat it.

For Reagan, anticommunism was an article of faith. His was the most ideologically motivated American presidency of the twentieth century, and he and his key aides were determined to act in what they believed to be in the nation's best interests. The circumstances of his election and the mood of the country strengthened their resolve. Undeniably, the long hostage ordeal and cumulative public sense of American weakness gave those in the Reagan group a stronger hand to play. They had every reason to conclude that Americans wanted to recapture a feeling of national strength and success and wanted them to act forcefully when challenged. It was by no means clear, though, that Americans of the post-Vietnam period wanted them to employ U.S. combat arms to overthrow or contain Communist regimes. In fact, public opinion survey evidence suggested the opposite: that Americans did not favor new military adventures that could entrap the nation in another Vietnam.

Intellectually Reagan's views on combating communism and terrorism *were* fundamentally different from those of Carter and numerous foreign policy experts who had served a number of presidents of both parties since World War II. The Reagan world view was expressed by Jeane Kirkpatrick, whom he appointed U.S. ambassador to the United Nations. She was a political science professor and former liberal Democratic supporter of her fellow Minnesotan Hubert Humphrey. Like Reagan and many others, Kirkpatrick had turned ideological conservative—or neoconservative—by the eighties. In a celebrated essay that had attracted Reagan's personal attention and praise the year before the election, she drew distinctions between the rulers of "authoritarian" and "totalitarian" governments. Good ones (authoritarians)—Nicaragua's Somoza, the shah of Iran—preserved "traditional" societies and encouraged capitalism and the profit motive. Bad ones (totalitarians)—Hitler, Stalin—ruled by iron force and controlled every aspect of a nation's political, social, military, and economic life. Such thinking became central in the policy-making rationale of the new administration.

It was against this backdrop that Reagan and his policy advisers began grappling with the immediate problem they faced in Central America, specifically in El Salvador. They were determined both to set a strong new example of U.S. willingness to meet force with force and not to permit a failure in their first foreign policy challenge.

Alexander M. Haig, Jr., the new secretary of state, shared Reagan's distrust of communism. But he was no ideologue. Haig was an anomaly among the Reaganites, an outsider among the key insiders and viewed with suspicion by them. A West Point graduate who had served with distinction in Vietnam and risen to rank of general and supreme commander of European forces, he had earned a special place in American history for his critical stabilizing role inside the White House as deputy assistant to the president for national security affairs during the Nixon impeachment trauma. In many respects he had acted as assistant president then, serving Nixon with loyalty but not permitting the impeachment crisis to bring the government to a halt. Later he sought the presidency, but that was not to be. He became Reagan's secretary of state without either man knowing much about the other or having developed any closeness.

Haig brought to his office a pragmatic, if cold-eyed, view of the world. On the subject of Castro's Cuba and spread of communism in the hemisphere, however, he was a hard-liner. As a young major in the Pentagon Haig had worked with Washington lawyer Joseph A. Califano, Jr., then counsel to the Army, in assisting the ransomed prisoners of Brigade 2506 upon their return to the United States after release from Cuban jails at the end of 1962. They had languished there for more than a year and a half after their disastrous Bay of Pigs invasion.

Many of the liberated Cubans immediately went into the U.S. Army. Others went into the CIA. Haig, like nearly everyone connected with the Bay of Pigs operation or its aftermath, had been affected by it and the reasons for its failure. In private he often talked about the lessons of the Bay of Pigs and referred by name to some of the Cubans involved whom he had come to admire. He viewed the expanding war in El Salvador, coming after the Sandinista triumph, as part of the same ideological struggle that had brought Castro to power. And he, too, was determined not to let another Central American nation fall to communism. Thus, he spoke of going "to the source," if necessary, to contain communism—that is, moving on Cuba to cut the flow of arms into the hemisphere. Haig ordered a contingency plan for a U.S. naval blockade of Cuba, a move that stirred high-level opposition within the Pentagon and among some in the Reagan inner circle. It was too warlike, too openly provocative. It reinforced the public image of Reagan as the reckless cowboy, whose ideology could get U.S. forces involved in another Vietnam. Talk of a naval blockade, employing open use of U.S. military force, was quelled. Concern about a threat to the hemisphere, however, did not abate. The question was over what means to use to achieve the desired end.

As the level of violence in El Salvador increased, Haig's State Department issued an official U.S. white paper detailing the American version of the source of conflict there and laying groundwork for possible U.S. retaliation. At the same time the Reagan administration poured military aid into El Salvador.

Within weeks of taking office, Reagan increased aid to El Salvador fivefold. He immediately approved twenty million dollars for shipment of arms and equipment there, sent additional U.S. military advisers to train Salvadoran forces fighting the rebels, arranged for additional millions in loan guarantees, and requested another twenty-five million dollars for more arms purchases.

Fifteen hundred Salvadoran soldiers were brought to the United States for special training in American military bases. The flow of arms, equipment, and economic aid increased monthly. By the end of 1982 the United States had sent more aid to El Salvador than to any other Latin American nation in that period of Reagan's presidency. While the focus was on El Salvador, the Reagan administration continued to condemn the Sandinistas and apply increasing public pressure on them. Days after the inauguration the United States publicly demanded that Nicaragua stop helping "their revolutionary brothers" in El Salvador and step away from their growing ties with Havana and Moscow. Economic screws were tightened. Fifteen million dollars in U.S. economic aid to Managua was halted. Millions of dollars of wheat shipments bound for Nicaragua were stopped. Breadlines sprang up throughout the country. Within months all U.S. aid to Nicaragua had stopped.

By then, in a major shift of U.S. foreign policy objectives in the post World War II era, the Reagan administration had elevated Central America into the nation's preeminent national security concern. Just two months after the inauguration Jeane Kirkpatrick, in a speech before the Conservative Political Action Conference, explained why Central America and the Caribbean had become "the most important place in the world for us." Echoing concerns expressed by Haig, she warned that failure to stop the spread of communism there would affect America's ability to play "a major role in the politics and security of countries in remote places and even Western Europe." The very security of the United States, she maintained, depended upon "not having to devote the lion's share of our attention and our resources to the defense of ourselves in our own hemisphere."

Here was a new and more threatening version of the domino theory come home to imperil the nation through America's backyard. And now the threat was occurring on Ronald Reagan's presidential watch.

Despite its tough anti-Communist rhetoric aimed at the Sandinistas and major new military assistance to El Salvador, the Reagan administration quickly found itself facing a familiar problem. Words and military hardware alone were not enough to affect the outcome of the struggle decades old with deep economic, political, and social roots.

In Nicaragua the Sandinistas reacted to the new U.S. sanctions by moving sharply left, tightening state controls, driving out private businesses, aligning themselves more closely to the Cuban and Soviet bloc, and embracing aid from radical terrorist third world regimes, such as that of Libya's Muammar el-Qaddafi. In El Salvador the rebels' final offensive had failed to achieve its objectives and gain victory over the Duarte regime. At the same time another deadly pattern recalling earlier U.S. experience in Vietnam was forming. The United States was learning again that power alone was not enough to prevail. The U.S.-backed Salvadoran Army of seventeen thousand could not suppress rebel forces one fourth its size. Stalemate. The prospect of another long, inconclusive struggle loomed.

Here, too, the American response was familiar. As diplomatic historian Walter LaFeber aptly observed, "The Reagan administration sought to fight fire by pouring on gasoline."

Instead of a public war against communism in Central America, the administration soon embarked on a path others had been down before, never with great success. It became involved in backing a series of secret wars in Central America fought in the main by proxy warriors.

First, the administration turned to the ruling Argentine junta of generals (an example of what Kirkpatrick viewed as a "good authoritarian" regime) for secret assistance. They, in turn, began secretly training Salvadoran forces and, more fatefully, dispatching military aides to train a new counterrevolutionary force of Nicaraguans opposed to the Sandinistas in Honduras, a nation that relied heavily on U.S. military and economic aid and one that had provided past sanctuary for U.S. covert operations. (The CIA operation that overthrew Guatemala's Arbenz in 1954 had used Honduras as a launching area for attacks.) Months after Reagan came to power, the Argentine military forces were on the ground training what became known as the Nicaraguan resistance, or contra, forces.

Second, as an implicit (and, later, quite explicit) quid pro quo price for such assistance, U.S. military aid to Honduras tripled in the first two years of Reagan's presidency. U.S. arms flowed into Honduras. A training camp for the contras was constructed near the Nicaraguan border.

By the time Reagan completed his first hundred days in office, administration focus of greatest danger to U.S. interests in Central America had shifted from El Salvador to Nicaragua. Now, internally, there was high-level talk of not just "checking" the Nicaraguan revolution. Reagan hard-liners were planning to overthrow the Sandinistas. The president himself reinforced that view. "I've got to win one," he said on more than one occasion in private to career U.S. ambassadors.

Although there is evidence that by the summer of 1981 Regan emissaries were privately telling friendly Central American leaders that the president intended to overthrow the Sandinistas, it was not until November 16, 1981, that Reagan formally approved a plan to provide twenty million dollars in covert U.S. aid to the Nicaraguan contra forces forming in Honduras. Two weeks later, on December 1, as required by law to give him authority to launch covert operations, he signed an official intelligence finding saying he had determined that secret aid to the contras was important to U.S. national security. Then, as also required by law, administration officials secretly informed appropriate congressional intelligence oversight committees of the finding and of the president's reasons for the covert operation.

The covert operation was specifically undertaken, congressional leaders were informed, *only* to interdict the flow of weapons from Nicaragua to El Salvador and to make the Sandinistas amenable to negotiations. Nothing was said about overthrowing the regime. Congress assented but adopted specific classified language limiting the covert operation to interdiction of weapons traffic in Central America.

This deception of Congress was the first of a series of lies that were to move the Reagan administration deeper and deeper into a web of secrecy. Each step required more cover, more secrecy, more U.S. surrogates. Each operation, fought on many fronts and many national territories with a plethora of presumably undetectable and deniable U.S. surrogates, raised new dangers of exposure and embarrassment. Each risk made the consequences of failure even greater.

Compounding the problem was an even more complex and potentially damaging set of circumstances involving the use of covert operations.

Despite the strength of his convictions, Reagan was faced with practical constraints on his use of power. These constraints were both political and public in nature. They were part of the legacy of suspicion and distrust that had intensified as his presidential predecessors had grappled with achieving public and political support for open warfare in Vietnam and secret military operations in trouble spots around the globe. As public disenchantment and cynicism over U.S. military and intelligence operations had grown, critical political reactions had inevitably followed. Greater congressional oversight of intelligence operations took place. Tighter legal restrictions for approval of them were imposed.

Just four months after the first false intelligence finding was signed by Reagan, a central part of the administration's secret plan to topple the Sandinistas collapsed. Argentina and Great Britain had gone to war over control of the Falkland (Malvinas) Islands, and the United States sided with Britain. In the debacle that followed, Argentina quickly lost the war. Its ruling junta of generals was overthrown. Gone with them was the Argentine leadership for training the contras.

Reagan officials were forced to find other ways to support the contras and keep their secret war alive in Central America. To do so, and keep their hand hidden from congressional overseers and public, they chose a method singularly in keeping with the spirit of the eighties. They decided to privatize their intelligence operations. Thus, they ventured even deeper into the subterranean world of covert operators, soldiers of fortune, mercenaries, international arms dealers, and smugglers.

Theirs would be a war without public accountability, fought by both people motivated by ideology and those motivated by profit. The two went together. Once again Panama and Colonel Noriega became a key to the secret struggle.

CHAPTER 21

HAVEN

On July 31, 1981, a helicopter carrying Panama's leader General Omar Torrijos crashed moments after takeoff under mysterious and never officially determined circumstances. Torrijos died instantly.

For most of that year there had been little contact between the new Reagan administration and Torrijos. The Reaganities were suspicious of Torrijos, for his close connections both with the Carter administration and with Fidel Castro. Some thought he was a crypto-Marxist. At the least he was believed to be untrustworthy by the new group in Washington.

With Torrijos gone, conditions in Panama suddenly took a different turn. The country fell victim to a vicious internal struggle within the armed forces. In the end a faction headed by Noriega (soon to be a general) prevailed. His military forces expanded their involvement in government on all levels. They assumed such normally civilian governmental responsibilities as control of immigration and customs, the ports, railroads, and airports. Handpicked civilians, operating under Noriega's direction and sufferance, were placed in key positions in the ministries and courts. They also controlled the Banco Nacional de Panama.

Noriega, who continued as chief of Panama's intelligence services and later assumed operating command of the armed forces, became the supreme dictator of Panama. He moved swiftly and aggressively to consolidate total control over the country.* In the process Noriega and his group succeeded in turning Panama into a gigantic machine for a wide range of criminal activities and enterprises.

By the end of 1981 two critical forces that strengthened Noriega's hand came together to make Panama even more central in the rapidly increasing flow of clandestine traffic that coursed through Central America.

First, Noriega had established a personal relationship with Reagan's new CIA director, William J. Casey. From that point on Noriega maintained close contacts with Casey and met personally with him on trips to Washington. What Casey wanted—and got—from Noriega was covert assistance in facilitating arms shipments to contra forces. Through his control of Panama's security apparatus, Noriega was now in a position to arrange Panamanian "end user" certificates that legitimized arms shipments to Panama. Once the arms had arrived in Panama, Noriega was then able to sell the weapons to the highest bidder, legally and with no questions asked about the supposed purpose for the arms as specified in the certificates.

Noriega's business in selling arms had been developed years earlier. It had flourished with the aid of his personal pilots, César Rodríguez and Floyd Carlton, and with the assistance of an Israeli based in Panama named Michael Harari, who purchased the weapons in Europe and worked closely with Noriega.† Soon Rodríguez,

*The ruthlessness with which Noriega asserted control was demonstrated by a notorious case in 1985, when, according to sworn testimony judged credible by U.S. authorities, Noriega personally ordered a rival leader seized, tortured, and, while still alive, beheaded. The victim, Dr. Hugo Spadafora, kept a notebook on drug dealing, with dates of flights and missions, in which Noriega was directly involved and intended to use it to expose and overthrow Noriega, according to congressional testimony. Two books about Noriega, published in 1990 after the U.S. invasion of Panama, are especially useful: Frederick Kempe, *Divorcing the Dictator: America's Bungled Affair with Noriega* (New York: G. P. Putnam's Sons), and John Dinges, *Our Man in Panama: How General Noriega Used the United States—and Made Millions in Drugs and Arms* (New York: Random House).

†José Blandón told me Harari was an Israeli intelligence officer with close ties to the late Israeli Premier Golda Meir who assisted the CIA in Central America, especially in the Carter period when CIA covert operations were dormant. The Senate report named him as someone who bought weapons for Noriega. Harari surfaced publicly in the 1989 U.S. invasion of Panama and mysteriously escaped to Israel after it was announced that U.S. authorities had arrested him.

Carlton, and other Noriega pilots were flying missions carrying arms for the contras.

The second critical event that occurred in that period between the end of 1981 and the early months of 1982 involved Noriega's establishment of a formal, but secret, partnership with the newly consolidated drug lords who formed the notorious Medellín Cartel in Colombia.

After a bitter and bloody struggle in Colombia, pitting the organized drug leaders against the Marxist revolutionary group M-19, the Medellín Cartel forces had triumphed in 1982. After a struggle that had featured kidnapping, torture, and murder, the Medellín Cartel then forged a new relationship with the vanquished M-19 remnants. The newly empowered drug lords had raised a two-thousand-man private army (later expanded fourfold), equipped with automatic weapons, to crush the M-19 and assert control over Colombian life. It was more powerful than the government itself. The additional M-19 soldiers became, in effect, enforcers for the cartel, used both to protect narcotics shipments and to sow terror among Colombian government officials. In return the cartel gave them money and weapons.

This newly merged power created what official investigators called "the world's most powerful drug trafficking operation, the Medellín Cartel." The cartel dominated the illegal narcotics trade. It became the chief source of marijuana worldwide and, far more lucratively, for the burgeoning traffic in cocaine. Its greatest and most profitable market was in the United States. The Colombian cartel organized itself into elaborate conglomerates for purposes of growing, harvesting, processing, transporting, selling, and repatriating the profits from cocaine and marijuana. Coca processing centers were constructed in trackless rain forests of Colombia's Amazon River basin. These factory complexes were capable of converting a mash of coca leaves into a paste and then into crystalline cocaine in quantities of tons per week.

Toward the end of the eighties the cartel was estimated to supply between 60 and 80 percent of all the cocaine entering the United States. Earnings from cocaine alone were believed to be about eight billion dollars a year. So fabulous were the financial returns from this vast criminal enterprise, or complex of illegal businesses within businesses, that by 1988 *Forbes* magazine had listed two of the cartel's leaders, Jorge Luis Ochoa and Pablo Escobar, as among the richest men in the world.

The Noriega connection, a matter of documented record and sworn testimony, had begun before the final consolidation of the cartel's power. By 1976 Noriega had been supplying money-laundering services for Colombian drug dealers. Three years later, according to testimony of a Miami accountant and convicted principal money launderer for the cartel, a personal agreement was negotiated between the cartel and Noriega. Under its provisions, Noriega was to receive a commission ranging from one-half of 1 percent to 10 percent of each drug money-laundering transaction for his services in providing security and other assistance.

Noriega's assumption of control in Panama after Torrijos's death made him even more valuable to the cartel.

Even before Noriega's dictatorship Panama occupied a unique place in the complex world of high international finance. By eliminating its income taxes, it had become a tax haven. And by developing strict bank secrecy laws along the lines of Switzerland, it had also become a bank haven. Because it used the U.S. dollar as its official currency and then developed a legal system that allowed the formation of so-called bearer share anonymous corporations, Panama had become a perfect place for people and institutions worldwide to deposit money without having to worry about problems of currency convertibility, taxation, or disclosure.

By the early eighties illegal dollars were pouring into Panama by private planes, in passenger suitcases on commercial flights, and as airfreight. Eventually the Panamanian military facilitated this activity by supervising the off-loading of huge sums of cash into armored cars. U.S. investigators say that in the four-year period alone from 1979 to 1983, Noriega's satraps helped the Medellín Cartel launder billions of dollars in U.S. currency through Panama. As part of his payment from this process, Noriega was said to have received more than $2.5 billion in that time period alone.

The Senate Foreign Relations Narcotics Subcommittee report, a product of three years of investigation and sworn testimony and published on April 13, 1989, described how under Noriega's hand the military took increasing control over Panama's most important institutions and thus controlled the drug trade:

> Noriega gained control of the Customs, Immigration and Passport Services, Civil Aeronautics, the National Bank of Panama, and the Attorney General's Office, which together represented the major Panamanian institutions with jurisdiction over the narcotics trade. Noriega pushed legislation through the National Assembly consolidating the National Guard, Air Force, Navy, police and Customs under a single command called the Panamanian Defense Forces [PDF]. As head of the PDF, Noriega now controlled all elements of the Panamanian government essential to the protection of drug trafficking and money laundering, thus accomplishing two goals simultaneously: increasing his control over Panama and enriching himself. Noriega had turned Panama's political system into what one witness called a "narcokleptocracy," a political system in which Panamanian government became controlled by personal loyalties to Noriega, cemented by graft and corruption, and substantially funded with narcotics money.

Noriega was now in a position to turn Panama into an open, but secure, base for drug smuggling. Drug cartel leaders would transport the drugs and pay back a percentage of the returns, while he guaranteed safety—and secrecy—of operations.

In the next two years, the final ones of Reagan's first term, Noriega transformed Panama into a vast, illegal drug center. He even allowed the Medellín Cartel to establish a major and modern cocaine processing plant (complete with laboratory) in Panama's Darién Province, near the Colombian border.

Another moneymaking sideline of the drug dealers, the illegal trading and shipment of weapons between smugglers in the United States and the Colombians, developed during this time. Once again Panama's role was critical. The flow of weapons through Panama was far more extensive through the resources of the cartel. With the assistance of the Israelis, in particular Mike Harari, according to Blandón, weapons for the contras were purchased through a secret channel operating through the Soviet bloc. This was to eliminate the possibility of unauthorized U.S. combat weapons being discovered in the hands of contras, whose mission was supposed to be limited to interdiction of Communist arms into Central America. Furthermore, contras could claim to have captured the Communist weapons they were then using. The U.S. hand was thus supposedly further hidden.

Arms purchased in Yugoslavia were shipped to Panama, with appropriate end user certificates, through Paraguay and Bolivia. From there they would be transshipped secretly to the contras. (Later this same channel was used by the United States to ship arms to Iran.)

Noriega's assistance to the contras is a matter of record. Exactly how he made his decision to support them, however, is a matter of dispute. José Blandón says that he was briefed by Noriega immediately after a Panama visit between Noriega and Vice President George Bush in 1983. Bush, according to Blandón, made an appeal for Noriega's assistance and also delivered an implied warning about drug and money-laundering operations centered in Panama.*

Later Blandón was present when Lieutenant Colonel Oliver L. North of Reagan's National Security Council met with Noriega in June 1985 on a private yacht anchored off Panama City. There North asked Noriega to permit training of contra forces on Panamanian bases and to let contra leaders enter and exit Panama freely in furtherance of their war mission. Noriega agreed. Contra troops were in fact subsequently trained in Panama, though not at U.S.-controlled facilities. Blandón testified that at a second meeting between North and Noriega, Noriega suggested that Panamanian units might be employed for military operations in Nicaragua. They seem to have been.

It is also a matter of record that by 1985 Noriega had helped the contras "in blowing up a Sandinista arsenal" in Nicaragua. As the question of Noriega's role in drugs drew more public attention in the United States, it is also part of the same official record that Noriega offered the United States a quid pro quo deal of his own.

In August 1986, according to a document of facts certified as "true" by the U.S. government,† a Noriega representative told North

*Blandón's account reported here is from what he told me in 1989.

†This document was introduced at the trial of Oliver L. North early in 1989 as part of the agreement reached between prosecution and defense in *U.S. v. North,* D.C. District Court.

that "in exchange for a promise to help clean up Noriega's image and a commitment to lift the U.S. ban on military sales to the Panamanian defense forces, Noriega would assassinate the Sandinista leadership for the U.S. government." North responded that U.S. law forbade assassinations. Noriega's representative then "responded that Noriega had numerous assets in place in Nicaragua and could accomplish many essential things, just as Noriega had helped the previous years in blowing up a Sandinista arsenal."

The next month North secretly met Noriega in London. With the approval of his National Security Council chief Admiral John Poindexter, North told Noriega that if the Panamanian dictator had intelligence "assets"—that is, operatives—inside Nicaragua, they could be helpful. He further officially informed Nicaragua that the United States viewed favorably his offer to engage in sabotage operations. Noriega then agreed "to take immediate actions against the Sandinistas and offered a list of priorities, including an oil refinery, an airport, and the Puerto Sandino off-load facility."

Neither is there any question that by 1984 arms shipments were being flown from Panama to Costa Rica to assist the contras in their so-called southern front operations against the Sandinistas. At that same time, Noriega himself offered—and the United States secretly accepted—to provide contra forces there with one hundred thousand dollars in clandestine assistance. According to sworn testimony, many of the pilots flying arms missions between Panama and Costa Rica carried mixed cargoes of guns and drugs to contra bases there. They unloaded their weapons, refueled, then took off again, and flew north toward the United States.

The same planes that had carried contra weapons now carried illegal drug shipments into the United States. Pilots flying those missions included Americans, Colombians, and Panamanians. Sometimes they used contra airstrips to land and refuel on their U.S. drug runs even when they carried no weapons. They knew authorities would not check those airstrips because the contra war was "protected." They knew, too, that if arrested by U.S. authorities, they

---

Both sides stipulated it to be factual, though Bush administration officials later tried to back away from it.

could employ a familiar covert legal defense ("I work for the CIA" even though they didn't). Sometimes such claims of "national security" worked to short-circuit prosecution.

That such mixed missions, or missions for mutual interest and profit, took place are not disputed. "Individuals who provided support for the Contras were involved in drug trafficking, the supply network of the Contras was used by drug trafficking organizations, and elements of the Contras themselves knowingly received financial and material assistance from drug traffickers," the Senate Foreign Relations Narcotics Subcommittee report concluded. "In each case, one or another agency of the U.S. government had information regarding the involvement either while it was occurring, or immediately thereafter."

On the question of drugs and contras, José Blandón asserted that by the spring of 1984 the Medellín Cartel leaders in Colombia had made a deliberate decision to support the contras by supplying weapons and financial assistance. It was a decision motivated by pure self-interest. By their secret assistance of the United States, their drug shipments were exposed to less risk because they could use the very same bases employed by the contras. "Since March 1984," he said, "the financial support of this operation was the responsibility of the cartel of Medellín."

That cannot be proven. Nor has the charge been substantiated that the contra leaders themselves were directly and personally involved in drug profiteering.* There is no doubt, however, that there was a connection among drugs, arms, contras, and covert operators—and between public U.S. policy and many private dealers.

As Blandón put it, "So you have an illegal network that was supposed to support the contras but that was also used to buy drugs

*Substantial evidence has been accumulated, however, that adds much more detail to the Senate Foreign Relations subcommittee's finding of no direct involvement between contra leaders and narcotics trade. See Jonathan Kwitny's *Crimes of Patriots* (New York: W. W. Norton & Company, 1987). On May 18, 1990, after previously classified pages from North's notebooks had been made public through a Freedom of Information Act suit, Senator Kerry stated: ". . . The North notebooks confirm that high-level U.S. officials, including officials at the CIA and the NSC [National Security Council], knew about General Noriega's drug trafficking and corruption in 1986, kept him on the U.S. payroll, and discussed helping him clean up his image in return for his help for the contras. This evidence, contained in the Notebooks, was suppressed by the White House from January 25, 1988, when we first sought the information, until today."

that came from the cartel. So it was a good business for everyone. A lot of people were making a lot of money."

By his own testimony, toward the end of a business career that "went far beyond my wildest expectations," Ramon Milian Rodriguez was making between two and four million dollars a month as the Medellín Cartel's chief U.S. accountant and money launderer. That was his payment for laundering approximately two hundred million dollars each month in drug money. His personal life-style resembled that of a Boesky or a Trump. In the Cuban-American community of Miami, Milian Rodriguez was a highly respected professional who served on the boards of several banks and important companies. On his frequent trips to New York, he was met at the airport by a representative of one of the nation's great financial institutions and taken by limousine to transact important business at the bank.*

He was a special customer and granted special privileges. As he explained to fascinated U.S. senators, "they have a special representative for people like me." With good reason, for he controlled an estimated eleven billion dollars in drug money that had been properly laundered, and he dealt only with the biggest and best of the financial houses, banks that "courted my business" and "banks that can take a two hundred million dollar CD [certificate of deposit] easily. You just can't place that kind of money with a Ma-and-Pa bank in Des Moines, Iowa." If not in a CD, the laundered drug money was invested in real estate, stocks, and bonds. "You name it," Milian Rodriguez said cheerfully. "They [the cartel drug dealers] have a very diversified portfolio."

As for whether the great U.S. commercial banking institution with which he dealt knew what his money represented and where it came from, Milian Rodriguez certainly had no doubts. "They knew they were dealing with Milian Rodriguez," he said, "who repre-

*At the time he testified before the Senate Foreign Relations Narcotics Subcommittee on February 11, 1988, Chairman Kerry stressed Milian Rodriguez's credibility. "We have checked out a great number of the things you've said," he stated, "and obviously, you have corroborated other witnesses significantly, and they have corroborated you, both by having seen you in Panama, knowing you were engaged in this, and knowing of the detail. Also, you've given us privately an extraordinary number of names, actual corporations and so forth, which have checked out. And so this committee obviously has been comfortable in putting you on."

sented money from South America, and from their corresponding banks in Panama knew where the money came from. . . . They knew what they were doing. It was not . . . like they didn't have an inkling of what the purpose was."

"Money speaks?" he was asked.

"Marvelously," he replied.

How Milian Rodriguez arrived at such a powerful position and at such an early age ("I reached my peak at twenty-eight," he remarked) is a story perhaps even more complicated than that of the clandestine drug operations in which he excelled. It is a story that also directly connects criminal drug enterprises with covert wars fought by the United States.

Born in Havana, Milian Rodriguez was not quite eight years old when he and his family joined the tens of thousands of Cubans fleeing their homeland for the United States in the weeks immediately after Castro came to power early in 1959. Like many of the Cuban immigrants, Milian Rodriguez prospered. Upon graduating from the University of Santa Clara in California, he returned to the Cuban community of Miami to begin a career as a certified public accountant. Through "a very dear friend of the family" and especially close friend of his father's, he was retained in 1973 by a most powerful and influential client.

This was Manuel Artime, whom he described as "a hero figure" in the Cuban community "who had been involved in various anticommunist efforts." Artime was much more than this; the CIA had picked Artime as the civilian leader of the Bay of Pigs invasion, and later the United States obtained his freedom from a Castro prison by paying the five-hundred-thousand-dollar ransom price Castro had set for him.

Artime, as Milian Rodriguez explained it, needed someone he could trust, and who was ideologically in tune with his own beliefs. He knew young Milian Rodriguez to be such a man. "I fit those bills for him," Milian Rodriguez said. "He asked me to work for him on certain projects that involved the covert handling of money." Artime immediately arranged for him to start receiving training in rudimentary skills of handling money covertly. He provided expert teachers. Milian Rodriguez never knew their names. They never gave them; he never asked. "It's an interesting field," Milian Rodriguez said. "It requires expertise in accounting, banking, logistics, and security. And I received training in all of those areas. I had to learn about banking secrecy laws, the various vehicles, incorporation."

Melodramatic though it sounds, there was good reason for such secrecy.

"The very first project I ever worked on was delivering money to the families of some agents that had been captured, breaking the law in the U.S.," he said. "It's commonly referred to as 'Watergate.' "

His job was to deliver money to the Cuban families of the Watergate burglars (Bay of Pigs veterans with CIA connections, some on the payroll) who lived in Miami. Milian Rodriguez made deliveries of "a couple of hundred thousand dollars in cash" directly to the families' homes in Miami. This was for their living expenses and to defray their legal costs. "There were other cases where I made deliveries to accounts in specifically Nicaragua," then controlled by the Somoza dictatorship and a country with which Artime had established long and important covert ties and where he also trained teams of saboteurs with U.S. funds for operations inside Cuba.

Milian Rodriguez viewed his role in the Watergate affair with pride. "We felt that the Cubans had behaved well and they had done as they were ordered and they took their punishment and we felt that we owed them backing," he explained. "We felt that they had been mistreated."

It is his testimony that his own money-laundering career for drug dealers took a new, more profitable turn when he began representing more and more of these Cuban-American smugglers after Artime died of cancer in 1976. "Many of his people were left without a captain," he said. "They drifted into the smuggling business because they had assets, they had boats, airplanes, radio. . . . When you lose your ideological leader, you are somewhat disgruntled, and many of my countrymen feel that they have reason to be disgruntled with America. Like water always chooses the course of least resistance, at that time, the easiest way to make money, the fastest way, was through drug smuggling. And many of them went into that."*

*This may be so, but I have been told by people that I have excellent reason to believe that Artime, or operations in which he was personally involved, began dealing in drugs at least ten years before.

Now Milian Rodriguez branched out in his expanding money-laundering drug business. Three years after Artime's death he had established contacts in Panama. Until that point, he was, as he said, in the minor leagues. "Let's say that I was dealing in the tens of millions. I was going to shortly deal in [ten to twenty times] more than that."

It was then that he "sat down with General Noriega and reached an accord." His meeting with Noriega, then still a colonel, had been arranged by Colombian drug dealers.

"Through word of mouth and through success," he said, "I was referred to some Colombians who had a problem with their cash flow, not in the terms of business, but actually the flow of cash. . . . I very quickly got an idea who they were when we started discussing the amounts of money that they needed handled. Initially, I believe we were talking in the neighborhood of fifty to one hundred million dollars."

Toward the end of 1979 he made his business arrangement with Noriega on behalf of the cartel. Although Torrijos—a charismatic leader with strong popular support who "ruled from the heart, not from the brain," in Milian Rodriguez's view—was still in power in Panama, Noriega operated from a different kind of strength: cunning. "He had the intelligence training, and he fully recognized the value of the information he received, and he fully recognized how best to utilize that power. You had Noriega as the enforcer."

Noriega's involvement in drugs was well known to a host of U.S. agencies and has been documented by a number of official investigations, but for years this knowledge was put aside because Noriega was a means to an end.

Lee Hamilton, chairman of the House Intelligence Committee, had developed a close relationship with CIA Director William Casey that extended beyond professional dealings into personal friendship. Hamilton often pressed Casey to explain the U.S. connection with Noriega. Hamilton's recollection of those private conversations is most telling in explaining the rationale of high U.S. officials who knowingly dealt with Noriega:*

"Bill Casey's remark to me about Noriega sums it up. Casey must

*This is from an interview I had with Hamilton for this book on May 10, 1988.

have told me half a dozen times, 'He's a bastard, but he's our bastard.' That was the way Bill Casey expressed his view. Now the only thing wrong with that statement is he was not our bastard. He was only partly our bastard. But it expresses Casey's attitude. Noriega helped in several ways. He gave us a lot of information with respect to Castro; he's close to Castro, and our information about Cuba and Castro is not as good as you would think it should be. Noriega was an important source for us about a guy that we dislike above all others in the hemisphere. Secondly, Noriega told us a lot about the drug problem. He was a double-crosser. He probably double-crossed—and I'm reasonably sure he did—people who didn't pay him off. So he would tip our law enforcement people off about somebody he didn't like for whatever reason. And thirdly, he was very, very, important to us in Nicaragua in support of the contras. He did a lot of little things that helped us there. Now those three things were enough—and there may have been others—to justify anything in terms of our relationship with Noriega. There can have been no reasonable doubt in anyone's mind . . . that this guy was a drug dealer and he was a thoroughly, thoroughly reprehensible man. But we chose to deal with him because of the assets. We paid him. We paid him handsomely [some estimates are as much as two hundred thousand dollars a year]. . . ."

While arms and military aid flowed secretly to the contras, in part assisted by people like Noriega and covert operatives from Bay of Pigs days, drugs and other illegal cargo stemming from the same source moved into the United States.

For such as Ramon Milian Rodriguez, a businessman with a strongly held political ideology ("as a Cuban, I cannot accept dealing with Communists"), the secret illegal dealings with Noriega had their own poetic justice. In 1983, after paying off Noriega on behalf of the Colombian cartel at an average rate of ten million dollars a month for four years, Milian Rodriguez was arrested by members of Vice President George Bush's South Florida Drug Task Force.

He believed he had been betrayed by Noriega, and the circumstances of his arrest suggest he was right. "I believe General Noriega very adroitly used the American law enforcement agencies to surgically extract me from the operation while leaving the operation intact for him and his cronies to continue working," he testified, explaining his rationale for becoming a public witness against Noriega after he had been tried, convicted, and sentenced to a combined total U.S. jail sentence of forty-three years. "A telex was sent out of Panama to the South Florida Vice Presidential Task Force identifying me as a major money launderer. I think it's important to note that prior to that telex they didn't know who I was. And the Vice President's Task Force immediately—you know, for a government agency—within two or three months arrested me without doing very much investigative work or any of the things that I would expect from that type of agency. By doing that, and by taking me out of the picture, without hurting the system that was working, I think they were used by General Noriega."

If so, it was not the first time. It was only one more case of many people engaged in secret Central American activities playing one side against another.

José Blandón drew part of the lesson: "For me, the U.S. government fought a war against the Communists that everyone in Latin America knew didn't work. The U.S. lost both the war against the Communists and the war against the drugs and is now paying a high price in its society at home. For us in Panama, the result of all this policy is that we have a civil system weaker than ever and a military system stronger than ever."

CHAPTER 22

APRIL AGAIN

All was not what it appeared to be in Central America. For months, as spring approached in 1984, senior members of Congress had been receiving reports from many sources that raised questions about the true U.S. role there, but none of them was conclusive.

In the Senate the chairman and vice-chairman of the Select Committee on Intelligence, Barry Goldwater and Daniel Patrick Moynihan, "kept tugging at the CIA to tell us what was going on in Central America," as Moynihan later put it. It seemed evident something was, but they were unable to find out what. The administration tried to reassure them. In response to their request months before that the president submit a new intelligence finding detailing any new Central America actions, a second finding that Reagan signed was presented to their committee secretly on September 20, 1983. Still, new reports kept coming in, raising even more questions.

Goldwater and Moynihan, prototypical conservative and liberal politicians of national standing, had served together in a spirit of bipartisanship for the last four years, and even the intelligence community conceded their committee had functioned with fairness and discretion since its creation in 1976. After years of recrimination and disrespect among the intelligence agencies and Congress, trust had been rekindled. Now there were new doubts.

Similar doubts a year before in the House had led to passage of a bill sponsored by the laconic Representative Edward Boland of Massachusetts, chairman of the House Select Committee on Intelligence.

What came to be known as the Boland Amendment barred U.S. covert actions "for the purpose of overthrowing the government of Nicaragua," thus expressly putting into law what the president had secretly informed lawmakers were the limitations of U.S. clandestine operations there: to cut the flow of arms from the Sandinistas to El Salvador.

There the uneasy situation stood in April 1984.

For some reason, April has always been a fateful month in the capital. It was the month in which the great war presidents, Lincoln and Franklin Roosevelt, died; of America's entry into World War I; of the Bay of Pigs disaster; of bloody riots that left the capital city in flames following Martin Luther King's murder seven years later; of the disintegration of Nixon's presidency as the Watergate crisis came to a head; of the debacle in the Iranian desert during the attempt to rescue American hostages; of the terrorist bombing of the U.S. Embassy in Beirut that marked the worst attack against American targets in Lebanon.

Now it was April again, and Reagan's turn. On Thursday, April 5, at a Georgetown University forum, Pat Moynihan offered a Democratic view of the topic, "Forging a Bipartisan American Foreign and Defense Policy." Moynihan, whose impish charm and wit sometimes hide his intellect and scholarship, was entirely serious on this occasion. He struck a statesmanlike position: "To the degree that law is seen to be and is the basis of our international conduct, a bipartisan foreign policy does not require a party out of office to agree with policies of the party in power, but rather simply to agree with the principles of law on which those policies are based."

Speaking at the same forum the next day, Reagan echoed Moynihan's themes, also stressing the merits of bipartisanship, saying "an effective foreign policy must begin with bipartisanship. . . . The sharing of responsibility for a safer and more humane world must begin at home."

Three days later that spirit of bipartisanship was shattered. The *Wall Street Journal,* in a story with explosive impact, reported that U.S. CIA agents, acting in the name of the contras, had mined the harbors of Nicaragua, endangering not only its shipping but that of the Soviet Union and the innocent passage of commercial ships of third parties. Agents who took part in the mining operation included

Salvadorans, Hondurans, Argentinians, Chileans, and Ecuadorans—but no contra Nicaraguans in whose name the mines had been laid. It was disclosed, too, that a CIA training manual that described sabotage and assassination methods had been prepared and distributed to contra forces.

Goldwater was outraged. Moynihan was stunned. Neither they nor their committee had been informed in advance about this dramatic escalation of the conflict in Nicaragua. Goldwater, with Moynihan's strong backing, responded with an extraordinary letter of outrage to CIA Director William Casey. In his "Dear Bill" letter of April 9, 1984, Goldwater was even more blunt than usual. He began:

> Dear Bill:
>
> All this past weekend, I've been trying to figure out how I can most easily tell you my feelings about the discovery of the President having approved mining some of the harbors of Central America.
>
> It gets down to one, little, simple phrase: I am pissed off!

He went on to say:

> During the important debate we had all last week and the week before, on whether we would increase funds for the Nicaragua program, we were doing all right until a Member of the Committee charged [after the *Journal* story was published] that the President had approved the mining. I strongly denied that because I had never heard of it. I found out the next day that the CIA had, with the written approval of the President, engaged in such mining, and the approval came in February!
>
> Bill, this is no way to run a railroad and I find myself in a hell of a quandary. I am forced to apologize to the Members of the Intelligence Committee because I did not know the facts on this. . . .
>
> The President has asked us to back his foreign policy. Bill, how can we back his foreign policy when we don't know what the hell he is doing? Lebanon, yes, we all knew that he sent troops over there. But mine the harbors in Nicaragua? This is an act violating international law. It is an act of war. For the life of me, I don't see how we are going to explain it. . . .
>
> I don't like this. I don't like it one bit from the President or from you. I don't think we need a lot of lengthy explanations. The deed has been done and, in the future, if anything like this happens, I'm going to raise one hell of a lot of fuss about it in public.

Even those facts that Goldwater had just learned proved to be incorrect. Presidential approval for the mining operation had been given *nine months* before (and nearly three months after the latest presidential finding about Central America covert operations requested by the committee, which had *not* disclosed the mining operation). The first mines were laid on January 7, 1984. They were American mines, laid by an American vessel, under American command.

Moynihan, believing he had been betrayed, announced his resignation as vice-chairman of the intelligence committee. Eighty-four of his fellow senators, exactly half of them Republicans and half Democrats, in an unusually strong expression of bipartisanship voted that the mining should stop. Moynihan, commenting publicly, declared that "the rest of the president's Nicaragua program is in ruins."

Casey wrote to Goldwater and apologized, Moynihan was prevailed upon to stay on the committee, and within two months the first of what came to be known as the Casey Accords were signed by Casey for the CIA and by Goldwater and Moynihan on behalf of the Select Intelligence Committee. Supposedly this agreement ensured that a similar breakdown in reporting or a deliberate presidential failure to notify Congress of covert actions would not recur.

For his part, Casey, acting for the president, pledged to provide the committee with the written text of any new presidential finding concerning covert action, unless otherwise agreed to by both parties. Along with it would be a "scope" background paper spelling out the operational plans as well as its purpose and rationale. He agreed to inform the committee of "any other planned covert action activities for which higher authority or presidential approval has been provided, including, but not limited to, approvals of any activity which would substantially change the scope of an ongoing covert action operation." Such notification, he further pledged, would be provided "as soon as practicable and prior to implementation of the actual activity." Casey also promised to brief the committee on "all important elements of the [planned covert] activity, including operational and political risks, possible repercussions under treaty obligations or agreements, and any special issues raised under U.S. law."

There was more, in similarly clearly stated language. For its part, the committee leaders agreed to maintain strict procedures to prevent unauthorized disclosure of such sensitive U.S. secrets.

In the tenth and final clause, the congressional and executive representatives agreed they would "jointly review these procedures no later than one year after they become operative, in order to assess their effectiveness and their impact on the ability of the DCI [director, Central Intelligence] and the Committee to fulfill their respective responsibilities."

Those secret protocols were signed on June 6, 1984. They seemed to guarantee there would no repetition of the Nicaraguan mining deception.

A year passed. The promised review did not take place. It kept getting put off. Another year went by. Goldwater and Moynihan no longer were leading the committee. Their successors as chairman and vice-chairman respectively were Minnesota's David Durenberger, a Republican, and Vermont's Patrick Leahy, a former prosecutor.

In June 1986, exactly two years after the original agreement, the long-delayed review finally took place when a second accord was signed by the heads of the committee and CIA Director Casey.

Both parties solemnly agreed that "the Procedures have worked well and that they have aided the Committee and the DCI in the fulfillment of their respective responsibilities." In the new accord Casey made a new pledge. He promised that the committee would be informed when "significant military equipment actually is to be supplied for the first time in an ongoing operation, or there is a significant change in the quantity or quality of equipment provided."

That solemn promise was made five months *after* Ronald Reagan had signed an intelligence finding authorizing the shipment of arms to Iran. In that finding Reagan specifically ordered such information to be withheld from the U.S. congressional intelligence oversight committees. Congress was not to be informed.

Much later, when he learned of that presidential order, Pat Moynihan wrote: "What we had here, however unwitting, was an effort to subvert the Constitution of the United States. Such is the fruit of contempt of government."

Two months after the public controversy over mining harbors, a CBS News report described the CIA's use of a private cargo line called Southern Air Transport (later identified in hearings as being used in both Iranian and contra activities) to transport arms, airplane parts, and soldiers to the contras by way of Honduras. During this same period the name of Oliver L. North, a young Marine lieutenant colonel assigned to Reagan's National Security Council staff, began to surface in Associated Press reports about administration contra aid efforts. North at that time was virtually unknown to the general public.

It was in this context that in August the House of Representatives passed a definitive legal act barring the CIA from future support for the contras. The full Congress adopted this new Boland Amendment, or Boland II, as it came to be known, and Reagan signed it into law on October 12, 1984.

This Boland Amendment unambiguously cut off *all* funding for the contras. It specifically prohibited any administration agency involved in "intelligence activities," citing by name the CIA, the Defense Department, and "any other agency or entity," from "supporting, directly or indirectly, military or paramilitary operations in Nicaragua by any nation, group, organization, or individual."

Passage of this law, Boland stated, "clearly ends U.S. support for the war in Nicaragua. Such support can only be renewed if the President can convince the Congress that this very strict prohibition should be overturned."

That seemed to end it. It did not, for the administration merely continued doing in private what it had already been doing for most of the past two years. By then the Reagan administration had already made the decision to continue supporting the contras by any means necessary. That decision emanated from Ronald Reagan himself.

Reagan was the driving force behind efforts to keep the contras alive, with or without appropriated funds, with or without congressional and public approval, and regardless of legal and political risks. He personally directed his National Security staff, in the words of his national security adviser Robert C. McFarlane, to keep the contras together "body and soul." McFarlane's principal deputy, and the person who succeeded him, the dour Admiral John Poindexter, clearly understood the president's desire. Reagan, Pointexter later said, "wanted to be sure that the Contras were supported."*

To accomplish this day-to-day operational task, McFarlane turned to his fellow marine, the energetic and ambitious Oliver North. "I was given the job of holding them together in body and soul," North later said, employing the same phraseology as McFarlane.

North had no doubts, either, upon whose orders he was acting. The commander in chief was calling the shots. North's charge in assisting the contras, as he understood it, was: "To keep them together as a viable political opposition, to keep them alive in the field, to bridge the time between the time when we would have no money and the time when the Congress would vote again, to keep the effort alive, because the President committed publicly to go back, in his words, again and again and again to support the Nicaraguan resistance."

Finding ways to secure financial support for the contras outside public channels began inside the White House at least as early as February 1984, when McFarlane came up with an idea that fitted perfectly with Reagan administration philosophy. He would privatize the secret support effort, "contract it out." In effect, that meant "farming out the whole contra support operation to another country, which would not only provide the funding, but give it some direction."

McFarlane turned first to Israel, already a source of great help to the administration in facilitating weapons shipments clandestinely. Would Israel have any interest in instructing "the contras in basic tactics, maneuver[s], and so forth?" Not exactly, came back the equivocal response. For its own interests, Israel did not wish to play the full Argentinian trainer role for the contras but was anxious to help.

By the end of March McFarlane discussed another approach with the CIA's Casey: to let foreign powers friendly to American

*Unless otherwise noted, all quotations and memorandums cited herein are taken from the sworn testimony and documents introduced during the Iran-contra congressional hearings, published as *Report of the Congressional Committees Investigating the Iran-Contra Affair. with Supplemental, Minority, and Additional Views* (Washington, D.C.: U.S. Government Printing Office, 1987).

interest fund the contras secretly. Casey liked the idea. "I am in full agreement," the CIA director wrote in a memorandum of March 27, "that you should explore funding alternatives with Israel and perhaps others."

As the contras were about to exhaust the last money Congress had appropriated for them, McFarlane met with Saudi Arabia's ambassador to the United States. It was "almost inevitable," he told the Saudi representative, that the administration would fail to win congressional support for the contras. The Saudi diplomat was most solicitous and generous, offering to make a "contribution" of a million dollars a month to support the contras for the remainder of the year. It was a "humanitarian gesture," not a solicitation, merely a gift from a goodhearted friend, McFarlane later maintained.

McFarlane received the initial million-dollar contribution and so informed Poindexter, his deputy. Once again final responsibility fell on Oliver North. McFarlane instructed North to contact contra leaders "and to find out where the[ir] bank account was kept." North reported back with the name of the bank, its address, and the contras' account number. Not surprisingly, the contra bank was located in Miami.

Next North established an "offshore" banking account for the contras and gave the Swiss account number to the Saudis, enabling them to make their monthly million-dollar contra "gifts" directly into an undetectable international account.

McFarlane reported this good news to Reagan in somewhat melodramatic style. He chose not to tell the president privately, alone, but slipped a note card describing the Saudi deal and payment inside the morning briefing book that Reagan referred to during his daily senior staff meeting. When that meeting was over, McFarlane was called back to the president's office "to pick up the note card." The president, he was pleased to discover, had registered his personal appreciation by jotting down a note that, as McFarlane recalled, "expressed the President's satisfaction and pleasure that this had occurred." Nothing had been said; nothing needed to have been.

Later McFarlane testified that "within a day or so" he also informed Vice President George Bush, Secretary of State George Shultz, and Defense Secretary Caspar Weinberger of the secret Saudi funding arrangement. The contras would be "provided for" until the end of the year, he told them. It was "possible," he said later, that he also informed Edwin Meese, then Reagan's presidential counselor.

None of this was communicated, as solemnly pledged, to congressional intelligence oversight committees. The omission was deliberate and made with full recognition by these highest U.S. officials, including the president, that such a deception could have the most grievous political consequences. Reagan himself, and his top aides, were well aware that public disclosure could result in impeachment proceedings against the president. They chose to proceed anyway.

On June 25, 1984, in the same month that the so-called Casey Accords were signed, pledging full disclosure of further covert actions to Congress, the subject of impeachment was specifically raised with the president during a critical high-level White House meeting about other contra matters. Besides Reagan, those attending this June 25, 1984, National Security Council meeting were Casey, McFarlane, Meese, Shultz, and Weinberger. When Casey urged Reagan personally to seek third-country aid for the contras, Secretary of State Shultz warned it would be an "impeachable offense" if the U.S. government acted as a conduit for such secret funding. Shultz said he was passing on the opinion of White House Chief of Staff James A. Baker III, a lawyer.

According to official notes taken during that meeting, Reagan warned the group: "We'll all be hanging by our thumbs in front of the White House . . ." if word leaked out that they had discussed third-country funding for the contras.

That same day Oliver North secretly informed the contra leader Adolfo Calero that Saudi funds would be transferred to the contra account "w/in 24 hrs.," as he recorded in his notebook. He also warned Calero of the crucial necessity to keep everything secret. "Never let agency [CIA] know of amt, source, or even availability" of the Saudi funds, he wrote, adding: "no one in our govt. can be aware." Referring to the contras, he said similarly, "Your organization must not be aware."

Despite what North informed the contras, of course, the highest U.S. officials were *all* aware of his secret efforts. To give the administration further legal protection, Casey received a favorable legal interpretation from Attorney General William French Smith a day after possible impeachable offenses had been raised with Reagan. A memorandum of that Justice Department session recorded the attorney general as stating:

> that he saw no legal concern if the United States Government discussed this matter with other nations so long as it was made clear that they would be using their own funds to support the contras and no U.S. appropriated funds would be used for this purpose. The Attorney General also said that any nation agreeing to supply aid could not look to the United States to repay that commitment in the future. The DCI made it clear that if there is a possibility this option might be used, he would advise the CIA oversight committees.

Casey never did advise them. Instead, to ensure that the contra operations continued despite present and possible future congressional restrictions, he set about creating the most remarkable secret operation in U.S. history, a covert operation within a covert operation, worldwide in scope and operating without constraints inherent in constitutional checks and balances.

To create this extralegal operation, Casey turned to the NSC's ubiquitous Colonel North. In effect, as North later explained it, Casey was "handing off" CIA functions to him in the way a football quarterback hands off the ball to a running back.

Acting through Casey's guiding hand, North began forming what came to be called, among operatives involved, the Enterprise. These men became the private brokers who carried out secret foreign policy goals of the Reagan administration. Arms merchants, former CIA and Pentagon operatives, expert international financiers, soldiers of fortune, and Bay of Pigs veterans formed the ranks of this secret Enterprise. Gradually they expanded their activities into fields other than contra support. In a matter of months they had at their disposal what amounted to their own private air force, navy, offshore bank accounts, private companies, and private operatives. They carried out their missions through a network of shadowy figures who operated in the netherworld of third world intrigues and revolutionary movements, skirting or actually dealing with terrorists, hostage takers, and drug dealers.

Though aid to the contras was the initial impetus that led to creation of the Enterprise, Casey apparently had in mind something far more ambitious. As North explained Casey's thinking, he envisioned the Enterprise as an all-encompassing, fail-safe intelligence operation, one that would enable top U.S. policy makers to carry out their covert plans without being limited by congressional restrictions or public reactions. "It was always the intention to make this a self-sustaining operation and that there always be something there which you could reach out and grab when you needed it," North said, in recalling his sense of numerous conversations with Casey. "Director Casey said he wanted something you could pull off the shelf and use at a moment's notice. . . . Director Casey had in mind, as I understood it, an overseas entity that was capable of conducting operations or activities of assistance to U.S. foreign policy goals that was a stand-alone . . . self-financing, independent of appropriated monies and capable of conducting activities similar to the ones that we had conducted here."

It was Casey who supplied names of people that North could use for the operations. One whom Casey recommended was Richard V. Secord, a tough-talking former Air Force general who had been involved in special operations with the CIA in Laos and also in the disastrous Iranian hostage rescue mission.

The way in which Secord helped create the Enterprise reflected Casey's wishes. It was to be a private concern, carrying out secret missions with public purposes but without public accountability. As an inducement, members of the Enterprise, unlike their counterparts in public life, would be amply rewarded financially. "He agreed to establish, and did, private commercial entities outside the United States that could help carry out these activities," North said of Secord. "It was always viewed by myself, by Mr. McFarlane, by Director Casey, that these were private commercial ventures, private commercial activities. . . ."

As such, they were presumably freed from legal restraints and review imposed by congressional laws and regulations.

By the summer of 1984 Secord was buying weapons for the contras with Saudi funds. Assisting him was his business partner, Albert Hakim, an international arms dealer who was a naturalized American of Iranian descent.

From that point, the Enterprise carried out presidential wishes that the CIA and other U.S. agencies could no longer legally fulfill. The burden for overall direction for contra aid now fell on North and the National Security Council. To limit potential political embarrassment, if not impeachment, one more safeguard for NSC activities was sought. First the NSC's legal counsel gave an opinion stating that the NSC staff was *not* an intelligence agency under the definition adopted by Congress. Reagan himself said the Boland Amendment restrictions did not apply to members of his staff. By such reasoning, both the NSC and the president's staff were exempt from its prohibitions.

Thus North and the Enterprise were ostensibly free to act, and they did.

In addition to Israel and Saudi Arabia, other countries, including Taiwan, the People's Republic of China, South Korea, South Africa, and Brunei, were approached for aid and "contributions." Money from these countries moved into Swiss accounts and returned in the form of arms to the contras. Continuing to expand his search for new sources of funding, North tapped into a network of private foundations and organizations, met with conservative contributors, and invoked both the cause of the contras and the name of Ronald Reagan. Through the cover of "independent" and private fund-raising organizations he coordinated White House briefings and arranged private sessions between Reagan and contra contributors. At least ten million dollars were raised through this effort.

North's activities ranged even wider. He was instrumental in carrying out a secret propaganda operation, again through use of congressionally prohibited federal funds, to influence public opinion favorably toward the contras. This was conducted through the State Department's Office of Public Diplomacy for Latin America and the Caribbean. Subsequent investigation showed that the public diplomacy office, working with North's coordination of the NSC, financed so-called white propaganda, or pro-contra articles for submission to editorial pages of major U.S. newspapers, without disclosing a government background or interest in their preparation.*

*This does not appear to be the only connection among government money, covert propaganda operations, and the U.S. press. North also was involved with a Project Democracy operation using U.S. Information Agency funds and with an Afghan Media Project in which government grants were made to colleges and news organizations to send journalists to report on Afghan rebel actions against Soviet forces. The head of Boston University's College of Communications, H. Joachim Maitre, became intensely controversial during the Iran-contra

The president continued to be deeply involved in efforts to secure secret contra aid. Within four months after passage of Boland II, Reagan approved what McFarlane later described in court as "very secret" plans by which the United States offered "incentives" in the form of economic and military aid to Honduras, El Salvador, and Guatemala in return for their covert support of the contras.

These were specific quid pro quo arrangements in which the president played a leading part. On February 7, 1985, senior administration officials agreed to seek Reagan's approval of a three-part deal to persuade Honduras not to abandon support for the contras. Twelve days later Reagan approved this plan and authorized $174 million in economic aid to Honduras, speeding deliveries of U.S. military aid there and increasing the scope of covert CIA programs to help that nation. These were specific "incentives," as McFarlane's memo put it, that the United States would offer the president of Honduras in return for his government's continued and secret support of the contras. The memo suggested that Vice President Bush would be sent as an emissary to complete this deal with the Honduran leader. Bush did meet with the Honduran president one month later but strongly denied he had been involved in a quid pro quo deal when the memo was made public four years later.

Other White House documents that later came to light portrayed Reagan as having ordered military support to the contras after the Boland Amendment had prohibited all such assistance. One memo showed that he authorized an airdrop of two antitank weapons for the contras in this period. After a Honduran military official seized ammunition intended for the contras, Reagan personally phoned the president of Honduras and succeeded in getting the ammunition released for delivery to the contras.

When the need for even more contra funds arose, Reagan met with Saudi Arabia's King Fahd in the family quarters of the White House. There the Saudi ruler agreed to make another twenty-four-million-dollar payment (later raised to thirty-two million). As the year passed, the war continued, and the contra force grew from a

---

disclosures for contributing to a documentary about the contras that received government funding and for his association with North, with whom he attended several White House briefings on Central America.

force of nine thousand to sixteen thousand, Secretary Shultz was instructed to prepare a list of other countries that Reagan could solicit for funds. Additional millions were raised from these third-country solicitations.

Under North's NSC supervision, and with the help of other U.S. agency officials, the Enterprise funneled more weapons, supplies, money, and military intelligence to the contras. All this took place for two years after Congress had specifically banned such activity and during a period when administration officials issued repeated denials to Congress and press that any such U.S. government assistance was occurring.

By the summer of 1985 press accounts in such newspapers as the *Washington Post* and the *New York Times* reported that North had given the contras "direct military advice" on attacks and strategy and also was said to have "facilitated the supplying of logistical help" for them.

After a *New York Times* story in August 1985 cited "administration officials" as its sources for those charges about North, Reagan responded with an unequivocal public denial. "We're not violating any laws," he said. In a follow-up statement later that day, he pledged to continue working with Congress "as effectively as possible and take care that the law be faithfully executed."

Congressional officials were not satisfied. Representative Michael Barnes of Maryland, who chaired a Foreign Affairs subcommittee, wrote McFarlane on August 16 to say that press reports about NSC support for the contras "raise serious questions regarding the violation of the letter and spirit of U.S. law" and requested information about whether NSC staff had provided "tactical influence on rebel military operations," whether it had "engaged in facilitating contacts for prospective financial donors," and whether it had been involved in "otherwise organizing and coordinating rebel efforts."

That same week Representative Lee Hamilton of Indiana, chairman of the House Select Committee on Intelligence, also wrote McFarlane and demanded "a full report on the kinds of activities regarding the contras that the NSC carried out and what the legal justification is for such actions given the legislative prohibitions that existed last year and earlier this year."

McFarlane, in the first of six letters that North drafted for him to answer similar congressional questions, answered that he had "thoroughly examined the facts and all matters which in any remote fashion could bear upon these charges" and told Hamilton: "I can state with deep personal conviction that at no time did I or any member of the National Security Council staff violate the letter or spirit" of the congressional ban on contra aid. He added: "I am most concerned ... there be no misgivings as to the existence of any parallel efforts to provide, directly or indirectly, support for military or paramilitary activities in Nicaragua. There has not been, nor will there be, any such activities by the NSC staff."

This "deliberate attempt to deceive Congress and the public," as congressional investigators later put it, was successful. The denials, if not completely believed, were accepted, and the contra secrets remained secret.

An even greater and politically more explosive secret was then being tightly held within the highest levels of the administration, but not a hint of it had surfaced. Ronald Reagan had approved secret shipments of arms to Iran.

His action came against a backdrop of another wave of terrorist incidents and the taking of new American hostages in the Mideast that year. That June, after Shiite terrorists murdered a U.S. Navy diver who was a passenger on a hijacked TWA flight in Beirut, Reagan repeated the same vows he had made since his presidential campaign of 1980. "The U.S. gives terrorists no rewards, no guarantees," he said. "We make no concessions. We make no deals." The next month, while he and his aides were denying involvement in contra operations, Reagan continued to lash out at terrorists, calling both Iran and Nicaragua part of "a new international version of Murder, Incorporated." Linking Iran and Nicaragua with Libya, North Korea, and Cuba, Reagan described them as "outlaw states run by the strangest collection of misfits, Looney Tunes, and squalid criminals since the advent of the Third Reich."*

*Reagan's public stance toward Iran was extremely harsh. In December 1983, amid public fanfare, the United States began Operation Staunch, in which it urged allied nations to "stop transferring arms to Iran." A month later, on the third anniversary of Reagan's presidency, the United States officially branded Iran a sponsor of international terrorism. Restrictions on export to Iran of aircraft, spare parts, and high-powered outboard motors were announced

Three weeks later, on August 2, Reagan secretly approved the first shipment of 100 U.S. TOW missiles to Iran by Israel, promising the Israelis that the United States would replenish the weapons Israel transferred to Iran from its stocks. Twenty-eight days later Israel delivered those arms to Iran for the United States. Two weeks later a second Israeli shipment of 408 U.S. TOW missiles was made to Iran. The next day, September 15, an American hostage, the Reverend Benjamin Weir, was released by his captors in Lebanon.

By November the Israelis had stopped shipping the missiles, partly because of problems over immediate U.S. replacement of the weapons and also because direct flights from Israel to Iran would almost certainly attract wide public attention, especially in view of the poor relations between those countries. Richard Secord was dispatched to Europe to resolve this problem; the mission of shipping arms was taken over by the Enterprise. Again North was instrumental in arranging for the covert shipment of weapons.

On November 25 Secord made the third delivery of American arms to Iran, this time transporting eighteen U.S. Hawk missiles. No legal authority existed for shipment of these weapons, and within high U.S. government circles concern was expressed about these illegal acts. After CIA lawyers had argued strongly that covert shipments of U.S. arms required specific written approval by the president to make it legal, Reagan signed a new intelligence finding that *retroactively* authorized the three weapons transfers to Iran that had already taken place since August. This finding, signed by Reagan on December 5, 1985, was titled "Hostage Rescue-Middle East." It explicitly spelled out the purpose of those shipments as a straight arms-for-hostage deal between the United States and the government of Iran and stated:

> I have been briefed on the efforts being made by private parties to obtain the release of Americans held hostage in the Middle East, and hereby find that the following operations in foreign countries (including all support necessary to such operations) are important

---

along with the ban on weapons and other matériel with military use. The next fall Secretary of State Shultz promised "swift and sure measures" against terrorists, saying, "We cannot allow ourselves to become the Hamlet of nations, worrying endlessly over how to respond."

> to the national security of the United States. *Because of the extreme sensitivity of these operations, in the exercise of the President's constitutional authorities, I direct the Director of Central Intelligence not to brief the Congress of the United States, as provided for in Section 501 of the National Security Act of 1947, as amended, until such time as I may direct otherwise* [italics added].

It was never disclosed to Congress.

The privatizing of U.S. foreign policy continued, carrying with it yet another secret within a secret and, despite all the revelations that followed, in circumstances that remain murky and complex. The Enterprise had raised the price on arms sold to Iran, deliberately overcharging the Iranians an average markup in price of 38 percent. A percentage of the arms proceeds, the result of the sale of U.S. government property, was set aside for the personal profit of the Enterprise operators. Other sums were diverted to Enterprise bank accounts to provide cash for operations the Enterprise chose to mount. A lot of cash was held back, for purposes that have never been identified. Aid to the contras was one use of funds raised by overcharging the Iranians and, in terms of the actual amount of money raised, a modest one. Money from this source was used to buy arms for the contras. It was, as North later said of the diversion of those funds, "a neat idea." Now the same Enterprise charter planes that shipped arms to Iran flew back with weapons for the contras. The two secret paths had joined.

The old C-123 cargo plane took off from a secret contra supply airfield called Ilopango in El Salvador at 9:50 A.M., Sunday, October 5, 1986, carrying a crew of four and ten thousand pounds of ammunition, uniforms, and medicine. The ammunition and supplies were to be dropped to contra forces operating inside Nicaraguan territory. By then these clandestine flights were routine. Just days before, after completion of another successful contra supply drop, one Enterprise operative at the Salvadoran air base had written to another in Washington: "Ho-hum, just another day at the office."

To avoid Sandinista guns, the cargo plane flew a southern route across Costa Rica and over Nicaraguan territory. Around noon, after two and a half hours of flight and some thirty miles past the Costa Rican border, a patrol of Sandinista soldiers, resting in the jungle after straying from their command, heard the sound of an approaching plane. Through a break in the clouds, they saw the old C-123 moving slowly toward them at an altitude of about eight hundred feet. Nineteen-year-old José Fernández Canales quickly set up his shoulder-carried Russian-made SAM-7 missile launcher. He fired. Seconds later the missile hit the plane's right wing. As the plane began spiraling down toward the jungle, a former U.S. marine named Eugene Hasenfus, standing by the cargo door from which he was supposed to kick out supplies for a parachute drop, made an instantaneous decision. He jumped. While Hasenfus floated to the ground by parachute, the plane crashed into the jungle. Three Americans died. Hasenfus survived and was captured.

In the wreckage Sandinista soldiers found logbooks and other documents linking the dead Americans with Southern Air Transport of Miami, an airline identified in the earlier CBS reports as involved in contra operations and well known as a former CIA charter airline. They also found an ID card that had been issued to Hasenfus by Salvadoran authorities. It identified him as an "adviser" in the "Grupo USA" group at Ilopango. Other documents recovered linked the crew with an office in Washington, D.C.

Soon Hasenfus told his captors that his real employer was not the "dummy" Enterprise company in Panama called Udall Resources, Inc., that ostensibly paid the bills; he believed he was working for the CIA on missions to drop arms to the contras. This news was immediately flashed to the world by the Sandinistas.

Hasenfus also identified the man who commanded the secret contra resupply missions in El Salvador for the Enterprise, a veteran Cuban-American former CIA agent whose code name was Max Gomez. In reality, he was Felix Rodriguez, another in the long line of Bay of Pigs connections with U.S. secret operations in Central America in the 1980s. Rodriguez had been in charge of Brigade 2506 infiltration teams for the Bay of Pigs invasion and continued anti-Castro clandestine work with groups headed by Manuel Artime in later years. José Blandón, the close aide to Panama's Torrijos and afterward head of Panamanian political intelligence for Noriega, said that Rodriguez had been involved with Israeli Mike Harari in the early guns and drugs smuggling operations for the contras. Ramon Milian Rodriguez, the Cuban-American drug cartel money launderer from Miami and former accountant for Artime, also claimed that Felix Rodriguez had requested and received a ten-million-dollar contribution in drug money for the contras. This cartel money was funneled to the contras, Ramon Milian Rodriguez said, through a series of "front" companies he controlled in Miami. Felix Rodriguez denied it.

Moments after learning that an American had been captured after the plane crash, the CIA station chief in El Salvador dispatched a secret message to Richard Secord's top deputy in Washington: "Situation requires we do necessary damage control." Felix Rodriguez also immediately placed an urgent call to Washington, trying to reach his old friend and former CIA colleague from Vietnam duty Donald Gregg, then the national security adviser to Vice President George Bush. Gregg had worked closely with Rodriguez and North but denied that he was aware of the extent of the secret aid efforts for the contras; he knew firsthand only of U.S. covert assistance against the Salvadoran rebels. He emphatically denied that Vice President Bush, a former head of the CIA, knew or had been briefed about the contra operations that Rodriguez directed.*

In Washington Secretary of State Shultz flatly denied any U.S. involvement. The Hasenfus aircraft had been "hired by private people," he said, "who had no connection with the U.S. government at all."

Questions continued. So did the predictable barrage of press stories raising still more embarrassing ones. When Reagan next met with reporters, he was asked if the downed aircraft had any connection with the U.S. government. "Absolutely none," he told White House reporters. The president also said: "There is no government connection with that at all. . . . We've been aware that there are

*Later it was determined that Rodriguez had met three times with Bush in Washington while he was directing contra resupply operations from El Salvador. There had also been seventeen contacts or meetings between Rodriguez and the vice president's office. On May 1, 1986, Rodriguez and Bush met in Washington for what the vice president's scheduling memo described as: "To brief the Vice President on the status of the war in El Salvador and resupply of the Contras." Three years later Gregg testified that the memo must have been the result of a typist's error. Instead of "resupply of the contras," he said, the subject for discussion might have been "resupply of the copters."

private groups and private citizens that have been trying to help the contras—to that extent—but we did not know the exact particulars of what they're doing."

But the story could not be contained. Official investigations were looking into the circumstances of the flight. North tried, with some success, to stop them. He called FBI Executive Assistant Director Oliver ("Buck") Revell and told him that Southern Air Transport had been involved in carrying out a highly secret presidential intelligence order (the shipment of arms to Iran). North assured the FBI official that Southern Air had not been involved in illegal activities.

Next North tried to halt a U.S. Customs Service investigation of the crash. He was concerned that a Customs Service subpoena for Southern Air Transport records would lead to disclosure of two of the Enterprise's secret Swiss bank accounts, Lake Resources and Hyde Park Square, which had paid for the shipment of arms to both Iran and the contras. North told the Customs enforcement director, William Rosenblatt, that Southern Transport people were "good guys" who had done nothing illegal. He said he had double-checked into the cargo the C-123 had carried. No matter what the Sandinistas claimed, he could assure Customs that there had been no arms aboard. Customs narrowed the scope of its investigation.

John Poindexter, who had succeeded Robert McFarlane as the president's national security adviser and was North's immediate superior, added his authority to the cover-up attempt, phoning Attorney General Meese to request that FBI and Customs investigations into Southern Transport be delayed. Saying their employees were needed for the "Iran initiative," Poindexter warned the investigations could compromise "sensitive hostage negotiations." FBI Director William Webster ordered the FBI investigation delayed for ten days.

CIA Director Casey conferred with North. As far back as the early spring of 1984 Casey and North had discussed the necessity to have a "fall guy plan" in the event the secret operations were exposed. "It was seen that there would need to be someone who could . . . take the fall," North remembered Casey's telling him. That way the highest officials, starting from the president down, would be provided "plausible deniability." The time to implement the plan was approaching, Casey told North; it was time to begin cleaning up the files. Wholesale destruction of documents and evidence began.

Casey had another grave concern that he did not share with North. Two days after Hasenfus was captured, threatening to expose the secret contra operations, Casey received a blackmail threat as the price for silence about the Iran arms sales. This direct threat came from two Canadian businessmen who had advanced money for the Iranian arms sale and had not been repaid. Unless they received ten million dollars in repayment, they would make public what they knew.

This warning came from an old Casey friend and former client in New York named Roy Furmark, a business associate of the Saudi Arabian international financier Adnan Khashoggi, who was instrumental in providing financing for the purchase of arms sold to Iran. When Casey and Furmark met in New York two days after Hasenfus was captured, Furmark warned his old friend that unless the Canadian businessmen received the ten million dollars, they would not only disclose their knowledge of the Iran arms sales but also reveal that proceeds from those arms-for-hostage deals had been used to buy arms for the contras.

Bill Casey was "deeply disturbed." This whole thing was coming unraveled, he told North. Things ought to be "cleaned up."

Early that October North began, as he put it, "cleaning things up." He shredded documents and destroyed the ledger book in which he kept records of payments and disbursements of funds, including the names and addresses of "everybody" involved.

The White House had positive news to announce on Monday, November 3, 1986. Another American hostage, David Jacobsen, had been released in Lebanon, the third American to be set free since the arms-for-hostage shipments began, though the public then knew nothing about those secret deals. Within twenty-four hours the good news about Jacobsen had been overtaken by the worst political news the Reagan administration had experienced in its six years in office: On that election day Republicans lost control of the U.S. Senate. It was a personal blow to Reagan, who had campaigned actively for Republican candidates that fall, and marked an ebbing of power that had begun in 1980 when Republicans, riding Reagan's popularity, won back control of the Senate for the first time in nearly thirty years. Newspapers and network television broadcasts were filled with commentary about the political implications.

Attracting scant attention that same day was a brief wire service report from Beirut. An obscure Lebanese magazine named *Al-Shiraa,* in an edition published the day that hostage Jacobsen's release was announced in Washington, reported that the United States had secretly shipped arms to its enemy Iran.

These allegations were briefly recounted in the wire service report from Beirut, along with even more unbelievable details of the supposed secret shipments: that Bud McFarlane, who had left the White House in December 1985 as the president's national security adviser, had made a secret mission to Teheran the previous spring to meet representatives of Ayatollah Khomeini. Furthermore, the article said, McFarlane had come bearing gifts. Among them were a chocolate cake with a confectionery key—a symbol of a new relationship—and a Bible personally signed by Ronald Reagan.

At first the White House offered no response. The report was too ludicrous for discussion. By Thursday, however, questions about possible arms sales to Iran had intensified to a point where Reagan was forced to respond publicly and authoritatively. These press reports about sale of arms to Iran had "no foundation," Reagan said.

Key members of Congress, already incensed by the Hasenfus disclosures, were not satisfied. They demanded answers. If the charges were true, Reagan had violated both his pledge never to make concessions to terrorists and the law by selling arms to Iran.

One week after his first denial the president again attempted to defuse the controversy. In a televised speech to the nation, Reagan acknowledged that secret diplomatic contacts had been taking place between the United States and Iran for eighteen months. The purpose for what he called the Iran initiative was fourfold. First was to deal with "moderate elements" within Iran and forge a new relationship with them. The second purpose was to end the Iran-Iraq War honorably, the third, to end state-sponsored Iranian terrorism. Mentioned last, and almost in passing, was another motivation: Through this new relationship and the good offices of Iran, release of Americans held hostage in Lebanon could be won.

To further these objectives, he told the American people that he had authorized "the transfer of small amounts of defensive weapons and spare parts" to Iran. The actual amount of arms shipped was insignificant. They were, he said, "modest deliveries" that "taken together could easily fit into a single cargo plane." He maintained that all these activities had been conducted in full compliance with the law, and he attacked "the wildly speculative false stories about arms for hostages and alleged ransom payments."

Reagan gave unequivocal assurances: "We did not—repeat—did not trade weapons or anything else for hostages nor will we."

Every one of these assertions was false.

Six days later, on November 19, after more reports of secret administration Iranian arms dealing had surfaced, Reagan denied at a news conference that there had been any involvement by a third country in the arms sales. "We, as I say, have had nothing to do with other countries or their shipment of arms or doing what they're doing," he said. This, too, was false.

By then a crisis atmosphere had settled over the administration. Top officials conferred at tense private meetings. Attorney General Meese, recalling those days in mid to late November, said the president's top advisers feared that further disclosures could lead Reagan's political enemies to begin impeachment proceedings.

North, whose destruction of contra arms supply evidence had begun weeks earlier, now dealt with the more inflammatory Iranian arms secrets. Even more documents were destroyed. Computer files were purged. He prepared false chronologies of the background of the Iran "initiative." These, for use by high officials to brief congressional intelligence oversight committees, contained supposedly accurate accounts of events and decisions and offered background and rationale for what had taken place.

They also contained a long-standing and agreed-upon cover story—and a major omission. The cover story had been hatched to deal with arms shipments that took place *before* Reagan signed any presidential finding making them legal.

Months before, Casey, North, Poindexter, and other officials had agreed that if the initial Israeli arms shipments to Iran were disclosed, they would deny advance knowledge of them. If pressed, they would say that the Israelis just "went ahead on their own." If pressed further, they all would say that they had told the Israelis they disagreed with their action as soon as they learned of it. All this was an entirely false account.

A different cover story was prepared to deal with the November Hawk missile shipments made by Secord and the Enterprise. U.S. officials would claim that they believed the shipment to Iran had carried "oil drilling equipment" instead of arms. This, too, was false.

Omitted from North's chronologies was any reference to the diversion of Iranian arms sales proceeds for use by the contras.

With these chronologies as their guide, the CIA's Casey and National Security Adviser Poindexter prepared to testify secretly before the House and Senate Intelligence committees on November 21. The two officials met the day before to coordinate their testimony along with Meese, North, and others. A draft of Casey's proposed testimony that they discussed included the "oil drilling equipment" fiction. North suggested the language be changed to say that "no one in the United States government" knew at the time that the November Hawk shipment contained arms. His suggestion was accepted.

Poindexter testified first the next day. He stuck to the story. The United States had learned of the early Israeli shipments only after the fact, and he knew nothing at the time about the November Hawk deliveries. He would check further into the facts about possible U.S. involvement and report back, he promised.

Casey, too, stuck to the prearranged script. He testified that the crew of the plane that flew the mission to Iran in November had been told the cargo consisted of spare parts for oil drilling fields in Teheran. Three weeks later, while preparing to testify again before the Senate Intelligence Committee, Casey suffered a brain seizure. He was taken to the hospital, operated upon for removal of a tumor, and died five months later, taking with him secrets that would likely never be revealed.

That same Friday morning Attorney General Meese, even more concerned about the political damage Reagan was sustaining and worried about the possibility of impeachment, convened his top advisers. Meese told them he wanted to reconcile the conflicting versions of administration officials so that the administration would be "speaking with one voice." He then called Poindexter on a secure telephone line and requested that he schedule a White House meeting later that morning with Reagan, himself, Poindexter, and the president's chief of staff, Donald T. Regan.

The meeting took place at 11:30 A.M. Meese said he told Reagan they needed to have a more coherent account of the Iran arms dealings; the operation had been so compartmentalized that they lacked a clear overall picture. Acting, he said later, in his capacity as "legal adviser to the president," he requested that he be given authority to gather facts over the weekend and report back to present his overview the next Monday. Then the president would be able to present the story to the public. The president agreed.

A singular lack of curiosity about what had actually transpired characterizes the separate accounts officials later gave publicly of this critical meeting. According to their individual testimony, no questions were asked. No one made any attempt to find out what others present might have known about events that had occurred secretly during the past six years of their administration and that were creating such explosive problems for them and the president.

Poindexter, who had already given his false testimony to the intelligence committees earlier that morning, left the Oval Office meeting, returned to his office, opened his safe, and destroyed documents secured inside. Among them was the arms-for-hostages intelligence finding Reagan had retroactively signed authorizing the November shipments and the earlier Israeli ones. He tore up the finding and the notes he might have used to brief the president about those missions. Then he disposed of the paper in his National Security Council office "burn bag."

Others involved were also meeting privately. Among them were Bud McFarlane and Oliver North. Early that afternoon, after they discussed the arms sale deals for an hour and a half at a private home in the Washington suburbs, McFarlane offered to drive North back downtown to his office. He remembered North's telling him he was going to have a "shredding party that weekend."

In the space of two hours North met twice with Poindexter. He brought with him his spiral notebooks in which he had recorded in minute detail daily events during the complex secret dealing. Inside those notebooks was contemporary written evidence that directly contradicted Poindexter's congressional testimony hours earlier that no one in the government knew about the November Hawk missile shipments. North's notebook entry written at the time read: "R. R. [Ronald Reagan] directed operation to proceed. If Israelis want to provide different model, then we will replenish."

After informing Poindexter that he intended to destroy his notebooks (but he did not), North returned to his own office. With the help of his secretary and another aide, he withdrew classified National Security Council documents from his safe and began to destroy or alter them.

While that was taking place, General Secord and his secretary were busy destroying Enterprise records, including steno books, telephone logs, and telexes, at his office in nearby McLean, Virginia. Though more and more of the Iran-contra story was surfacing hour by hour, the public and private operators of the Reagan administration were still attempting to keep the secrets secret.

CHAPTER 23

ON THE HILL

In 1987, the year *Rolling Stone* magazine called a "year without heroes," the U.S. Congress was faced with a challenge that demanded, if not heroes, the best the country had to offer. With a self-imposed and constricting time limit of only a few months, the Republicans and Democrats of the Iran-contra investigating congressional committees were asked to provide definitive answers to some of the most complicated political questions any of them had faced. In addition, they were expected to resolve one of the nation's most confusing scandals. Through televised hearings witnessed daily by some fifty million people, they had a chance to do something rare in modern government: to educate the public about the political process, to distinguish between political right and wrong, and to draw lessons that would be learned far beyond the Washington beltway.

When it was over, despite great efforts to determine the truth, it was at best an open question whether their labor had been appreciated or understood by the American public. It was an even more dubious proposition that their attempt to set—or reestablish—highest standards of governmental and political behavior had a lasting impact on public attitudes. It might have had just the opposite.

When I talked to the men of the Iran-contra committees a year after their inquiry had passed into history, it seemed possible that the worst had happened: that they had little to no impact at all, except perhaps a negative one; that their laborious examination into a disturbing affair, a sign of something seriously amiss within the body politic, had produced a bad and unsuccessful investigation, one that would be reduced to a footnote in the public's mind. What would people remember? A televised summer soap opera at best—Oliver North and Fawn Hall, a glimpse into the secret world of covert operators with the mystery and intrigue surrounding Swiss bank accounts, and well-intended, if misguided, attempts to free American hostages. But did people understand that subversion of the Constitution lay at the heart of the affair? Did they recognize the tragedy of what had happened to the government? Did they realize what it meant to have indispensable communication and trust among the branches of government break down? Did they understand that this was a very real casualty of the affair, one that would certainly have consequences for the country for a long time to come?

Among those who sat in judgment on their system were people destined to be America's political leaders. Some of them rose superbly to the challenge; others did not. Like the system they all represented, and were representative of, they produced a spectacle deserving of praise and condemnation. Herewith, to begin at the beginning, are some of those principals as they began their process.

In the Cabinet Room, shortly before a Reagan news conference that Tuesday morning, November 25, 1986, congressional leaders sat around the table awaiting the president's arrival. They didn't know why they had been summoned to the White House but suspected it might have something to do with the Iran arms sale stories.

As usual, Reagan didn't greet them personally but went directly to his chair. After a brief welcome he told them he had just learned some disturbing information from the attorney general. He turned to Meese, who gave the congressional leaders startling news: Meese's inquiry into the arms sale situation had discovered that proceeds from the secret sale of U.S. arms to Iran had been diverted to assist the U.S.-backed contras fighting in Nicaragua. Meese emphasized there were many things he didn't know; it was an ongoing investigation.

Members were taken aback, and their expressions reflected surprise and shock. Few questions were asked. It was obviously a matter of major importance, one with potentially far-reaching implications for Reagan and the country.

Sitting near the president was Lee Hamilton of Indiana. He was quiet and studious by nature. His spectacles, crew cut, and conservatively tailored dark blue suit gave him the appearance of a high school civics teacher in the fifties. At the meeting he remembered thinking:* Obviously, this is a very, very serious revelation. Hamilton thought the policy decision to sell arms to Iran was incomprehensible. But now the diversion! This was infinitely more tangled and complex, far beyond his imaginings. He spoke up. Would there be criminal indictments as a result of the diversion? he asked Meese. The attorney general didn't know. That was being looked into.

Since coming to Congress twenty-one years before, Lee Hamilton had served with five presidents and found Reagan the most inarticulate by far, a man who seemed unable to formulate any problem precisely. As Hamilton observed him, Reagan had little information about decisions that he made and delegated his authority to an extraordinary degree. Basically Reagan had no interest in the ordinary problems of government. Hamilton got the impression that Reagan, unlike the genial, avuncular Reagan of television appearances, didn't like most of the congressional people with whom he dealt. That was most unlike Lyndon Johnson, who genuinely liked people and reacted with them. Even Carter and Nixon forced themselves to engage in displays of camaraderie, although obviously that wasn't their natural instinct. Reagan didn't even make that effort.

Hamilton noticed that if you sat around the table and talked about a problem with Reagan, the president asked few questions and showed little interest in what was being discussed. To the extent that Reagan *did* display interest in a subject, it was in how to communicate about it. He remembered a White House meeting with Reagan on the subject of the MX missile that summed up for him Ronald Reagan's operational style. That time, too, the room was filled with congressional leaders and the secretaries of state and defense and other high officials. After reading words of greeting from three-by-five cards, Reagan turned the meeting over to his national security adviser, Bud McFarlane. "Reagan's only contribution throughout the entire hour and a half was to interrupt somewhere at midpoint to tell us he'd watched a movie the night before," Hamilton remem-

*All comments of principals involved in this chapter are from tape-recorded conversations for this book.

bered, "and he gave us the plot from *WarGames,* the movie. That was his only contribution."*

But there was no question that Reagan had a few passionate beliefs. Anticommunism infused his administration. Hamilton observed that Reagan spoke about the contras with an intensity absent from his discussion on arms control or anything else. To Hamilton, Reagan had an unsubtle, incurious mind; he clearly didn't worry much about ends and means. So long as he believed the goal a worthy one, he didn't seem troubled by the way it was achieved.

All this combined to create the most frustrating political phenomenon Hamilton had confronted. It was a case, he thought, of trying to deal with the popularity of a man who knew so little and was so little interested in knowing.

Also reflecting on the Reagan phenomenon, and equally disturbed by this latest disclosure, was another serious congressman. Richard Cheney of Wyoming served with Hamilton on the House Intelligence Committee as the ranking Republican and occupied the number two leadership position in the by then virtually permanent Republican minority in the House of Representatives.

Ten years before, at the age of only thirty-six, Dick Cheney had completed an unusually varied Washington governmental experience. He had come to Washington while still a graduate student at the University of Wisconsin, worked on Capitol Hill as an aide to a Republican congressman from that state, served in the federal bureaucracy at the Office of Economic Opportunity, and twice held posts in Nixon's White House before becoming chief of staff for President Gerald R. Ford.

Like many survivors of the Nixon White House, Cheney was keenly aware of the potential for abusing power, personal as well as political power. After Ford's defeat in 1976 he left Washington feeling considerably more conservative and less optimistic about the ability to manage the government than when he arrived. "Sometimes I think the best solution for government is to do nothing," he said then. "Maybe you have to measure success in terms of what didn't

*Countless officials who met privately with Reagan during his presidency told similar anecdotes about him.

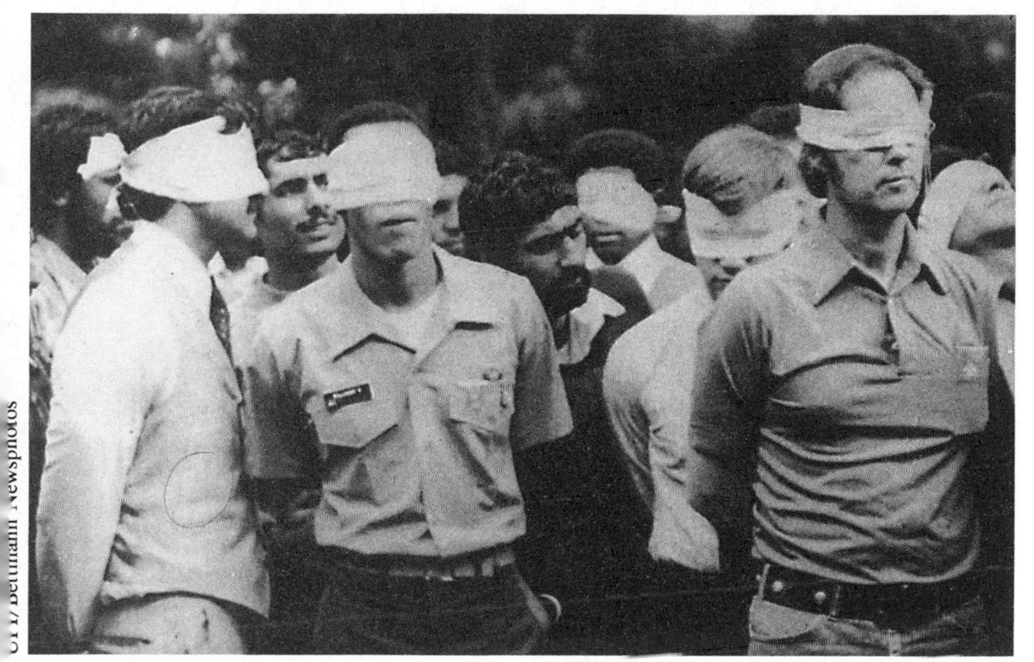

UPI/Bettmann Newsphotos

Blindfolded American hostages are led outside the U.S. Embassy compound in Teheran by Iranian captors on November 4, 1979, beginning the hostage ordeal that shapes the 1980 election.

An abandoned U.S. helicopter stands behind wreckage of another U.S. chopper in the Iranian desert after a hostage rescue attempt fails disastrously in April 1980.

James K. W. Atherton/The *Washington Post*

Jimmy Carter, in the closing moments of his presidency, stares grimly ahead while Ronald Reagan displays the look of the winner just before taking his presidential oath on January 20, 1981. Nancy Reagan, seated behind the new president, savors the moment along with Barbara Bush, wife of the new vice president.

Reagan becomes president while Vice President Bush watches in the background.

AP/Wide World Photos

Upper left: Reagan's inaugural coincides with the release of the hostages, leading to rare newspaper "extra" editions. *Above:* Crowds cheer the returning hostages as buses carry them down Pennsylvania Avenue to a White House reception six days after Reagan's inauguration.

To the blare of trumpets and amid a blizzard of flags, Reagan strides out of the White House to greet the returned hostages.

AP/Wide World Photos

Reagan grimaces after being shot in an assassination attempt on March 30, 1981, outside the Washington Hilton Hotel.

Nancy and Ronald Reagan's smiling demeanors reassure the nation during his recovery but obscure the seriousness of his wound.

Ronald Reagan Library

AP/Wide World Photos

Supply-side economics gets a preview as David Stockman briefs Reagan and displays a graph giving optimistic forecasts. Among those watching is Treasury Secretary Donald Regan, gesturing.

The boom of the eighties generates heavy trading like this in a New York securities firm.

Dennis Brack/*Time* Magazine

American soldiers move across the desert sands after being dispatched to Saudi Arabia to check Iraq after the invasion of Kuwait triggers the first crisis of the post-Cold War era in the summer of 1990.

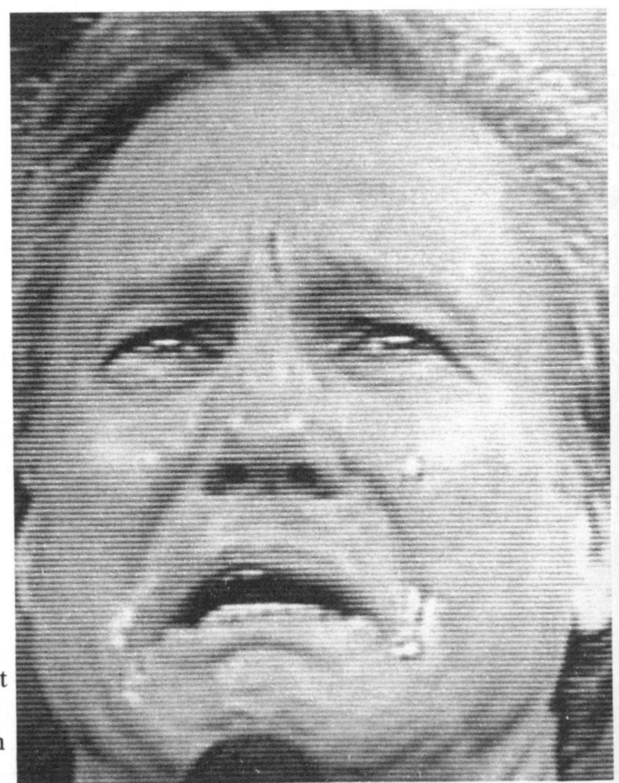

Televangelist Jimmy Swaggart sobs as he confesses over television to having been with a prostitute.

Televangelist Jim Bakker makes a "prayer line" fund appeal while his wife, Tammy Faye, wipes away her tears.

Jessica Hahn, the church volunteer whose sexual assault by Jim Bakker leads to his downfall, meets reporters after testifying before a federal grand jury on September 21, 1987.

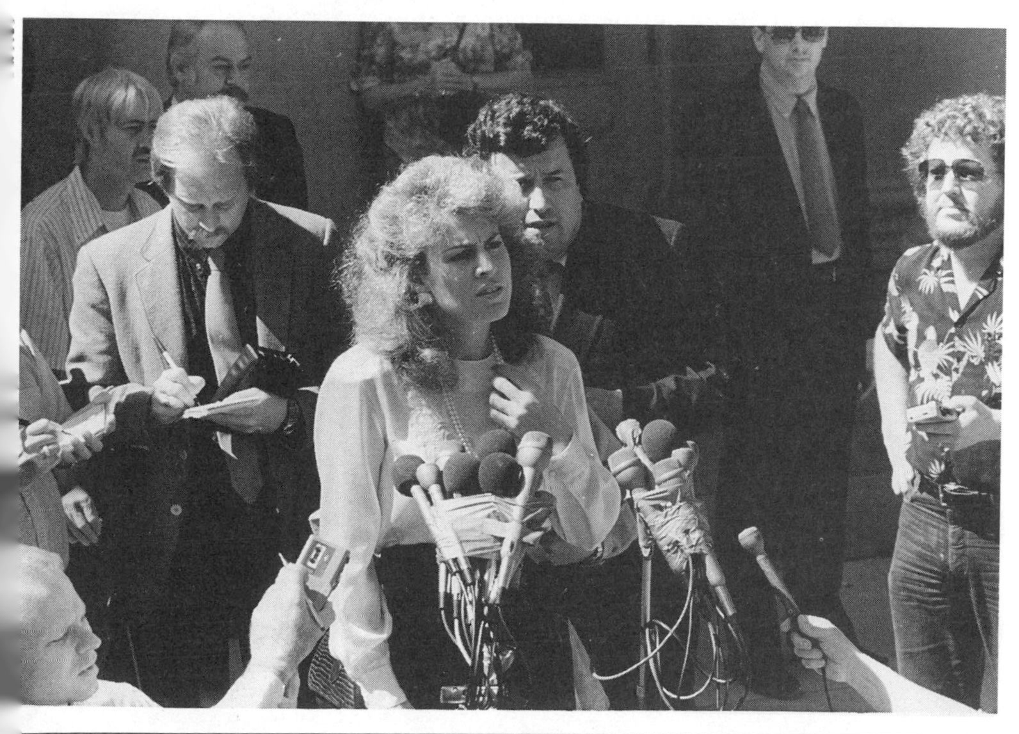

James K. W. Atherton/The *Washington Post*

AP/Wide World Photos

Left: Oliver North takes the oath before pleading the Fifth Amendment in front of a congressional panel investigating the Iran-contra affair. *Right:* Admiral John Poindexter puffs on his pipe during his appearance before Iran-contra congressional investigators.

Counsel Arthur Liman (left, first row facing camera) questions North, seated before him on July 10, 1987, during the Iran-contra hearings. Next to Liman is Senator George Mitchell, and on the extreme right is counsel John W. Nields, Jr. In the row behind them are Senators Warren Rudman (extreme left) and Daniel Inouye (beneath flag) and Representative Lee Hamilton (taking off glasses).

Banner headlines tell the story of the crash.

Left: A dejected stockbroker reflects the shock of the crash on October 19, 1987. *Right:* Ivan Boesky, looking like Rip Van Winkle, returns to Connecticut on furlough from prison in November 1989.

Paul Adao of The *New York Post*

Reuters/Bettmann Newsphotos

Michael Milken and his wife are surrounded by reporters as he prepares to enter court in New York and plead guilty on April 24, 1990.

Left: Manuel Noriega poses for a prison mug shot in Miami after surrendering to U.S. authorities in Panama on January 3, 1990. *Right:* Willie Horton, convicted murderer and rapist, becomes a symbol of the "prison furlough" issue used by George Bush in the 1988 presidential campaign.

AP/Wide World Photos

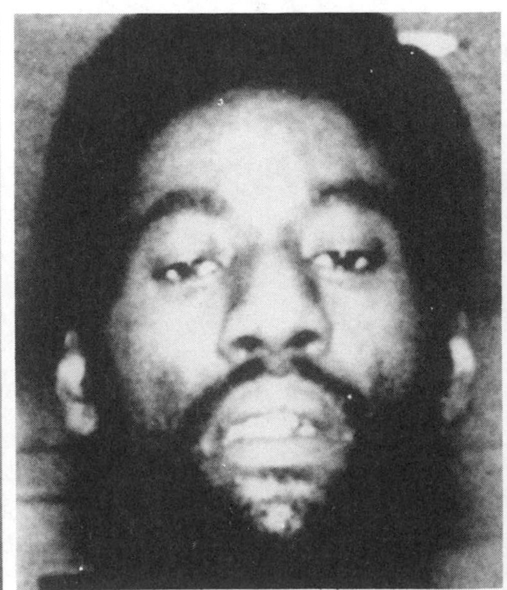

James K. W. Atherton/The *Washington Post*

Bush takes his presidential oath on January 20, 1989. Behind him is the new vice president, Dan Quayle.

Ronald Reagan Library

Mikhail Gorbachev views the Statute of Liberty with outgoing and incoming U.S. Presidents Reagan and Bush on December 7, 1988.

Prodemocracy Chinese students demonstrate beneath their Goddess of Democracy emblem in Tiananmen Square on May 30, 1989.

East German police watch as a youth carrying flowers is hoisted atop the Berlin Wall.

East Germans rush through the newly opened wall into West Berlin.

The nineties begin with a New Year's Day fireworks celebration of freedom before the Brandenburg Gate in West Berlin.

James K. W. Atherton/The *Washington Post*

Czechoslovakia's new president, Vaclav Havel, flashes the V for Victory sign before addressing a joint meeting of Congress. Applauding are Vice President Quayle and Speaker Tom Foley.

Donald Trump, deal-maker of the 1980s, poses to promote one of his properties, the Trump Parc.

January 20, 1989: With a final salute, and final presidential photo opportunity, Ronald Reagan prepares to board his helicopter on the Capitol grounds after the Bush inaugural ceremonies.

happen." Cheney was not unhappy to leave and expected not to come back. "I have a strong sense of this town," he said at the time. "This city is full of people who sit around waiting to be called to serve again. They're like ghosts waiting for life to be infused. You've got to remember you don't get all these phone calls, all these invitations to parties, and all that attention from the press because of yourself personally. It goes with the turf, and it ends when you leave. To some extent the value of the experience in Washington depends on being able to know when it's over."*

But like many others who thought they had left forever, he found the lure of Washington was strong. Cheney returned as a member of Congress from Wyoming and quickly rose among Republican ranks.

Cheney was a believer in a strong presidency. He believed Congress had exceeded its authority in the seventies in limiting presidential power in foreign policy. To him, and many like him, Reagan represented an opportunity to reclaim some of that authority for the presidency. Until the Iran arms sale crisis erupted, Cheney believed Reagan had been successful in restoring and strengthening presidential powers. Cheney also felt strongly about the need for the United States to have covert action capability and was a staunch defender of Reagan's use of covert operations to assist anti-Communist insurgents around the globe.

With this kind of background, Cheney was more than inclined to give Reagan his strong support as problems arose. When the Hasenfus plane episode stirred controversy, Cheney backed the White House. He accepted official assurances given him during a private briefing then that "this was not an official U.S. operation."

Cheney had scheduled an elk hunting trip to Wyoming after the fall elections with his friend and fellow Wyoming Republican Senator Alan Simpson. He had barely left Washington when Iran arms sales disclosures blew up, forcing him to return and attend the first White House briefing given to only four congressional leaders, Speaker Jim Wright of Texas and Senator Robert Byrd of West Virginia representing the Democrats, Senator Robert Dole of Kansas

*This is from a conversation I had with Cheney in his last days as Ford's White House chief of staff, later published in my book *In the Absence of Power: Governing America* (New York: Viking, 1980).

and Cheney for the Republicans. (The Republican House leader, Robert Michel of Illinois, was unable to attend.)

Present in the White House Situation Room, the inner sanctum of critical presidential decision making, were Reagan, CIA Director Casey, Attorney General Meese, Secretary of State Shultz, Defense Secretary Weinberger, and National Security Adviser Poindexter.* It was, as Cheney put it, "the national security establishment, and they laid on us the basic story."

The story they presented, in a united front from the president down, was in the context of a strategic initiative toward Iran and, to some extent, the hope that with a new U.S.-Iranian diplomatic relationship American hostages would be freed. Cheney's initial reaction was to be supportive. While he had doubts about the wisdom of the policy of selling arms to Iran, he didn't view it as a scandal. It wasn't another Watergate. There was no hint of corruption connected with it.

Like his Democratic colleague Lee Hamilton, Cheney found Reagan a study in contradictions and different from other presidents with whom he had worked. Personally he thought Reagan one of the most charming people he'd met. Ronald Reagan, in Cheney's opinion, was a thoroughly decent man. Honest and honorable, he held a few strongly felt convictions. As a president Reagan had a capacity unexcelled in modern times to use the symbolic power of the presidency to lead the nation. Cheney was far from alone in believing that Reagan's speech delivered on the fortieth anniversary of D Day from the bluffs of Normandy demonstrated the rarest kind of ability to evoke the spirit of America.† Reagan could harness it, move the country with it, and, most important, build support for his policies. Those were his pluses, and they were considerable.

His negatives were also considerable. Without either being aware of the other's views, both the conservative Republican Cheney and the more liberal Democrat Hamilton saw Reagan's weaknesses in strikingly similar light.

*Cheney, like many others who participated in important Reagan administration meetings, could not remember whether Vice President Bush attended or not.

†It was written by White House speech writer Peggy Noonan.

To Cheney, Reagan was both uninterested and too tolerant of incompetent subordinates, a failing that Cheney recognized the president shared with Gerald Ford. Cheney also thought Reagan failed to set standards and hold people accountable for their performance. Reagan was not, as Cheney said, "intellectually curious." Then, carefully ticking off other aspects of what he called Reagan's "down side," he listed them as: "Mostly listens instead of asking questions. Passive, except for some things he cares deeply about. When he decides he's going to work for tax reform, he can aggressively pursue tax reform. When it's time to support the contras, you can get him worked up on that kind of issue. But he's not the kind of guy, in my opinion, who reads the morning newspapers and says, 'Goddammit, what are those guys over at Transportation doing?' Ford used to read the *Grand Rapids Press,* or Nixon, you know, those newspapers would come by every morning and he'd circle articles in red ink that dealt with federal agencies fouling up and throw it in the out box and it'd land on my desk and I'd have to go find out what the hell was going on. None of that with Ronald Reagan. I think he deeply believes everything he says. That doesn't mean it's always right or that it's all that carefully thought out. He gets himself psyched into defending what it is he wants to defend, and he can rationalize why a tax increase is not a tax increase."

All this had been surmountable throughout Reagan's first six years as president. Now, as he listened to his latest crisis, Cheney wondered if Reagan's good luck would hold. "It really started to become unraveled," Cheney said. "Clearly what we'd been told was not yet the complete story. It was clear that it kept getting more and more complicated and that there were more and more things we didn't know."

Uh-oh, Daniel Ken Inouye thought, here we go again.

Like most of Washington and much of the country, Inouye had been watching Reagan deliver a prepared statement before the assembled press corps in a live telecast from the White House that Tuesday. The president was saying he had learned only yesterday the results of a fact-finding inquiry that he had directed Attorney General Meese to conduct over the weekend into "the implementation of my policy toward Iran." He had not been "fully informed" about the nature of one of the activities undertaken. It raised "serious questions of propriety."

Facing the TV cameras, Reagan said he had just met with his national security advisers and briefed congressional leaders about the action he was taking to deal with it. Further investigation and review would be undertaken by the Justice Department. He was appointing a special review board to examine the role and procedures of his National Security Council staff in the conduct of foreign and national security policy. His national security adviser, John Poindexter, had asked to be relieved of his presidential assignment, and Lieutenant Colonel Oliver North had been relieved of his duties on the NSC staff. After stating that information brought to his attention only yesterday had convinced him that "in one aspect" implementation of his policy toward Iran had been "seriously flawed," Reagan turned the press briefing over to Meese.

From private briefings that he had received the day before about the Iranian arms sales, Inouye, the senior senator from Hawaii, knew that the sales had violated congressional mandate, if not actual law. There was sure to be a congressional investigation. Then he heard Meese make his stunning announcement about the diversion of arms sale funds to aid the contras. The Justice Department was beginning an investigation to determine if there had been criminal involvement in this diversion of funds generated by the sale of U.S. property, Meese said.

"When he made that statement, everything blew up," Inouye recalled. "Combined with what I had heard the day before, I reached the conclusion that uh-oh, here we go again. I was absolutely certain at that point that a special committee would be formed. It was obvious that this was going to be a big thing."

Thirteen years before, Inouye had attracted national attention for the firm but fair manner in which he asked questions during the televised Senate Watergate Committee hearings that laid the groundwork for impeachment proceedings against Richard Nixon. The experience deeply affected him.

Though he was a strong Democrat, Daniel Inouye was first and foremost a patriot. Like many Americans of Japanese descent, he found World War II to have been a torturous experience. After Pearl Harbor, 110,000 Japanese-Americans, a majority of them American citizens, were placed behind barbed wire in U.S. detention camps. Some 30,000 members of those same families volunteered for active military duty. Among them from the Hawaiian contingent was eighteen-year-old Dan Inouye, whose grandfather had migrated to Hawaii seeking opportunity to pay off a family debt of honor.

Inouye became a member of a famous Nisei combat outfit. He was barely twenty when he won a battlefield commission in Italy. Nine days before the end of that campaign, he led an infantry assault against a German position. Forty yards from German bunkers, he hurled a grenade into a machine-gun nest. Although hit in the stomach by a bullet, he continued leading the charge, firing his automatic weapon and lobbing two more grenades into another machine-gun emplacement. From ten yards away a German rifle grenade all but tore off his right arm. Picking up his own grenade with his left hand, Inouye killed the German who had severely wounded him. He was hit with another bullet in his right leg while directing the final assault that took the ridge. For this, Captain Inouye was awarded the Distinguished Service Cross to go with an earlier Bronze Star for heroism.

At war's end, on the way home to Hawaii, his empty right sleeve pinned to his beribboned officer's uniform, he stopped to get a haircut in a San Francisco barbershop. "We don't serve Japs here," the barber told him. It was a theme that haunted his life.

Loss of his arm ended his dream of becoming a doctor. Instead, he studied law, became a public prosecutor, and entered politics. After statehood in 1959 he was elected Hawaii's first U.S. congressman and three years later was elected to the U.S. Senate.

Inouye had strong feelings about the way the Watergate hearings had been conducted and was concerned that the all-consuming television atmosphere would be even greater this time. Privately he sought out both leaders of the Senate, the Republican majority leader, Robert Dole of Kansas, and the Democratic minority leader, Robert Byrd of West Virginia. "I was concerned that if this became a circus, or if it resulted in a partisan battle," Inouye said, "the consequences may be very bad."

The phone call from Washington came while Arthur Liman was preparing to try a case involving impressionist paintings for Christie's in New York. In his painstaking style, Liman had been talking to experts about Monet and Manet and learning how to pronounce van Gogh properly for an expert in Dutch art when his secretary said that Senator George Mitchell was calling from Washington. Liman didn't know Mitchell personally and only barely knew his name. He was a not a Washington type; he had never practiced in the capital, had never worked with the Congress, and had only visited there on rare occasions.

Mitchell was direct and brief. Would Liman come down to Washington and talk with a select group of officials about the possibility of directing the U.S. Senate's investigation into the unfolding Iran-contra affair? Liman said he didn't think he was the right person for that task, but he would be happy to discuss it.

For Liman, one of America's leading criminal lawyers and an expert on securities fraud cases, this was the second such call from Washington in recent weeks. He had first been approached about representing the downed American pilot Eugene Hasenfus when the Sandinista regime announced that Hasenfus would be tried in Nicaragua. Liman was not interested in representing an American mercenary. The Senate investigation into Iran-contra was another matter.

Liman had followed the arms sale news with special interest. Years before, as chief counsel of the committee investigating the New York penal uprising at Attica, when guards were held as hostages, he remembered Governor Nelson A. Rockefeller's lecturing him strongly about the necessity never to negotiate over hostages.

Here we go again, Liman remembered thinking when he first heard the news that the administration appeared to have sold arms to Iran in exchange for American hostages. It was obvious to him, as he watched Meese's television announcement about the diversion of Iranian arms proceeds, that the government had been involved in a sordid operation. He wondered whether it was possible, as Meese had suggested, that a lieutenant colonel in the Marines could have done all this without the president's knowledge.

He was still mulling over that question, and many others involving the secret arms-for-hostage deals, as he traveled to Washington to meet with a group of senators in George Mitchell's office.

After intently watching Meese's televised news conference disclosing the diversion, Senator Warren Rudman immediately tried to call Senator Paul Laxalt. Rudman liked Laxalt enormously, and he knew that Laxalt was closer personally to Ronald Reagan than any Republican in the Congress. Several hours later he reached Laxalt in Bermuda, where the senator was playing tennis. "Paul," he said, "I used to be attorney general in New Hampshire, and I've got an old prosecutor's instincts. I think I can tell when something is really bad. And, Paul, this is not only bad. This is going to be a disaster. I don't like what I'm hearing. I don't like what's going on. I don't think there's much political sense being used here. I don't think there's any damage control. The whole thing ought to be laid out. As a matter of fact, it's a lot like Watergate, Paul."

"Is it really that bad?" he remembered Laxalt saying.

"Worse," Rudman replied.

Aggressive by nature, a Reagan loyalist elected to the Senate in the Reagan sweep of 1980, Rudman urged Laxalt, as someone Reagan listened to and trusted, to use his influence to get the word to the right people that this was a serious matter. It was a small fire now. Unless Reagan and his White House team acted immediately, it was going to be a conflagration.

Weeks later, near midnight, Rudman received a call from Senate Republican leader Bob Dole during a snowy evening in New Hampshire. Dole said he was appointing Rudman to the Iran-Contra Committee. A few minutes later Dole called back to say he was naming Rudman ranking Republican member. The news left Rudman sleepless and in turmoil. He knew he would face a terrible conflict, a conflict between what a U.S. senator was elected to do and his loyalty to the president and his party. His first meeting with Inouye, whom the Democrats had picked to head the select committee investigating the Iran-contra affair, was, he realized, potentially part of that conflict.

Inouye told Rudman he was determined that unlike Watergate, there would not be majority and minority staffs with separate payrolls and differing backgrounds pursuing different agendas, interviewing different witnesses, holding different caucuses, and sometimes not sharing all their information. He wanted one highly professional unified staff that would work together and strive to be bipartisan in nature. Inouye also told Rudman he also wanted to avoid another problem that had rankled with him since his Watergate committee service. As a freshman senator then, by seniority pecking order Inouye had been assigned last to ask questions of witnesses. This time he wanted to ensure that every member, whether senior or freshman, would have equal opportunity for questioning—and not just with lesser witnesses, as in Watergate. He wanted them all to take turns at questioning principal figures.

Like Inouye, Rudman had served with honor as a U.S. Army combat infantry officer, winning a bronze star for valor in Korea and emerging as a captain. Toward the end of their long private session Rudman was stunned to hear Inouye say "one last thing." Impassively Inouye said: "You're not going to be the ranking minority member." That's really not your choice, Rudman thought, waiting for Inouye to go on. "You're going to be the vice-chairman," Inouye continued, "and I'm going to tell all the Democrats on the committee that as far as I'm concerned, when I'm not there, you will preside."

It was an extraordinary gesture. Rudman was moved. He threw himself into the process of forming a bipartisan unified staff.

George Mitchell is a quiet-spoken, deliberate sort of man who comes by his judicious air naturally. Most of his adult life was spent in the legal process in Maine, although like Dick Cheney, he had a solid background in Washington long before being elected to the U.S. Senate in 1980. His first job after law school was as a Justice Department trial attorney during the Kennedy years; then, for three more years, he was executive assistant to Maine's Senator Edmund Muskie, a leading Democrat nationally and later secretary of state. In 1965 Mitchell returned to Maine, where he served as a local prosecutor, defense attorney, federal prosecutor, and finally federal judge. At Inouye's request, Mitchell and another former federal judge, Alabama Senator Howell Heflin, headed a group to screen candidates for chief committee counsel and staff director of the new Senate investigating committee.

With his understated personal demeanor and cautious political approach, George John Mitchell of Maine appeared to be another in a line of Yankee legislators who became public servants. His actual background was more complicated.

It was not until his father died in 1972 that Mitchell learned his father's real name was Joseph Kilroy. It was then, too, that he learned for the first time many of the circumstances of his father's early life. His father, the son of Irish immigrants who never knew his own parents, had been adopted by a childless elderly couple by the name of Mitchell in Bangor, Maine. They in turn had emigrated to the United States from Lebanon. At an advanced age they decided to adopt a child and picked one of many lined up at an altar rail after Sunday mass to which orphans were brought by nuns from a Boston foundling home. The Mitchells changed the name of the orphan they adopted—though never legally—and then moved to Waterville, Maine, where a large community of Lebanese immigrants worked in the textile mills. Mitchell's father, who had a limited formal education, grew up speaking Arabic fluently. He met and married another Lebanese immigrant who had come to the United States in the last year of World War I at the age of eighteen unable to speak a word of English. Not untypically in such a family background, Mitchell's parents placed great store on education and perseverance—traits that Mitchell had demonstrated repeatedly throughout his public career.

With typical attention to detail, Mitchell began the task of finding the best person to head the committee's investigation. After personally contacting scores of individuals, Mitchell was ready to interview his first prospective candidate, someone whose name had been recommended by several people, the New York lawyer Arthur Liman.

Mitchell had never heard of Liman, but Rudman knew about him. He had read Liman's law review pieces, had heard him speak once, and admired him as being among that select class of American attorneys that could accurately be described as superlawyers.

Rudman, Mitchell, Heflin, and the few other senators present were impressed with the forthright way in which Liman spoke. He told them immediately that he thought their investigation faced major problems. First, he said, Reagan enjoyed great popularity. Second, even in liberal New York City people were not preoccupied by the Iran-contra affair. Furthermore, this appeared to be the kind of case in which it would be difficult to determine the truth. Liman's experience had taught him, he said, that when you are dealing with evidence controlled by subordinates of a chief executive, you never had any assurance you will get the truth. Everyone tends to be protective of superiors. Besides, in this case they faced an additional burden of dealing with Swiss bank accounts, and he told them of his experience in trying to penetrate Swiss secrecy. All in all, it was going to be a most difficult investigation, and they were likely to be caught in the middle. They would be accused both of failing to disclose the full story and of persecuting the president for political purposes. Liman said he didn't envy them.

As for himself, two things should make them hesitate even considering him. He had no prior Washington experience, and there was much to be said for having a lawyer well versed in the ways of the capital. His greater concern, he went on, was the fact that he was Jewish. Would that influence the way he conducted the investigation? they asked him. No, he said, but appearances are important. "I think you will never satisfy people that a Jewish chief counsel could do the job objectively," he said.

This remark touched off a strong reaction. From the way the senators spoke, Liman felt they thought him almost un-American. "Well," Rudman said, "I'm Jewish!" Liman looked surprised. He had not known.

Liman explained everyone knew Israel was involved in the arms sales, and questions were being raised in the press, planted and encouraged by the Reagan administration, about whether the diversion had been Israel's idea. If the investigation failed to document Israel's role clearly, would it be said that Liman had tried to whitewash Israel because he was a Jew? If he came down hard on Israel, would he be accused of trying to prove that he was uninhibited by being Jewish? Either way, it was a problem. The fact that he was Jewish *was* a factor. The senators would not hear of it: If support for Israel was a disqualification, they told him, then they ought to disband the committee. The session ended with Liman being impressed with the senators and the senators impressed with him.

Much later Mitchell realized that he had never considered one aspect that might influence public judgment on the investigation: How would Arthur Liman come across on television? No one raised that question or thought to weigh the impact of personality on the televised inquiry they would conduct.

In New York Liman quietly sought the counsel of people he most respected. Foremost among them was his senior law partner, Simon Hirsch Rifkind. Liman revered Rifkind, a Russian Jew who became a naturalized citizen in the mid-twenties, then legislative assistant to New York's Senator Robert F. Wagner, Sr., and an ardent New Dealer whom Franklin D. Roosevelt had appointed to the federal bench in New York, where he had a distinguished career before returning to private practice.

Rifkind urged Liman to accept the committee job if it was offered. There are some calls you cannot reject, he said. This was such a call. Liman owed this service to his country. Another law partner, Theodore Sorensen, former special assistant to President Kennedy, gave similar advice.

A third person whose advice he valued highly strongly disagreed. William S. Paley, board chairman of CBS and for years the most influential person in U.S. television, urged Liman not to accept if asked. He had spent all his life in the media, Paley reminded Liman, and this situation involving Reagan and Iran-contra was going to be exceedingly difficult. This is a very, very popular president, and you're going to be crucified if you take on that job. Paley repeated his warning: You're going to be crucified.

When Mitchell called to offer Liman the job, he accepted and immediately went back to Washington, where he had a brief but intense conversation with Inouye. Once more Inouye stressed his desire that the committee be bipartisan. Then he talked about himself. He had been in Congress nearly thirty years, Inouye said, and his experience was that whenever a president was under attack, it invited adventures by the Soviet Union. Therefore, he said, it was important for this problem to be resolved promptly.

If the evidence demonstrated that the president should be removed, then he should be removed promptly and America would get a new president. If the evidence didn't warrant his removal, Inouye added, then we should end this investigation, report the facts, and let the country continue with its business. In the months to come, this was a discussion that Inouye and Liman had privately on at least a dozen occasions, and Inouye consistently expressed the same philosophical point of view: The country could afford to remove and replace a president, he would say. The country could also survive having this particular president remain in power. What the country could not endure was to have a president so crippled that in effect no one was in charge.

Liman left that first session with Inouye deeply impressed. "Inouye was perhaps the most patriotic person I ever met in the sentiments that he had expressed," he said, "and I wondered how they chose this chairman—somebody who was prepared to truly be as above partisan politics as he was in this kind of affair."

CHAPTER 24

THE INVESTIGATION

The calendar favored the president. When the investigation began, Reagan was entering the last phase of his second full term in office. Completion of his term would make him the first president to serve for eight years since Dwight Eisenhower nearly three decades earlier. By the time the congressional investigation and hearings were finished, another presidential election cycle would have begun. Thus, everyone involved in the investigation felt a need to complete the task quickly. If there were to be an impeachment proceeding, it would come at the very end of his presidential tenure. This was the opposite of the Nixon impeachment crisis, which began building immediately after his second inaugural with appointment of the Senate Watergate Committee and impaneling of a grand jury to look into criminality.

Watergate and Nixon left another legacy. The public had been conditioned to find a "smoking gun" in deciding whether to impeach a president.

With Nixon, it finally came down to whether clear evidence existed that he had lied and covered up criminal activities. His secret Oval Office tape recordings provided that conclusively. With Reagan, public attention focused almost exclusively on one question: Had the president approved the diversion of Iran arms sale funds to the contras?

This was never the most significant aspect of the secret activities that constituted the Iran-contra affair. But from the moment knowledge of a diversion was announced from Reagan's White House itself, it was the topic that dominated press reporting and political debate. In a real sense, near-exclusive focus on the diversion was itself a diversion from more troubling questions.

Paradoxically Daniel Inouye's admirable desire for bipartisanship and political unity contributed to a fundamental flaw in the investigation: the combining of both houses of Congress into a single joint select committee with members of the House of Representatives and the Senate sitting in judgment. Not only was this cumbersome, but institutionally combining these distinct political bodies also did not work well. In the Senate the tradition of comity and civility was long established and long observed. In the House a far more contentious spirit prevailed. The House was polarized politically. Partisanship reigned, and a partisanship especially acute during the Reagan years. Republicans chafed with frustration and fury at their inability to crack the lock the Democrats held on control of the House while their own party dominated presidential elections. As Dick Cheney remarked, "Republicans have to fight for their rights in the House, and they do it day after day after day."

Despite talk of bipartisanship, House Republicans sought to defend the president and avoid weakening his authority in foreign affairs. Democrats saw the issue as usurpation of constitutional authority by the president, failure to notify Congress, abuse of power. "We were like two ships passing in the night," Cheney said. "In a sense, we headed one investigation and they headed another."

It was Inouye who prevailed in combining the two committees into one overall investigatory unit and Inouye who set an October 1987 deadline for completion of the committee's work to enable both political parties to begin the new presidential nominating process. He did so with the best of intentions. It would be unacceptable, in his view, to have two simultaneous hearings into the same intensely controversial subject. "Imagine witnesses running back and forth, vying for headlines," he said. "It would have been a circus of the worst type that you can think of."

The same concern for fairness, decorum, and national unity motivated his attitude toward Ronald Reagan. Inouye knew that the question would ultimately come down to the president. Were all those subordinates acting under the orders of the commander in chief? With that question in mind, Inouye told the committee privately that he was opposed to any move to subpoena the president or the vice president. Nor did he wish to issue an invitation for them to appear. If they declined and word got out, unbelievable pressures would be placed on the president. His ability to lead and govern would be irreparably damaged.

Inouye was haunted by the picture of having to put the president through the indignity of being sworn as a witness amid the full glare of the television cameras. "I could just not see this picture of myself standing up there with the president down below with raised hand administering the oath: 'Do you, Ronald Reagan, swear to tell the truth, the whole truth, and nothing but the truth?' This would have torn the country, just ripped it apart. It would have projected a terrible picture to the outside. You know, what's gone wrong with this country? The chief executive has to be called to testify."

Admirable as this attitude was, especially in the concern for fairness, at heart Inouye's was an old-world view of politics and leadership, the view of an insider who lacked taste for a difficult conflict and sought to reconcile rather than confront. Inouye did not bring to his task the passion and indignation, say, of a Sam Ervin during the televised Watergate hearings; he brought to it the cast of mind of a conciliator. It was Inouye, too, who also prevailed in acceding to conditions imposed by Oliver North's attorney, Brendan Sullivan, Jr., on the terms of North's public testimony. North's position, as articulated by his lawyer, was that he would refuse to appear unless granted immunity from criminal prosecution for congressional testimony that he might give. He also demanded that the committee limit length of its questioning of North in number of both days and hours per day.

George Mitchell, for one, strongly opposed meeting North's demands. He was convinced that North was bluffing, that in fact, North wanted to testify and would have testified because it gave him a public opportunity to vindicate himself as well as a chance to defeat subsequent criminal prosecution by having his testimony "immunized" and thus inadmissible in a criminal trial.

Others felt equally strongly that the committees had no choice but to agree to North's demands. A cloud unfairly hung over the president's head, they argued, and Congress had an obligation to determine as quickly as possible what Reagan's role really was. That could not be done without the testimony of Oliver North. Furthermore, the congressional bodies had pledged to complete their investigation by October. If North continued to refuse to testify, the only congressional recourse would have been to institute contempt proceedings and compel him to testify or go to jail. Those proceedings would likely have dragged through the courts for months, extending the investigation far beyond the October deadline. Such delay would be unfair to the president and the country. Inevitably a greater divisive and destructive partisanship would result as the investigation became enmeshed in the presidential politics of 1988.

This, at least, was the view of Inouye, Rudman, and others, and they prevailed. The question never even came to a private vote. North's demands were met. Mitchell remained troubled and doubtful. "I'll always to the day I die wonder what would have happened had I pressed it to a vote and we'd prevailed," he said. "I still think North would have testified."

John Nields was frustrated. After two months of intensive work that began formally on January 10, 1987, it seemed to him that the investigation was never going to get off the ground. As Liman's counterpart for the House committee, chief counsel Nields had immersed himself in seven-day-a-week sessions that seemed to last around the clock. He had hired staff and investigators but was still unclear of the scope and complexity of their investigation. In the beginning all they had was a box of newspaper clippings and no paper clips. For two months they didn't even have offices. They couldn't get security clearances or physical custody of documents they sought. It was taking, he realized glumly, a shockingly long time to gather their basic material. Still, there were enormous gaps. Obviously there were many new fields to explore. It was a morass.

Aside from intense pressure from committee members and the press for faster action, there were also other major problems. An independent counsel, formerly called a special prosecutor, the distinguished New York lawyer Lawrence Walsh, had been appointed simultaneously to investigate possible criminality in the Iran-contra affair. Walsh and his staff maintained that the congressional investigating committees were obligated to turn over to their inquiry everything they found and all documents they obtained. At the same time the special prosecutor took the position that under the law his investigation was obliged not to share *its* findings with the congressional groups. It was a classic conflict. Nields, and the committees, were caught in the crossfire. And even as their investigation was struggling to begin moving, a widely publicized special presidential commission issued findings that seemed to exonerate Reagan from responsibility for the Iran-contra fiasco.

When the so-called Tower Commission report was issued on February 26, 1987, nearly two months after the congressional committees had begun their task, its findings were regarded as strongly critical of Reagan.* In fact, the commission that Reagan had appointed contributed strongly to a public impression that Reagan had been duped. The impression was left that Reagan had been a victim of his own inattention and lax "management style."

The Tower Commission, headed by the diminutive and scrappy former Texas Senator John Tower, a strong Republican conservative, was also composed of the Democrat Edmund S. Muskie and Gerald Ford's former national security adviser Brent Scowcroft. The commission had operated with no legal authority to subpoena documents, compel testimony, swear witnesses, or grant immunity. Its final report, the product of three months of investigative work, concluded that the Iran-contra matter "still is an enigma." Some individuals might have "concealed evidence or deliberately misled the board," it suggested, but it said such possible behavior could not be confirmed. Neither was the commission able to resolve conflicts in testimony. While it criticized the internal Reagan White House decision-making process as "too informal," the commission was unable to determine how North first became involved with the contras during the congressional ban on U.S. assistance to them. It concluded that the National Security Council operation was "very unprofessional" but could not determine whether the 1985 shipments of arms to Iran were approved in advance by the president. As for Reagan himself, the commission credited him with being motivated by his "intense compassion for the hostages." He was, it found, essentially

*The Tower Commission findings were published on February 26, 1987, in an official presidential office report containing 185 pages, plus an appendix of 42 more pages, and entitled *Report of the President's Special Review Board.*

unaware of the way in which the operation was implemented and of the full consequences of U.S. participation. While it criticized the president's "management style" for putting "the principal responsibility for policy review on the shoulders of his advisers" and said Reagan "must bear primary responsibility for the chaos that descended upon the White House when such disclosure did occur," it left the impression that Reagan was more victim than victimizer.

This portrait of a detached, uninformed, inattentive, passive Ronald Reagan fitted with the image the public had already formed about the president and was, in the context of the Iran-contra affair, a political plus instead of a negative. Reagan simply hadn't known what was happening. Others had.

For Nields and the congressional investigators, the Tower Commission report made their job all the more difficult.

John W. Nields, Jr., whose long hair and lean, youthful looks made him resemble a sixties student in a Brooks Brothers suit, was a lawyer with considerable prior experience on Capitol Hill. Lee Hamilton, who picked him as the Democratic chief counsel, had been impressed with Nields's work as chief counsel for a House Ethics Committee investigation of congressional misconduct involving contributions from Korean lobbyists—the so-called Koreagate affair. Nields was a man of even temperament who seemed mild and self-effacing. Beneath his calm demeanor, however, was a passion about injustice. Nields was the kind of person who entertained friends by singing Irish and American folk songs of protest and rebellion and who exhibited strong feelings about social inequity and public impropriety.

He was fully aware his committee assignment would be difficult and demanding, but now, two months later, he was beginning to doubt his own abilities. So much time had passed, and the deadline for public hearings was fast approaching; but he still believed he didn't have a grasp of the subject or where it was heading. He lashed himself for failing to do the job properly. In that frame of mind he asked his investigatory staff to pull together all significant material it had gathered so he could read it and prepare a private briefing of the full House committee.

As he began reading, two things immediately hit him. These were the altered documents that North and McFarlane had prepared and McFarlane's two letters to Representatives Hamilton and Barnes falsely claiming that no National Security Council members were involved in assisting the contras. "Looking at these things as an investigator," Nields said, "I was absolutely flabbergasted. I could not conceive of someone writing those letters to Congress. To me it was a shocker."

He read on and grew even more disturbed. Committee investigators had uncovered computerized PROF messages that North thought he had purged. They were devastating and damning.* Nields could hardly believe what he was reading when he studied PROF messages between North and Poindexter about the November 1985 Hawk shipments juxtaposed with the false secret testimony about oil drilling equipment that both CIA Director Casey and Poindexter had given the congressional intelligence committees. "Again, I was shocked," Nields said. "I just didn't think I would ever find national security advisers participating in that kind of a fraud. That was the point at which the whole thing changed for me. I had a totally different impression of what we were doing and what it meant, what conduct we were likely to find. The way I thought of it was that it was *my* government that was being dishonored and deceived. That's what shocked me. The dishonesty hit me a lot harder than the diversion. I don't understand why it didn't hit other people harder."

Privately Nields gave an evenly stated factual briefing of these preliminary findings to the full committee or those members who attended. A number did not. Carefully, nonjudgmentally, he stressed the factual conflicts between what Reagan officials had said privately among themselves and what they had claimed in both secret congressional testimony and public comments. The absence of much reaction from the committee further frustrated him. Nields had the feeling he hadn't captured their interest, and he wondered if perhaps he

*The PROF, or Professional Office System, was an interoffice mail system run through an IBM mainframe computer and managed by the White House Communications Agency for the National Security Council. All NSC officers had personal passwords that enabled them to send and receive messages to each other from terminals at their desks. As a civilian McFarlane continued to use the PROF system from his home to write memos to Poindexter, North, and others after leaving the NSC.

himself had misunderstood the seriousness of the material already uncovered. Maybe it wasn't as important as he had thought. Maybe he needed to work harder.

Paul Barbadoro would never forget that Saturday when the first shipment of National Security Council documents was delivered to Senate committee investigators. There were in all some twelve thousand documents, and all from Oliver North's NSC office safe. Only three committee lawyers were then cleared to see the documents, Arthur Liman, his executive assistant, Mark A. Belnick, and Barbadoro. They all went immediately to the committee room. For the next fifteen hours they sat together reading documents and, as Barbadoro said, "just being shocked at the things we were reading." Every so often one of them would pull out a document, read it aloud, and say, "Can you believe this?" To Barbadoro, "It was very revealing and very frightening. This thing was much bigger than we had anticipated."

Barbadoro had been a prosecutor in the criminal division of the attorney general's office in New Hampshire when he first attracted Warren Rudman's attention. He came to Washington on Rudman's personal staff for a two-year assignment that ended the day of the Meese press conference announcing the diversion. Listening to Meese, as he prepared to return to New Hampshire and begin law practice, Barbadoro was "totally shocked that something like that could go on."

Three weeks later, after Rudman had asked him to become deputy counsel of the Senate Iran-Contra Committee, Barbadoro returned to Washington and met Liman. "Look," Liman told him, "We're partners in this thing, and I want to work together." Barbadoro was impressed. Here he was, only thirty-two years old and working with one of the top trial lawyers in the country, someone who took a cooperative, equal-partners approach.

It quickly became apparent that their greatest challenge was obtaining information from the government. Barbadoro had dealt with the CIA before and knew it was slow to produce documents. With the CIA, if you didn't know what question to ask, you weren't going to get the right answer, and even if you did ask the right question, you might have to ask it thirty times to get the right material.

Dealing with Justice Department lawyers was even worse. After the committee staff argued paragraph by paragraph over documents sought, there would still be weeks of delay. The experience left Barbadoro more suspicious of the Justice Department than of the CIA. Preoccupation with secrecy at the CIA was more understandable than that at the Justice Department. In taking depositions from career CIA people, Barbadoro came to appreciate the difficulty of keeping one's moral compass oriented when one's daily job involved lying and deceit. It took a unique person to live the life the CIA sometimes required. A CIA agent lived his life in total anonymity. If he ever died on the job, he'd get a star up on the wall at CIA headquarters. That was it—just a star, no name. Whoever was comfortable with that kind of life had to be either a real patriot or someone who enjoyed the power that came from the possession of secrets. Maybe both, Barbadoro thought.

Misuse of secrecy was the problem. It didn't seem possible that Oliver North could have done what he had without the protection of someone like William Casey. Barbadoro was convinced that the CIA station chief in Costa Rica was taking instructions directly from Casey. It was his theory that Casey appointed people he knew he could depend upon; then he instructed them to circumvent the normal chain of command. That was Casey's style. The problem was how to prove it. It was just a theory of the case, and a theory was not good enough. The staff lawyers could demonstrate some level of knowledge of Casey's part, but not the kind of direct involvement they suspected.

After immersing himself in the case, Barbadoro believed the CIA had suffered under Bill Casey's rule. It was not intended to be a place where unsupervised James Bond types ran wild. While Barbadoro believed in the need for limited covert operations, tightly supervised and clearly defined, the more he learned, the more he was struck by the dangers of secrecy. A perfect example was the story they uncovered about the U.S. Drug Enforcement Agency (DEA) and two hundred thousand dollars in hostage ransom money that was paid to informants and then lost by DEA agents assigned to North.

It was an incredible episode. There had been no accountability for where the money went. "These guys would just go wherever they wanted to go," Barbadoro recalled, "go spend a week at the beach in

Cyprus. . . . It's frightening that this kind of thing can go on in government, that the DEA could just assign two people to North and look the other way and let him misuse those people, that they would let themselves be misused."

That's not the way government should work, Barbadoro thought. You can't practice covert operations on your own government and have a democracy.

Like most people his age, W. Neil Eggleston had followed Watergate, and from the moment he first heard about the Iran-contra scandal, he knew there would be hearings. He phoned John Nields, who years before had held his job as chief of the appellate unit in the southern district, in charge of criminal appeals for cases prosecuted in New York.

Though colleagues of his were already working with the independent counsel, Lawrence Walsh, Eggleston was more intrigued with Congress. After having served six years in the Department of Justice, he was interested to see how Congress would handle such a problem. Shortly after Nields was appointed chief counsel for the House majority staff, Eggleston was hired as majority deputy chief counsel with principal investigative responsibilities for National Security Council operations inside the White House and the CIA. His first deposition was that of Eugene Hasenfus, the downed Enterprise pilot.

Eggleston, a man in his thirties of medium height, slim build, and fair complexion, quickly came to respect House Chairman Lee Hamilton. As he studied the available record and began to form his ideas about their investigation, Eggleston became indignant at repeated criticisms of Hamilton's failure to exercise effective congressional oversight of North and NSC operations: "People talk about the oversight being flimsy, but I have to tell you, I don't know what more you would have wanted that guy to do. He was chairman of the Intelligence Committee, and he would read in the newspaper that all this stuff was going on. He wrote letters from one constitutional branch of government to another and asked, 'Is this going on?' And he got letters back saying, 'No,' . . . and he didn't stop with one letter. He wrote another letter, and another letter, and he'd say, 'Now you say this isn't going on, but I've got some more questions for you. Is this going on? And this? And this? . . .' He's asking people who are supposed to be in charge if these things are going on, and they tell him, 'No, it's not, the papers aren't telling you the truth.' . . . Everybody's asking if this is going on—and they're all lied to. . . ."

To Eggleston, it came down to a fundamental point: The two branches of government should be able to believe that they were not lying to each other. Like Barbadoro, Eggleston wasn't opposed to covert operations. But what happened in Central America was different. It was not covert action; it was covert policy inspired by a secret decision to support a group that the American people had decided overwhelmingly *not* to support.

What was worse, no one was ashamed. Nobody was ashamed for the lies or the shredding of documents. The argument about vagueness of the Boland Amendment was no excuse. It was not ambiguous or hard to follow. Oliver North simply took the position that the law did not apply to him, and others gave him what he wanted.

Charles M. ("Chuck") Kerr, a Baltimore lawyer, came to the committee through Democratic Senator Paul Sarbanes of Maryland. He took leave from his law firm, set up shop in Washington, and, as he said, "I basically spent six months in the bowels of Langley dealing with defensive people. That in and of itself probably made the trip worthwhile and convinced me that I never would have anything to do with intelligence operatives again if I can avoid it."

Kerr and the other lawyers in his group handled the CIA "piece" of the committee's inquiry, reviewing the CIA's people involved in both the Iranian and Central American operations.

From the outset it was difficult to appreciate how dedicated the CIA was to making sure that nobody, including fellow CIA people, knew what CIA people did. It was a different world; Kerr had never experienced anything like it. "I came down with naive notions that the CIA was composed of, if not dedicated patriots, at least hardworking, honest bureaucrats," he said. "I left with a view of the agency as an extraordinarily sinister, dangerous cancer on the government. . . . Getting a sense of what they do and how they do it ultimately just kind of sickened me. Little things like learning what they had done to people . . . it just kind of turned your stomach."

To survive in that business, Kerr concluded, you had to be something of a manipulator, and when it came to a congressional investigation, the agency had mastered the art of damage control. Bales of documents were delivered with everything but the identifying number in the upper right-hand corner blacked out. "I don't think we discovered anything more than what they let us discover," he reflected. "And much of what we discovered was that fascinating amalgam of fact and fiction that is damage control as it is carried out by the CIA. . . . There's no way one develops any kind of hard sense of that palace of mirrors."

Some of the people at the top were among the most engaging, delightful people Kerr had met—the kind of people you'd like to have over for a drink. It was only when he began to measure the tale that was being told orally against the documents that were obtained—those bits and pieces of objective reality— that he realized he had been magnificently spun. They were better at manipulating interrogators than people like Kerr who were professional interrogators. During one deposition he confronted an operative with an undeniable lie. Suddenly Kerr thought he had discovered the real agency. It was as if the air had begun to crackle. "It became apparent to me," Kerr said later, "that there wasn't much percentage in pursuing that fellow. He was more than capable of taking care of a Baltimore lawyer who got in his way. It was not the kind of thing where one had much incentive to pursue it."

C. H. ("Bud") Albright, Jr., began the inquiry with a decidedly open mind. If anything, he was skeptical. "I am a Republican, and a strong supporter of this administration," said Albright, a Justice Department lawyer who had been approached by Republican Senator Paul Tribble, Jr., of Virginia to work on the committee. "So my bias was with the administration. . . . I've been politically active enough to know when there's vulnerability, so I was skeptical as to motive on the investigation. Here we had a very popular president who was riding high. . . . Here was an opportunity for the Democrats."

Albright was assigned to areas of the Pentagon and Oliver North. From the start, covering the Pentagon was an exercise in frustration; many of the programs he examined led him around in circles. With North, it was easy, just a matter of going through his notebooks.

As Albright studied North's notebooks, he didn't see how North ever got away from them. Everything was recorded in them: every meeting; every phone call; even, it seemed, every fragment of conversation. The same extraordinary diligence was true of North's prolific performance on the PROF computer electronic mail and memo system. He recorded anything and everything that was happening. Reading through this voluminous material, Albright began to get a sense of the driven nature of the person he was investigating. Often late at night or into the dark hours long after midnight, North would still be writing his revealing personal messages. Sometimes they seemed like cries from the heart or cries for support and understanding. He hadn't slept for two or three days, he would write, but had to keep on, had to keep trying, had to keep driving for the hostages. If anyone was listening or receiving, he would say, offer them a prayer. It was both surrealistic and disturbing. Oliver North, self-appointed superpatriot, endlessly writing into a void.

Jamie Kaplan had been following the Iran-contra affair since it broke in November, long before he was asked by George Mitchell to serve on the committee. Affable and serious, quick to laugh, James E. Kaplan had clerked for Mitchell when he was the U.S. attorney for Maine, had been in Washington for a decade, and knew Capitol Hill and government agencies well. Once he was hired by the committee, his principal area of investigation was Admiral John Poindexter.

His first impression of Poindexter, after studying the initial secret deposition of the admiral, was of a most uncomfortable witness. Kaplan was surprised to find that Poindexter had given a number of halting replies to basic questions that had obvious straightforward answers. Poindexter struck Kaplan as a by-the-book character, not someone who was likely to have had a lot of experience at being questioned by New York and Washington counsel—or topflight lawyers like Arthur Liman. He was someone for whom the whole Iran-contra affair and the investigation were obviously a very unpleasant experience.

Neither did Kaplan think that Oliver North would present much of a problem for the committee and its stable of talented lawyers and interrogators. From what Kaplan had learned of North, he was merely a junior officer who had attended the Naval Academy, served well in combat, and faithfully carried out orders of superiors like

Poindexter. So what's he going to know about responding to prepared questioners? Kaplan thought. Sure, Americans liked a uniform, he knew, but he didn't believe that Poindexter or North would be in a position to control the committee or dominate its counsel.

What bothered Kaplan most was what they began to uncover about the Enterprise—and what they still didn't know about the Enterprise. Kaplan and others believed that the Enterprise had carried out projects that hardly anyone in the American government knew about and operations that would probably never be known to the public. As Kaplan said, "It's a frightening prospect, the notion that there are people, some within and some outside of the American government, who are making foreign policy decisions and implementing them by covert operations funded by some sort of surplus money floating around in Swiss bank accounts. . . . It means that American policy makers can never be taken at face value because you've got these other people running around with at least some approval from within the government somewhere—even if it's just simply from the director of Central Intelligence, which isn't such a simply!"

Tim Woodcock seemed happy to be back in Bangor. With the straightforward, clear manner common to many northeasterners, Woodcock was a young lawyer with a bright and curious mind. Though he was a native to Maine and comfortable in the small-town setting of Bangor, the complex workings of national government were not unfamiliar to him.

Working first for Republican Senator William Cohen in Cohen's 1978 Senate election campaign, Timothy C. Woodcock had gone on to serve on the Indian Affairs Committee, becoming staff director in 1980. It was an active committee, with more than one hundred hearings in the span of two years. In those two years Woodcock received a complete, if informal, education on the substance and structure of legislation. In 1983, after four and a half years of working in Washington, Woodcock returned to Bangor, where he became assistant U.S. attorney, concentrating on criminal drug prosecutions. Four years later, through Senator Bill Cohen, he returned to Washington to work on the Senate Iran-Contra Committee and was assigned to "CIA/Iran," or the aspect of the investigation that involved Iran.

Like Chuck Kerr, he found that some people within the CIA let foreign policy objectives obscure their understanding of how the domestic political process was supposed to work. Consequently, they were less than forthcoming and often sought to impede disclosure of information. Woodcock believed a number of them had been outright untruthful, particularly in their protestations of lack of memory. "From a criminal prosecution standpoint, when people start having enormous memory problems, your antennae go up," Woodcock said. "And chances are, the person is trying to hide things. There were a number of people that we came across who had failures of memory at crucial points. And the matters which they were saying they could not remember were matters you wouldn't forget."

Woodcock was struck by how the CIA functioned in the Casey years. Under Reagan, the CIA had cabinet-level representation, and it was led by a strong covert operative who was personally and politically close to the president. Both president and director had a contempt for the normal processes of government. Ideologically and operationally they were kindred spirits. These connections provided Casey an unprecedented opportunity, and he took full advantage of it. If Congress imposed restrictions, Casey, with Reagan's blessing, would create his own worldwide covert agency and carry out actions that he and the president believed to be in the best national interest. In Woodcock's view, this method of operation and the ideology that created it permeated the entire administration, starting with Reagan himself. What went wrong with North went wrong all the way up the line to the president.

Maybe the *real* problem, Woodcock thought, was that the charges against North & Co. were made on the ground of bad government, as distinguished from bad policy. Bad government was bad procedure, illegal procedure, but the policy of selling arms to Iran for the release of the hostages was a policy the president himself had approved. In actuality, it might have been both bad government *and* bad policy, and illegal to boot.

CHAPTER 25

OLLIEMANIA

Warren Rudman was nervous. He administered the oath to Admiral John Poindexter amid circumstances melodramatic for their secrecy and then returned to his Senate office and waited, and waited, and waited.

It was Saturday, May 2, 1987, three days before the congressional hearings were to begin, and Poindexter's deposition was being taken upstairs in the presence of Arthur Liman, John Nields, and two of Poindexter's lawyers. Until that moment no one knew what Poindexter would say, under oath, when asked whether Ronald Reagan had authorized the diversion of Iranian arms sale funds to the contras. Many believed he would say the president had been fully briefed on all such matters and had approved the actions of Poindexter, North, and other NSC operatives. At an earlier congressional hearing his refusal to answer questions by taking the Fifth Amendment strongly suggested that he had incriminating knowledge damaging to the president.

Rudman, among many, had studied Poindexter's background. People who had been the admiral's commanding officers described him as a perfect subordinate. A painstaking officer with a formidable memory, who paid meticulous attention to detail and procedure, Poindexter always carefully briefed his superiors and was noted for his desire to bring any possible troublesome matter to their immediate attention. Was it conceivable that such an officer, not only graduated first in his class academically at the Naval Academy but also holding the number one leadership position in the brigade of midshipmen, would not have immediately brought to the attention of the president of the United States any matter that might create problems for him and the nation?

To assure maximum secrecy, Poindexter's deposition was taken in a specially constructed ninth-floor Senate Office Building security vault called the bubble. Made with panels of aluminum on the outside, with an air-conditioning system composed of special "sound baffling" materials, it was so security-proof that laser devices could not penetrate it. The CIA used something like it for its special interrogations, and this bubble, like theirs, was filled with sophisticated electronic antibugging devices.

On this day Rudman, representing the Senate committee, and Thomas E. Foley of Washington, a former West Coast prosecutor and son of a noted judge, representing the House, led the small group inside the fifteen-by-eight-foot bubble. The big heavy door closed behind them. They proceeded to the long table in the center of the room and administered the oath to Poindexter. Then Rudman and Foley departed, leaving behind Liman, Nields, Poindexter, his lawyers, and a stenographer.

Unless Poindexter's testimony presented major problems for the president, his deposition would be sealed and not made available to any members of the committees, including the respective chairmen and vice-chairmen. If Poindexter did offer explosive testimony about Reagan's role, Daniel Inouye had promised to inform White House Chief of Staff Howard H. Baker immediately, and privately. Inouye wanted to make sure that the White House and president would be prepared for another looming impeachment trauma.

As he left the bubble, Rudman thought, Today we're going to find out whether or not Ronald Reagan is going to finish out his term. We're going to find out whether we're going to have a tumultuous period of time or whether we're just going to have a difficult period of time.

From the beginning Rudman held the view that the diversion was the crucial problem. Selling arms to the ayatollah was a dumb thing to do, but presidents had done dumb things before. But when funds began flowing from taxpayer-owned assets for purposes that were both private and clearly contrary to congressional wishes, this was not just a stupid action. If the president had approved of this, it was an impeachable offense. John Poindexter held that key.

Rudman waited for hours without word of what was taking place upstairs. An entire day passed. Still no word, no signal from what was being disclosed inside the bubble. Finally he could stand it no longer. He went upstairs and arrived just as Poindexter was leaving. John Nields was walking out, too.

"Hi, John," Rudman said.

"Hi, Warren," Nields answered. Nields kept on walking without saying another word.

Rudman entered the bubble. "How're you doing, Arthur?" he said to Liman.

"Fine," Liman said. Liman told him that they were going to have to continue with Poindexter's testimony for another day.

"Okay," Rudman replied. He paused, then asked: "Anything you want to talk to me about?"

Liman said no.

Fine, Rudman said. At that moment he knew there would be no smoking gun. The admiral had absolved the president.

Within weeks after beginning his investigation, Arthur Liman had come to a conclusion about the case: The Tower Commission's findings about Ronald Reagan were completely wrong. The commissioners had, as Liman put it, concluded that the president was essentially like a child who needed a nursemaid. The reason Reagan made those mistakes, their theory went, was that he didn't have the right nursemaids. Secretary of State Shultz, Defense Secretary Weinberger, Chief of Staff Regan all were the wrong people for this kind of president. They hadn't been forceful enough; they hadn't brought matters to his attention; they hadn't objected strongly when they learned of covert operations running wild.

That theory was a fraud, Liman concluded, "not a deliberate fraud by them, but a fraud when it came to Iran and the contras." It had not been a case of Shultz or Weinberger's failing to argue hard enough with Reagan or of the president's missing the point they were making. Reagan knew what he was doing, Liman came to believe; he was in charge, even if he operated with disdain for the law.

For the first time it struck Liman that what he was seeing was a manifestation of what should have been apparent for the previous seven years. When the president didn't approve of a law, he didn't execute it. Instead, he impounded funds or appointed people hostile to the purposes of the regulatory agency or government department they headed and ideologically opposed to the laws they were supposed to enforce.

Reagan had done this repeatedly, Liman thought, in his environmental appointments, in his ideological battles over the Legal Services Corporation, in a host of other domestic areas. The president had raised no constitutional objections to any of those laws. He purported to enforce them; then he appointed people to circumvent them.

In the notes of Reagan's interview with the Tower Commission the president stated he didn't know that his National Security Council staff had been supporting the contras. Soon, however, Liman learned that Reagan had received a pledge of twenty-five million dollars to assist the contras directly from King Fahd of Saudi Arabia when the two leaders met alone in the upstairs family quarters of the White House. Moments after this meeting Reagan briefed his two key aides Shultz and McFarlane on what had happened but made no mention of money for the contras. McFarlane later learned this momentous news from the Saudi ambassador to the United States. Shortly thereafter the money was in McFarlane's hands, and it became his responsibility to see that it was deposited in Swiss accounts for the contras.

After learning this, Liman concluded that the president was not the puppet many believed him to be. Reagan had not been ill advised (except by Attorney General Meese), and he had received sound advice from people he chose to ignore. In the case of the contras Reagan had people who were more than willing to circumvent the law for him. In the case of Iran there were those who humored him in the fiction about establishing "moderate" relationships but knew that they were actually trying to buy back the hostages.

Liman was convinced that the Iran arms deal turned into something different after the initial attempts to free the hostages had failed. The Americans realized that they were not, in fact, dealing with "moderate elements" and that prospects for freeing the hostages were dim at best. At that point, Liman believed, Casey, Poindexter, and North continued to support the sale of U.S. arms to Iran because it was a source of money. The arms sales would generate a huge black operational fund for a number of special covert operations. It was a perfect means to fulfill Casey's desire for an off-the-books covert operation capacity that could be controlled outside normal U.S. government channels.

To Liman, the fragments of Reagan's diaries that he read made clear Reagan's strong wishes and personal involvement in illegally supplying the contras. Liman concluded that however misguided, however wrong, Ronald Reagan had acted like a president—a strong, bold, risk-taking president, not a detached, passive, uninformed one.

In the case of the arms sale diversion, it was more difficult to prove Reagan's direct involvement. Casey was unable to testify, pertinent documents had been destroyed, and there were doubts about the critical testimony that Admiral Poindexter and Colonel North might give.

Liman misjudged both men. Poindexter struck Liman as a man strongly indoctrinated by the Naval Academy code of honor. A number of Poindexter's military superior officers reinforced that impression. John Poindexter, they all said, was incapable of doing something of major consequence without informing his superior officers. They explained that there were different kinds of staff officers. Some will run with the ball, try to be manipulative, and operate in a political manner. That's not what John Poindexter was like. One officer who had been Poindexter's immediate superior told Liman that Poindexter had carefully briefed him on every issue of consequence. He was convinced that Poindexter, of all officers, would not make a decision without telling the president. If Poindexter knew of the diversion, he would immediately inform the president.*

Hoping to create an opportunity that would get Poindexter to talk, Liman arranged for a private meeting between Daniel Inouye and the admiral before the committee granted him immunity for his testimony and after he had taken the Fifth before another congressional panel. Liman hoped the two principals could meet alone, just

*This same officer, whom I have known for a number of years, told me exactly the same thing, in more detail, within weeks of the announcement of the diversion and before he was interviewed by Liman.

the chairman and the admiral. But both Poindexter's counsel and Liman were present.

It hurt him, Inouye began, to see a man in uniform taking the Fifth Amendment, and he spoke about his pride in the uniform and what it represented. This had to work, Liman thought. He appreciated, Inouye continued, that Poindexter had all the rights of a citizen, but sometimes you were thrust in a position in which you had to be willing to waive those rights. That's what the country expected.

Poindexter's face was hard to read. Listening to Inouye, he did not seem disturbed. When it was his turn to speak, he simply said, "I'm not going to wear my uniform." He had been looking steadily at Inouye the entire time.

Liman was astounded. Obviously Poindexter thought that a plainclothes politician was free to do things that an honorable uniformed man of the Navy was not. Without the uniform Poindexter could tell whatever story he wanted. To Liman, that insight into Poindexter's character was one of the most poignant and powerful revelations of the investigation.

Still, as a professional interrogator he thought he might be able to get Poindexter to be more forthcoming in their session in the bubble. After much thought he decided that Poindexter would expect him to go immediately to the central question of the diversion. Liman did the opposite. He began his questioning at the end instead of the beginning, focusing on Poindexter's destruction of the signed presidential finding that clearly stated Reagan had approved a straight arms-for-hostage swap.

By questioning Poindexter on this area, Liman thought he might avoid a prepared reply and just possibly might get the admiral to say things he had not intended. It did not work. After Liman attempted to pin Poindexter down about the motives that led him to destroy the finding, Poindexter changed the subject and then quickly volunteered his version of the diversion. He hadn't told Reagan, the admiral said, because he was certain that Reagan would have approved the idea—enthusiastically. Poindexter wanted to keep this critical knowledge from the president so Reagan could honestly deny knowing about it if it became public.

During a break in the long first day of examination inside the bubble, Liman turned to one of the other lawyers present. Poindexter was like Billy Budd, Liman said. He was going to go to his death saying that he loved his captain. From that time Liman thought of Poindexter as the stout, doomed Billy Budd.

Liman remembered when Poindexter had told him about his sons, Annapolis graduates. If Poindexter fingered the president, he might survive, Liman thought now, but he might destroy the careers of his sons. They would be regarded as Benedict Arnold's children.

There was the essence of tragedy: an officer of distinction whose career was destroyed because of his willingness to bend a historical fact in order to protect a president and save his sons.

Putting himself in Poindexter's head, Liman concluded that the admiral had been unable to say to the president, "It's your decision. You have to bear the responsibility for your actions. I must live by the code of honor that I am sworn to uphold."

At first Liman felt he understood Oliver North. People like him are bond salesmen, he thought. They believe in what they sell, and they ultimately go broke because they buy it. But the more Liman studied North, read his notebooks and PROF messages, and interviewed his close friends, he came to hold a different view. North was not the zealot that he was portrayed to be. Oliver North could have worked for almost any White House and done exactly what he did for the Reagan group.

Liman had seen many people like North. They could not distinguish easily between fantasy and fact. Their great strength was their total belief in their mission of the moment. He learned something else about North. Despite North's public claims to be willing to be fall guy for the Iran-contra fiasco, Oliver North had no intention of taking the fall.

In his testimony North repeatedly pointed toward the president as the responsible character. It was North who kept insisting that he regularly and repeatedly sent memos up the chain of the command for presidential approval, North who kept letting it be known that he believed every single act he had undertaken had been officially authorized. Once North even volunteered damaging information about Reagan. He had stood near the president after a national security planning group meeting, he recalled, and had then said aloud to Poindexter how ironic it was that the ayatollah was funding the contras. He didn't think the president had heard him, North said, but believed Poindexter would recall the conversation.

Why did North volunteer that? Liman wondered. No one had asked him about it. No one knew about the incident.

North seemed to be the kind of person who needed a father figure, a strong authority model. Originally Liman believed that Bud McFarlane filled that need in the early White House period. North even seemed to adapt certain of McFarlane's personality traits then, and his internal writings reflected them: a studied kind of intellectualism, the professional air of the important person who wrote significant policy memorandums for most important people. Then North seemed to drop McFarlane, appearing to have lost respect for his old national security boss and former ranking Marine Corps officer. Maybe North found McFarlane weak, Liman thought, especially after McFarlane attempted to commit suicide when the Iran-contra net was closing and McFarlane's record of deceiving Congress was about to be exposed.

Next, North seemed to adopt as his role model Richard Secord, the hard-bitten retired general who became the private operations officer for the Enterprise, courtesy of Bill Casey. Liman observed that North assumed a number of Secord's characteristics.

Then, of course, there was Casey himself. That was perhaps the most complex relationship of all, though Liman was never as sure as others that theirs had been a father-son kind of relationship.

It was speculation, to be sure, this fathoming of character, but Oliver North was a remarkably revealing person. His notebooks were a gold mine. They provided leads for countless new lines of inquiry. It was all there to be pursued.

Bud McFarlane seemed to offer the key to the case. In studying the North-McFarlane documents the investigators had discovered, and after talking to North's secretary, Fawn Hall, Liman realized that McFarlane had written out the numbers of the documents that North had altered. They were in McFarlane's handwriting, and McFarlane didn't know that the investigators knew that. Here is a man I can break, Liman thought. He has the whole story; he knows it all.

In that spirit Liman conducted some "bloody" interrogations with McFarlane. But McFarlane was not broken. The longer the questioning continued, the more McFarlane seemed to retreat into a fog of rationalization that he himself seemed to believe. Merely thinking about it later made Liman uncomfortable. But he had realized, when he looked at McFarlane during their private interrogation, that he had gone as far as he could go.

In the midst of one of their intense sessions Liman felt great sympathy and compassion for McFarlane. It was when McFarlane turned to Liman and said in an anguished voice, You have no right to judge me because you have never had to deal with this president. You have not been in sessions with this president where you describe this to him and you describe that to him and find that he has absolutely no interest whatsoever in those matters of policy. All he wants to do is talk about the contras. You don't have to deal with the ideologues in this White House. You don't have to deal with this president's uninterest in matters of real importance.

With immense frustration, McFarlane recalled how he had asked Reagan to choose his next foreign policy objectives after the 1984 landslide. McFarlane gave Reagan a list of twelve objectives, asking the president to pick only two or three to ensure success. Reagan picked all twelve.

Unless you were exposed to that kind of environment and those kinds of people, McFarlane said to Liman, his voice rising, you have no right to sit here and judge me.

The hearings began with Richard Secord. Short, stocky, with a square face and a cocky manner, Secord bristled with self-assurance and contempt. He was not matinee idol material, and it seemed unlikely that he would make a sympathetic witness for the millions who turned on their television sets to watch the opening of the Iran-contra congressional hearings on Tuesday, May 6, 1987.

Heavy red draperies covered the high vaulted windows of the hearing room to better the backdrop for the television lights that burned brightly. Committee members and staff occupied two long rows which rose up like steps before the single desk at which the witness sat. It was an intimidating array of political power massed above and looking down on the witness, who seemed, from the view captured by the television lens, like a defenseless gladiator.

Secord, setting an example that was followed throughout the hearing by succeeding witnesses, took the offensive. As arms dealer and covert operator for the Enterprise, the general aggressively attacked his accusers, including those in the Reagan administration who had allowed him to be humiliated in so public a fashion. By his own account, Secord was a selfless patriot, a man who had served his country long, honorably, and well. He was proud to have risen to the rank of major general, proud to have been asked to serve on secret missions in his country's interest. He was a man wronged, falsely accused of misdeeds. The same was so, he said, for the other men with whom he had come in contact during his efforts on behalf of the Enterprise. He singled out Oliver North and John Poindexter as "dedicated and honest men." Everything, he insisted, that he and the others had done had been sanctioned by Reagan administration officials, who "knew of my conduct and approved of it."

Returns from the television soundings and instant polls sampling public opinion on the hearings all were favorable to Secord. Critical mail and calls began flooding into the congressional offices. Many were abusive and angry. Committee members were criticized personally and their motives impugned as the public demanded to know why the politicians were attacking this patriot.

My God, one of the committee lawyers thought, watching what was happening on the first days of his testimony, we've succeeded in turning Secord into James Bond. Now all the public is waiting for is for us to crown him.

The worst was to come. During the last two of Secord's four days on the witness stand, Arthur Liman played an essential but unflattering role of the heavy. In what amounted to a cross-examination of Secord, Liman vigorously attacked the general's credibility and his motivations. He came at Secord from a familiar angle given Liman's background in numerous securities fraud cases. Secord, he amply demonstrated, had been motivated by something other than patriotism. He was interested in profits, big profits.

Liman: Each time that you were selling arms [to Iran], you were charging a sufficient markup to cover the cost of [insuring] the plane, weren't you?

Secord: We still had that commitment, and it went up. And, Mr. Liman, this is not a hard concept to understand. I don't understand why you keep heckling me on this point. It's not a hard concept to understand. . . .

Liman: And your position is that the $4.6 million you had to keep in this Enterprise?

Secord: My position is as I stated it, not as you state it. So stop trying to change my story and move my story around. The facts are the facts.

Liman: And the facts are that at the end of this transaction, when you returned the plane, you had $4.6 million left. Isn't that the fact?

Secord: Yes, fine. Get off of it. You know, that's fine.

Liman: Is that the fact?

Secord: Yes, I'll accept your construction. Go ahead, please.

Liman: Is it the fact? I'm not interested in a construction.

Secord: I said, we had $4.6 [million] left. I tried . . . to explain to you that we had $2 million in a CD [certificate of deposit]. You don't want to credit that? So, don't credit it. I do.

On it went, with Secord growing more belligerent and Liman drawing more admissions of destruction of evidence, details of secret bank accounts, and profit motivations. Again, public response as measured in immediate polls was overwhelmingly supportive of Secord, the patriot and private entrepreneur. Liman began to receive and outpouring of vile anonymous phone calls and hate mail, many of them viciously anti-Semitic. They included numerous death threats.

A sense of unease spread through the committee. On the House side the veneer of bipartisanship was quickly sundered. House Republicans began employing their time before the cameras to launch a spirited defense of Secord and, through him, a strong attack on the president's critics. "I think you're being charged with the high crime of ambiguity of intentions," remarked the cherubic-looking conservative Henry J. Hyde of Illinois. Hyde, in a pattern that continued, offered Secord and his attorney gratuitous public advice. Don't claim to have been involved in a diversion of funds to the contras, he suggested. "That wasn't a diversion of somebody else's funds. That was an allocation by the Enterprise of funds over which it had dominion and control. . . . I would choose allocation of funds rather than diversion."

Week after week the hearings produced similar scenes of defiant, proud witnesses and increasingly divisive partisanship within the House committee. Some witnesses were more sad than belligerent.

Bud McFarlane, his face set in a solemn mask and his tone sepulchral, told a story that matched his demeanor, the story of a lifetime public servant and son of a public servant, who walked the line for a president into personal disaster even though he knew the secret policy being pursued was dangerously flawed and had forced all involved to take "fatal risks." For McFarlane, those risks and inner conflicts between personal honor and political obligation became too much to bear. They led to his suicide attempt.

Fawn Hall, North's national security secretary, an intense and confident young woman, was anything but sorry for her actions. She testified proudly that she had helped North alter, shred, and destroy documents and even described how she had smuggled out incriminating classified documents past White House security guards by hiding them inside her dress and stuffing them down her boots. She hadn't been involved in a cover-up, she said sharply. "I looked at it as protecting." Protecting whom and from what? she was asked. "I was protecting the initiative," she replied. Again the question: "From whom?" Her answer, one of deceptive simplicity that went to the heart of the affair: "From everyone, because I felt that I knew that we were trying to get back the hostages, and I also knew that we were dealing with moderates and if this whole thing was exposed, there could be . . . lives . . . lost. . . ."

At that point Tom Foley of Washington, admired for his evenhanded approach and mastery of legislative process, asked a question that drew a revealing reply.

"Did you not know that alteration of existing documents in a major, fundamental way was a violation of the responsibility of those who possess those documents?" he asked Hall.

She did know, she conceded, and admitted to feeling uneasy about it. But she believed in Colonel North and was certain he had a "very solid and very valid reason" for altering classified documents. Then she said: "Sometimes you have to go above the written law, I believe."

Bill Cohen had an inkling of what to expect when Oliver North took the stand. The Maine senator, though another Republican supporter of Ronald Reagan, felt the country was going to pay a heavy price for the administration's growing disdain for law. Disrespect for national institutions was being created, making it ever more difficult to maintain ethical standards.

Cohen had risen to national prominence through the independent manner and eloquent turn of phrase he exhibited while sitting in judgment of Richard Nixon on the House Judiciary Committee's impeachment hearings. His was an unusual range of talents and interests. Published poet, collaborator on a spy novel with his Democratic Senate colleague Gary Hart of Colorado, son of a Jewish father and Irish mother, Cohen had also been an effective prosecutor in Maine before entering political life. He possessed both a philosophical turn of mind and a realist's political view.

Cohen would always remember where he was when he first learned about the Iran-contra affair. He was in Beijing, China, on a Senate trip when he read about Attorney General Meese's announcement of the diversion in the *International Herald Tribune.* He recognized instantly that if Reagan hadn't authorized it, the president should have known about it.

It was incredible that such a thing could have happened, Cohen thought, especially as the United States was lecturing its allies against dealing with the Iranians. This would seriously undermine the U.S. position in attempting to take the international lead against global terrorism. By doing what it accused others of doing, the United States would be seen as a hypocrite: selling arms to a terrorist regime, albeit clandestinely, through the back door.

Cohen knew little about Oliver North, but what he did know set off internal alarms. An attorney on the House Foreign Affairs Committee had told him of an incident when North was called to testify earlier before that committee. North and his attorney, Brendan Sullivan, were sitting in this man's office waiting to testify after Admiral Poindexter completed his appearance that day. North and Sullivan were discussing whether to demand that television cameras be banned when North was called to the stand and would, like Poindexter, take the Fifth Amendment. Sullivan wanted no cameras present to record that moment. North was in an ebullient mood, joking, laughing, obviously at ease. "Don't worry, counselor," he said to his attorney, "I can handle it."

With that, North walked into the hearing room. Immediately his demeanor changed. Instead of being cocky, lighthearted, cavalier,

North suddenly appeared soulful, sad. His facial expression was one of pain and sorrow.

The House lawyer, in recounting this to Cohen, warned that Oliver North was highly capable of turning emotion on—and off.

North did both when he was finally called to the witness stand in the old Senate Caucus Room to begin four days of televised testimony the first week in July.

His eyes glistening with emotion, North "handled it" well. His demeanor sorrowful, his manner open, his voice husky and cracking at times with emotion, he was the wounded warrior willingly prepared to take, as he put it, "the spear in my chest" for mistakes that might have been made in the national interest. Dressed in his Marine uniform, his chest filled with campaign ribbons and decorations, he was on the offensive, but not sullen like Secord, arrogant like Hall, or pathetic like McFarlane. He admitted to error, falsehood, obstruction, destruction of evidence, and all for a higher cause. "Lying does not come easy to me," he confessed. "But we all have to weigh in the balance the difference between lives and lies."

The country was enthralled by North. Here, at last, was a genuine hero. Even the childishness and bungling that typified much of his and the Enterprise's dealings were cloaked with a kind of exuberant innocence. So here, in the flesh, was a true secret operator, wearing medals no less. The public learned a tantalizing new vocabulary. North called hostages Zebras. The United States was Orange. Israel was Banana. Iran was Apple. Missiles were dogs. Nicaragua was Eden. Reagan was Joshua or Henry. North's young aide Robert W. Owen was the Courier. Secord was Major General Adams or Copp or John. The State Department he derisively tagged as Wimp. A secret Swiss bank account was Button. His wife, Betsy, was Mrs. Bellybutton. As for himself, Oliver North adopted the white hat. He was, in code terminology, either Mr. Goode, Mr. Green, Mr. White, or Steelhammer.

It was a remarkable show, better than the soaps, many thought, and it was all live on television.

"Olliemania," as it was instantly dubbed in the press, gripped America. Flowers poured into the Senate for North. They were stored in a room near the hearing chamber. Telegrams of support flooded the Capitol. Brendan Sullivan, his lawyer, shrewdly placed stacks of them on the witness table where they would be photographed. Outside the Senate Office Building, where he was testifying, large crowds of supporters cried out his name, "Ollie, Ollie, Ollie." At a break in the hearings one day North and his wife went to a Senate balcony and acknowledged the support of his legions by waving toward them. The Iran-contra committees reeled. Some members stumbled over themselves to pay tribute to this American hero for the eighties.

Once, during his days on the stand, a different North appeared. Bill Cohen and a few other committee members had gone to a closed room at night to be briefed by North on other covert operations in which the Enterprise had been involved.* Cohen was struck by the dramatically different atmosphere between the private session with North and the public ones and realized what a mistake the committees had made in staging the hearing. Through television, it had appeared that the committee members were sitting up on their high platforms like Roman potentates while down below the lone noble Christian faced the lions. In the small private setting, without the TV cameras, it was an entirely different feeling—and a different North. This North was relaxed, casual, a storyteller approaching them in the manner of an exclusive men's club. Okay, fellas, here's the way it really was on the front lines, he seemed to imply, and he shared confidences and sought their approval. No speech making now, Cohen noticed, not little sermonettes of the kinds he had been delivering before the cameras.

North profited from another structural problem inherent in the

*The range and scope of its activities were never fully determined. Some knowledgeable people interviewed for this book referred to black operations that included assassination plans and defended them as necessary for national security in an age of terrorism. In the Casey off-the-book concept of unaccountable covert operations, the central idea was to "farm out" to other parties, or countries, actions that the United States wished carried out but that were either illegal or judged too politically explosive if the U.S. role were detected. See, for instance, Bob Woodward's account of the attempted assassination of the fundamentalist Muslim leader Sheikh Muhammad Hussein Fadlallah in Beirut. U.S. intelligence agencies believed Fadlallah had been connected with three bombings of American facilities in Beirut and should be killed, a plan for which operational control was given to the Saudis. Woodward's account is in his *Veil: The Secret Wars of the CIA, 1981–1987* (New York: Simon & Schuster, 1987).

hearings. In the televised committee hearing format, it was difficult for either the chair of the committee or the committee itself to seem impartial. Of necessity, the chair acted not only as the head of the inquiring body, which was the committee, but also as the judge. Thus, he embodied functions of both inquisitor and judge. It was one more aspect that helped create an impression that power was arrayed unfairly against a single witness, especially so earnest and compelling a one. In such a setting no wonder Americans were ignoring disturbing truths that were being uncovered.

For Arthur Liman the worst moment came on the last day of his questioning of Oliver North. Nothing had been going well. House Republicans on the committee were openly attacking Liman, almost without defense, as a partisan liberal Democrat biased against North and Ronald Reagan. They were interrupting his questioning, criticizing his tactics, playing to the cameras. And hate mail and threatening phone calls increased by the hour. He wasn't worried so much about the threats; most of them, he realized, were from kooks. But he was worried about the effect on his wife, Ellen. Several years before, the Limans had been assaulted and nearly killed by a mentally disturbed person in New York. Memories of that traumatic experience were rekindled by the increasingly vicious threats Liman was receiving. Now the Limans had police stationed all night outside the home they had leased in Northwest Washington.

The lunch break came with North still testifying. Liman had one more hour to go before turning the interrogation over to the committee.

After a hurried lunch Liman returned to the Senate Caucus Room. It was still locked to the public. He walked into the room and was shocked by what he saw. There, before him, was what appeared to be the entire Senate police force lined up before the committee platforms. Along with them were other committee functionaries. In front of them was a Senate photographer. And there, standing in the center, posing like a president, was Oliver North.

One by one each member of the Senate security force, and the committee functionaries, moved forward toward North, paused to shake his hand, and posed for a picture with him taken by the Senate photographer.

Liman gazed at the scene and couldn't take it anymore. He walked back into the Senate anteroom behind the chamber and sat alone, his head bowed.

Warren Rudman's office was logging between 125 and 200 phone calls a day during the hearings. As with the others, many were critical, some threatening. The volume of calls and mail increased immediately after Rudman, in an indignant tone, had taken the microphone at the beginning of a committee session and decried the hate unleashed at Inouye, who for the first time in his public career had been forced to have his telephone number unlisted. Inouye was a dirty Jap, the callers said. Why didn't he go back to where he came from? Now, the callers said, Rudman was a Jap lover.

It didn't bother Rudman. Nor did the daily pummeling he was talking in his home state's major newspaper, the *Manchester Union Leader.* In a thirteen-day period that July, while North and Poindexter were on the stand, the paper published nine editorials excoriating Rudman for his behavior in the hearings. Some of the headlines reflected the tone of the editorial comments. RUDMAN'S TREACHERY, one said. RUDMAN'S CHEAP SHOT, read another. NORTH MADE HIM "SICK" was a third. The paper had been especially incensed at Rudman's praise for and defense of Inouye. "No tactic employed to date in the Iran-Contra hearings," the paper commented, "has been more contemptible than Rudman's move . . . to cheapen the debate by using Inouye's splendid military record as a rhetorical weapon with which to attack North."

Rudman would read the New Hampshire paper each morning, joke about the editorials to his staff, and return to the hearing room.

It had been an entirely new audience watching North on television, John Nields realized afterward. Countless numbers of Americans turned on their sets only when North appeared before the cameras on Capitol Hill and were thus unprepared for the background facts that had already been established in the previous two and a half months of televised hearings. For them, the story began with North—North the passionate defender of truth and honor against the hostile congressional inquisitors.

Nields could understand what had happened. Here was this attractive person, with what appeared to be the world's most sincere pair of eyes, proudly wearing his country's uniform and being subjected to rude and accusatory questions and bravely responding with moving speeches. Television was marvelous in many ways, Nields thought, but it wasn't good at conveying a full picture. People tuned in and out. They waited for the drama, then clicked off their sets and went shopping. In the end they were left with appearances and impressions. That's why he should have approached North differently, Nields came to understand. He should have laid a stronger foundation for his questioning. That's how he would proceed if he had it to do over. But there was no more second chance. It was over.

CHAPTER 26

POSTMORTEMS

In their individual postmortems, committee members realized how much information they had made public and how much they still did not know. They didn't know about Casey: Casey's true relationship with Reagan; Casey's full dealings with North. They didn't know a great deal about the Enterprise and what else it had been doing. "Frightening" was the word used again and again to describe this unaccountable entity that carried out worldwide national security missions with neither direct political scrutiny nor public knowledge. They didn't know what Reagan really knew and what Poindexter had really said to him. They were certain, though, they had not obtained the complete story—especially from an admiral with a reputation for always fully briefing his superiors, an officer with a fabled memory who on 184 separate times during his public testimony said he could not remember events about which he was questioned. There had been a cover-up, and in ways still not fully understood, it had worked.

Nor had they been able to pin down the connection between drugs and the multiple covert operations in Central America. They hadn't determined who pocketed how much money or discovered where the remaining tens of millions or more went. They weren't able to examine sufficiently the so-called black operations that were being conducted by the U.S. military. Congressional oversight in that area was notably weak; it fell between the cracks, lying somewhere outside the jurisdiction of the intelligence committees. The role of Vice President George Bush was still largely unknown. Former CIA

Director Bush's personal staff had maintained close contact with covert operatives in Central America, and Bush himself had been the U.S. intelligence chief during the early contacts with Noriega in the seventies. During the Reagan years Bush headed governmental task forces on both terrorism and drugs. Beyond this, little else was known, and the committees studiously did not focus on his role.

These all were mysteries, and many would remain so. In their final public report that November the committees characterized the Iran-contra affair as one marked by "pervasive dishonesty and inordinate secrecy." Individually, leading committee members had come to other conclusions about what the affair meant.

To Dick Cheney, it had been a fundamental mistake and a major policy failure, but it probably would not have any significant historical impact; it hadn't been that grave a crisis. The key, Cheney thought, had been Bill Casey's role, and the committee had understated it. Casey had been crucial; he had been at the heart of the Enterprise and most influential with Ronald Reagan. The trouble was, they couldn't prove it.

To Lee Hamilton, a remark that Poindexter made during his testimony summed up the larger abuse of power problem. "I really did not want any outside interference," Poindexter had said in explaining why he held information and secrets so closely. That kind of attitude was the real danger, Hamilton thought, and it was a state of mind that became pervasive during the Reagan administration. From the president down, the Reagan people viewed Congress with deep distrust, if not contempt, while at the same time celebrating expansive powers of the presidency. In view of such an outlook, it was inevitable that such a president and such a group would try to find ways to carry out policies themselves. Nor had the members done a good job of oversight in the Congress, Hamilton thought; they weren't tough enough; they hadn't been skeptical enough or asked the right questions.

To Nields, it was about secrecy. The more you entered the world of the intelligence agencies and covert operators, he thought, the more you realized how widespread was the belief that secrecy was an appropriate way for America's government to conduct its affairs. Now that same kind of mentality was creeping into the political realm. Especially dangerous in the Reagan years was the way the administration exaggerated the international threat and played upon the public's latent fears. Maybe the greatest danger, Nields thought, was that the public was being conditioned to accept all the secrecy and lying as necessary to combat a threat to the nation. Deception was being institutionalized.

To Inouye, it had been about trust. Trust was the essential ingredient, the lubricant that made possible the workings of a democracy. For such a system to work, the executive branch must trust the Congress, the Congress must trust the executive, the Congress and the president must trust the judiciary. They all must trust one another. But most important, the government must trust the people and the people must trust the government. When that chain of trust was eroded, American democracy was endangered. That was what had happened in the Iran-contra affair, Inouye concluded.

Americans had such a short view of history, Inouye thought. They measured things in increments of years or at most five- or ten-year spans. With the Chinese, when you talked about history, they viewed the Boxer Rebellion as though it happened yesterday. For better or worse, Americans didn't have that reflective cast of mind. Already, Watergate was ancient history for them. Soon Iran-contra would be. Already, Inouye heard other politicians saying, "Who the hell cares about it? People are going to forget about it." They were probably right, too, Inouye thought. Fifteen years later power would likely be abused again, and then, in different times and circumstances, the country would have to grapple with the same kinds of problems.

To Rudman, greed and zealotry carried to their logical conclusions will break any system that has ever been devised. That was the danger of Iran-contra, and that, to Rudman, helped explain other breakdowns that had occurred in the eighties both on Wall Street and in Washington. History was Rudman's hobby, and he had been reading about the early Franklin Roosevelt period and FDR's choice of able governmental lieutenants. Look back at the Teapot Dome, at the stock market crash of '29, at Watergate, or at any other major problems the country had experienced, he observed. It wasn't so much a breakdown of the system that produced those traumas; it was the behavior of people that created the difficulties. Sometimes it was lust for money; other times it was ideological fervor. Both had been exhibited in the Iran-contra affair, though it was zeal that ultimately carried the country into a constitutional crisis. Zealots always get the United States in trouble, Rudman thought.

To Mitchell, it was a reminder of the weakness of human nature in succumbing to the arrogance of power. The constitutional framers had been correct: Abuse of power required constant checking and vigilance. However the public initially viewed the hearings, Mitchell was convinced that the record established would affect history's judgment on Reagan's presidency. That record stood as a severe indictment of Reagan's attitude toward the rule of law. It was Reagan who set the climate in which illegal acts flourished, Reagan who made it clear to subordinates that he didn't care how they accomplished his objectives so long as they were successful. Reagan consistently refused to condemn those who had been involved in lawbreaking; in fact, he consistently defended those who *were.* Lack of respect for law suffused his administration, Mitchell believed. *That* was what had created the problems. Something that Liman said during the hearings stuck in Mitchell's mind. Liman had quoted Supreme Court Justice Louis Brandeis as warning that crime was contagious. If the government became involved in lawbreaking, it bred contempt for law. It invited every person to become a law unto himself or herself. Down that path lay anarchy.

To Liman, it was a manifestation of a deeper, more troubling national phenomenon. America had experienced a revolution in values in the eighties, Liman came to believe, and "revolution" was not too strong a word to describe it. Protective mechanisms put into place after the Great Depression were dismantled in the eighties. Laissez-faire economic theories discredited for nearly half a century were reestablished, and people again came to believe in the invisible hand theory of government: If government could be kept out of the nation's affairs, the free market would take care of any problems. Reagan and North personified the antigovernment attitude, Liman thought. North, in his testimony, described the need to go around the CIA. Richard Secord castigated the agency and its leaders as a bunch of shoe salesmen. Albert Hakim, the private international arms dealer, contemptuously testified that he could negotiate better than the secretary of state. Reagan adopted the secret policies he did to circumvent laws that Congress passed. When Reagan spoke with such contempt of Congress, he was doing nothing more than manifesting and encouraging a pernicious public attitude that government was evil, therefore Congress was evil, therefore laws were evil. To Liman, that was the deadly syllogism that symbolized the Iran-contra affair.

To Cohen, it had been a dangerous national episode, this tale of two governments, one elected, the other unelected, and a serious threat made even more so because people did not perceive it as such. Cohen wondered why the American people considered Watergate serious, and not Iran-contra. Why had one led to impeachment and the other to, well, nothing? Personality was a part of it. Nixon had seemed dark, defiant, and withholding; his manner inspired the suspicion that he was leading a cover-up.

With Reagan, an opposite impression had been created. In effect, Reagan pleaded ignorance before the American people. He was unwitting but sincere, and he seemed so open. And unlike Nixon, Reagan did not "stonewall" the investigators or retreat into "executive privilege" to withhold information. Come, look at everything, Reagan said. Here are my records, portions of my diary even, discover the truth and then tell me what was going on in *my own* administration. "I'm still trying to find out," he said several times publicly when questioned about damaging new disclosures. His reputation of *not* being in charge had saved him. It was extraordinary, Cohen thought, but there it was. Besides, in Watergate, people could easily grasp presidential abuses of power in such acts as turning the force of the Internal Revenue Service on political critics, compiling political enemies lists inside the White House, attempting to use the FBI to impede the investigation, and sanctioning break-ins in private offices of political opponents. Compared with these flagrant violations, Iran-contra seemed academic, an institutional struggle between a highly popular president and a deeply divided Congress quarreling about complicated foreign policy issues.

The public misunderstood the gravity of the scandal because they liked the president. But the geniality of the president was not the issue. The hand that steals the Constitution comes in a velvet glove as dangerous as that which appears in a mailed fist, Cohen thought. People did not understand the implications of disrespect for law that took root inside the White House. In the Reagan White House, laws were something to be evaded rather than faithfully executed. Instead of trying to change a law by pointing out its inadequacies, the Reagan people chose either to disregard it or find a way to get around it.

Maybe that's the metaphor for the times, Cohen thought. Don't worry about process and procedure. Don't worry about laws. Just get the job done. In the ethical wasteland of the eighties that was the bottom line.

CHAPTER 27

CRASH

. . . the snow of twenty-nine wasn't real snow.
If you didn't want it to be snow,
you just paid some money.

—F. Scott Fitzgerald,
"Babylon Revisited"

There was no end in sight. Up and up the averages went. Record after record was set and smashed. By the last week in August 1987 the market had established its fifty-fifth record close of the year. Five records were set in June, nine in July, and eight more before the end of August. Still, the boom continued. At that present rate of increase, in only four more months the Reagan bull market would set a record of expansion for the century, supplanting the sixty-three month surge that lasted from 1924 to 1929.

Now, as Labor Day approached, the Dow stood at 2722.42. Experts were predicting it would rise another thousand points within the coming year. Some predicted even greater gains.

There was, one Wall Street analyst thought that summer, a useful comparison. Japanese investors had recently paid a record art auction price of $39.9 million for van Gogh's *Sunflowers.* If they could pay that much for a painting, he reasoned, why couldn't they pay a comparable 3990 for the Dow-Jones average?

As the most important savers in the world the Japanese were pouring much of their excess cash into U.S. markets. In this they were joined by capital from around the world. And look, the analyst added, America's leading corporations were buying in more shares than they were selling. The correct analysis was inescapable: Pressure on stock prices remained upward. For the smart investor, there was still time to climb aboard.

There were some dissenters and a few Cassandras.

A year before, in the spring of 1986, one Wall Street investment manager privately advised his clients in a newsletter that they should take into account "whether or not we are repeating the mistakes of the 1920's."*

Nobody knows for sure, he wrote, "but the parallels are spooky: the financing of prosperity by insupportable debt, the erosion of the assets supporting that debt (e.g., farmland and oil), the difficulty in keeping the boom going late in the decade, the flow of wealth to the rich and the stock market boom are just some of the similarities."

He was far from alone in raising alarms, particularly about debt. In the United States, domestic debt, to say nothing of the rapidly increasing foreign trade deficit, had begun shooting upward at the very time the stock market surge started in 1982. The trouble was, overall debt was rising much faster than the nation's gross national product, reversing a thirty-year trend of debt increase being in line with economic growth. Now both domestic and foreign debt was rising at historic rates and far exceeding the GNP.

The year 1987 began with an ominous warning by the author of *The Great Crash,* the definitive account of the 1929 debacle. Writing in that January's *Atlantic* about what he entitled "The 1929 Parallel," the eminent economist John Kenneth Galbraith described the similarities between then and now. "There is a compelling vested interest in euphoria, even, or perhaps especially, when it verges, as in 1929, on insanity," he wrote. "Anyone who speaks or writes on current tendencies in financial markets should feel duly warned. There are, however, some controlling rules in these matters, which are ignored at no slight cost. Among those suffering most will be those who regard all current warnings with the greatest contempt."

With that gloomy caveat, Galbraith proceeded to describe unsparingly the parallels between 1929 and 1987. The first involved "the dynamics of speculation."

In the twenties speculative fever fueled by the stock market boom attracted more and more institutions and ordinary people to invest in the belief they could profit quickly and always get out before the fall. The permissive economic and political laissez-faire climate of the times contributed to hunger for cashing in on the boom. Coolidge-Hoover prosperity was judged unique and lasting. A business-ori-

*This was Alfred Gray Parmelee, of New York's Parmelee Management Corporation.

ented administration presided over the nation's affairs from Washington and, as Galbraith recalled, had taken positive action to foster the trickle-down theory of economics: "The infinitely benign effects of the supply-side tax reductions of Secretary of the Treasury Andrew W. Mellon, who was held to be the greatest in that office since Alexander Hamilton," were certain to lead to a more prosperous future. New technology stocks, like that of RCA, offered a favored and surefire speculative investment. Speculators, professional traders, and hordes of amateurs flocked into the market.

Those same kinds of "speculative dynamic," as Galbraith put it, were present again in the late eighties—and, as in the twenties, such "speculative episodes never come gently to an end."

He drew other, even stronger, parallels with '29. Once again, "seemingly imaginative, currently lucrative, and eventually disastrous innovation in financial structures" were in vogue. In the twenties it had been the proliferation of holding companies and investment trusts that existed not for practical product purposes but mainly as investment profit centers. They operated by incurring debt that was used to buy stock in other companies and ultimately to control them. "Pyramiding" it was called. Here, Galbraith wrote, was the most striking parallel with '29, the "rediscovery of leverage." He wrote:

> These lie in the wave of corporate takeovers, mergers, and acquisitions and the *leveraged* buy-outs. And in the bank loans and bond issues, not excluding the junk bonds, that are arranged to finance these operations.
>
> The common feature of all these activities is the creation of debt. In 1985 alone some $139 billion dollars' worth of mergers and acquisitions was financed, much of it with new borrowing. More, it would appear, was so financed last year. Some $100 billion in admittedly perilous junk bonds (rarely has a name been more of a warning) was issued to more than adequately trusting investors. This debt has a first claim on earnings; in its intractable way, it will absorb all earnings (and claim more) at some astringent time in the future.

Galbraith predicted that the time would come when the wave of mergers and their resulting debt would be "regarded as no less insane than the utility and railroad pyramiding and the investment-trust explosion of the 1920s."

His final parallel involved tax reduction and investment incentives. In the twenties cutting taxes on the wealthy, hailed as a means to stimulate the economy, had the hidden purpose of lessening "the tax bite on the most bitten." Rather than promote savings to spur future investment and growth, the evidence was that much of the tax cut revenues of the twenties went directly into the stock market in hopes that individuals would further be able to cash in on the boom. The same phenomenon was at work in the eighties. People were not saving; they were accumulating debt, plunging deeper into the markets, seeking ever-greater personal gains. At the same time, real capital spending, which induced genuine economic growth, was declining. In the end the merger craze and piles of new debt it induced did not improve the nation's industrial capacity and competence. It did not result in overall economic benefit to the nation.

It was a brilliant and prophetic article, but its warnings were largely ignored. Galbraith was, people said, an unabashed liberal and unreconstructed New Dealer. He was out of date, a defender of Keynesian economics trying to cling to the past. He didn't understand the new age.

Increasingly, from late summer into the fall months, cautionary warnings about problems to come were offered from respected economists and analysts and were quickly drowned out amid the greater glow of optimism that emanated from Wall Street and Washington. Here the similarity to 1929 was most striking of all. Those with longer memories, or historical perspective, recalled uneasily the description of the public climate in the late summer and early fall of 1929 given by Frederick Lewis Allen in *Only Yesterday* and wondered:

> As people in the summer of 1929 looked back for precedents, they were comforted by the recollection that every crash of the past few years had been followed by a recovery and that every recovery had ultimately brought prices to a new high point. Two steps up, one step down, two steps up again—that was how the market went. If you sold, you only had to wait for the next crash (they came every few months) and buy in again. . . . Time and again the economists and forecasters had cried wolf, wolf, and the wolf had made only the

> most fleeting of visits. . . . What the bull operators had long been saying must be true, after all. This was a new era. Prosperity was coming into full and perfect flower.

As the boom continued from summer into fall of 1987, with increasingly steep and volatile swings in the daily market closing, supply-siders prepared to celebrate their success. In Washington the supply-side forces had formed their own political group, something they called the Prosperity Caucus. These members of what Jude Wanniski, with typical bombast, called the true church met informally to plan the next mission for their supply-side revolution. Now they talked about carrying the word to other countries. The newly formulated goal was to reform the world's monetary system by installing supply-side doctrines and switching to currencies linked to gold. Their movement, which some of them described as having represented "creationist economics," had come of age. The great market boom and the economic expansion of the Reagan years proved it; the supply-siders were the mainstream now.

Writing on the *Wall Street Journal*'s editorial page on October 12, 1987, the U.S. Chamber of Commerce's chief economist, Richard W. Rahn, took the occasion to crow about the success of supply-side economics. Despite predictions of failure from liberal/Keynesian economists, he said it was time to mark "the longest American peacetime economic expansion since 1796." He hailed the supply-side economists and their political converts as "the intellectual Contras, if you will, who fought on the bloody fields of *The Wall Street Journal* editorial and op-ed pages for freedom against greater government control and for economic opportunity," and he offered a tribute to the fashioners of this triumph.

"Let me not be alone in the back of the crowd," he wrote, "as I tip my hat to my longtime colleagues on the economic barricades: Thank you, Mr. Gilder, Mr. Kemp, Mr. Laffer, Mr. Mundell, Mr. Roberts, Mr. Ture, Mr. Wanniski, and all the others who helped invent this economic miracle."

Exactly one week later letters were mailed from New York to leading supply-side gurus, their supporters, and selected national journalists inviting them to attend a special anniversary luncheon.

It had been six years, the letters from the conservative Manhattan

Institute announced, since George Gilder had delivered a celebrated luncheon address at New York's venerable Century Club. Then the famous supply-side theorist spoke in glowing terms about his topic, "The 1980s: Era of Success." Although Gilder's remarks about "the shape of the Roaring Eighties" had been lampooned at that time and he had been criticized "for romanticizing concepts like entrepreneurship, technological innovation, and incentive economics," his thesis had been amply proven: "George's bullishness was indeed prophetic."

People were invited hear Gilder mark "the fifth anniversary of the nation's economic expansion" by giving his forecast for "the Roaring Nineties."

The letters containing that invitation were postmarked in New York on October 19, 1987.

John Phelan had been up throughout the night in his Manhattan apartment monitoring the bad news that was moving, like a tidal wave, toward the United States that Monday, October 19, 1987. Tokyo exchanges had closed after sustaining a record collapse in prices amid panic selling. The collapse triggered others around the globe. Disaster followed the sun and inexorably exacted its toll from Asia through Europe and then on to New York. Hong Kong was wiped out. In Australia the nation's leading market index lost 20 percent of its total value in the first forty minutes of trading. In Rome, Frankfurt, Amsterdam, and Paris record losses were recorded. Down and down the prices plunged. In London the stock exchange was experiencing the single worst day in its history.

At one point, as the grim reports kept flooding in, Phelan, the chairman of the New York Stock Exchange, moved to a window overlooking the darkened New York skyline. He wondered if the world as he knew it was coming to an end. Before dawn he telephoned some of the most influential men in U.S. finance and asked them to assemble in his sixth-floor stock exchange office.

Half an hour before the opening trading bell sounded, these heads of America's leading investment banks and brokerage houses, controlling among them hundreds of billions of dollars, gathered around Phelan's desk.

No one knew for certain what they would face that day, but they all knew it would be bad. A dramatic drop in the markets had occurred before the weekend close the previous Friday. Even before the other exchanges opened for trading that Monday, a torrent of sell orders had already poured into brokerage houses.

Phelan gave them his thoughts. No matter how severe the crisis might become, he told them, he intended, if at all possible, to keep the market open all day. He asked for their views. They agreed. Then they all returned to their executive suites to begin the most agonizing period of their lives.

Panic first swept Chicago. There, in the futures pits, hundreds of traders who gathered to hear the opening call before the mercantile exchange opened at eight-thirty o'clock central time (to coincide with the opening trading bell on the New York Stock Exchange) knew it was going to be a difficult day. Panic selling in foreign markets had braced them for even more tense and draining dealings than normal. No one, however, was remotely prepared for what happened as they awaited the opening call and the beginning of trading on Standard & Poor futures contracts—that new financial product that enabled them to speculate on the overall New York Stock Exchange movement, as measured by the S&P index of five hundred leading United States corporations.

Within five minutes after the pit's opening, the S&P index had plummeted eighteen points. That drop was more than had been recorded in all of the previous Friday's dramatic losses—and Friday had been the worst drop ever.

Panic selling developed. "Everybody just had sell orders," one trader told a reporter for the *Washington Post.* "We had huge, huge orders that we haven't ever had before." Another trader said, awestricken: "Brokers were saying, 'Give me a bid—anywhere.' It was an absolutely scary, horrible feeling."

The Chicago markets went into a free fall. Their collapse triggered a torrent of new sell orders in New York. Now computerized programming took over, registering sell orders for enormous blocks of stock held by the great institutional investors, controllers of mutual funds and pensions. In the first half hour of trading on the New York exchange, more than 71 percent of the total activity was done in block trading. The average trade that day exceeded three thousand shares—a 50 percent increase over the norm of the first three quarters of the year. Average dollar value per trade was more than one hundred thousand dollars. Never before had such massive dumping, on such a scale, been led by the big investors. Once the rush to unload began, it accelerated. In Chicago major fund managers attempted to save their holdings by buying the new supposedly fail-safe portfolio insurance that would enable them to offset stock losses by buying speculative futures contracts. They were too late. Everyone was selling all at once. The markets were overwhelmed. "These people were using us to write insurance in the midst of an earthquake," the president of the Chicago Merc said during the day.

In New York it was immediately apparent that this was no mere, if major, "correction" on Wall Street. This was a crash, and of a magnitude Wall Street and the world had not experienced since '29. From opening bell until frantic close, fear, if not panic, moved the markets. "There's no anchor to it," said Robert D. Hormats, an investment banker and economist who had been a high government official in Washington before becoming a senior executive with Goldman, Sachs and Company on Wall Street. "It's the same as a parachutist who drops and drops and drops and never knows when the parachute is going to open—or if it's going to open."

Never had the markets been so volatile. The Dow-Jones averages fell 508 points. By the time the final bell had sounded on Wall Street, stock market prices had dropped 22.6 percent, almost double the record losses in the crash of '29. An astonishing 604.5 million shares had been traded, more than double the all-time record. Stock prices had been rolled back so far that all the gains recorded between January 1 and August had been wiped out.

Something else about the market performance stirred fearful memories. As in '29, the market reports ran far behind the actual buy and sell times. If you tuned in to your television or radio to find out what was happening or went to your brokerage house to watch the ticker prices, no one could tell you with any accuracy where they stood. Prices quoted were at least an hour or more old. At times the sheer volume of sell orders delayed reports of brokerage trades by more than two hours. More panic was ignited. Brokers, weary or panic-stricken or both, finally even began failing to answer phone calls placed by major clients. Gallows humor was evident everywhere. "It's the traditional way to celebrate a disaster," wire services quoted one young London stockbroker as saying while he sipped champagne amid the debacle. "And believe me, today has been a disaster."

Analyses of what had happened, why, and what it meant began immediately, but of necessity, they took place amid extraordinary turmoil and anxiety. For the worst crisis did not come on Black Monday. It came on the next day—what the *Wall Street Journal* later described as Terrible Tuesday.

How close the New York Stock Exchange, and with it the world's financial system, came to extinction then was never appreciated by the general public. For obvious reasons, neither was it ever fully addressed publicly by U.S. business leaders and political policy makers. In this, they all had learned one major lesson from '29 and the depression: Fear *does* feed on itself and breed greater market instability and panic.

The best account of the near-deadly aftermath of the crash came a month later in a lengthy page one article in the *Wall Street Journal.* Carefully and persuasively the article detailed how the market nearly disintegrated—or approached a meltdown, as some leading inside figures described it—creating its most perilous day in half a century.*

There was a moment that Tuesday when it seemed as if the market had in fact died. Trading in stocks, options, and futures all came to a virtual halt. Corporate giants representing the most successful and powerful elements of American capitalism were unable to trade any of their stock. There were no buyers at any price. Banks called in major loans, threatening some of the most venerable securities firms. Despite desperate pleas from leading clients for credit extensions to weather the crisis, banks refused to grant them. Facing catastrophic losses if the market panic continued, some of the nation's most prominent investment banking houses privately urged the New York Stock Exchange to close. In fact, exchange directors convened

*This article, by James B. Stewart and Daniel Hertzberg, won a well-deserved Pulitzer Prize as the year's most distinguished explanatory journalism. Their reporting, along with a series of articles a month later in the *Journal* on Wall Street and the crash by a team of its reporters, Randall Smith, Steve Swartz, and George Anders, drew implicit official confirmation when the Brady Commission on the crash concluded in its report of January 8, 1988, that as of midday on Tuesday, October 20, "the financial system approached breakdown."

shortly before noon to deliberate precisely about taking such action—and as Chairman Phelan told the worried chairman of the Chicago Mercantile Market, Leo Melamed, in a phone call then, the prospect of such an extraordinary decision "was close." If they closed, Phelan believed, they might never reopen.

"I think we came within an hour" of a disintegration of the stock market, said Felix Rohatyn, a prominent partner of Lazard Freres & Company. "The fact we didn't have a meltdown doesn't mean we didn't have a breakdown. Chernobyl didn't end the world, but it sure made a terrible mess."

In that moment of maximum peril the Federal Reserve Board in Washington stepped in forcefully and dramatically. Reversing its policy of tightening a grip on credit to forestall another round of feared inflation, the Fed announced its "readiness to serve as a source of liquidity to support the economic and financial system."

It was as good as its word. Immediately it flooded the banking system with dollars. By purchasing government securities and guaranteeing banks that everyone in the system would remain liquid, the Fed succeeded in quickly driving down short-term interest rates and, most important, reassuring banks and investment houses.

Coinciding with this good news to offset the grim fears was a remarkable rally of the Major Market Index futures contract in Chicago, then the only major index still trading. In a span of five minutes beginning at 12:38 o'clock that afternoon, the Major Market Index on the Chicago Board of Trade rose the equivalent of a 360-point Dow-Jones averages increase. Whether this dramatic and sudden surge was caused by a burst of new investor confidence in the system, as some people later claimed, or was the product of deliberate manipulation by a few major firms in a desperate attempt to save the markets by inducing a rise in the Dow, as a number of experts believed had happened, was never determined. But this welcome reversal, coupled with the Fed's strong intervention and the simultaneous announcement that leading corporations were entering the markets to buy back their own stock, produced desired results.

Buying resumed. Credit restrictions were eased. New York's ten largest banks began a process that by week's end had nearly doubled their rate of lending to leading securities firms, permitting an extra $5.5 billion in borrowing. The markets rallied. The threat of closing the exchange passed. By day's end the Dow had recorded gains of 102.27 points. Coming after the worst drop ever, it was the largest single day's increase in stock market history. The volume of shares traded exceeded even Black Monday's. More than 608.1 million shares were traded. The next day, Wednesday, brought an even greater rally. This time the Dow was up 186.84 points. Inherent American optimism took hold. Things were coming back to normal. It wasn't going to be like the aftermath of '29 after all. So, anyway, many said, and wanted to believe.

Inevitably, the search for scapegoats also began. Some blamed the Democrats. On Wednesday before the crash, Democrats on the influential House Ways and Means Committee had agreed on a bill that, if enacted, would revise tax laws to make corporate take-overs less attractive. Investors who believed that the wave of take-overs and ensuing corporate restructuring had been propping up the markets saw this political action as a destabilizing economic threat. "That bill took a lot of value right out of the market," one analyst commented.

Possible elimination of corporate take-over tax benefits also coincided with release of negative economic figures. That same day U.S. trade deficit figures were shown to have been much greater than expected. Together, these two pieces of bad news eroded investor confidence and contributed strongly to the crash. Thus some experts theorized.

Others cited an ill-timed and careless remark by the chairman of the Securities and Exchange Commission as having made the fall immeasurably worse. After delivering a luncheon speech in Washington on Black Monday, the SEC's David S. Ruder told reporters clamoring for his reaction about Wall Street: "There is some point, and I don't know what point that is, that I would be interested in talking to the New York Stock Exchange about a temporary, very temporary, halt in trading." When that remark was reported through news service tickers, some said, it so eroded business confidence that what had been a steep fall was transformed into a historic crash.

Still others offered another villain—two, in fact, simultaneously working at cross-purposes.

Concern over a new surge of inflation had led West German bankers to raise their short-term interest rates—the fourth such increase in three months—sending ripples of concern among investors worldwide. Since foreign investors then held a third of all U.S. savings and investments, thus in effect financing massive American budget and trade deficits, this German action spurred fears that a new round of destructive inflation would result in higher long-term interest rates as well.

In a series of statements that ran from the Thursday to Sunday before the crash, Treasury Secretary James A. Baker III made clear that the United States vigorously opposed the latest German interest rate increase. Baker strongly hinted that the United States was contemplating "an abrupt shift in policy." He implied that the United States would retaliate against the Germans. Not only would the United States let the dollar fall, he suggested, to the detriment of German investors, but it would actively seek to drive down the dollar against the German mark in foreign exchange markets. Such a move would make American goods cheaper while hurting the exports on which West Germany depended. A threat of economic warfare was raised, some highly placed people charged. At the least, Baker's words were destabilizing, others alleged.

None of these instant explanations held up under serious examination. They failed to account for deeper economic problems that, as so many warned, had been increasing for years. Craig Drill, a respected Wall Street money manager, had been one of those wise enough to foresee the inherent problems and get his funds and those of his clients out of the market. Speaking several nights after the crash from an executive dining room overlooking midtown Manhattan, Drill expressed thoughts that went beyond the obvious contributing factors of highly overpriced stocks, rising interest rates, and speculative dealing.

"To me, it was like an avalanche," he said. "It was like snow on the side of the mountain. Something was certain to happen. There was something structural about it. You knew when the snow started to slide that it would come down very fast because the rest of the mountain was coated with ice. And it was coated with ice because the system had tremendous amounts of leverage. . . . People who are saying it's not like '29 are right. It's worse! The leverage now is worse than it was in '29 . . . So I saw all the snow on the mountain, and I saw all the ice. And it was just a question of what is the accidental noise in the valley that causes it to fall.

"Ninety-five percent of all the historians are going to write about what caused that noise in the valley. Was the noise in the valley West Germany raising rates? Was the noise in the valley the tax on M and A [mergers and acquisitions] activities? Was the noise in the valley Jim Baker's shouting at the West Germans? It's all irrelevant. The right analysis is not the random accidental trigger. The analysis should be the snow on the mountain and the ice. Because if those other things hadn't happened, a wisp of wind would have come through the valley, or a branch would have broken, and it would all have come down."

The game had shifted from a short-term speculator's sport to an infinitely more difficult long-term one. Would Washington and Wall Street understand this? Would they address deeper problems like America's new debtor nation status? Would they capitalize on this crisis by using it to create public consensus about the need to reduce the nation's debts by paying off creditors, to start the process of importing less than we export?

Even if these actions were taken, and problems squarely faced, there were other uncertainties. Suppose our export partners decided they didn't want to buy what we were making and selling? Suppose they concluded that America's products were inferior, that we were no longer able to compete in the new, tougher global marketplace? What then? These were troubling questions that needed to be raised.

"What we've seen essentially is the first global election," said American Stock Exchange Chairman Arthur Levitt, Jr., one of more than a score of leading figures on Wall Street interviewed in the aftermath of the crash. "By that I mean a very significant massive vote of no confidence in our Congress and in our administration. We're in a different world today than we were a week ago. We are because so many people have been hurt, so many myths have been punctured. I think a lot of what happened has yet to be learned."

One lesson yet unlearned involved the nation's growing debt. Throughout the eighties the United States had been unwilling to take action to reduce its rising debt. If the U.S. government had placed a tax of one trillion dollars on wealth of Americans before the crash and designated half of that trillion dollars to reduce the national debt, Americans would have been outraged. Yet the markets, in their brutal, inexorable fashion, had taken exactly that action and confiscated half a trillion dollars in national wealth. And the debt still remained.

In the days following the crash, an axiom as old as the Republic came into play once more. In good times Wall Street wanted Washington to leave it alone. In bad times it wanted Washington to act.

"They're looking to Washington," as Robert Hormats put it, "because there's nothing else to look to. . . . They're looking to Washington to say, 'We understand that there's an imbalance here. And we are damned well going to do something about it. We are going to deal with the budget deficit. We are going to deal with the trade imbalance. We're going to try to pull our allies together.' . . . And it has to come from the White House because it's a national issue. The psychology of it requires a president to play a role."

Reagan's reputation suffered grievously during the days of crisis. Even many of his strong supporters had come to accept the popular picture of him as a president *not* in charge created during the Iran-contra affair. His actions during and immediately after the market's near disintegration reinforced those impressions.

During the height of Black Monday's free fall, Reagan had dismissed the seriousness of what was happening. He attributed the drop in prices to "some people grabbing profits" that had accumulated during the great bull market rise. After the markets had recorded their historic losses that day, the president issued a statement saying that "the underlying economy remains sound"—words that eerily, and almost literally, echoed what Herbert Hoover had said after the crash of October, 1929. On Wednesday, during a press conference, Reagan remarked that the markets had experienced "some kind of a correction."

Reaction to these comments was the most harshly critical of his presidency. Writing in the lead article of *Time*'s cover story about the crash, Walter Isaacson began his biting introductory essay to the week's news with an extraordinary personal assault on Reagan, the man, and Reagan, the president:

> What crashed was more than just the market. It was the Reagan Illusion: the idea that there could be a defense buildup and tax cuts without a price, that the country could live beyond its means indefinitely. The initial Reagan years, with their aura of tinseled optimism, had restored the nation's tattered pride and the lost sense that leadership was possible in the presidency. But he stayed a term too long. As he shouted befuddled Hooverisms over the roar of his helicopter last week or doddered precariously through his press conference, Reagan appeared embarrassingly irrelevant to a reality that he could scarcely comprehend. Stripped of his ability to create economic illusions . . . he elicited the unnerving suspicion that he was the emperor with no clothes.

There was a double irony in this Reagan bashing. Reagan, far more than most presidents, had delivered precisely what he promised: a new permissive regulatory climate in which government's role palpably receded, tax cuts and policies that favored the wealthy, and a change in public attitudes that reflected his own repeated exhortations and that elevated personal greed and glory into national values.

Wall Street and the yuppie generation had cheered Reagan passionately—and profited from the speculative boom and stock manipulation schemes that flowered under his benign political stewardship. Then, when the dream of easy riches and endlessly rising stock prices and profits disintegrated with the crash, they turned on Reagan.

The greater irony, less noted, was that in the end what kept '87 from turning into another '29 was the very hand of the federal government that Reagan and the supply-siders had railed against.

CHAPTER 28

RECKONING

By normal political reckoning, 1988 was a Democratic year. Not since the twenties, when voters successively elected Warren G. Harding, Calvin Coolidge, and Herbert Hoover, had voters chosen Republican presidents for three consecutive elections. Though neither war nor depression gripped the country and the feeling of peace and prosperity abounded, a number of factors favored the Democrats.

The so-called Reagan economic recovery, following the 1982 recession, had set records as the longest peacetime economic expansion in the nation's history. Beneath the statistics, however, was another story. Nearly ten million Americans lost their jobs to plant closings and layoffs in the five years from 1983 to 1988, and about half of those laid off had held their jobs for three years or more. They were thus experienced, or "tenured," members of the work force—precisely the kinds of people most likely to register political protest against those in power. Of this group of nearly five million tenured workers, half of those who found other work were forced to take jobs that paid less. They were poorer than when the recovery began and had more reason to vote against those in charge. By politically wedding them to the ranks of those hurt by Reagan's budget cutbacks against popular social programs—blacks and other minorities, the poor, women's groups, those approaching retirement age and beyond—they had the ready-made potential of a formidable political opposition. While the stock market crash of a year before had not produced an economic tailspin, it contributed to growing public uneasiness about the future.

Virtually every political poll and grass-roots sampling of public opinion showed people becoming more pessimistic about economic conditions. The Iran-contra affair had reinforced a sense that conditions were in danger of slipping out of control. Reagan's lack of leadership throughout that episode left the public troubled. Polls showed people were looking for a different kind of president to lead America into the nineties, suggesting the public was ready for a leader who would make up for years of neglect in vital areas of education, health care, environment, and quality of public services.

Democrats benefited from other conditions. The numbers of Reagan administration officials either indicted or the subject of criminal and ethical investigations reached record proportions in Washington. On Wall Street as well, indictments of high-rolling financiers on insider trading charges multiplied. Here, in the much-talked-of "sleaze factor," was further grist for Democrats. In 1988, they could resurrect time-tested political themes, run against corruption, failure to provide critical public services, abuse of power and privilege. Concern about the future and the specter of America's decline completed their potential case for major national change.

They had still another advantage. This time they would not have to face the mesmerizing presence of Ronald Reagan. No one on the political landscape, in either party, held such a claim on public affections as Reagan. No one else was so well known or so commanding politically. Without Reagan, the Republicans were vulnerable to the record of the Reagan years.

Against that backdrop, repeated public opinion polls showed Democratic presidential candidates leading prospective Republican nominees. The trend continued until the Democratic National Convention in Atlanta, where the party nominated a son of Greek immigrants, Governor Michael S. Dukakis of Massachusetts.

Typifying the American dream, Dukakis's father had become a medical doctor after arriving in New England unable to speak English. His mother, who also emigrated from Greece unable to speak English, had been graduated from a New England private college and become a schoolteacher. Dukakis, a Harvard-trained lawyer and teacher of government and public policy at Harvard's John F. Kennedy School of Government, also possessed television age political credentials, having been host of a public TV program, "The Advocates."

Leaving Atlanta as his party's nominee that July 22, Dukakis held a seventeen-point lead over the man the Republicans were certain to nominate a month later in New Orleans, George Bush. And Bush, already so far behind in the polls, carried with him a historical political liability: No sitting vice president seeking direct presidential election had won since Martin Van Buren 152 years before. Since then vice presidents had ascended to the presidency only through deaths of chief executives in office or, in the case of Gerald Ford following Richard Nixon, through forced resignation under threat of impeachment.

Given those political conditions, the prospect was for an extremely close race, with Democrats holding the edge. As Michael Barone and Grant Ujifusa assessed the situation in *The Almanac of American Politics 1988:* "There is more than the usual uncertainty here, more than the usual inability to know who will win each party nomination and which party's nomination will turn out to be worth winning. That uncertainty was one of the things that made 1960 so thrilling that it inspired the highest voter turnout of the 20th century and Theodore White's first *Making of the President.*"

As America prepared to enter the post-Reagan age, many other political experts expected the 1988 election to produce such a close and exciting contest. It shaped up as another Kennedy-Nixon race, a race that was decided by a mere one-tenth of one percentage point, or 100,881 votes out of the nearly 69 million cast.

Yet within a month after the Democrats nominated Dukakis something had happened. Suddenly Bush and the Republicans held an overwhelming advantage in all the polls. By Labor Day senior members of the Dukakis campaign feared the campaign was virtually over—before it had even begun.

To increasing numbers of Americans, politics and national political campaigns had become irrelevant. Long and costly* presidential campaigns lasted for well over a year, and news about political strat-

*Presidential candidates spent more than $210 million in 1988 on their campaigns.

egy, tactics, and polls seemed more like an insider's game between politicians and press than about real people, real lives, and real concerns of home, job, and community. During countless interviews in homes across the country, people said they didn't believe there was that much difference between candidates or the parties they represented, and they added that what happened in Washington was unrelated to what mattered most to them. People understood that a president and members of Congress could affect their lives. The problem was they didn't believe politicians would always work for their best interests or that government could be expected to fulfill political campaign promises.

Cynicism had become deeply ingrained. So had the belief that government did not work. The last campaign of the eighties, instead of being a positive vehicle for serious debate about the nation's direction, became a campaign of division, suspicion, and fear. More than any presidential campaign in years, it left a well of anger and bitterness. Issues that promised to be central at the beginning of the year never materialized, for either lack of effective airing from the candidates or public uninterest, or both. Implications of the Iran-contra affair were never fully explored. Nor were the connections between it and General Noriega's drug empire. The criminal trial of Oliver L. North, originally scheduled to begin around Labor Day, a time when public interest in a presidential campaign begins to peak, was postponed until after the election. Fears of a severe recession, or even depression, triggered by the stock market crash proved groundless. East-West tensions were easing, bringing hopes for a new Soviet-American relationship and perhaps even an end to the forty-year cold war.

On the surface, normality prevailed. Neither candidate clearly spelled out a course of action for the future. Both candidates shunned specifics, Bush more notably. Their campaigns were cloaked in generalities and banalities. In so doing, they failed the ultimate test of political leadership: They did not prepare the public for the direction they intended to take the nation or generate a climate of support for hard and necessary choices that lay ahead.

Whether the public *wanted* to hear discussion of issues was a question often asked and never conclusively answered. But to reporters who had spent months, years even, listening to Americans articulate their concerns during conversations in homes with family members, friends, and neighbors, there was no doubt that people wished to hear serious and specific debates about issues that affected them and their country: about education, health care, day care, housing, pensions, the changing nature of work, a cleaner environment. Politically, however, candidates had learned to avoid them. One of the lessons of the Reagan years had been that politics of pleasure played better than politics of pain. Every candidate understood the price that Walter Mondale had paid for candor in his losing race four years before. Mondale had told Americans that taxes would have to be raised to pay for the services they wanted and that Reagan would also be forced to increase them even while denying it. That is exactly what happened, but Mondale barely carried his own state of Minnesota, while Reagan won all the rest.

The success of Reagan in avoiding accountability for political mistakes and in shunning hard decisions—his Teflon factor again—was not lost on the candidates either. It made them, and the pollsters and media consultants who developed their campaign strategy, more reluctant to address tough issues and propose potentially unpopular solutions. Slogans worked better than specifics, especially in the age of electronic abbreviation when politics as entertainment had become even more ingrained as central campaign technique.

Americans had become accustomed to seeing their candidates close up, in their living rooms, in ways never possible before. Yet this new intimacy between voter and candidate brought feelings of familiarity and demystification that contributed to a candidate's fear of offending. Natural political instincts to appeal to lowest common denominators and reduce complexities to simplicities were strengthened. As with Reagan, what seemed to work best politically were pleasing personality traits of informality, sincerity, charm, or that inadequate cliché charisma. None of these had much to do with the qualities of heart and mind necessary for great presidential leadership. Continual complaints about America's "lack of leaders" notwithstanding, there was excellent reason to wonder whether the great figures of the past could have become president in the television age. For example, consider the portrait of Jefferson drawn by Henry Adams in his *History of the United States During the Administrations of Thomas Jefferson:*

> According to the admitted standards of greatness, Jefferson was a great man. After all deductions on which his enemies might choose to insist, his character could not be denied elevation, versatility, breadth, insight, and delicacy; but neither as a politician nor as a political philosopher did he seem at ease in the atmosphere which surrounded him. As a leader of democracy he appeared singularly out of place. As reserved as President Washington in the face of popular familiarities, he never showed himself in crowds. . . . The rawness of political life was an incessant torture to him, and personal attacks made him keenly unhappy. His true delight was in an intellectual life of science and art. . . . That such a man should have ventured upon the stormy ocean of politics was surprising, the more because he was no orator, and owed nothing to any magnetic influence of voice or person. Never effective in debate, for seventeen years before his Presidency he had not appeared in a legislative body except in the chair of the Senate. He felt a nervous horror for the contentiousness of such assemblies, and even among his own friends he sometimes abandoned for the moment his strongest convictions rather than support them by an effort of authority. . . .

If such qualities were thought "out of place" in early-nineteenth-century America, no wonder they appeared in short supply among public leaders of the late-twentieth-century television age.

Prime among the public concerns that formed the backdrop for the 1988 election was the lurking fear that America was slipping. Talk about eroding educational standards and national competitiveness could be heard everywhere. Every factory worker now understood, and talked about, the relative position of the Japanese yen and the German mark compared with the American dollar. Every parent understood that there was more truth than rhetoric in official warnings of a "nation at risk" because of falling educational standards and achievements. They also understood that many nations were doing better than the United States.

Influential national groups attempted to alert the public to new concerns about the future. In the summer of 1987, the National Academy of Engineering released a disturbing report that described the growing provincialism of the U.S. scientific and engineering community and deplored technical deficiencies that kept American scientists and engineers trailing behind their counterparts in other societies. Books critical of American education and corporate structures, such as Allan Bloom's *The Closing of the American Mind* and Thomas Peters's *In Pursuit of Excellence,* became best sellers. So did Paul Kennedy's scholarly *The Rise and Fall of the Great Powers: Economic Change and Military Conflict from 1500 to 2000.*

During the election year a collection of essays from leading scientists, university presidents, and foundation executives, most with long and distinguished experience in advising presidents since World War II, contained remarkably similar thoughts, especially since none of the authors knew what the others were concluding. "The world has caught up with us," wrote S. J. Buchsbaum, of AT&T's Bell Labs and chairman of the White House Science Council. "We now have to react to agendas set by others. There is precious little opportunity to act on our own in relative isolation from the rest of the world. Issues are no longer as straightforward as placing a man on the moon or filling a missile 'gap,' real or imagined."

William D. Carey, former executive officer of the American Association for the Advancement of Science and publisher of *Science,* wrote:

> American science and technology have had things largely their own way during four decades of primacy with the rest of the world as followers. That scene is changing rapidly as the Europeans, the Japanese, the Soviets, and eventually the Chinese make their moves. It is all very well to treat ourselves to visions of SDI, an Orient Express fast airplane, and even the blessings of superconductivity. But we are seen as lax in science education, facing demographic cramps, protectionist toward our advanced technology, unreliable as international partners, and unbuttoned in our capacity for science policy. Today's text is borrowed from Thomas Wolfe: "A wind is rising, and the rivers flow."

There was no question that the public wanted to hear these themes addressed. Responsibility for the fact that they were not was widespread, but in the end political leaders failed the people. In a society that was still by far the world's wealthiest, still blessed with material abundance, personal energy, talent, and public awareness of complicated issues, politicians chose the easy course. Fearing that people would reject alternatives that might require sacrifice, they failed to propose them. They didn't even ask that they be considered.

From a political standpoint, responsibility for this failure rested with the candidates, for the kinds of negative campaign techniques and tactics they employed, and with the media and the public for the way they responded to them.

Long before Republican presidential campaign strategists knew who their Democratic opponent would be, they knew how they were going to run against him. As Lee Atwater, chief strategist for the Bush campaign, later said, "Whoever it was, we had to paint him as a frostbelt liberal who is out of the mainstream and is not in tune with the values of the mainstream voters. What we did was find the actual issues that allowed us to paint the picture."

By "issues," Atwater meant negative attitudes about an opponent identified through extensive polling. This information then would be used to create negative impressions about him in the minds of voters. Through constant repetition as campaign themes, these discovered negatives could destroy the adversary. That was how Atwater had operated throughout a spectacularly successful political career that had begun in college in South Carolina while Nixon was in the White House and the new ultraconservative and virtually all-white Republican party was on the rise in the Deep South. "Republicans in the South could not win elections by talking about issues," Atwater explained. "You have to make the case that the other guy, the other candidate, is a bad guy."

A trial of allegations of dirty campaigning—phony polling, appeals to racism, use of survey questionnaires to make clear to voters an opponent's Jewish religion in a district of Christian fundamentalists—followed in the wake of Atwater's rise from South Carolina operative to national political strategist.*

By the 1988 election campaign Lee Atwater had become the nation's foremost practitioner of the negative campaign. Pale, intense, still in his thirties, Atwater had developed a theory, as he was quick to explain to reporters, about the negative campaign. "Let me tell

*Ironically, in 1980 Atwater ran the Reagan GOP South Carolina primary campaign against Bush. When he learned that Bush had previously supported gun control legislation, Atwater seized on that issue and turned it into a negative against Bush. This was credited with helping Reagan carry the state and reversing the political momentum Bush gained after defeating Reagan in Iowa.

you about my negative theory," he said. "When a candidate reaches a negative factor of thirty-five percent in the polls, and his positive rating is within five points of that, he's terminal."

That was precisely the perilous situation that George Bush faced in May, two and a half months before his own nomination, and six weeks before the Democrats chose Michael Dukakis as their standard-bearer.

When Atwater, media consultant Roger Ailes, pollster Robert Teeter, and other key Bush advisers gathered that Memorial Day weekend to map general election strategy with the vice president at his vacation home in Kennebunkport, Maine, Bush's political prospects appeared bleak. The latest Gallup poll then showed Bush trailing Dukakis by 54 to 38 percent. More ominously, more than 40 percent of the voters held an unfavorable opinion of Bush—already approaching Atwater's definition of terminal status. Bush's negative rating at that point was the highest recorded for a presidential candidate before the fall campaign. Among losing candidates whose early negatives presaged a November defeat, the next highest previously recorded negatives had been those of Barry Goldwater (with 36 percent) in 1964. Three Democratic losers, George McGovern, Jimmy Carter, and Walter Mondale, had negative ratings of 27, 28, and 29 percent respectively in their unsuccessful campaigns of 1972, 1980, and 1984. Bush's negatives topped all of theirs.

Bush's favorable rating late that May was 53 percent, while Dukakis was viewed *positively* by a full *70 percent* of likely voters. Worse, Bush was plunging in the polls, while Dukakis was rising.

The Bush operatives presented a strategic campaign plan for his approval.* Bush must go on the offensive, they said, stress the powerful peace and prosperity themes that worked to his advantage, and, by constantly attacking Dukakis as an ultraliberal out of step with mainstream America, drive up his negatives and destroy him. They explained that those negative themes with which Bush could defeat Dukakis had already been found.

Two days before, two separate groups of fifteen New Jersey citi-

*The first account of this meeting was in a page one article by Paul Taylor and David S. Broder in the *Washington Post* on October 28, ten days before the election and four months after the meeting was held.

zens each had assembled for a private session in Paramus, after having been selected by a survey marketing firm retained by the Bush campaign. All the thirty "target" voters were Democrats, all of them had supported Reagan in 1984, and now all were inclined to move back to the Democratic party's presidential choice.

Seated around a fourth-floor conference room table, the Dukakis voters formed what political pollsters called a focus group—voters whose attitudes about candidates and issues could be tested to develop larger campaign themes and strategies, just as market research firms tested new products for public acceptance. A moderator led them through a previously selected set of carefully chosen topics culled from material the Bush people had been storing in their campaign research bank, to be used if Dukakis became the nominee. The subjects were designed to see if certain issues would make the voters think of Dukakis as an extremist, an ultraliberal.

Watching the groups through a two-way mirror, but unknown to the voters, were the three key Bush operatives—Atwater, Ailes, and Teeter. They eagerly assessed reactions, both oral and visual, that these voters gave to their chosen set of "issue" statements.

The voters that day in May were told these things about Michael Dukakis and asked what they thought about them: that as governor of Massachusetts, Dukakis had vetoed a bill passed by the state legislature requiring teachers to lead students in the Pledge of Allegiance;* that he had called himself a "card-carrying member of the ACLU," the American Civil Liberties Union; that through a furlough program for Massachusetts prisoners that he approved, a black murder convict named Willie Horton, sentenced to life without parole, had raped and stabbed a Maryland woman while on a weekend furlough from a Massachusetts jail; and that Dukakis opposed the death penalty for criminals.

After hearing that description of Dukakis's record, half of these thirty pro-Dukakis voters said they had changed their minds about him as a presidential candidate.

Months before the candidates were picked and the actual campaign began, Atwater & Co. had found their negative attack themes.

*This had occurred eleven years before, in 1977, but was treated throughout the campaign as a recent event.

If they could turn around New Jersey voters this way, Atwater reasoned, think what they could accomplish with such themes in other, more conservative parts of the country. "I realized right then," Atwater told Paul Taylor and David S. Broder of the *Washington Post,* "That we had the wherewithal to win . . . and that the sky was the limit on Dukakis's negatives."

Sinking in all the polls, written off by many of the experts, George Bush approved the campaign strategy presented to him that Memorial Day in Maine.

The negative campaign was hardly new. In the seemingly more innocent era of torchlight parades, political picnics, and stump speeches, dirty practices ranging from vote buying to ballot stuffing and false charges were commonplace. In the modern era, voters had been exposed to repeated examples of falsehoods and sowing of fear and division.

In the fifties Republicans exploited fear of communism, concern over crime, and frustration with the war in Korea to wrest back control of the White House. In 1960 the Kennedy campaign falsely accused the Republican administration of having left the nation in a weakened state militarily by having permitted a "missile gap" to develop between the United States and the Soviet Union. Four years later Lyndon Johnson's presidential campaign portrayed Johnson as the peacemaker while depicting Barry Goldwater as a reckless warmonger who would lead America into open conflict in Vietnam. The Johnson campaign's single most powerful TV commercial showed a young girl innocently reaching to pluck a daisy from a field of flowers against the sound of a countdown that ended in a nuclear explosion. Nixon's winning campaign of 1968 turned racial fears and prejudices to his advantage by employing "crime in the streets" rhetoric and appealing to "silent majorities" of whites angered by and fearful of race riots and civil rights marches.

The '68 campaign saw advertising techniques melded effectively into the negative approaches. That year Joe McGinniss wrote a best-selling book about the naked merchandising of the Nixon campaign, *The Selling of the President.* His theme became commonplace in much of the reporting, commentary, and books written about succeeding presidential races.

Television created unexcelled political opportunities for the new professional campaign consultants and their cynical anything-goes approach. These electronic media manipulators were expert at delivering the most effective political message to the widest possible audience—an audience unimaginable to earlier political practitioners, for it reached into virtually every dwelling in the land. Political consultants packaged their candidates for the cameras and crafted the most compelling message. They devised "attack" strategies that enabled them, as Atwater explained, to drive up opponents' negatives and crush them. The prevailing standard was to do whatever was necessary to win. Increasingly, that meant negative campaigning.

The campaign of 1988 degenerated into a battle of "sound-bite scenarios." Deliberate distortion was employed. Everything was aimed at gaining the 15-second lead spot on the evening network newscasts. In fact, even that minimal time allotted for a news sound bite on prime-time network TV newscasts had shrunk appreciably in the '88 presidential campaign. During the Reagan reelection campaign four years before, the average length of a television news sound bite had been 14.8 seconds. In '88, according to some studies, it had dropped to only 9 seconds—enough to convey a quick slogan from a candidate, as George Bush's near-daily repetition of "Read my lips: No new taxes" or his desire to achieve "a kinder, gentler America," but little else.

In his campaign appearances, Bush stuck to the strategy that his advisers had proposed. He made the Pledge of Allegiance the symbolic centerpiece of his campaign, contrasting his support with Dukakis's veto of legislation requiring students to recite it eleven years before. He recited the Pledge constantly and visited a factory where American flags were made. By figuratively wrapping himself in the flag, he injected the divisive issue of patriotism squarely into the campaign.

Coupled with this daily rendition was his charge that Dukakis was a "card-carrying member of the ACLU"* or an ultraliberal out of the mainstream of American values—another Atwater theme.

*In North Carolina a number of voters said they believed Dukakis was a Communist after seeing Bush TV commercials naming him as a member of the ACLU with a close-up of a card reading: "ACLU, American Communist Labor Union."

This, despite the fact that the American Civil Liberties Union had a long and honorable bipartisan tradition of upholding basic American constitutional rights and values. Again and again Bush attacked Dukakis as a liberal, turning "liberal" and "liberalism" into pejorative terms; they stood for alien, and therefore dangerous, ideas and values. By such claims and such emotional appeals to flag and country and conservatism, Bush in effect asked the American people to believe that he represented true patriotism while his opponent and the Democrats represented unpatriotic, un-American values.

Along with flags, he hammered Dukakis on another potent theme: that the Democrat was soft on crime and criminals. Bush embraced the death penalty, contrasting Dukakis's opposition to it, and pledged to give drug kingpins swift execution. He would show criminals no quarter.

His most powerful assault into this emotional area was over the prison furlough question and the case of the convict Willie Horton. Night after night Americans saw fearsome television commercials attacking the prison furlough program and Dukakis's support of it. Shot in ominous black-and-white instead of color, these commercials crafted by Roger Ailes showed a stream of prisoners entering and leaving jail through a rapidly revolving door. Dangerous men were on the loose and headed right toward you, the pictures implied, a point explicitly reinforced by the stark words superimposed over the screen. Hundreds of such prisoners had escaped, the words informed viewers, and "Many are still at large."

The Horton case was the other side of the flag issue, the dark and dangerous side. For in depicting Willie Horton as a symbol of Dukakis's alleged softness on crime, the Bush campaign fomented racial fears for political purposes and appealed to the worst elements of the American character. Campaign commercials directly linked Horton, the black murderer who raped a white woman, with Dukakis. So did campaign literature distributed under local, and sometimes national, GOP auspices.

On the day after the Republican National Convention ended in New Orleans, for instance, a young GOP operative walked up and down the aisle of a plane heading back to Washington, distributing small yellow cards to passengers. On the front of the card, alongside a drawing of a man flying from an open case like the picture in a

Monopoly game, was a slogan printed in bold letters: "GET OUT OF JAIL, FREE."* Underneath, the card read: "Compliments of Michael Dukakis. Distributed by College Republican National Committee."†

The back of the card contained the following political message: "Michael Dukakis's furlough plan allowed convicted murderers to take a weekend leave from prison. One, Willie Horton, left and never came back. He viciously raped and beat a woman while her fiance was forced to helplessly listen to her screams.

"This is only one example of many. In the last several years, Mike Dukakis has furloughed more than one murderer per day.

"Mike Dukakis is the killer's best friend, and the decent, honest citizens' worst enemy."

As the campaign progressed, similar literature turned up around the country. In Illinois the executive director of the State Republican Central Committee distributed campaign material that said Dukakis "basically sympathizes with criminals, sides with the criminals, bends over backwards to protect their rights instead of the victims." In Maryland the state GOP distributed pamphlets with pictures of Willie Horton alongside a smiling Dukakis. Television commercials showing Horton and Dukakis side by side also were run.

The use of Willie Horton, furloughed black murderer, was the single most powerful political device of the campaign. That its implicit message about Dukakis was as false as its latent appeal was racially polarizing was a point of no consequence to the Bush operatives. They knew that as governor Michael Dukakis personally had nothing to do with letting Horton out on a weekend pass. They knew, too, that Dukakis was not even responsible for setting up the furlough program in his state; the Massachusetts furlough program had been established by Dukakis's Republican gubernatorial predecessor, and it was only one of many in existence in other states, including California, where it was used during Reagan's governorship. They knew only that the tactic worked, and they continued to use it.

Another Bush commercial that accomplished the Atwater-Ailes

*I was handed this card by a young Republican operative on the plane back to Washington.

†Atwater headed this same Republican National Committee unit when George Bush was party chairman in the early 1970s.

team goal of driving up Dukakis's negatives was equally false and equally effective.

Viewers saw disgusting scenes of pollution fouling Boston Harbor. One scene showed clearly contaminated water with a sign saying: DANGER/RADIATION HAZARD/NO SWIMMING. That picture had nothing to do with Boston Harbor or Dukakis; it was taken at an abandoned New England nuclear submarine repair yard and used in the commercial to depict, falsely, Boston Harbor. Viewers of that regularly repeated commercial also saw Bush, who had made a widely publicized tour of the harbor (a sound bite winner that led evening TV network newscasts) attacking Dukakis's environmental record as governor. The commercial accused Dukakis of responsibility for failing to take action to stop Boston Harbor pollution. If he couldn't clean up the mess in his own capital city, how could he claim to be an effective environmentalist—and who was he to criticize the environmental record of the Reagan-Bush administration?

As with the Willie Horton case, this presentation was a deliberate distortion of the truth. If anything, Dukakis deserved praise for acting to resolve long-standing problems that were not of his making. At the end of 1978 Massachusetts officials in charge of the regional sewage system—not Dukakis—had applied to the U.S. Environmental Protection Agency for a waiver from federally imposed water treatment requirements mandated by the Clean Water Act. The waiver request was found to be reasonable by the court-appointed special master in complicated Massachusetts Superior Court litigation over Boston Harbor pollution, especially since a number of experts had testified such treatment was ill advised for Boston Harbor. It produced sludge; there were better ways to proceed.

During the presidential campaign Dukakis was accused of failing to see that Massachusetts obtained its fair share of federal funding for water pollution control from Washington. But as the special master in the case, Professor Charles M. Haar of the Harvard Law School, wrote in a *New York Times* article shortly before the election to rebut what he called "a damaging distortion" by Bush of Dukakis's environmental record, "The stern truth is that federal grant money under the Clean Water Act has been reduced to a trickle; funds have been halved for water treatment plants and the EPA's budget for water pollution control has been cut by as much as 43 percent. Moreover, the present administration led the fight that defeated Congressional efforts to appropriate money for cleaning up Boston Harbor. They have taken the bat away and now blame the player for not making a hit."

Furthermore, he said, Dukakis was the "unsung hero" in the affair. "Governor Dukakis was able to marshal the diverse interests—industry, environmentalists, a hesitant and skeptical state legislature, private funding sources—to shape an effective policy," Haar wrote, adding: "This is the reality—not the photogenic boatride or a hasty sound bite on TV."

However true, the other reality was that in the battle of sound bites and negative TV campaign commercials false symbols mattered more than complex, if accurate, substance.

Dukakis's failure to respond to these attacks and connect personally with voters by offering a credible message of his own completed the cycle. Until the final days of his campaign Dukakis remained above the fray, a distant, aloof figure who seemed disinclined to fight for what he believed. Long before the end, even some who had been strongly for him concluded that he lacked the essential qualities of strength, decisiveness, and vision that one wanted in a president. He permitted the Atwater negative campaign strategy to dominate the political debate and define him as a candidate. "Atwater was made for Michael Dukakis, and vice versa," observed William Carrick, a South Carolina contemporary and longtime political opponent of Atwater's, who had been Richard Gephardt's presidential campaign manager earlier in 1988. "Everything he is Dukakis is not, and vice versa. Lee was born to take Dukakis on. Dukakis was too good to be true."

Edward Kennedy pronounced the final assessment on the reasons for the failure of Michael Dukakis and his campaign. Marshall McLuhan's television age notion that the medium was the message wasn't true, he said. TV image makers notwithstanding, in American politics substance, not mere skill, remained the "the driving force of our public life." And it was here that Dukakis failed. Kennedy said he rejected the idea that the Democrats lost because of Willie Horton and the Pledge of Allegiance. To him, "those issues defined the contest primarily because there was no compelling Democratic message." He went on to rebuke Dukakis's convention speech, in which he had said that the presidential campaign of 1988 was about competence, not ideology: "Competence was not enough. Ideology—which is about ideas—was missing, and our opponents filled the gap with appeals to fear, only lightly sprinkled with the kinder, gentler seasons of . . . Bush's perorations. Or to put it another way: because we failed to gain the high road of ideas, the Republicans could run on the low road and win."*

Daily journalism is reactive by nature. It responds to and is limited by the ebb and flow of events in the daily news cycle. With notable exceptions, it is better at reporting what has just happened—what charges and countercharges have been made, who's up and who's down in the latest daily tracking poll commissioned by the press itself—than in explaining complicated issues or setting events in larger context. Television, with its time constraints and visual orientation, is particularly limited in this respect. But both electronic and print media have special difficulty in dealing with negative campaign tactics in the television age.

Journalistic form, admirable in its own right, to be objective, balanced, and fair, to give both sides equal time, runs into problems when confronted with the kinds of distortion practiced by the electronic media manipulators. Political journalism, in particular, operates in a climate that nourishes closeness between the campaign consultants and managers and those who report on their campaigns. Together, they exchange intelligence, share and rely upon excessive use of polls to tell the story of how the campaign is progressing—not only who's ahead but what issues are working and why. This leads to a natural symbiosis between the two. By 1988 their relationship had become even closer and more complicated.

Old lines separating political operatives and the press had crumbled. Unlike the past, when for the most part journalists rose through their own profession to become leading columnists, commentators, and editors, increasing numbers of the most influential members of the press achieved their positions through political, not journalistic, backgrounds. For such as Bill Moyers, George Will, William Safire,

*Kennedy's assessment was from his Chubb Fellowship lecture at Yale University, entitled "Politics and the Power of Ideas," delivered after the campaign on March 6, 1989.

Charles Krauthammer, and David Gergen, to pick distinguished examples, the path to journalistic eminence was through their political connections and work as advisers, press secretaries, speech writers, and strategists. Increasingly, too, campaign consultants whose candidates were defeated were hired as network consultants or commentators, often with dual media outlets through syndicated newspaper columns. It was not uncommon, either, for network news bureau chiefs to come directly from the world of politics without prior journalistic backgrounds.*

It was not that these people lacked talent and integrity. Some (notably Moyers, Safire, and Will) became among American journalism's brightest ornaments. Neither was it a case of the press's becoming a captive of the consultants, part of a conspiracy to manipulate the public for political purposes. Nor had political reporting in general become less critical and more unsophisticated. In 1988 major news organizations devoted enormous resources to go beyond the contrived staging of the campaign, to report on deeper public attitudes about leading issues, and to present well-researched portraits of the candidates and their principal advisers. In these important areas in the '88 campaign, journalistic performance had probably never been better. But increasingly in the era of electronic communications and blurring of roles between press and political operatives, the press also tended to celebrate the role of those master strategists who devised the tactics, plotted the moves, approved the commercials, and charted the course of the winning campaigns.

As Anthony Lewis of the *New York Times* later said, the press by 1988 had become ever more fascinated with the *process* of the modern

*My colleague David S. Broder in a widely noted National Press Club speech three weeks after the election, warned of the danger of "subversion by seduction" caused by this blurring of lines between journalism and politics and creating "a new hybrid creature, an androgynous blending of politician/journalist called The Washington Insider. One day, he or she is a public official or political operative; the next, a journalist or television commentator. . . . We all know them. The journalists who go into government and become State Department or White House officials, and then came back as editors or columnists. Or the editors who become ambassadors and ambassadors who do columns. Or managers of presidential campaigns who turn up as television analysts of their successors' tactics. The columnists who coach their favorite candidates and mobilize campaigns to purge the Senate of people who vote against their favorite Supreme Court nominees. Or the White House spiritual advisers who turn up next as moderators, if that is the word, of political talk shows where the meek not only do not inherit the earth, they are never heard on the air."

campaign, and coverage focused increasingly on process instead of *substance* and values:

> We celebrated Roger Ailes for his craft as a maker of television ads that created a picture of Michael Dukakis as a friend of murderers and rapists. There were lots of stories about the superiority of the technicians on that side: value-free stories. One newspaper analyst even wrote a piece arguing that the inferior quality of Governor Dukakis's television ads had "disturbing implications about Dukakis's leadership."
>
> I wonder how Thomas Jefferson, an introspective man, would rate as a political leader by that standard? Perhaps our democracy has been so corrupted by technology that a sensitive person, a Jefferson, can no longer hope to lead it. That may be. But I do not think the press should be cheering the corrupters for their efficiency. I say all that not out of concern for Michael Dukakis, who should have replied to the smears long before he did. My concern is for our business. There were times in this campaign when we looked like theater critics—critics interested only in the artfulness of the scenery, not in the message of the play.*

Another problem influenced public attitudes during the campaign. By staging events for the cameras, making strong political attacks, and leveling controversial charges close to network deadline times, the campaign managers sought to dominate daily network newscasts and put the opponent on the defensive. The Bush people also successfully employed the tactic of not having press conferences and keeping their candidate removed from the media. The combination of these tactics produced political unaccountability beyond even the old Rose Garden strategy, in which a president campaigned away from the Oval Office only in a series of small appearances and took no questions from reporters. Bush largely got away with it for two reasons: Dukakis failed to rebut the charges and launch his own attacks immediately, and the media, notably television, were too often willing accomplices in a policy of unaccountability.

In researching his book about the role of the media in the Reagan presidency, *On Bended Knee,* author Mark Hertsgaard cites a reveal-

*From the annual Frank E. Gannett Lecture that Lewis delivered in Washington on November 28, 1988.

ing interview with Jeff Gralnick, executive producer of ABC's "World News Tonight." Gralnick was asked how he, as a news executive responsible for deciding which stories appeared on the air, responded to administration efforts to restrict journalists' access to Reagan. According to Hertsgaard, he answered: "It's not my job to respond to it. . . . It's not my position to say, 'For shame, public agency.' It's my job to take the news as they choose to give it to us and then, in the amount of time that's available, put it in the context of the day or that particular story."

The shame was the media's for failing to label as false what was false and in conveying half-truths often uncritically. Too often the media permitted themselves to be used as pawns by cynical political consultants.

Even when the media *were* exemplary in their dealings with distortion, there were additional difficulties. One that figured significantly in the '88 campaign involved the old problem of how to deal with rumors. In the interim between the two national political conventions that summer, rumors about Dukakis began to circulate throughout the country.* Virtually every national political reporter heard them. None could be substantiated; therefore, none was reported. One of the most widely circulated rumors was that Dukakis had twice undergone psychiatric treatment for depression—first, after the death of his older brother in a car accident in 1973 and five years later, when he was defeated for a second term as Massachusetts governor. Then, on August 2, these rumors were discussed at a presidential news conference and could no longer be ignored.

At that time, two weeks after he became the Democratic nominee, Dukakis had not released his full medical records. That day in Washington a representative of Lyndon H. LaRouche, a political extremist, asked Reagan during a news conference about Dukakis's fitness to be president. How could Dukakis be "fit to govern," Rea-

*One day then, for example, I received two calls from prominent people whom I knew well on Wall Street and who had no connection with each other. Each wanted to know whether the stories they had just heard about Dukakis were true. One was that Dukakis had murdered his brother, who had been killed in a car crash, and the other was that Dukakis was a homosexual. Each man said they had heard these stories from political people they had reason to believe. It was in this same time period that rumors were circulated that Dukakis's wife, Kitty, had participated in a flag-burning protest during the Vietnam War demonstrations. All these were false, and all widely disseminated.

gan was asked, if the governor didn't release his medical records?

"Look, I'm not going to pick on an invalid," Reagan replied.

Though he later said he intended the remark as a "joke," Reagan's televised conference comment lent credence to the rumors about Dukakis's mental health and stability.

On the network news broadcast that night CBS correspondent Bruce Morton showed a better way to report rumors. "This story is about a rumor," Morton began his report after the Reagan press room statement. He labeled it an unsubstantiated rumor and said flatly that Reagan administration officials had attempted to peddle the story to CBS. Morton thus performed two important journalistic services: He let the public know the falsity of serious allegations and identified the source of them. The problem, of course, was that the rumor had surfaced, had been given widest possible public distribution, and would be certain to have an afterlife. Subsequently, Dukakis's physician of seventeen years made public a medical report saying the candidate never sought or received psychiatric counseling and "has had no psychological symptoms, complaints or treatments." Damage, however, had been done. In a matter of days Dukakis dropped eight points in the polls.

By late October the Gallup poll reported a "stunning turnaround" from its presidential campaign surveys taken in the spring. Now Dukakis carried the burden of overwhelmingly negative opinions from voters. His unfavorable rating had more than doubled, rising from 20 to 43 percent and putting him over Atwater's terminal standard for a candidate. In the same period Dukakis's favorable rating had sunk from 70 to 20 percent. Bush was the beneficiary of this remarkable swing. His negatives had dropped from 40 to 35 points, while his positives had risen by six points to 59.

On election day, November 8, George Bush carried forty of fifty states with nearly 54 percent of the votes cast. Instead of a great surge of voters to the polls, along the lines of the century's highest presidential turnout figures in 1960, only 50 percent of eligible voters chose to exercise their franchise. The voter turnout was the lowest since Calvin Coolidge was elected in 1924, succeeding in his own right Warren G. Harding.

BOOK FOUR

AMERICA JAN. 20, 1989

CHAPTER 29

CAPITAL OF SUCCESS

Larry Stone was mayor of Sunnyvale again. In between his two terms that began and ended with the decade, Stone's own real estate and investment business had flourished, yet he found himself troubled.

"I think back when you were here in 1980 and this was a thrilling place to be," he said, "and it was almost like the gold rush. We talked about how this place was recession-proof. It had nonpolluting industry. It was going to go on forever. This was *the* golden egg. And when Ronald Reagan repeated in 1984 what he had said in the 1980 campaign—'Are you better off today or not?'—I remember screaming at the television set: 'You bet your ass I am.' "

He paused. "I'm better off today than I was in 1980, but I don't feel better. I don't feel that the future is as secure as I did then. This place has changed. We've got a lot more problems today that we didn't know about then. We *do* go through recessions. We *do* pollute the ground. We *do* do all these types of things that we didn't think we did and that make this a much more complex area. It isn't as easy as I thought it was in 1980 and I was hoping it was in 1984. So while I feel better about where *I* am, I'm not sure I feel better about the area. The learning curve is so fast out here. This isn't a Detroit, where it takes you forty years to deteriorate. It could go very very fast here, and we're setting ourselves up for a lot of it."

In Silicon Valley 1989 began with sales down and growth projections unfavorable in the semiconductor industry, makers of the silicon microchips that were the building blocks (or brains) of modern computers. Already a new wave of layoffs swept the valley in the wake of industry losses. The last downturn, four years before, had forced U.S. chip makers to lay off thirty thousand employees as their industry ran up two billion dollars in losses. High tech electronic industrial complexes that had sprung up almost overnight throughout Sunnyvale and the valley sat empty, their production lines stilled.

To those like Larry Stone who remembered the glory days when the valley between San Francisco and San Jose was the envy of the world as the place where millionaires were made overnight, the contrast was acute. In the early eighties Silicon Valley growth was so great and workers were so scarce that firms doled out free trips to the tropics as incentives to keep employees from defecting to other high tech companies. The last recession was the second for the valley in the eighties. The first, beginning in 1982, had paralleled the national downturn. But the second, beginning in 1984 and lasting through 1985, was prompted by a more disturbing development: the increasing intensity of international competition, especially from Japan.

Figures released around George Bush's inaugural day showed a significant change in America's competitive high tech position worldwide in areas ranging from military technology to consumer electronics. Japan, in just a decade, had overtaken and begun to solidify its dominance of the semiconductor industry. Of the world's ten top chip manufacturers, now six were Japanese, and only three American. Ten years before, the United States controlled 55 percent of the world market. By 1988 its position had sunk to 37 percent. Increasingly U.S. commercial and military manufacturers were dependent on overseas suppliers for key parts. Ominously, the U.S. share of the world's electronics production had dropped dramatically while Japan's share rose from 21.3 to 27.1 percent and Western Europe's increased from 23.5 to 26.4 percent. Latest trade figures showed significant increases as well in Hong Kong, Singapore, Korea, and Taiwan.

Loss of world market share was not the only reason for concern in Silicon Valley. In the eighties the valley benefited enormously from the other side of high tech industrial production, defense. Sunnyvale and Silicon Valley were loaded with defense firms that did highly classified contract work for the federal government, building high tech systems for satellites and missiles and for naval vessels, aircraft, and land vehicles.

These firms had profited from the virtual blank-check expenditures for "Star Wars" research and new space age weapons systems during the Reagan era. Now, as power again shifted in Washington, it was obvious that the day of unlimited defense spending was over. Constraints imposed by the federal budget deficits, coupled with rising demands for new nondefense domestic spending, meant that defense no longer could expect to be as dominant. Firms were pulling in, anticipating slowdowns and cutbacks in government contracts. Wall Street, which had looked so favorably on the hot new high tech growth stocks, no longer judged Silicon Valley and its spectacularly successful start-up electronics firms to be such a surefire investment. Besides, the mergers and acquisitions and take-over craze had also cut into the long-term viability of some of Silicon Valley's companies, leaving their futures less certain.

Other problems had been created. Production lines that first gave the valley its preeminence were long gone. Factory jobs had moved either "offshore," where lower-paid labor provided the work, or, for the same reason, to such new high tech centers as Austin, Texas, Phoenix, Arizona, and Boise, Idaho, where the labor, land, and other living costs were still relatively low compared with California. Left in Silicon Valley at the end of the eighties was a place for the most expensive side of high tech: for the brain trust of the electronics and computer industry, for research and development, and for marketing. Sunnyvale had become a place for only the most successful. Houses that at the end of the seventies had sold for one hundred thousand dollars now went for four hundred thousand—and still there were more buyers than sellers.

A flood of new immigration had entered the valley. Mainly Asian, many from Hong Kong, these were not the impoverished refugees who had sought entry to America in the past few decades but wealthy people from the Pacific Rim looking for a secure place to invest their money. To them Silicon Valley prices seemed cheap. Many paid hundreds of thousands in cash for houses, driving prices even higher. When a local school district decided to raise money for needed educational improvements by subdividing and putting up for sale quarter-acre lots carved out of a vacant school property, the results were startling. Before a spade had been turned on that undeveloped land, six-hundred-thousand-dollar bids had come in, and some of those lots were sold for that much or more—in cash!

Beyond economic and sociological changes, Silicon Valley's vital high tech industries faced a more competitive world. The contest intensified in pace with the ever-greater diversity among companies. Fifteen years earlier an IBM might have had fifteen competitors; by the end of the eighties it had more than two thousand. Technology had become widely accessible. In any market, businesses found themselves up against fifty or a hundred different rivals. "The term I use is that 'other' has become the major market share category," said Regis McKenna, who had become a leading figure among Silicon Valley entrepreneurs in the eighties. "The largest share of the personal computer marketplace is 'other.' Not IBM, not Apple, but 'other.' If you look at other markets, 'other' is the expanding category. So competition has become the watchword of every business today. And of course, that has spread internationally as well. Going into business today means the moment you open your door you're in fierce competition not only with the guy down the street but with the guy across the ocean and on both sides of both oceans."

It was a reunion of sorts. Seated around Larry Stone's living room in Sunnyvale were some of the same people who had gathered in 1980 to talk about their area and its future. Like Stone, each person had done well, but like Stone, each was troubled about the future. One of them put into words what they all felt. "If it is true that nothing happens in America until it happens in California," said Dave Baram, a senior executive with Apple Computer and a statewide leader in education, "then nothing's going to change in America now because California's still in the grip of this no tax, no spend, great contentment period. Until that changes, there will be no change."

There were expressions of agreement around the room. "People have found a reason to rationalize the I've-got-mine-and-everybody-else-forget-it attitude," said Dr. Elliot Lepler, a pediatrician. "We don't want to raise taxes. We don't want to spend money. Everybody wants his mother to have the very best health care and to have somebody else pay for it."

Dave Baram offered another thought. "From my perspective, I see a real quieting of the governmental/political stew that was going on in 1980 and the late seventies," he said. "In part, that's because the Reagan philosophy pervaded and dampened activism. A lot of people just settled back. What's been interesting to me about the eighties is education. California is just woefully underfinancing education. The people of California, when polled, admit that and are willing to spend more on it. Our political leadership has been saying no. No more taxes, no nothing. So we have this incredible stalemate, and it's frustrating. We continue to vote down local bond issues or local tax overrides for education left and right even while we want to spend more."

Nodding her head was Dianne McKenna, who had served a term as mayor of Sunnyvale in the eighties and gone on to become Santa Clara County supervisor. "There are an awful lot of people trying to explain why I've got mine and why I don't have to worry about anybody else—or I shouldn't worry about somebody else," she said. "It goes back to what Dave says about education: People want it, but they don't want to pay for it. It's pervasive."

They were concerned that the quality of life of the valley and the state was diminishing. They were concerned about the lack of leadership necessary to address, and reverse, it. As one of them said, they were concerned that what they saw happening in the valley might be representative of the country at large. "You know," said Larry Stone, "when I moved here in the sixties, Pat Brown was running against Ronald Reagan. Reagan hammered Brown and won. At that moment I think the state of California with all its institutions was better off than it's ever been, before or since. It had the best highway system. It had the best junior college system. The University of California system statewide was outstanding. The criminal justice system was the best in the country. It had the best public school system, and it did nothing but go downhill from that moment. Yet Reagan was able to convince the people of California that Pat Brown, through eight years, had done an atrocious job. In fact, this state was probably better off at that point in time than it had ever been."

In Sunnyvale and Silicon Valley, as in the nation, the gap between the new abundance and new problems had widened. All but the very rich were being priced out of the valley. Service industry people—hotel and restaurant workers, those who provided maintenance services, manned the laundries and sanitation trucks—could no longer afford to live there. Finding replacements for them became more difficult and promised to be more so in years ahead.

At the same time the rapidly expanding Hispanic population in Santa Clara County, which encompassed Sunnyvale and Silicon Valley, experienced new strains and pressures as public services deteriorated and quality of education diminished. Among Hispanic public school students in Santa Clara County, the dropout rate had risen to 50 percent. For them, like blacks in America, those kinds of statistics indicated a bleak future. They were falling farther behind their more privileged contemporaries. Conditions in the public schools made their plight worse.

In California, and across America, minorities, black and Hispanic, were the fastest-growing proportion of the population. But they were also the poorest, least well-educated segment, and generally less able to compete in a technical world. Already, half the public school students in California came from minority groups: black, Hispanic, or Asian. And in Los Angeles six out of ten public school students were from minorities.

Demographic changes also meant that public schools were being forced to pay another kind of price in attempting to maintain standards. As the population aged, a higher proportion of adults had no children in school. There were also more single heads of households, more couples with no children, and more single-parent families. Public schools were composed of expanding minority groups, many of which tended to vote less and were less able to provide adequate funds for education. Because the better-off, mainly white population group that traditionally had offered more support for education politically and financially no longer had many children in public schools, it was not inclined to vote to pay for the education of the poorer minority groups.

This situation promised to grow more severe as the majority of white Californians became a minority by the end of the nineties. In Silicon Valley thoughtful people understood that the very future depended on a strong educational system. The entire society needed strong public services, including a good health system, a good road system, a clean environmental system. But lack of public support placed all these in jeopardy, and even if support was there, the federal budget deficit sharply limited funding for them. Urban America faced new strains as local governments failed to assume the burdens for maintaining necessary levels of service. From roads and highways to schools and hospitals, services were deteriorating. Everyone knew it. The particular tragedy was that the decline hit hardest those who could least afford it.

"I can say from the perspective of a county government that had been dependent on state and federal funding, the haves have gotten better and the have-nots have gotten worse in the eighties," Dianne McKenna said. "That's so whether you're talking about health care, the criminal justice system, the transportation system. All of it has gotten worse for the middle class and on down. For example, I'm responsible for county hospitals, and we're now seeing nationwide thirty-seven million people without health insurance. And those numbers are going up. There is no competition in the health care world for uninsured patients. We're seeing this at all levels, in all of our clinics, in all of our hospitals. The eighties have really shown a dramatic change between people that have and those that don't."

She expressed another kind of problem, involving attitudes, not money. "I'm seeing too much of what I call the disposable society," she said. "That is, if the kids get too tough, you take them; I don't want them. If the parents get too sick, you take them; I don't want them. If the relationship gets too bad, well, dissolve it, and we'll go our own ways. We have moved to that point where we dispose of people the way we disposed of appliances in earlier days. Do you know that eighty-five percent of fathers stop paying child support after two years? Where's the responsibility? Look at people who put parents in nursing homes. We get rid of people real easy in our society."

Silicon Valley's success derived from a combination of talent and willingness to take risks and to invest in the future. New industries that made the valley famous were the result of investments in basic research that created technological breakthroughs ten, twenty, or thirty years later. The Silicon Valley that had emerged as a capital of success in 1980 was created by investments made in the fifties, and historically, government funding had played a major role in developing those new technologies and products. Half of America's research and development money had come from the government and the federal labs; in the sixties it had been as high as 70 percent. But recent years had seen a decline in such research funding.*

The lesson of Silicon Valley at the end of the eighties was that the country was in danger of shortchanging itself. By failing to make long-term investments in basic commercial and university research, instead of in weapons development, it left the nation in a weakened competitive position at a time when other societies were moving forward.

*A National Science Foundation study showed that the amount American companies spent on research and development had increased by 5.5 percent in the first half of the eighties but had declined by more than half in the closing years of the decade. The study attributed the decline to company desires to enhance immediate shareholder value and stock prices at the expense of longer-term basic research investment.

CHAPTER 30

SUNBELT

One night in the midst of the eighties a Houston businessman met a visitor at the airport. "How do you like my car?" he said, opening the front door to a blue Mercedes. After receiving murmured pleasantries in response, the businessman added: "I got it secondhand. They're a glut on the market now. You can get them remarkably cheap."

At the beginning of the decade, while other sections of the country experienced economic distress, Sunbelt businessmen made plans based on a doubling of oil prices. For a time conditions seemed to prove them correct. The price of oil kept rising; many believed it would go beyond its high of forty dollars a barrel, climb on to fifty dollars, and stay there. Millions of feet of new oil holes were drilled on those assumptions. Oil field rigs were being built as fast as possible.

Then, suddenly, the boom turned into a bust. Driven by declining demand and worldwide overproduction of oil (the so-called oil glut), oil prices dropped more than two-thirds in less than a year. Starting in late 1982, oil prices began falling—and kept falling. They sank below the thirty-two-dollar-a-barrel mark and spiraled downward. Down to twelve dollars, and even to eight and five dollars on the spot market, the prices dropped. With production costs running at eighteen to twenty-five dollars a barrel, oil producers found themselves in a desperate situation. Production ground to a halt. Everything tied to the oil business—from manufacture of drill bits to tubular steel, from cement companies to electronics firms, from trucking to shipping—

was affected. Money for drilling all but ceased. Oil rigs were stacked and put out of commission. A ripple effect set in, sweeping across the Gulf Coast states. Unemployment rose. The population boom ended as workers left.

The worst was yet to come. Middle West aside, the rest of the country had recovered from the recession of 1982, but in Texas and the Gulf states the economic slide accelerated.* In the West Texas oil fields around Midland, where oil executives had happily gathered on Ronald Reagan's inaugural day with a cake in the form of the U.S. Capitol and the word "ours" on it, millionaires became paupers overnight.

In 1986 alone, one hundred thousand people lost their jobs in Texas. At more than 10 percent of the work force, Texas's unemployment rate was well above the national average. At that point the Texas real estate market and banking industry suffered a massive crash. Major construction projects were left unfinished. New office buildings, if completed, had more vacant space than tenants. Homes, shopping centers, and malls stood empty. In some areas, real estate prices fell 30 percent. Overnight, it seemed, Houston alone registered an average of three thousand foreclosures per month on homes and businesses. Soon a new inducement was used to lure businesses to Texas: unoccupied buildings and vacant office space, which now could be leased cheaply.

Texas financial institutions had gone on a speculative binge in the eighties, making bad loans to real estate and oil entrepreneurs. The extent of corruption involved was immense. Dozens of financial institutional lenders became targets of one of the largest campaigns against white-collar crime ever mounted by the federal government. Kickbacks on loans made, falsification of net worth statements by banking officials, false appraisals to inflate real estate values, and a conspiracy involving a band of savings and loan owners and execu-

*In a little-noted but significant change, by the Bush inaugural the United States was importing more oil than it produced for the first time in a decade. The rate of energy consumption was steadily rising, and at a greater than expected rate. Diminishing public concern over fuel conservation was cited as the principal reason. Prices were also rising, along with consumption, of copper, aluminum, nickel, zinc, specialty steels, and other metals. All this suggested that the old American tendency to live for the moment continued. The Iraqi invasion of Kuwait, in August 1990, again hammered home the dangers of America's rising dependency on imported oil and the lack of a comprehensive national energy policy.

tives who made multimillion-dollar loans to one another—all were subjects of major criminal investigations. "A lot of money got put into people's pockets and they've rat-holed it somewhere," H. Joe Selby, former chief regulator of the Federal Home Loan Bank of Dallas, told the *New York Times* ten days before the Bush inaugural. "Some of it is in artwork, fancy homes, fancy airplanes, and Rolls-Royces. Some of it went to Rolex watches, lizard shoes, hunting parties, and yachts."

As the oil and real estate markets collapsed, a wave of bankruptcies swept Texas. By some estimates, as much as a hundred billion dollars had been squandered on uncollectible real estate loans. The state's savings and loan institutions foundered. Hundreds of them closed or were emerged, and survivors looked to Washington to bail them out. Early in the decade Texans had boasted that they were financing their own destiny through Texas banks owned by Texans. By decade's end most of the state's major banks were no longer locally owned; outside interests controlled them, and major banking houses were forced out of business. Even as late as 1988, 113 banks closed in Texas. The economic effects of the downturn multiplied and spread to service industries providing food and clothing. Texas's economy hit bottom. Not since the thirties had economic conditions been so dismal.

Of all Americans, Texans had exhibited perhaps the greatest belief in their destiny. Independence, self-reliance, willingness to take on the hardest tasks—this was their legend, and Texans, with good reason (and a good dose of braggadocio), unquestionably believed in it.

Part of that legend was the idea of the "good partner," the notion that Texans took care of their own. But in terms of supporting public services, Texans did not. Social, health, and welfare programs in Texas lagged far behind those of other areas. Some of this stemmed from the old legacy of poverty and exploitation that Texas and the South suffered after the Civil War. But some of it came from deeply ingrained attitudes about the need for individuals to solve their own problems. A familiar contradiction marked the Texan (and, in this respect, American) attitude toward taxes and expenditure of public money: Although Texans railed against big government and Washington interference, they aggressively sought and gladly accepted federal funds. In the New Deal era and beyond, the state had profited from federal spending for public works projects and federal grants that helped create defense, space, and medical research centers. The eighties were marked by a continuing infusion of defense money from Washington into Texas. Yet in the early Reagan years Texas still stood last in the nation in percentage of per capita income spent for education. Though major efforts were made to redress that situation in the eighties, by the time George Bush became president Texas still ranked no better than thirty-third out of the fifty states in percentage of per capita income spent for education. Other public services also ranked far below the national average. The economic downturn thus exacerbated the existing problem caused by low state support for public services.

This meant that citizens in Texas and similar Sunbelt states ended up paying a heavy price for years of neglect. All citizens were affected by a combination of hard times and less federal funds from Washington, but the burden fell most heavily on the poorest and fastest-growing segments of the population. In Texas, as elsewhere, two groups were hit hardest: blacks in the urban centers and Hispanics in the Rio Grande Valley.

Nearly half of America's Hispanics, some ten million people, lived in two states of vital importance to America economically and politically, California and Texas. Between the two of them, those states held 76 of the 270 electoral votes needed to win the presidency. In each, the plight of Hispanics was severe. Texas, with its huge and growing numbers of Hispanics, most of Mexican-American ancestry, provided a case study of what had happened to this group in the decade.

In the Rio Grande Valley, a fertile but impoverished flat stretch of land dotted with mesquite and palms and forming a crescent where the United States and Mexico converge, population growth had been explosive in the last half of the century. From 1950 to 1980 its population had doubled from about one hundred thousand to two hundred thousand. In the eighties it doubled again.

Though earlier decades brought significant progress in reducing poverty, eliminating disease, and providing greater opportunities, by the time Reagan left office there was undeniable evidence that the valley and its growing minority were in worse condition than when his presidency began. "It's like any gains that had been made were frozen as of 1980," said Professor José Hinojosa, chairman of the political science department at Pan American University near the Mexican border and a recognized authority on the status of Hispanics. "The other thing that bothers me is that the gap has grown tremendously, not only here, but nationwide. Figures will prove that major differences can be shown between the upper class and the middle class and the lower class. They will show, too, that part of the middle class is disappearing and slipping into the lower class. The Reagan administration has probably been the most antilabor, anti-middle- and lower-class administration we've had in our history. It has been disastrous for us as far as education is concerned, from kindergarten to graduate education. Many students have been saddled with very large debts and will have to spend the next ten or fifteen years getting out of it. It's a modern version of indentured servitude. That has hurt a lot of our people, especially since education has been the major vehicle for our upward mobility."

Public programs that had been judged successful when Reagan came to power were slashed or eliminated for lack of funds. Where positive results had been achieved in getting people off welfare rolls and onto tax rolls, the situation was reversed. Block grants of federal money that filtered down to the valley through state and local agencies were cut sharply and, in some cases, eliminated entirely. Services to the indigent, the ill, and the infirm were affected. With less money and manpower, clinics in the valley were asked to operate around the clock. At a cancer clinic in McAllen, on the border, director Petra Reyna cited intensifying problems in providing treatment and said bitterly: "We provide treatment for a very high number of medically indigent patients. But we're limited in what we can do because insurance rates are high. It borders on a moral issue. You provide cancer treatment services if the patients have insurance. They have a chance to live. If you don't have insurance, and you're poor, you die. It comes down to that. There's just no money available."

CHAPTER 31

RUSTBELT AND FARMBELT

Along Lake Michigan, twenty-five miles east of Chicago, smoke rose from what was the nation's largest surviving steel mill, the Gary Works of USX, formerly United States Steel. In the early eighties the Gary Works in Indiana symbolized the declining fortunes of America's steel industry and the country's heavy industrial manufacturing base. It was then losing nearly a quarter of a million dollars a year, and hopes for revival were dim.

By George Bush's inaugural day a notable turnaround had occurred, and the Gary Works was cited as a symbol of industrial regeneration and Rustbelt success achieved during the Reagan years. Now these works, which accounted for nearly half of USX's steel production, generated annual profits of more than three hundred million dollars. Nor was this an industrial aberration. Near decade's end, U.S. domestic steel mills were operating at 90 percent of capacity. In the four-year period preceding the inauguration, steel prices had risen by 42 percent. American mills were producing better steel in less time with far fewer people than at the beginning of the Reagan years. From being among the least productive and technologically inefficient, they had become among the most productive mills in the world and ranked among the top in technological proficiency.

All this was evidence that American industrial leaders and their work force had not lost the capacity to respond to adversity, learn lessons from mistakes, and change. At the same time these achievements did not reflect the economic calamity that had befallen the old industrial empire and the once-leading role that steel played in it.

A smaller, more efficient American steel industry had emerged, but one that in no way held its former dominant position and one that faced tougher questions about its long-term competitiveness and survival.

Japanese firms had penetrated the domestic American steel market, and Japan itself made more raw steel than the United States. In one case Japanese acquired a 50 percent interest in the nation's sixth-largest steel producer, National Steel, which in turn provided more than 40 percent of its production to the American auto industry, into which the Japanese also moved aggressively through establishment of Japanese-owned but American-produced automobile factories on American soil.

The disastrous recession of 1982 dealt even heavier blows to the steel industry and the major manufacturing businesses it supplied. Cumulative steel industry losses were staggering, reaching nearly twelve billion dollars in the period from 1982 through 1986 alone. Total steel employment fell by 58 percent. New and better technology notwithstanding, along with the employment decline came a sharp drop in the nation's raw steelmaking capacity: from 154 million tons per year at Reagan's inaugural to 112 million tons by January 1989. Workers fortunate enough to survive in the industry found their wages did not keep pace with inflation. Tens of thousands who lost jobs either headed south and west or stayed in the Rustbelt and settled for "service jobs" paying perhaps a third less than what they had previously earned. For those in their forties or fifties, there were few jobs available at any salary.

On top of this was another concern: that new trade wars could further erode the U.S. position. While steel had been helped by the falling dollar, that was only another signal of America's deteriorating trade position worldwide as the United States fell from world's leading creditor nation to world's leading debtor. Perhaps most troubling for the future was the steel industry's decision to adapt new technology by buying available foreign technology rather than developing its own. Steel essentially had chosen to rely on West German and Japanese technology. In the short term, purchase of this technology was unquestionably helpful by reducing long-term research and development costs. But it also made American industry more dependent on foreign competitors. This threatened to transform basic

American industry into Japanese-American or German-American hybrids.

Decline of America's basic industries—steel, rubber, autos, machine tools—was the price of years of complacency, of inefficient, outmoded labor-management practices, and of stiffer foreign competition that provided the kinds of manufacturing and personal goods Americans increasingly preferred. Nor did economic problems in the Rustbelt region end there. The decline of American agriculture was slower developing, but the crash of the Farmbelt was even more disastrous.

Until the early eighties America's farmers enjoyed a boom that seemed to guarantee ever-rising levels of prosperity. Long years of inflation led to ever-increasing value of farmland and an accompanying speculative fever. As the price of land kept rising, farmers went on a spending spree and plunged more heavily into debt, thanks to easily arranged financing from bankers eager to accommodate them. As a Kansas farm economist later observed, "People became accustomed to inflation being a way of life. They couldn't imagine life without inflation." More and more heavy equipment was bought, more major home and personal purchases were made, more expensive Caribbean and Hawaiian vacations taken, and all by putting up surefire land as collateral and counting on rising land and commodity prices to keep the new debtors ahead. Even if commodity prices fell, farmers were sure that land would never depreciate.

And indeed, this seemed the case. In the seventies midwestern farmland rose from an average price of $193 to $725 an acre. The eighties promised more of the same. Young farmers had no memories of the harshness of the depression, nor did they share their parents' or grandparents' depression-created habit of vowing never to incur debt. Suddenly all that changed, and in ways that even the pessimists could not have foreseen. Both farm prices *and* the value of land began falling, but real interest rates remained historically high. Across the Farmbelt conditions began to resemble the thirties in a rash of bankruptcies, forced auctions, foreclosures, falling land values, lower commodity prices, lack of cash flow, and production surpluses.

In the thirties the farm depression pulled down the rest of the economy. That didn't happen in the eighties for a good reason: America's farm population had dwindled from 25 percent in the thirties to 3 percent in the eighties. In a nation of nearly 250 million people, there were only 2.3 million farms. To put it another way, 700,000 farmers were responsible for producing a majority of the nation's food and fiber. So while the foreclosure rate was not far behind that of the thirties, there were far fewer farmers to start with. Those being forced out were the good farmers, not just the marginal or unproductive ones; there simply weren't any other kinds left.

Farm income, after increasing in the early Reagan years, had been cut in nearly a third by decade's midpoint and was actually lower than it had been in 1970. Not only were farmers earning less than before the boom, but they were now burdened with immense new levels of debt. Only the intervention of the federal government kept this disaster from being worse. By 1986 and 1987 government payments to the Farmbelt had reached record levels and were largely responsible for bolstering the farm economy. Even so, it was then estimated that one in every six farmers was in grave financial straits.

Simultaneous industrial and agricultural decline wrought severe hardship throughout the Middle West. In factory and farm communities, cases of human suffering multiplied, and the Middle West's unemployment rate was twice that of the national average. America's central region became a place apart from the prosperous America of East and West coasts. Funds to provide basic services were scarce, and thousands of jobs had been lost permanently from the area. Young people were moving away, leaving behind an aging population less able to provide for itself. There was talk among social workers that a "new poor" was emerging in the nation's heartland.

These were not the tragic losers of the inner cities, blacks born into a pathology of poverty generations in the making. By contrast, these new poor of the Rustbelt and Farmbelt had been winners, or so they thought. They had made the "right" economic moves, had progressed and become confident that tomorrow would always be better than today. Suddenly their life's hopes were dashed; their once highly paid blue-collar jobs were gone, their farms sold. Many were forced to take jobs paying little more than the minimum wage, without health insurance or other benefits they had counted on. In the Midwest soup kitchens appeared for the first time since the depression.

A mood of painful introspection developed. Factory workers, farmers, and businessmen alike talked of America's place in the world changing; they all were aware that they were linked, as never before, to a new world economy, an economy and world order in which they were no longer the unchallenged masters. Many learned to develop a kind of survivor's instinct, a desire to cling to what they had rather than attempt something new. This was understandable, especially among those who came from the ranks of the labor and farm force and had taken for granted their continuing prosperity. Among many, one such was Bob Hogan, who had spent his life in the steel valley around Youngstown, Ohio.

Hogan was a locomotive engineer, a union president, and a state representative from Ohio's Fifty-second District in Youngstown. In barely a generation Hogan had seen the industrial empire nearly disappear, its blue-collar work force disintegrate, the role of the unions diminish, and shared certainties about the future erode. Looking back, Hogan expressed, in somewhat wistful fashion, how great a change had taken place, and he also offered an insight into why it became increasingly difficult in the eighties for politicians to achieve consensus to deal with the many consequences of change: "I was fourteen when I moved into Girard, which is right along the river, and every night you could hear the whistles of the steel mill and the whistles of the trains, and when I got out of high school, I immediately went to work in the steel mill and I learned to run to those whistles. Five whistles were to call the electrician; two, to start the mill up; one, the mill was down. From there I started working in a factory, and from there on the railroad. And I got involved in the union. Now the union is in a terrible state. It's devastated. . . . So what happens now? What do you give workingmen and women?

"I spent a lot of money on my last political campaign, and it was all TV. When people saw me, they'd say, 'I saw you on TV.' Not what did I say; it was: 'I saw you on TV.' It was like advertising yourself. People were voting for me because they saw me on TV. You get frustrated sometimes because you're not able to explain the way you feel or because people don't know that the bills that you pass really *do* affect their lives. My frustration is we have to be convincing in our argument but we can't go too far because you put 'em to sleep. The American people want to watch TV, and if you can get your message in just after the movie and before the commercial, you've reached their minds. I probably sound very cynical about it. But I mean we really are a media generation."

That world of train and factory whistles would not return. The future lay in different kinds of industries requiring more technical skills and preparation. New technology had altered both the way businesses were conducted and the kinds of businesses that existed.

By the end of the eighties more than 40 percent of all new investments in plant and equipment were for what was called information technology—for such products as computers and copying machines. That rate of investment was double what it had been a decade before. Other countries were outstripping the United States in advanced technologies and in the quality of education required to achieve them. This was true not only among the United States' European and Japanese competitors but even more strikingly among nations not thought to be in a serious competitive position relatively few years earlier.

In 1970, for instance, only 40 percent of South Koreans of high school age were enrolled in school. Twelve years later 82 percent of that age-group were enrolled, and the quality of the education they received was as high as—or higher than—that of comparable U.S. students. Toward the end of the eighties approximately 30,000 Americans were attending foreign universities, but only about 3 percent of them were even studying technical subjects. By contrast, there were then more than 317,000 foreign students in the United States, and of them 180,000 were studying engineering and science.

Looking ahead to the next century, the U.S. Office of Technology Assessment (OTA) raised a challenge and a warning to the older industrial workers of the Rustbelt. The OTA report concluded:

> Change can lead to wrenching dislocation and pain for workers with obsolete skills, for management unable to recognize opportunity, and for communities where traditional businesses have failed. Change can create an America in graceless decline—its living stan-

dards falling behind those of other world powers. This could mean an America less able to ensure the operation of free international markets and less able to ensure the security of the free world. Change can weaken the bargaining position of some groups while strengthening that of others. Change can result in a growing gap between those fortunate enough to have the talents, education, and connections needed to seize emerging opportunities and those forced into narrowly defined, heavily monitored, temporary positions. This latter group could be forced to bear most of the costs of uncertainty.

CHAPTER 32

WALL STREET

Four days before Christmas and a month before the new presidential inaugural, the Wall Street firm of Drexel Burnham Lambert, Inc., agreed to plead guilty to six U.S. felony counts of mail, wire, and securities fraud and pay a record $650 million in fines and restitutions. Terms of the settlement stipulated that Drexel would fire Michael Milken, its junk bond genius, and withhold his 1988 bonus (alone estimated to be $200 million). Although Milken had not then been formally charged, his spectacular relationship with Drexel was over. With him went a large piece of the financial history of the decade and the single most vivid example of the kinds of success that some individuals had achieved in the big deal atmosphere of Wall Street.

Until the settlement plea Drexel and Milken maintained a united front in denying wrongdoing. A key part of the case against Drexel involved charges that the firm had engaged in a secret arrangement with Ivan Boesky to defraud Drexel's clients. Much of the evidence was from Boesky himself, who, though in prison, cooperated with the government in the apparent hope of parole. When charges were first brought against Drexel, the expectation was that Boesky would be the government's star witness against the firm responsible for revolutionizing the way many of those financial deals were made. Now it appeared that Milken, the greatest financial innovator of the times, would face Boesky, the greatest deal maker, in court. Two months later that prospect became more possible when Milken was indicted on ninety-eight instances of fraud, racketeering, and illegal insider stock trading.

The Drexel settlement, with its accompanying reams of documented evidence, provided, as Steve Coll and David A. Vise noted in the *Washington Post,* the most extensive portrait of widespread corruption operating at the heart of the U.S. financial markets since Joseph P. Kennedy's famous Securities and Exchange Commission investigation in the early New Deal years had exposed market manipulation that contributed to the stock market crash of '29.

In Congress there was talk about instituting new regulations and imposing tougher penalties for criminal behavior on Wall Street. Business and law schools offered new courses on ethics. "Students coming out of law school today are substantially more aware of nuances of ethical issues than I was twenty years ago," Professor Stephen Gillers of New York University Law School told Sarah Bartlett of the *New York Times.* "That's a first step."

Prodded by public disgust with the greed that permeated financial markets (and highlighted by such popular films as *Wall Street* depicting anything-goes practices), Wall Street firms reexamined personnel policies and ethical codes. Like the Iran-contra affair, belated official response to the scandal, however inconclusive, showed that there was a price to pay for skirting the rules—even if it was limited to defending oneself at heavy expense amid unwelcome publicity. Also like Iran-contra, and Watergate earlier, memory of the price of scandal was likely to induce a self-policing atmosphere on Wall Street, at least for a time. Already there was talk of a "post-Boesky morality."

However welcome some of these developments, they more resembled treatment of symptoms rather than causes. Even as the Drexel case possibly checked future insider trading scandals, the business methods Drexel employed continued unabated. The leverage buyout craze reached new levels. One great corporation after another was swallowed up by raiders who acquired and dismantled them through immense amounts of debt—raised, to large extent, by the same kinds of junk bond financing that Milken and Drexel had pioneered.

From 1981 through 1988, the volume of leveraged buyouts rose from $3.1 billion to $67.4 billion a year. Airlines, clothing chains, tobacco companies, oil corporations, media concerns, publishing houses—all were acquired for higher and higher prices. In the bidding wars that ensued, take-over targets saw their stock prices suddenly double. Billion-dollar corporations that seemed impervious to control by raiders found themselves overtaken and then dismantled as winners slashed costs and sold off large parts of newly acquired business to raise cash to make interest payments on the huge debt level incurred to gain their prize.

Prices paid for these corporate giants escalated throughout 1988 and culminated in the greatest of all buyouts, the take-over of RJR Nabisco. Itself the product of a huge merger between corporate giants, RJR Nabisco was acquired by Kohlberg Kravis Roberts & Company for a price of nearly twenty-five billion dollars. At that point it was the largest corporate transaction in financial history.

To reach that pinnacle, and along the way become a billionaire, Henry Kravis demonstrated how the take-over game was played. Starting as a young financier in the late seventies and expanding his tactics rapidly in the eighties, Kravis became rich beyond dreams by borrowing, buying, and dismantling corporations. In 1984 his firm accomplished the first billion-dollar buyout—of Wometco Enterprises. Two years later it established a record by borrowing $5.8 billion to acquire Beatrice Foods for a price of $6.2 billion. Using the same technique of borrowed money, it acquired, among others, Safeway Stores for $4.1 billion, Owens-Illinois for $3.7 billion, Jim Walter for $2.4 billion, and, finally, in late 1988, the capstone buyout of RJR Nabisco. The multiplicity of such deals and the debt they incurred were becoming a major issue in Congress and the press, an issue that gained greater urgency because it coincided with new public awareness of the danger facing the nation's savings and loan institutions.

Suddenly the public became aware that it had a financial crisis on its hands—and aware, too, that taxpayers would likely be forced to pay the price for bailing out S&Ls that had, to large measure, created their own problems through bad management and corruption. By the new year of 1989 government regulators reported that hundreds more thrift institutions were in danger of bankruptcy. Total losses were estimated at a billion dollars a month.

The S&L debacle provided a case study of a system gone awry and the eighties' most vivid example of how the public repeatedly was let down by those charged with seeing that the institutions dealing with the public were run honestly and efficiently. For month after month, year after year, the S&L situation festered. When confronted with evidence of wrongdoing, executive branch regulators and congressional overseers of the financial institutions involved chose not to sound the alarm. Instead, the watchdogs looked the other way. So did the great mass of the press that should have been reporting on it but did not. Nor did the gathering S&L crisis receive public airing during the 1988 presidential campaign. In the absence of scrutiny, and flourishing amid the deregulated, insider atmosphere of the times, the S&L situation mushroomed into the single worst financial scandal in U.S. history—worst in the losses to the federal Treasury and the taxpayers, worst in numbers of institutions involved, worst in the extent of fraud uncovered. In their final White House annual report (the *1990 Economic Report of the President*) issued days before the inauguration, Reagan's own economists warned that the public would have to pay for much of the cost of saving the S&L industry. This report implicitly criticized such Reagan era deregulatory actions as removing ceilings on interest that S&Ls could pay depositors and congressional action raising the federal insurance limit to one hundred thousand dollars per person. It also complained about ineffectual regulatory policies from officials who had themselves been appointed by the Reagan administration. "The irony is that Federal Government policies have led to this debacle," the report concluded, reinforcing the administration's responsibility for these problems without addressing or assigning blame for them. The Reagan economists estimated that the S&L bailout price might be as high as fifty billion dollars—another grievous misjudgment, for the cost would be in the *hundreds* of billions.*

Public awareness of S&L problems, with costs to be borne by the public Treasury for decades, raised concern that one day the public

*By April 1990 this figure had soared to half a *trillion* dollars. Testifying before Congress, the head of the General Accounting Office said the taxpayer bailout would be "bigger than all the bailouts of New York City, Chrysler, and Lockheed put together" and far exceed the cost of the Marshall Plan, which rebuilt Europe after World War II. He also said taxpayer S&L payments would greatly raise the budget deficit and take thirty-three years to complete. Five months later the estimated S&L cost had doubled again to one trillion dollars. Some experts reckoned the overall cost to be twice as much as the entire Vietnam War in comparable dollars and nearly four times that of the Korean War!

would also be required to bail out some of the huge new leveraged buyout (LBO) corporations whose heavy debts could throw them into bankruptcy during a recession. This long had been a worry, and countless warnings had been issued about it. A belated national debate about the LBO situation had begun among leading financiers as Bush became president.

Wall Street's respected Henry Kaufman wrote in the *Washington Post* on New Year's Day:

> We are rapidly evolving into the kind of free-enterprise system that speaks loudly in public of market discipline but whispers in the closet that the government will always bail people out if anything really nasty happens. That is not the kind of system we ought to have. But it is the kind of system we will end up with unless Congress and President-elect Bush promptly throw some cold water on the hot game of mergers, acquisitions and leveraged buyouts. As we enter the new year, the M&A and LBO mania has become so fevered that each week of delay can add new threats to the health of U.S. corporations, financial markets, and the federal Treasury.*

Others disagreed. Leveraged buyouts were actually good for American business, they argued, because they transformed inefficient conglomerates into efficient entities by removing layers of bureaucracy and uncompetitive internal corporate divisions. Thus, they became more productive and competitive, not less.

That debate would be resolved only when it became known how these leveraged buyout firms fared during recessionary times such as 1982, when the greatest number of bankruptcies since the depression had occurred. There was no doubt, however, that leveraged buyout deals and their accumulation of long-term corporate debt already had negative impact on one critical aspect of U.S. competitiveness: basic industrial research.

In streamlining, or "restructuring," corporate operations after a

*By late August 1989 the number of defaults of debt-laden leveraged buyout companies was reported to be the greatest ever. Most troubling to financial analysts was that these defaults were occurring during a surging stock market and a stable economy. At the same time defaults on junk bonds for the first half of the year were estimated to be $3.2 billion, more than double a year before. In an ironic twist, the same investment banks whose funds had arranged LBOs now sought to profit in reverse by forming "turnaround departments" to rescue companies in danger of bankruptcy because of their excess debt.

leveraged buyout, new managements needed to raise capital immediately to pay their big debts. To do this, they sold or eliminated entire divisions. Among the first to be cut were industrial research laboratories producing basic corporate research and development for the future. They produced no current income, so they went.

Thus, when General Electric took over RCA, it shocked veteran employees by "donating" RCA's venerable Sarnoff Labs to a nonprofit group, eliminating three hundred positions. It was a step taken "to create a more competitive cost structure," according to a GE announcement. When the Borg-Warner Corporation experienced an LBO, it decentralized its research and development functions and closed its central lab in Des Plaines, Illinois. When the B. F. Goodrich Company became a chemical and aerospace producer after an LBO, its industrial rubber research lab, founded in 1895 as the first such in the United States, was eliminated. "I'm not interested in Nobel Prizes," the chairman of the Uniroyal Goodrich Tire Company was quoted as saying. "I want to focus on market requirements."

When Polaroid, a company built by basic research, faced a takeover threat, it shifted its R&D toward shorter-term needs. "The pressure to produce short-term profits runs counter to the investment the company has to make in the future," a Polaroid spokesman told a *Washington Post* reporter. "But we feel if we are going to be competitive now and in the future, we have to strike a balance between those things."

As Walter Adams, professor of economics at Michigan State University, observed of the long-term effect of leveraged buyouts: "One of the things that gets squeezed is R&D because that's an investment in the future. Whatever costs are postponable are likely to go by the boards." Put another way, as one company analyst did, it meant that "the manipulators, not the innovators, are getting the rewards."

Quick sale of assets to service often staggering debt after a leveraged buyout became even more necessary because the same companies were often sold several times within a short period during the LBO craze. That leveraged buyouts limited long-term research and development was shown in results of the National Science Foundation study cited earlier examining the amount American companies spent on R&D in the eighties. In the first half of the decade R&D expenditures had increased by 5.5 percent. In the closing years of the decade those expenditures were more than cut in half.

A few reformers sought remedies in legislation to curb the excesses of LBOs, but the real solution lay in attitudes and behavior, not in new laws. Americans, and American businesses, had become used to planning for the short term, not the long, and both individuals and the country appeared caught up in a credit card mentality.

America had become a country where debt was no longer seen as bad, but good. Writing in the *New York Times,* James Grant, editor of a financial newsletter, provocatively expressed America's growing debt predicament at the end of the eighties. "These are odd times but there is a coherence in their strangeness," he wrote. "As the economic expansion rolls on, so does borrowing on ever more liberal terms. In the 1920's, the term of the average auto loan was one year. In 1955, it was three years. In 1989 it is five years and going on six. In 1946, fewer than nine thousand Americans filed for personal bankruptcy. In 1987, nine thousand filed a *week.* In the shank of Reagan prosperity, there are record bank failures."

Only a change in attitudes would reverse this trend, and such a change could realistically be expected only when Americans recognized they faced a crisis. As Grant observed, "Laws don't make lenders and borrowers conservative. Recessions do."

CHAPTER 33

WASHINGTON

Once again corporate jets were parked wing to wing on the tarmac. Men deplaned in tuxedos. Women in mink formed what one writer described as "a parade of skins" as they moved through National Airport's Butler Terminal toward waiting limousines. An airport official with a long memory surveyed the scene and drew a historical comparison. "Even the *men* wore mink coats in '81," he said, settling conclusively any doubt whether Ronald Reagan's first inaugural eclipsed George Bush's for opulence.

The price was greater, though, and airport official notwithstanding, the display of wealth at least as ostentatious. Where Reagan's most-expensive-ever inaugural cost five times that of Jimmy Carter, at more than thirty million dollars, most of it paid by corporate contributions, Bush's was twice as costly. Prices were up, too, for the main events. For nine hundred guests invited to attend a dinner at the National Building Museum, the cost was fifteen hundred dollars per plate. One limo driver, after dropping off guests there, shook his head at the expense. "I mean, the food can't be that good," he said. Still, he couldn't complain. Business was brisk, and one limousine service charged twenty-seven hundred dollars to lease a stretch limo for the inaugural festivities. For "only" sixteen hundred dollars, one could lease a town car. There were takers at all prices.

There was one difference between the Bush inaugural and Reagan's first: Concern about Washington's having become "Murder Capital, USA" because of drug-related violence led out-of-town guests to seek extra protection, and the limo services complied. "We prefer not to call them bodyguards, but executive protection people," one limo office manager explained. "They're highly trained professionals. Actually, they're sort of James Bond types. Very discreet. They'll go to the inaugural with their protectee and fit in perfectly. They're not types with cauliflower ears. They don't look like ex-boxers. They look perfect."

As always, an American inaugural was a time for celebration, and if this one lacked the exhilaration, the sense of ideological triumph, it was understandable. George Bush's assumption of power did not represent a break with the past, as had Reagan's, but was more a continuum. Power was being passed, but it was also being consolidated, and in a way that had not occurred between a sitting president and vice president in a century and a half. And if excess marked Bush's inaugural, as it had Reagan's, there should have been no surprise. Public excess had become the standard.

Bush inherited a Dickensian best-and-worst situation. He became president of an America enjoying peace and prosperity, confronting no immediate crisis, domestic or foreign, and amid unusual, perhaps historic international opportunities for American leadership. Around the world, old animosities appeared to be easing and a tantalizing possibility of new relationships existed. Behind the iron curtain, moves toward more democratic governments proceeded with what seemed to be a new spirit of acceptance from ruling hierarchies. Similar stirrings were occurring inside China, where students demonstrated for democratic reforms. From North and South Korea came the most positive signs of rapprochement since the war thirty-six years ago had left those nations divided at the thirty-eighth parallel.

In the Mideast the head of the Palestine Liberation Organization for the first time unequivocally stated the PLO's acceptance of Israel's right to exist and renounced terrorist acts. Those actions immediately led the United States to announce that its reservations about direct talks with the PLO were removed.

Beyond all else was the stunning new Soviet leadership. Mikhail Gorbachev, backing up his dreams of *glasnost* (openness) and *perestroika* (economic restructing through "new thinking") with deeds, announced the withdrawal of Soviet troops from Afghanistan, ordered Soviet tanks placed on railcars in East Germany and moved back to Russia, called for greater liberalization and openness within the Soviet Communist system, and proposed significant reductions in both nuclear and conventional weapons. Then, in a United Nations address a month before the inauguration, Gorbachev boldly articulated a vision of a "new world order" that would redefine international relationships. Resolving fundamental economic and environmental questions, he said, would require new methods of international cooperation in order "to put an end to an era of wars, confrontation, and regional conflicts, to aggressions against nature, to the terror of hunger and poverty as well as to political terrorism."

Gorbachev presented this visionary approach in a refreshingly nonideological manner. In referring to the longing of people everywhere for "independence, democracy, and social justice," he proclaimed that "today, the preservation of any kind of 'closed society' is hardly possible" and added that "the formula of development 'at the expense of others' " was on the way out while "the principle of freedom of choice is mandatory." Implicit was the idea that there is no one way to work, no one way to live, no one system that must prevail; international cooperation was the only feasible solution. His words, if taken at face value, signaled an end of the cold war era.

Suddenly there were rare diplomatic opportunities for a new president of the United States. Not in the post-World War II period had the prospect for fundamental change in world relationships been so strong.

Yet Bush had little time to savor his victory. The weeks between his election and inauguration were not marked by celebration, as was the case with Reagan. Past national bills were coming due, and the necessity for making difficult choices seemed inescapable. The savings and loan crisis had hit with a vengeance and required resolution. At the same time had come public pressure to modernize and make safe the nation's deteriorating nuclear plants. Hundreds of billions of dollars would be required for these two problem areas alone.

Demands increased for additional services in health, education, child care, public facilities, and environmental protection. Bush was being asked to do more to assist the homeless, fight crime and illegal drugs, construct new federal prisons, combat the AIDS epidemic, repair the nation's deteriorating infrastructure, generate greater research and development efforts, strike a better balance between private and public sectors, restore relapsed regulatory oversight functions, establish stricter governmental ethical standards, and meet continuing pressures to maintain the high level of military spending achieved during Reagan's presidency.

These were daunting challenges. Meeting them and fulfilling the few worthy, if vague, pledges of his presidential campaign (to become the "education president" and the "environmental president") would be difficult under the best of circumstances. Those favorable conditions did not exist on January 20, 1989, because funding for these myriad needs would take place in an administration facing the most severe budgetary constraints since the Great Depression, a specific result of the near tripling of the national debt in the Reagan eight years. The bill alone for modernizing America's badly neglected infrastructure upon which the nation's commerce moved—its highways, railways, airports, seaports, and mass transit facilities—was staggering. Expenditure of between *$1 trillion to $3 trillion* would be required for this over the next twenty years, it was officially estimated, with annual outlays running as high as $150 billion. Nor was the need to spend such vast sums to put the nation's transportation system in reasonable condition profligate; it was critical to America's future competitiveness as a trading nation.

Besides the soaring national debt, two other factors made solving these problems more difficult. Bush took office against a backdrop of an America conditioned during the Reagan years to think of addressing personal opportunities instead of national problems. For most of the decade, president and Congress had avoided acting on many difficult issues. Precious time and opportunities were squandered as problems were allowed to fester. That was the case with, among others, the budget and trade deficits, the S&L debacle, the nuclear plants, the infrastructure, and the third world debt crisis that continued to mushroom, threatening international economic stability.

In addition, Bush as president would run head-on into his most firmly stated and best-remembered political pledge: "Read my lips: no new taxes." Money alone, of course, was not the answer. Attitudes had to change; a new national consensus had to form, demonstrating public and political willingness to pay the price to solve tough problems. Without such changes, and without necessary funds, the prospect of seriously addressing them was slight.

Bush had another problem. It was his fate to follow, and be compared with, the most popular president since Franklin D. Roosevelt, one who, for eight years, escaped the blame for creating new problems or the responsibility for failing to solve old ones.

For Bush, extricating himself from the long shadow of Reagan was both delicate and necessary if he was to exercise strong leadership in his own right. On his inaugural day the new president sent a subtle but strong signal that he was in fact attempting to distance himself from his predecessor. He made known to congressional leaders that he would not continue to press the ideological battle to support the contras; that battle was over, part of the Reagan past. His new nominee for secretary of defense, the Texan John Tower, let it be known publicly that another cherished Reagan goal—"Star Wars," or the Strategic Defense Initiative—was both too costly and impractical, an unattainable dream. And now, on his inaugural day, the new president's words, themes, and actions all suggested that the change in power represented something more fundamental than a mere shift in focus from the larger-than-life figure of Ronald Reagan to the more circumspect one of George Herbert Walker Bush.

In numerous ways Bush's inaugural message was a break from the Reagan years. After years of ideological warfare Bush sounded a call for bipartisanship and cooperation between the Democratic Congress and the executive branch. After a decade of presidential attacks on the federal government for being, as Reagan put it in his first inaugural, the problem, not the solution to national problems, Bush reversed the priorities and placed public interests over private ones. He sought to establish a new tone for government and public service and rekindle belief in the honor, and honesty, of government.

His greatest departure from the prevailing ethos came in the most striking passage of his inaugural address, a summons for the nation to turn away from the greed and materialism of the eighties.* "My friends, we are not the sum of our possessions," he said, ". . . We cannot hope only to leave our children a bigger car, a bigger bank account. We must hope to give them a sense of what it means to be a

*Once more, Peggy Noonan's speech-writing talents were employed to craft a presidential address.

loyal friend, a loving parent, a citizen who leaves his home, his neighborhood and town better than he found it."

Such words had not been uttered from the Reagan White House in the eighties.

Bush's theme was public generosity, not selfishness, and the need "to initiate a new engagement in the lives of others." That meant attending to "the homeless, lost and roaming." It meant remembering that in history's verdict America's success would be measured by the need not "to be more driven to succeed than anyone around us" but "to celebrate their quieter, deeper successes that are not made of gold and silk but of better hearts and inner souls."

He continued to articulate these themes in his first appearances as president. To senior civil servants gathered before him later in Constitution Hall, he sent a strong signal of appreciation for service rendered (they were true heroes, he said) and called for a greater sense of selflessness. To his senior staff in the White House, he stressed the necessity to adhere to the highest ethical standards, to avoid conflicts of interest, to bend over backward "to see that there's even not a perception of a dual standard." To military personnel assembled aboard the carrier USS *America,* he called for rigorous oversight in seeing that weapons systems are procured honestly, at a fair price, and without unduly enriching contractors.

Through specific words and symbolic gestures, Bush was appealing to the best, not the worst, in America, to altruism instead of egoism, and in so doing, he sounded the note that public interest was paramount. While he was scrupulously careful not to make invidious comparisons, his initial actions contrasted with the ethical record and political philosophy of the Reagan years. Whether Bush's record ultimately matched his rhetoric would, of course, remain to be seen. But for now he held out promise that a new national era had dawned.

Through it all at Bush's inauguration Ronald Reagan sat stiffly off to the side, bareheaded, bundled in a white scarf that contrasted with his navy blue overcoat, his left hand wrapped in bandages from an operation for Dupuytren's contracture, or curling of the finger, a hearing aid visible in his left ear, and a distant, unfathomable look on his face.

Suddenly he looked old and diminished. While the wind swept

across the inaugural stands on the West Front of the Capitol, rippling his hair, he barely moved, staring straight ahead.

Three times he had delivered what the White House described as a "farewell address" to the nation. Given over a period of weeks before the inaugural, these addresses offered his views of America at home and in the world and, finally, his vision of America in the future.

They were self-congratulatory and sweeping in their claims of presidential success. "We are the change," he proclaimed, adding: "What a change it's been." He took credit for all the good that had ensued in the eight years since and laid blame for all the failures at the feet of others: Congress; the press; special interests in Washington. He accepted no responsibility for massive federal deficits, conceded no errors in judgment about them, continued to defend the supply-side economic theories that produced them, maintained he was still trying to find out what really had happened in the Iran-contra affair and who had been responsible for it, and, rhetoric aside, offered no new vision for the future, except a familiar Reaganesque vision of America, a land evoked by fables and mythology, by symbols and patriotic dreams.

In his final days as president, he also gave a series of interviews, attended lavish formal dinners, encouraged a sense of nostalgia about his pending departure from Washington by the manner in which he repeatedly referred to it, and made himself more accessible to the press and public than at any point in months.

His purpose was self-evident and natural: He was polishing his image and attempting to secure a positive historical "legacy" for himself. At his last formal press conference the first question asked was how he could square the huge budget deficits with his pledges to balance the budget. Typically he blamed not the tax cuts that slashed public revenues by a third at the same time that he doubled defense spending but the Congress and the Democrats who controlled it, ignoring the facts that as president he never *once* submitted a budget to Congress that was in balance and that for six of his eight presidential years Congress had actually *cut,* not increased, Reagan's own budget.

It was Congress that moved to redress the fiscal shortfall caused by the combination of huge tax cuts and defense increases by passing legislation raising new taxes, and it was Reagan who signed those tax increases year after year after year from 1982 through 1988. Of eighteen tax bills he signed as president, thirteen of them called for *increases,* facts that Reagan always conveniently ignored in his public statements while blaming "big spenders" for creating the deficit.

In those closing days of his presidency Reagan returned to California for a last vacation, marking, as one of his biographers, Lou Cannon noted, the 458th day he had spent in California during his two terms as president. There the Reagans stayed for the first time in what would be their new home—a Bel Air mansion in the same neighborhood as such Hollywood stars as Zsa Zsa Gabor and Elizabeth Taylor.

Here, too, was a reminder, for those who cared, that Reagan was leaving politics the way he entered it. The same wealthy Californians (among them Holmes Tuttle and Earle Jorgensen) who had purchased a private home for him to use as California's governor, later sold for a profit, had again pooled their money to purchase the Bel Air mansion and leased it to the Reagans. Thirty months before Reagan's second term was to end, eighteen of these Californians contributed a reported $156,000 apiece to buy the seventy-two-hundred-square-foot property, set on one and a quarter acres and overlooking Beverly Hills and all of the Los Angeles Basin. The price was $2.5 million. By inaugural day the land value alone had appreciated to more than $3 million, and the property itself was estimated to be worth more than $5 million. Reagan had also recently completed a multimillion-dollar book deal to write his memoirs and publish a collection of his speeches and was preparing to sign an exclusive agreement with a Washington lecture bureau. (At the same time Nancy Reagan signed a $2 million book contract and was retained by the same lecture bureau.) Reagan was to be paid an estimated $50,000 for each speech inside the United States (and double that overseas), making him the highest-paid speaker in the country. For only two speeches a month he could make more than $1 million a year. This, of course, was in addition to his presidential pension of $99,500 a year for life and his annual pension as a former governor of California of $30,800. In addition, he received Secret Service protection from forty full-time agents and other security at a cost to the government estimated at $10 million annually, more than double that of other living presidents. A suite of offices atop a new thirty-four-story office building twenty minutes from his home, commanding a view that extended from the Pacific Ocean to the towers of downtown Los Angeles, cost the government $173,000 a year to lease. From the government he also got use of a $1.25 million presidential transition fund for six months and $150,000 a year to pay staff.

All this provided more grist for his critics, who pointed out, not inaccurately, that when it came to cashing in on public service, Reagan, who more than any president in history railed against government benefits and spending, set the standard for all members of his administration. From Reaganomics to Reagabucks, one writer noted wryly.*

Naturally the departure of this star, so permanently fixed in the public galaxy, produced an outpouring of preliminary assessments of his place in history. The most provocative was by Frances FitzGerald, who pointed out that the public already had been given revealing insights into his presidency through a number of memoirs from top Reagan aides—among others, his budget director, his press secretary, his domestic policy chief, his treasury secretary and chief of staff, and his secretary of state—published even before he left office. Never had there been such a rush to place before the public "inside" accounts from a presidency, and never so early such an unflattering presidential portrait.

Writing in the *New Yorker,* in its issue published four days before the inaugural, FitzGerald described what these books told the public about their president and life inside his White House. His former domestic chief and fellow Californian Martin Anderson speaks of Reagan as an "ancient king," FitzGerald observed; David Stockman says he is like a "ceremonial monarch." In these books, however, FitzGerald concluded, Reagan resembles not Louis XIV, as Donald

*On May 11, 1989, William Safire of the *New York Times,* commenting on published reports that the Fujisankei Communications Group of Japan had hired Reagan to make two speeches and attend ceremonies that fall, reported that Reagan's weekly fee was about two million dollars, more than he earned during eight years as president. Safire also reported that Reagan's two jobs, as president and later master of ceremonies at the Japanese business event, were not unrelated. In 1983 Reagan had "favored the founder of the Fujisankei conglomerate by agreeing to an exclusive interview in one of his newspapers, and in 1988 brought him into the Oval Office to discuss the possibility of the visit that turned out to be so lucrative." He gave the lecture, and took the two-million-dollar fee, later that year.

Regan imagines, or a "Turkish pasha," as Anderson does, but, rather, the elegant, slim-waisted boy-king Tutankhamun:

> In the friezes, Tutankhamun is depicted in his golden chair on the royal barge, his wife kneeling beside him in profile, her wide gaze fixed upon him. Dozens of servants file before him, some holding out wild ducks, others holding trays of fruit on their shoulders: a banquet is in the offing, and the service will be of alabaster, the cutlery of gold. Below decks, one imagines, a hundred slaves are rowing this eternal boy upstream; they are sweating, their sinews stand out like ropes, and occasionally they curse at him. But, of course, he cannot see them—he cannot turn his head—and he may even think that the barge moved against the current by itself. On the banks, the priests of Amon are waiting for him. Not long before, they were training the soldiers, collecting the taxes, and fighting among themselves. But now, their heads slightly bowed, they are preparing for the ritual of deference suggesting that they believe it is the boy-king who calls the sun up in the morning.

Taken together, the memoirs contributed to the picture that had already begun to form about Ronald Reagan: of the disengaged, uninterested, genial old man (the "amiable dunce," Clark Clifford had called him) who presided, by luck and happy instinct free from major problems, over America's destinies in the eighties.

Some people, in retrospect, would conclude that they had been had. Reagan, the wizard, had deceived them. The pictures he had painted for the country had taken on a life of their own; they had replaced reality. It was the *pictures* they had believed in. Maybe that was it. For the past eight years the country had been staring up in some kind of trance at pictures in the sky. Now Reagan would be gone and people were left with the memory of how he had made them feel better. His departure was like the end of a fireworks display when the colors and trails and sparks fade, leaving nothing but a dark sky.

Reagan's ability to show Americans what they wanted to see had been perfect at a time when America wanted to escape past problems and growing national doubts. Maybe Ronald Reagan was just another sound bite in a series of prime-time programs that America was addicted to, registering as smoothly and securely as the characters in "Dallas" or "Dynasty," and with the same degree of shallowness. Maybe the lasting memory of Reagan would be not of substance but of image, and with the same ease with which it arrived, his image would be replaced by another. America was primed for that, too. It was like nonnutritive food, the refined sugars that picked you up at first and then dropped you, leaving you more exhausted than before. There had been no challenging third dimension to Reagan or Reagan's America. No complex carbohydrates.

In the course of their triumvirate alliance in the eighties, Reagan, television, and America had steered away from complexity. Not that Americans were unaware of complexity or uninterested in understanding what was happening in the country. But high technology was moving things so fast that they couldn't always keep up: test tube babies, heart and organ transplants, artificial limbs, life-sustaining machines. Problems abroad were so complex as to make them seem unsolvable: hostage taking, reemployment of poison gas and chemical weapons, peoples rejecting modernity and moving backward into a medieval past; plagues and famine, new diseases, and new starvation. There were times, too, in those same years, when many Americans displayed a noticeable loss of appetite for real issues and information. They opted for predigested packages, the kind that made no demands. Who was to blame for such a downward spiral in a supposedly thinking democracy? Was it Reagan? Was it television? Was it the press that reported favorably on Reagan and his times? Was it the politicians who failed through lack of will or fear to offer real alternatives? Or were the people themselves responsible? These were questions without answers. Blame could not be neatly consigned. All were responsible.

Reagan's ebullient brand of no-problems presidential leadership made dealing with complicated national issues more difficult. He was able to put off action on them because he presided in a time of perceived success. By Bush's inaugural that no longer seemed as certain. For weeks after the election one report after another reinforced the feeling that the day of reckoning was approaching—and in areas other than the widely publicized S&L and nuclear plant problems.

Evidence of gradual national decline had accumulated,* and

*Typical of assessments was a paper for the *Harvard Business Review* around the Bush inaugural by Clyde V. Prestowitz, Jr., a former Reagan official and counselor for Japan affairs for the U.S. secretary of commerce from 1981 to 1986, who wrote: "For the first time in the

some of the statistics were startling. In 1950, for instance, the United States had produced 33 percent of the gross national product of the world; by 1989 it produced only 26 percent, and its share was continuing to decline. In Reagan's last year as president, Japan replaced the United States as first in per capita GNP, with $19,462, while the United States slipped to $18,463. Real incomes, which rose steadily between 1963 and 1973, had stagnated since then, while real income of U.S. competitors regularly increased. Advancing rapidly were the nations of the European Economic Community. Four Asian nations (the "other tigers," as they were beginning to be called popularly)—South Korea, Taiwan, Hong Kong, and Singapore—were growing at an annual GNP rate of 6 to 8 percent, and their share of world trade had tripled since 1960.

All these were signs that Europeans and Asians, who once had studied American business and production methods and boasted that they were doing it the "American Way," were now celebrating their own successes. Now it was the European Way or the Japanese Way that was studied and emulated.

How great a decline the United States experienced was shown in the shift away from American-produced goods to foreign ones.

In the mid-seventies American companies made 95 percent of the telephones and 80 percent of the television sets used in American homes. By the end of the eighties American companies made only one in four telephones and one in ten TV sets sold in the United States. Similarly, the U.S. share of world automotive output declined from 52 percent in 1960 to 23 percent in the late eighties. By then one of every four cars driven in America was foreign-made. During that same period the U.S. share of world steel production dropped from 26 to 11 percent. In the battle for world markets, other nations—among them Japan, West Germany, France, and Canada—were drawing even with the United States in shares of markets and in some cases capturing them.

Making these conditions more difficult were the U.S. trade and budget deficits. With the United States importing about $150 billion

experience of Americans, our country is in serious decline and we are facing a question we have only faced twice before, once in 1776 and again in 1861. That is: 'What kind of country do we want to have?' "

more in products and services at the end of the eighties than it exported each year, this deficit was a sign that the historic American trade surplus was gone. Gone, too, was the American role as the world's biggest lender of capital. Now the United States was the world's biggest borrower of capital, and the comfortable day of the dominant American dollar with its predictable exchange rate appeared gone forever. The budget deficit was equally alarming. Rising at a rate of $12 billion a month by 1989, the budget deficit represented a debt of about $45,000 for every family in America. Not since 1969 had any Congress or any president been able to balance the annual budget. The result was that every American worker was paying an average of $4 *a day* in taxes just to pay interest on his or her share of the federal government's debt.

Debate about whether or not the deficit was as dangerous as critics alleged missed the larger point. That was: The *pattern* of increasing national debt demonstrated beyond question that something was grievously out of order. By 1989 annual interest on the debt *alone* had nearly reached two hundred billion dollars and was rising rapidly. One of every seven federal dollars was then being spent just for interest on the debt, and one-third of the interest Americans paid was leaving the country as "a sort of financial tribute to wealthy strangers in Japan, Germany, and the Middle East."

In a bipartisan report they prepared for the next president, Gerald Ford and Jimmy Carter warned: "We must borrow from abroad, because all the savings of Americans are not enough to support the Treasury's *weekly need for more money* [italics added]. As a consequence, some of the biggest decisions about the financial future of the United States are now in the hands of foreign investors."

Looking at the world, America faced many new challenges. One was the prospect of a unified Europe without borders, operating with a common currency, and trading in world markets as a single entity. Better educated, technologically more skilled, culturally and racially more homogeneous, possessed of greater population than America and with enormous resources, a true European Economic Community would provide the United States with even sharper competition. A United States of Europe was by no means settled, however; historic rivalries and ancient grudges still existed, and it was yet to be demonstrated that Europe could in fact sublimate its traditional differences and emerge as the unified world power of many dreams. Even if it did, another great question loomed: the prospect of a unified Germany forming a superunit within the emerging new Europe and stirring memories of the rise of German power.

Beyond Europe, America faced other challenges. Japan continued to be on the rise, in both its expanding economic power and its military potential, and not far behind it were the other ascending powers of Asia. India appeared to be emerging as a major international service industry supplier. If China held together, after its bloody internal explosions in the spring of 1989 between forces of the old regime and the rising young student class that sought a more democratic society, it also had the potential to become a formidable competitor.

At home America's unmet domestic agenda was immense. The poverty rate, running at 14 percent of the population and embracing some thirty-three million people, was one of the highest in the industrialized world. A child born in the United States was between two and three times as likely to be poor as one born in Germany, Sweden, Norway, or Canada. The dropout rate of entering high school freshman had reached 26.7 percent and was greater among some groups. Among eighteen- and nineteen-year-olds studied in 1987, only 77 percent of whites, 65 percent of blacks, and 55 percent of Hispanics had completed high school. By 1989 the government reported that *half* of America's black children lived in poverty. Each year half a million teenagers dropped out of school to take menial, low-paying jobs, drift into unproductive idleness, or fall into the brutal world of the streets.

Family structures were further sundered. Demographics projected that at least half of recently married couples would end in divorce, the highest such rate in the world, and the U.S. divorce rate had increased fourfold since 1960. One of five American children lived with a single parent, and that parent was likely to work, leaving children even less supervised than in the past. Thirty-seven million Americans had no health insurance; the cost of health care was rising sharply and public facilities to provide for it were declining in quantity and quality.

Thirteen percent of the nation's seventeen-year-olds were "functionally illiterate." By such definition, they were unable to read job notices, fill out job applications, make change correctly, or read a bus schedule.

Violence in America had increased. The annual murder rate of over twenty thousand was by far the world's highest, and half of those deaths were the result of gunshot wounds. Despite the assassinations of major public figures and the murders every day of ordinary citizens from handguns, the numbers of guns in public possession continued to rise, approaching nearly one hundred million. Statistically, the most dangerous parts of the country were not in the great urban centers, but in the American West. There citizens stood one chance in eight of being attacked, robbed, or raped, and one chance in four that someone would break into their homes or steal their cars.

Appalling lack of knowledge existed. In 1986 a study of high school juniors showed that only 15.5 percent knew that Alexis de Tocqueville had written *Democracy in America.* Only 21.4 percent knew that "Reconstruction" referred to the readmission of the Confederate states into the Union. In one survey only half of California adults could identify Japan on a map. Of those responding to another survey, 25 percent did not know the difference between north and south on a globe. In 1989, three out of every four liberal arts college faculty members surveyed nationwide believed that undergraduates at their institutions were "seriously underprepared in basic skills."

In a survey of American companies, 50 percent reported that their managers and supervisors were unable to write paragraphs free of grammatical errors and that their skilled and semiskilled workers were unable to use decimals and fractions in math problems. That group included company bookkeepers.

While America urgently needed more engineers, computer operators, and electronics technicians, the society was not creating them in nearly sufficient numbers to remain competitive. While the nation needed greater educational skills, it was doing less well in providing them. American high school students knew less math and science than they did in 1975. An international survey of twenty-four thousand students, aged thirteen, financed by the National Science Foundation and U.S. Department of Education and made public in 1989, showed that Americans scored last in mathematics and were among the worst in science.

Looking ahead and examining the demographic trends, the United States faced additional challenges. The nation was aging rapidly, and its population growth was slowing. The Census Bureau predicted for the first time that the U.S. population would peak at about three hundred million and then decline after the first third of the next century. Soon the United States would become the first country where one in five citizens was over the age of sixty-five. Already Americans over sixty-five were increasing as a percentage of the population at a rate more than twice as fast as other age-groups. The country was rapidly entering a period when it would need many more workers to carry out essential jobs in the society. Given the prevailing birth and death rates, with fewer people being born and people living longer, population growth would have to come through immigration. Throughout the nineties it was expected that a full third of America's growth would come from immigration, mostly from Mexico, the Caribbean, and Asia. By the year 2000 one new worker in three would be a member of a minority. Assimilating, training, and educating these new immigrants, as well as caring for older Americans leaving the work force and living longer, would place a greater strain on the nation's public facilities and services. Demographic trends also suggested that the nation faced new tensions between the generations as younger Americans would have to pay increasingly heavier costs to provide for the larger numbers of older citizens living longer.

Even if he wanted to, Bush would find it harder to continue postponing action on these national problems and also find resolving them more difficult, especially if there were a recession.

In that context, assessments of Reagan's presidency further contributed to the negative impression already created by the memoirs and kiss-and-tell accounts. New stories of his ignorance, insensitivity, and inattentiveness surfaced. Jokes about "while Reagan slept" and "while Nancy consulted her astrologer,"* some of which

*Donald Regan's memoir, *For the Record,* published in the spring of 1988, first reported that Mrs. Reagan regularly consulted a San Francisco astrologer, Joan Quigley, for guidance

he disarmingly told on himself, made the rounds. Some were fanciful and good-natured. Others were serious and disturbing. For example, his former doctor Brigadier General John Hutton said Reagan had not realized the seriousness of AIDS until July 1985, when he saw a news report disclosing that the actor Rock Hudson had died of the disease. This was more than five years after AIDS had been identified, thousands of Americans had been infected, and AIDS had been the subject of intense national publicity. When Reagan saw the news report about Hudson's death, he asked General Hutton to tell him about the disease. After listening to a long explanation, the general said the president replied: "I have always thought the world might end in a flash, but this sounds like it's worse."

Troubling as that kind of story is for its revelation of a president's ignorance and isolation, it did not come as a surprise to those who thought they knew what Reagan was like. Yet in fundamental ways they did not. The real Reagan, the Reagan behind the self-deprecating anecdotes and jocular manner, remained as elusive as he had been to those who realized, years before in California, that they had not been able to penetrate his many public masks.

At a Georgetown dinner party during the Christmas holiday period before the inauguration, Michael Deaver was seated at a table among guests who had been named to high positions in the new Bush administration. Inevitably the conversation turned to Reagan. After years of almost daily association with Reagan did Deaver think he really knew him? Deaver was asked. Deaver was silent, looking thoughtful. No, he finally said. After twenty years of close contact, he had come to realize that probably no one knew Ronald Reagan, with the single exception of his wife, Nancy. In all those years, Deaver went on quietly, he had seen Reagan shed tears in public on numerous occasions but never once in private. No, he said again, he didn't really know him. No one did.

That aspect of Reagan was less well known. The side that people thought they knew, that of the comical but affectionate political

---

while in the White House, relying on Quigley's astrological advice to such an extent that it affected timing of presidential speeches, appearances, meetings with heads of state, airplane travel schedules, and even discussion topics. Later Quigley's published account claimed her astrological advice had even greater impact on Reagan's presidency.

bumbler, was no less illusory. In many respects it, too, was false. To the end, Reagan was misjudged.

It was easy to snicker at the old actor, to deride his act and miss the meaning and consequences of his actions.

Ronald Reagan was a consequential president. Of the thirty-eight men who preceded him as presidents of the United States,* he was among the few who truly altered the condition of the country and affected the way people thought about it. Nor, as we've seen, was it all for the better. For years to come the social and economic costs would continue to accumulate.

Judged by his own terms, Reagan's presidency was a success. He accomplished much of what he set out to achieve a quarter century before in California, when liberalism and the Great Society were in full flower. He had cut taxes, redistributed wealth to the immense advantage of the wealthy, reordered spending to pour billions upon billions into the Pentagon, and checked, if not reversed, the domestic expansion of the federal government. In his time the Progressive Era did appear to come to an end. From health to housing, from the environment to consumer protection, from education to child nutrition, from deregulation of financial markets to public transportation, every aspect of the domestic ledger had been affected. The poor *had* been left poorer, the rich, richer; the social compact, if not broken, *had* been severely weakened. In fundamental ways America was more divided into its many racial, ethnic, and regional groupings than when he became president.

Greatest of all was his imprint on political attitudes. He had deprecated the belief that government held the answer, or even part of the answer, for solving public problems. In so doing, he contributed to more cynicism. His success in securing the appointment of strongly committed conservatives to the federal judiciary guaranteed that his beliefs would be reflected in legal decisions, from the Supreme Court down, for decades to come.

By personal example and the tone he set, he encouraged individualism and made more difficult the role of the public servant. No

*While Reagan is officially listed as the fortieth president, he was the thirty-ninth person to hold the office. Grover Cleveland, who was elected to terms in 1884 and 1892 and was defeated in 1888, is listed twice.

president since Harding had set so low a standard for public behavior; the ethical problems that multiplied during his administration were the inevitable outgrowth of permissive attitudes toward personal enrichment through public service and public contracts that stemmed from the top. All these could not be attributed to Reagan. The congressional ethical climate was also low, a fact underscored when the Democratic speaker of the House and the Democratic majority whip both were forced to resign under ethical misconduct clouds during Reagan's last year. But Reagan's appointments brought into government an unusually high number of people who seized opportunity for personal gain. In this, the comparison between Harding and Reagan was not invidious.

As the Housing and Urban Development scandals showed, agencies of the federal government that existed to help the needy became places of political influence peddling for a profit, and at the expense of the average citizen. Reagan alone could not be blamed, as he was regularly by his harshest critics, for fostering the new climate of racial hostility and hatred in America. But through a pattern of indifference and insensitivity, through calculated policies that worked against the interests of the poor and minorities, through repeated and open political appeals to ideologically divisive groups, he added to these new tensions and made them worse.

Reagan's was not a generous-spirited presidency; it was characterized by its small-mindedness and even at times by its meanness. However inadequate the definitions of "liberal" and "conservative" had become in his America, he intensified an already growing public mood of "conservatism."

This was especially notable among young Americans, who saw in him their only successful presidential model and the one who repeatedly prevailed over his critics. Not that he was a leader who broke new ideological or intellectual ground. His ideological rhetoric notwithstanding, he was not the kind of visionary public figure who lent his name to an age of new behavior through imposing a Code Napoleon. He was more a chaplain to believers, someone who addressed those already converted; but he possessed the political ability to intensify the feelings of those who wanted to be warmed up, and his powers of persuasion were such that he drew into his camp many who were reluctant to embrace all of his expressed ideologies. Either from disillusionment or desire for a different public approach, old liberals and socialists, Democrats and past reformers, joined him.

Even his critics had to acknowledge his influence on public attitudes. "I remember when I was in college, everyone seemed pretty Democratic and liberal," a young woman remarked to a group of friends during a conversation about politics in 1988. "Then I spent some time away from school. When I came back, in the last election year [of 1984], ninety-five percent of the student body had voted for Reagan. It was a shock. We called them the Nazi youth."

"It's amazing to see the change in our parents," one of her friends said. "I mean, my parents are so much more conservative than they were."

"What do you mean?" someone asked.

"I mean, in terms of passing judgment as opposed to having judgment. Somewhere along the line another value system came into play."

In no small measure, it was a value system for which Ronald Reagan could take credit—and blame for the public problems it fostered.

He was a strong president, not a weak one. Despite his assaults on government—his calls for reducing its powers and returning to the states, municipalities, and private interests responsibility for setting their own course—he greatly expanded the powers of the presidency and the executive branch. Under him, the influence of the Pentagon and the various intelligence branches increased greatly. Secret operations were undertaken beyond the scrutiny of a legislative branch charged by the Constitution with the *exclusive* power to raise armies and navies, see to the general defense of the nation, and in the American system granted the only legal authority to declare war.

Reagan bent the Congress to his will, succeeded in spending astronomical sums for defense, even if that meant years of national fiscal gridlock, if not bankruptcy. And he could argue that it was his defense buildup that compelled the Soviet Union to seek a new relationship offering improved peace prospects and that it was his strong anti-Communist resolution that opened the way for democratic governments to rise dramatically out of the ashes of the cold war in Eastern Europe.

Certainly, there was truth in the claim. By the end of Reagan's term the bankruptcy of the Soviet system was transparent; but its problems long predated the Reagan era, and many of them stemmed from internal causes. While for decades world attention had focused on the external Soviet threat, it was internal failure that threatened the disintegration of its empire. In a real sense the Soviet system had sown the seeds of its own destruction. Not only was the Soviet system cumbersome, corrupt, and repressive—a police state that failed to produce necessary consumer goods and provide adequate standards of living for its people—but it was also poisoning itself. Long before the Soviet nuclear disaster at Chernobyl in April 1986, the air, streams, water tables, and soils of the Soviet bloc were becoming contaminated through hopelessly inadequate environmental controls and bureaucratic bungling. Gradual recognition of these conditions, coupled with more obvious economic and societal problems, produced explosive pressure for change, especially in Eastern Europe but also within the Soviet borders themselves. And, as was so often overlooked, with no little irony, the great American defense buildup had begun in the last year of Carter's presidency, and the cold war policies of containment had been pursued vigorously by *every* president since Harry Truman.

Nonetheless, in this, Reagan was among the most aggressive of his presidential predecessors. He was a president willing to take great risks to carry out his objectives, including the ultimate one of impeachment. In an era of high rollers, he may have been the boldest risk taker of all. As Arthur Liman said of him, in judging his actions during the Iran-contra affair, "The president acted like a president." That does not mean his actions were always right, wise, truthful, or even lawful. They were not. Nor does it mean that he paid attention to the business of governance. He did not. His was a lax and largely inattentive presidency. But in the areas that he cared about, he was a useful simplifier who knew what he wanted and how to get it. To these ends, he was stubbornly determined to achieve his goals. When it came to those few things in which he was deeply involved, Ronald Reagan was a strongly committed president, and he prevailed.

To a degree that should have been evident, but did not always seem so, Reagan's life and public career reflected many of the changes America had experienced in the last half century or more.

Garry Wills, in his *Reagan's America,* expressed this thought about Reagan best:

> He spans our lives, culturally and chronologically. Born in the year the first studio opened in Hollywood, he reached that town just two years after Technicolor did. His second term as president runs through 1988, the two-hundredth anniversary of the ratification of the United States Constitution, and his life spans over a third of that history of constitutional government. . . . He began his regular radio career the year Franklin Roosevelt delivered his first fireside address. An adult during the Depression and World War II, he has known union crusades and corporate worries, spoken for civil liberties and for red hunting. He has been a Hollywood success and a Las Vegas flop. After two victories by wide margins in California, he went down to two defeats as presidential candidate. He died for victory as the Gipper and won personal glory in the defeat of Barry Goldwater. We have been through it all with him.

However historians would judge him, Reagan had stayed the course, and his presence would be felt long after he was gone. In terms of his appointments to the courts alone, his stamp on government and American life would continue well into the next century. A country that celebrated youth and change had found comfort and security in this oldest of leaders, who in an age of increasing complexities had offered simplicities and who for the first time in nearly thirty years had returned full two-term presidential stability to the land.

One last act was staged.

Network camera crews, alerted in advance by the White House, were ready to record that final scene on the East Front of the Capitol after power was again passed peacefully before watching millions. There, as a Marine helicopter waited to carry the old president on a last "flyover" of the capital, the outgoing and incoming presidents of the United States would take their farewells by saluting each other before the whirring cameras.

The exchange of salutes, as promised, took place. The boarding of the helicopter and the last wave, as planned, followed. It all was part of the script. The helicopter carrying Ronald Reagan slowly lifted off as the wind generated by its blades blew off women's hats in the Capitol Plaza below. Then he was gone. With him went the eighties.

EPILOGUE

I began this book in the spring of 1987 in the belief that America was passing through a period that increasingly resembled the moral slackness of the spendthrift twenties, a new Gilded Age, and one that, like then, would extract a price for its excesses. That belief has been borne out, but there the comparison ends. Unlike the twenties, the eighties were not a romantic period, and it's doubtful that the characters who gave it special flavor will be remembered with nostalgic affection. Oliver North and Ronald Reagan, Michael Milken and Ivan Boesky, Jim and Tammy Faye Bakker, Arthur Laffer and his curve, the yuppies and the LBO kings, the hustlers and quick-buck promoters—all typified a self-indulgent and imitative age when entertainers became public leaders and when celebrities, not pioneers, scientists, or artists, became cultural heroes.

Neither was it an age of originality and experimentation, like the twenties, when artistic talent flowered and people saw in the new architecture or new music or new literature a wellspring of cultural vibrancy. In the eighties few scientific eminences were produced, no Einsteins or Marconis, to lead an age of advance. It was more a time when deal makers, money managers, and paper shufflers flourished. Their lasting imprint would be minimal, if not negative.

By decade's end some of these tendencies appeared to have run their course. The great consumption boom seemed over, as flatness of the real estate market, declining department and specialty store sales, collapse of the junk bond market, rising inflation and interest rates, and severe new bank credit restrictions nationwide showed. Caution and circumspection were becoming more evident.

Like Arthur M. Schlesinger, Jr., I am a believer in cycles of history in which periods of reaction are followed by periods of reform. But there is nothing to indicate that a new cycle has emerged, or, if so, what it will bring, and much to suggest that underlying attitudes of the eighties are still exerting a powerful influence on Americans in the nineties.

In these pages I have enumerated a number of problems that threaten America's standing and continued prosperity. Positive elements, of course, exist. As dramatic events around the world have shown, the American system remains the model for others. America's resilience in the face of national tragedy, its capacity to assimilate diverse cultural and racial groups, its expansion of freedoms and individual rights in the face of the most reactionary administration of the century, its ability to provide opportunity for those who start at the bottom—all remain the envy of the world.

For two hundred years, as it grew from a nation of 3.9 million people, 20 percent of whom were black slaves, clustered along the eastern seaboard in a land still untamed and a continent still unexplored to 250 million people in a society whose influence was felt throughout the world, America has experienced a continuing revolution. But with the exception of its own Civil War (the "second American Revolution"), in all those years it has never fallen into the kinds of violent convulsions that have led to the overthrow of governments. It has had numerous demagogues and knaves in its national life; it has never had a dictator, never had a king, and, for all its failures, its society remains the freest and fairest on earth. Despite the ethical lapses, public and private, of the Reagan years, criminal and civil prosecutions did result and dirty linen was aired. On Wall Street the junk bond kings fell, the insiders were punished. If not over, the outpouring of greed was checked, and the symbols of that greed, the Trumps, the Helmsleys, the Boeskys, became public objects of derision. Televangelists still rattle their electronic tambourines over the public airwaves and still entice the unsophisticated to contribute to their personal wealth. But they, too, were brought low. Religious bigotry is not on the rise. Zealots who sought to impose their minority views are not in the ascendancy. Abortion rights are more secure, not less, as the public, through the ballot, decisively rejects legislative attempts to limit individual freedom of choice. The executive and legislative branches of government, responding to scandals and public pressure, have adopted new ethical standards, and Congress has even renounced the practice of taking outside honoraria from special interests. This kind of self-corrective record suggests that there is nothing beyond America's ability to accomplish—if it chooses to do so.

Therein lies the problem. With all its talents and resources, America at this juncture has not decided what it wants to do with all the great things it possesses. Consequently, its problems multiply as resolution of them continues to be postponed.

Despite its achievements, the plain fact is that the American political/governmental system is not working as it should. A breakdown has occurred, and a breakdown all the more troubling because it comes when the American people and their leaders seem even more unwilling to face long-term national problems. A peculiar mood of public passivity still envelops the nation, a mood of disengagement typified by the tepid American reaction to the international events at the end of the eighties that made it seem as if the historic revolutionary cycles of 1789 and 1848 were being replayed before the eyes of the world on television. In daily procession passed the faces of a new generation of Europeans laying claim to the future by burying their past. Not since the Russian Revolution seventy-two years before had popular movements of such size and strength sprung spontaneously from the ranks of the people to overthrow entrenched regimes. Yet this extraordinary drama only sharpened the contrast between what appeared to be America's diminishing world leadership role and its self-indulgent actions at home. In the new world being born, America no longer seemed as relevant.

America was not, of course, irrelevant, as the world learned when the United States took the lead in imposing international economic sanctions on Iraq after the Iraqi invasion of Kuwait in August 1990. In the Iraqi crisis the United States assumed the leading role in forging a unified international effort to counter aggression. But that crisis also underscored its vulnerability in the new post-cold war world. Mounting economic problems at home, driven by a deepening budget deficit crisis and new historic levels of debt, forced the United States to plead with its allies to cover its costs in deploying troops to Saudi

Arabia and naval and air forces to the Persian Gulf. The lesson was clear: America's internal problems had lessened its ability to act abroad, not only in the Mideast but in assisting the nations of Eastern Europe to fulfill their dreams of becoming democracies.

That leads me to this conclusion: America's greatest test in the nineties lies not beyond its borders, as two generations of Americans were taught during the cold war era, but within. If America falls, it will likely be from internal causes and probably because of four factors: from its failure to address long-festering social and economic problems and growing divisions among its citizenry; from subversion of its constitutional system, as in the Iran-contra affair; from the corruption and ineffectiveness of its government; and from the cynicism and inattention of its people.

All these elements are present in the nineties, and neither public will nor political consensus has formed on how to address them. There is not even agreement that America faces fundamental problems. In fact, euphoria over the crumbling of the Soviet empire seems to have strengthened a sense of complacency about the future. While the end of the cold war holds the greatest promise in half a century, it also presents America with great new challenges.

For East and West, the cold war became more than a way of life; it became a state of mind that led America and Russia to divert their energies into unproductive areas that sapped the strength of both societies. Policies and attitudes shaped by that war became as hardened as the underground silos that encase nuclear warheads aimed at Soviet and American targets. Decade by decade, the range and destructive capacity of these weapons increased. A single American Poseidon submarine, for example, carries more explosives than were used by both sides in World Wars I *and* II. By the nineties the United States had thirty-two such submarines and, in addition, more than one thousand land-based missiles and six hundred bombers. As the British statesman David Lloyd George once said, "There is no greater fatuity than a political judgment dressed in a military uniform," and for two generations America and Russia fashioned their policies and allocated their wealth according to higher military priorities. That no longer needs to be so. But if winning the cold war was difficult, winning the peace will be more so, and the sad fact is that after spending more than a trillion dollars on preparation for nuclear war, the United States is not prepared for that greater effort for peace. For nearly half a century it has had extensive plans for nuclear war,* but it has had no plans for peace.

During the long cold war the United States came to resemble the Soviet Union in its reliance upon military force, covert operations, expanding arsenals, and allocation of increasing national resources for defense. Like the Soviets, the United States adopted the devices of the National Security State, a state in which official secrecy, rationalization, propaganda, and an expanding bureaucracy wedded to the status quo thrived. The other side of national security—improving economic performance, raising educational standards, developing new technologies for peaceful and productive endeavors, combating hunger, poverty, disease, environmental degradation—received secondary consideration.

In the nineties and beyond America will have to address those neglected areas in a world in which the United States no longer holds unsurpassed superpower status and in which many of the old national, racial, ethnic, and religious problems that have beset the world in the twentieth century still smolder and at times flare into warfare. That is the current lesson of Armenian-Azerbaijan, Lithuanian-Russian, Serbian-Croatian, Irani-Iraqi, Irish Catholic-Protestant, Arab-Jew, Muslim-Christian, Shiite-Sunni, Hindu-Sikh, and black-white relationships.

Iraq's invasion of Kuwait was a perfect example of the kinds of problems the United States and the industrial societies would confront. That crisis also demonstrated the heavy price America would have to pay for past policy failures. In the eighties the United States had tilted toward Iraq in Iraq's bloody war with Iran even as the United States was secretly selling arms to Iran. The United States had substantially helped Iraq economically and militarily and, through CIA Director William Casey, had passed on important in-

*The SIOP, or Single Integrated Operations Plan, is the plan that provides for the use of nuclear weapons by all U.S. forces, including those in Europe, Britain, and Korea. Over the decades this plan, which defense experts tell me has been reviewed by virtually no members of Congress, perhaps only one president (Jimmy Carter) since Truman, and apparently few secretaries of defense, expanded from initial designated targets of a few hundred to more than forty thousand targets. Total destruction of the enemy is to be achieved by drawing upon a nuclear stockpile that grew from a number below fifty under Truman to more than twenty thousand warheads by the nineties.

telligence information useful to Iraq in fighting its war with Iran. It had removed Iraq from the list of nations it branded as terrorist states and failed to denounce Iraq's use of chemical weapons and its efforts to produce nuclear weapons through technology provided, in part, by the United States. Then, in 1990, the United States had misread or ignored intelligence reports clearly warning of Iraq's intent to seize Kuwait by force, thus jeopardizing vital oil reserves.

These failures pointed toward even greater ones. The sudden crisis in the summer of 1990, which took both America and the world by surprise, showed that the United States had pursued no coherent Middle East policy. Nor had it taken steps to ensure its energy independence. Iraq brought home the lesson that America still had no comprehensive national energy policy and was even more vulnerable to disruption of oil supplies and to hostage taking than it had been when the eighties began. Nor had the great U.S. military buildup of the eighties prepared the nation to deal with this latest Mideast crisis. Despite all the money spent on stealth bombers, missiles, and "Star Wars" technology in the eighties, when the first military crisis came in the nineties, the United States found itself still without the rapid deployment force that it had boasted of forming to use in such a situation. It did not even possess adequate transport ships and planes for its new emergency mission of instantly ferrying troops and supplies.

Most critical of all, the cost of its massive military deployment in the gulf underscored the consequences of failing to resolve its domestic economic problems. The Iraqi crisis struck when the nation appeared to be sinking into a recession, with the national debt rising to greater heights and the Congress seemingly more paralyzed over meaningful action. By then the federal Treasury had been drained by the necessity to provide additional tens of billions of dollars for escalating S&L bailout costs. Any economic "peace dividend" resulting from the end of the cold war had already been wiped out. The unexpected tens of billions needed to meet gulf military expenditures immediately negated projected savings that Congress and the Bush administration had hoped to achieve from new defense spending cuts.

The Iraqi crisis taught other lessons, among them that America would have to operate in a world facing a new interdependence of critical issues. Solving them will require new forms of international cooperation. Iraq is only one example. Environmental degradation is another. Twenty years before, despite popular attention to environmental concerns through such television age events as Earth Day, the environment was still viewed as a local or even a national issue, but not an international one. That is no longer so. From destruction of the Brazilian rain forests to depletion of the world's ozone layer, from global warming to Sahara drought and famine, awareness is growing that environmental problems on one part of the globe affect the destinies of people elsewhere.

Other issues demand world action. Nuclear proliferation, the spread of terrorism, and the rapidly increasing world population pose threats that promise to grow more dangerous. How long will debt-laden third world societies, falling further and further behind advanced industrial countries, wait for their share of prosperity before embarking on more destructive courses of action? How long will it be before they, or the terrorist states like Iraq, or the shadowy terrorist groups present a claim for more of the world's wealth while armed with nuclear weapons? How will leading powers stop a Brazil from ravaging its rain forests or prevent other nations from polluting the atmosphere? How will they halt the expanding international arms trade that funnels an ever-increasing flow of destructive modern weaponry and military technology into tinderboxes like the Middle East?

Perhaps, as optimists believe, the end of the cold war signals a new golden age, but these kinds of unresolved complicated issues also suggest that the world faces new forms of vulnerability at a time when the two great powers that provided an uneasy stability for half a century are less able to control events as the Soviet Union approaches disintegration and the United States stands in danger of decline.

As I write, near the halfway point of the Bush administration, the American condition at home remains bogged down by petty squabbles and lack of political will. President and Congress spar inconclusively over old questions of taxes, deficits, and public funding. The deficit, driven by the savings and loan bailout and Mideast troop deployment, continues to rise. Political leaders in both White House and Congress conceal their failure to act by employing false accounting methods and sleight of hand budgetary devices. Growing surpluses accumulated in the Social Security trust funds are used to mask the real deficit. Instead of preserving those funds, as intended by law, for the large numbers of baby boomers when they reach retirement age in the next century, they are spent to meet daily demands of the federal government. Major spending items totaling hundreds of billions of dollars (as in the savings and loan bailout) are declared "off budget" and therefore not accountable in legally required actions to reduce the budget deficit, through either spending cuts or increased taxes, or a combination of the two.

Political timidity still prevails. Members of Congress cower before the prospect that a vote to raise needed funds by increasing taxes will provide political opponents with material for negative thirty-second television commercials. The Bush administration has been typified by a passive/reactive approach to foreign and domestic challenges and its frank admission that there aren't the resources to deal with many of them. In fighting a "war" on drugs and in fashioning new public initiatives in education and the environment, Bush identifies the problems but doesn't propose spending to solve them. Sloganeering continues to take the place of substance.

American life grows increasingly fragmented and divisive. Along with this comes a further tendency of people to withdraw from public affairs and distance themselves from public questions.

They have good reason to do so. The performance of the American political system inspires more cynicism. Negative TV campaign techniques are more pronounced as campaigns grow even dirtier and personal attacks stronger. There's no doubt that this climate contributes to destroying careers, driving good people from public service, and inducing even more cynicism. Special interests possess greater power over the process, in part because of societal fragmentation and because politicians are increasingly beholden to lobbyists and political action groups that provide them with the immense sums needed to run for and hold their public offices. Campaign funding is a national disgrace. For members of Congress, more and more time is spent raising the funds necessary to run their reelection campaigns, and the very schedule of Congress is set not by deliberation of issues but by political fund raising.

Congress schedules no votes on Mondays because that day, and especially that night, are set aside for fund raising, and it takes no votes on Fridays so that members can visit their home districts for more fund raising. Increasingly, campaign money comes not from constituents at home but from political action committees based in Washington, and the cost of campaigning soars. Since 1976, for instance, the cost of winning a U.S. Senate seat has gone from an average of six hundred thousand dollars to over four million dollars—an increase of 470 percent in just fourteen years. This cost, and the source of the money, make members all the more obligated to the special interests. By contributing disproportionately to incumbents and protecting their congressional seats (political action committees give to incumbents at a rate of four to one in the Senate and eight to one in the House), the prevailing system perpetuates the status quo and keeps out people with fresh ideas and new approaches to public problems.

America's presidential election process is also too long, too costly, and too driven by public opinion polls and advertising tactics. It need not be, but campaign conditions are likely to worsen until the political parties rewrite their rules to shorten the interminable length of election campaigns and agree in advance to hold a series of true nationally televised debates for their presidential candidates and until lawmakers require networks to make available free airtime for political commercials over the publicly licensed airwaves.

While American politics operates in an increasingly negative atmosphere, with politicians hostage to moneyed interests, the American press, preoccupied with scandal, more and more practices celebrity journalism in which entertainment masks as news. The press's critical role of rigorously holding public officials accountable and, perhaps more important, of establishing the truth and falsity of political campaign claims assumes greater importance. But the recent record of the press in this area is one of inconsistency and lack of aggressiveness. Not only did regulatory and congressional overseers fail to detect abuses in the savings and loan institutions, in the Department of Housing and Urban Development, in the National Security Council, on Wall Street, and in the religious broadcasting operations over the public airwaves, but in the eighties the press, too, failed to pay attention to these areas until they reached crisis proportions.

American life is more divided in other ways. Racial tensions have intensified. In the eighties it became more acceptable to express prejudice openly. Nor are expressions of racial hostility coming solely from whites; perhaps inevitably, black demagoguery is on the rise, and open resentment or hatred of whites appears to have increased. Further exacerbating racial tension is the rising level of violence in every American city. Assaults between mobs of blacks and whites become more common—or at least attract more press attention—while the pathology of the inner cities with its deadly cycle of drugs and crime grows worse.

Theodore Roosevelt's old problem of "hyphenated Americans"—putting one's ethnic or racial group before one's nation (African-American, Italian-American, Mexican-American)—is more pronounced and makes reaching consensus more difficult. So are distances between other groups of Americans: between white and blue collar, college and noncollege, civilian and military.

The growing stratification of American life leads more people to associate within their own social, economic, and racial groups and to grow more removed from those outside them. Here, too, such separation makes more difficult the forging of public consensus necessary to set national goals. Proposals for mandatory public service are one way of easing cultural divisions, bringing disparate groups closer, and encouraging a shared sense of national purpose. Requiring young Americans to choose among service in the military, environmental cleanup projects, drug clinics, or public hospitals can be seen as American society's price for the benefits of citizenship and a way to help dissipate some of the negativism and cynicism that surrounds the idea of government and those who serve the public. This is an idea whose time should have come long before and that needs to be implemented.

About government, the question is not whether America needs less government at the expense of more private operations; obviously it needs both, and the best of each. In the eighties it had the worst of both. That there is even an argument about the *need* for a federal government, or the *need* for reasonable regulation, in late-twentieth-century America shows how serious this problem has become.

Just as obviously, America needs to do a better job in strengthening educational standards. The need goes beyond improving science and math achievements. Equally important, if not more, is the need to provide a better historical perspective so that young Americans understand the constitutional principles of their democracy and the forces that shape the modern world. The woeful response of young Americans to the events in Eastern Europe indicates that many do not understand them.

One lesson of Iran-contra is that Americans need to appreciate why checks on power are essential and why excessive secrecy *always* poses a threat to liberty. In my experience, a shocking number do not. Too often they are ignorant of American history—real history, not romance and political fables. A survey of college freshmen toward the end of the eighties revealed that two out of three did not know the dates—or even the decades—of World War II, World War I, or the Civil War. As one scholar said, in reflecting on those findings, "In such a context of ignorance, it follows that millions of Americans admire Clint Eastwood and Jane Fonda and are oblivious of General George Marshall, President Woodrow Wilson, and General Ulysses S. Grant." Dr. J. S. Holiday added:

> In considering why so few Americans admire George Washington or Booker T. Washington, why the absence of heroes is a mark of our times, why celebrity status has replaced heroic virtue, I must emphasize that professional historians are part of the cause. In his book, *The Death of the Past,* British historian J. H. Plumb points out that under the influence of New History, Psycho-History, and Revisionist History, timeless heroes have been replaced by impersonal forces, or they have been denigrated by New Truths that have opened the way for impressionable students and cynical adults to think that maybe Betsy Ross was a lesbian, Abraham Lincoln a racist, Thomas Jefferson a hypocritical slave owner who had a black mistress, and Booker T. Washington an Uncle Tom.

Television, with its false "docudramas" and the growing trend of network news programs to "reenact" or "dramatize" actual news events with actors, further blurs the distinction between celebrities and true national figures of distinction. And by its nature, television is a poor vehicle to provide understanding of the deeper forces that made the society function. That has to come from education, from a sense of community, from a shared common understanding of what is worth celebrating about America, and, perhaps most important, what is *not.*

Real patriotism involves much more than jingoistically evoking past glories, whether real or fanciful, or invading small states like Grenada and Panama with overwhelming power. As thoughts of decline and awareness of growing problems have filtered into national consciousness, part of the destructive legacies of the Vietnam and Watergate years, Americans and their leaders seem to need to prove that they, alone in the weary world, are unique. They proclaim, romanticize, and grow lyrical over their country's great power and wealth and possessions and in the process make it appear that America is different *because* of these assets and *because* they assert love of country so loudly. In this, Americans are no different from Romans cheering their legions, Russians extolling their motherland, Germans hailing their fatherland. They loved their countries, too.

The greatness of America stands for none of these things, not for its power or its possessions and its wealth, national or individual. Its greatness derives from the simple but powerful idea that America represents something more, a promise to do better for its people through its freedoms, its tolerance, its decency, its originality and, by its example, to hold up an emblem for the world. It was this idea that first created the nation, caught the world's attention, and in time formed what the sociologist Gunnar Myrdal called the American Creed. The essence of that creed, as Myrdal defined it, was both moralistic and morally conscious. "The ordinary American is the opposite of a cynic," he wrote. "He is on the average more of a believer and a defender of the faith in humanity. . . . We recognize the American, wherever we meet him, as a practical idealist."

These are old-fashioned notions, I realize, and perhaps I cherish them because I have been shaped by an America that no longer exists. Born in the depression years, affected by awareness of World War II when my father was overseas, coming of age during high school, college, and Korean War Army service in years that mirrored the cold war era, witnessing personally as a young reporter the epic civil rights struggle that proved America had the capacity to be true to its own principles of equality and justice, I have seen my country, for all its mistakes, forge a bright chapter, one that became an inspiration for the world.

Perhaps these notions of mine are generational and no longer as relevant to younger Americans looking ahead to the new world forming in the nineties and beyond, though I doubt it. And obviously those values still have powerful applicability in the world of the nineties. From Tiananmen Square to East Berlin, expressions of democratic ideals vibrate throughout the consciousness of people seeking the same kinds of freedoms that Americans take for granted. The question is whether they continue to have equal applicability for Americans at home.

I believe they do. I believe the much-maligned "yuppie" generation, a generation imbued both with fiscal conservatism and practicality and with social liberalism and individual tolerance, shares those same values and, when challenged, will respond positively to fulfill them. As yet American leadership to summon them has not emerged.

It is a curious aspect of American life, and perhaps the genius of its system, that its people always expect too much of their leaders when the very nature of the democracy dictates that leaders follow more than they lead. That is not as negative as it seems, nor does this mean that strong leaders with vision are incapable of setting goals by appealing to *national* over parochial interests, to the most generous instincts in people instead of the most selfish. It does mean that politicians act when forced to; they respond, as in the example of Eastern Europe, when pressure from below becomes so great it can no longer be ignored. For two centuries, great issues that transformed American life were resolved only when they reached critical public mass. That was the case of antislavery in the early years of the Republic, of civil rights and segregation more than a century later, of equality for women, which proceeded from suffragettes battling to win the vote to the broader struggle for full equality. All these were accomplished over time, not overnight, and often took generations instead of decades to achieve. This has also been true of other issues that gradually formed powerful political forces for change: consumerism, the environment, and the antiwar movement that ended American involvement in Vietnam after more than a decade of public pressure. It will be true of American problems of the nineties and beyond. They will be solved only when—and *if*—sufficient public pressure demands it and leadership then emerges to fulfill it.

For at least a decade Americans have had to look abroad for inspiration. It was the voices of such people as Russia's Andrei Sakharov, Poland's Lech Walesa, China's Fang Lizhi, South Africa's Nelson Mandela and Desmond Tutu, and Czechoslovakia's Vaclav Havel that provided examples of vision and daring.

No American voice in the eighties rang with such universal appeal as theirs. None approached the public candor and eloquence expressed by Havel, the playwright and former imprisoned dissident. Upon delivering his New Year's Day message of 1990 as Czechoslovakia's new democratically elected president, Havel referred to the cold war leadership that had preceded him: "I do not think you put me into this office so that I, of all people, should also lie to you." Their country was not prospering, Havel said bluntly, and their creative and spiritual energies were not being used to their full potential. "Not even all of that is the most important thing," he said. "The worst thing is that we are living in a decayed moral environment. We have become morally ill, because we have become accustomed to saying one thing and thinking another. We have learned not to believe in anything, not to have consideration for one another and only to look after ourselves. Notions such as love, compassion, friendship, community, humility and forgiveness have lost their depth and dimension, and for many of us they represent merely some kinds of psychological idiosyncrasy, or appear to be some kind of stray relic from times past, something rather comical in the age of computers and space rockets. . . ."

He then issued a summons that Americans never heard from their leaders in the eighties. It was in their hands alone, he said, whether they had the courage to reawaken, cast aside the self-defeating negative spirit of the past, and rekindle their civic, national, and political self-confidence in a historically new way. The same applies to America. It, too, needs to reawaken and apply fresh thinking and actions to the task of building the future.

In the end, America needs have no "Grand Design" to impose on the world, as some of our critics urge. America needs nothing more than to be true to itself, to its ideals and to its values, and to work to create a more just, humane society at home and join others in working toward a freer, more open world. This is not a matter of romantic idealism; it is a case of practicality. There is no better way for America to meet its challenges at home and abroad than by being realistic, by remaining faithful to truth, by not living with illusions, and by working to perfect an imperfect society.

PLAYERS OF THE EIGHTIES

Roger Ailes, who produced the Bush prison furlough/Pledge of Allegiance negative campaign attack commercials, continued to employ similar negative tactics as media consultant to national Republican candidates. In press interviews he insisted that 85 percent of his TV political commercials for candidates were positive.

Air traffic controllers numbered twenty-five hundred people fewer employed at decade's end than their peak strength during the 1982 strike before Reagan fired them. In the same period, U.S. air traffic increased from sixty million flights to more than eighty million annually. Controllers continued to complain about unsafe air conditions resulting from too many planes and too few controllers. Early in 1990, after experiencing one of the worst safety records in some time, federal airline safety inspectors cited a shortage of inspectors (then 20 percent fewer than needed) as a contributing factor.

Lee Atwater became chairman of the Republican National Committee and chief strategist for Republican candidates nationwide. In March 1990, at the age of thirty-nine, he underwent radical treatment for a brain tumor.

Jim Bakker was sentenced to forty-five years in prison on October 24, 1989 and fined five hundred thousand dollars after his conviction on all twenty-four fraud and conspiracy counts during a trial in Charlotte, North Carolina. Bakker blamed his downfall on rival televangelist Jerry Falwell, the devil, greedy aides, and a scorned secretary. After the verdict his wife, Tammy Faye, sang a hymn before the TV cameras and paraphrased Yogi Berra, saying, "It isn't over till it's over." Bakker appealed his sentence.

Robert Bartley remained editor of the editorial page of the *Wall Street Journal* and a staunch defender of supply-side economics. Editorially the *Journal* continued to be the nation's most influential voice of conservatism.

Ivan Boesky was furloughed from prison on November 15, 1989, the third anniversary of his plea bargaining agreement. He had then served a year and a half of a three-year sentence at California's minimum-security Lompoc Federal Prison, popularly known as Club Fed West because of the high number of federal people sent there and for its pleasant Southern California climate.

George Bush maintained an even higher popularity, as measured by the polls, than Reagan during his first two years as president. His popularity rating increased after he ordered an American invasion of Panama in 1989 and sent U.S. troops to the Persian Gulf a year later. Then, in the fall of 1990, he experienced a dramatic drop in the polls after he agreed to include new taxes in a bitter battle with Congress over the budget. Bush's strongest opposition came from his own party and led to threats that a Republican would challenge him on his renomination in 1992.

Jimmy Carter remained active in public affairs, playing major roles as a mediator in international disputes and winning praise for his skill in handling delicate situations in Africa and Central America. Among trouble spots to which he traveled were Panama and Nicaragua, where he headed teams monitoring elections. In 1990 polls showed Carter with a more favorable public rating than Ronald Reagan.

Richard Cheney, vice-chairman of the House Iran-Contra Committee, became secretary of defense under President George Bush. His first crisis in that job came during a controversy over the extent of U.S. involvement in an unsuccessful coup attempt to overthrow Panama's Manuel Antonio Noriega in October 1989. After acknowledging that the United States had been more involved in the covert operation than it said publicly, Cheney accused some members of Congress of attempting to micromanage U.S. foreign policy, the same argument made by the Reagan administration during the Iran-contra hearings. Later Cheney oversaw the Pentagon's massive deployment to the Persian Gulf and carried out personal missions there for President Bush.

William S. Cohen continued to serve in the U.S. Senate, where he became vice-chairman of the Senate Intelligence Committee. The chairman of that committee was another member of the Iran-Contra Committee, Senator David Boren of Oklahoma.

Michael Deaver received three years' probation and was fined one hundred thousand dollars after being convicted for lying to a congressional subcommittee and a federal grand jury about his lobbying activities after leaving the White House. He resumed his Washington consulting business.

Drexel Burnham Lambert, Inc., the firm that virtually created the two-hundred-billion-dollar junk bond market that financed the decade's giddy corporate take-over business, filed for bankruptcy on February 13,

1990, after defaulting on payment of more than one hundred million dollars in loans. The end came after the near collapse of the junk bond market, resulting in failure of great corporations and unraveling of the Campeau Corporation's retailing empire. By then Wall Street employment had dropped by thirty thousand since the crash, with an additional twenty thousand expected to lose their jobs.

Michael Dukakis served out his term as Massachusetts governor, scheduled to end in January 1991. His popularity in the state plummeted to only 15 percent approval ratings in polls after he faced a budget crisis and a legislature that would not raise taxes. Exactly one year after he lost the presidential election, his wife, Kitty, was hospitalized when she ingested rubbing alcohol, an act caused in part, doctors said, by a recurring depression.

Jerry Falwell disbanded the Moral Majority on June 10, 1989, ten years after founding it, explaining that the organization had accomplished its goal of getting conservative Christians involved in politics. Donations to the Moral Majority had dropped following the widely publicized sex scandals involving fellow televangelists.

Thomas Foley, who asked Fawn Hall the question that drew the memorable response about the need sometimes to go "above the written law" during the Iran-contra hearings, became speaker of the House of Representatives and thus the nation's ranking Democrat and constitutionally second in the presidential succession line after the vice president. His predecessor as speaker, Jim Wright of Texas, was forced to resign during a congressional ethics investigation.

George Gilder was among the "celebrity" authors who signed contracts in 1989 to write brief hard-cover books that contained corporate advertising and would be distributed to subscribers. Before that he charged that several prominent publishers had backed off plans to reissue a revised edition of his book *Sexual Suicide* after protests from feminist editors. His next books were *Men and Marriage,* and *Microcosm: The Quantum Revolution in Economics and Technology.*

Mikhail Gorbachev, after becoming Soviet president and Communist party general secretary and the figure most responsible for permitting the peaceful move toward democracy in Eastern Europe, became locked in an increasingly difficult struggle for his own survival as protests mounted in the Soviet Union, food shortages led to panic buying and runs on stores, and independence movements gained strength in the Baltic states. He continued, however, to exhibit a visionary strain as he told Americans during a 1990 summit visit that "the cold war is now behind us." He pressed for further reforms and urged radical new alliances with the West to create "a new civilization." To an audience of cheering Stanford University students, he said, "My friends, your generation will not only create a new world order, but live it."

Jessica Hahn, the church secretary from West Babylon, Long Island, who said she was raped by televangelist Jim Bakker, sold her story to *Playboy,* for which she posed topless, for a fee reportedly between five hundred thousand and one million dollars. "She's an American phenomenon," her lawyer said, explaining her value as a TV miniseries subject. "She's not just the person who had sexual relations with Jim Bakker, but she grew up in the church. She was one of the sheep. The fact that she was abused is very telling about this society."

Fawn Hall, Oliver North's secretary, who helped shred secret Iran-contra documents and removed other classified material from the National Security Council White House complex, left the government to pursue a television/show business career. The idea of a political career had "crossed my mind," she said, adding that she was considering becoming a TV talk show host.

Lee Hamilton continued to serve in Congress from Indiana.

Willie Horton remained in prison. In an interview after the 1988 presidential election had made his name known across America, Horton was quoted as saying of Bush, "He may be just a cheap political opportunist. But I can't help but question his moral judgment."

Daniel Inouye was defeated by George Mitchell when he attempted to become Senate majority leader. He remained in the U.S. Senate.

Jack Kemp, the original supply-side politician, failed to gain the Republican presidential nomination in 1988 and left Congress. As Bush's new secretary of the Housing and Urban Development Department, Kemp inherited the HUD scandal from the Reagan years.

Ayatollah Ruhollah Khomeini died on June 3, 1989, in Teheran after a heart attack at the age of eighty-six (some reports said eighty-nine). At the time of his death eight Americans were still held hostage in the Mideast by pro-Iranian terrorist groups.

Arthur Laffer ran a financial consulting business out of California and often logged more than ten thousand miles a week in speaking appearances. His own attempt at politics failed when he sought the Republican senatorial nomination from California in 1986. Two years later he was a national cochairman for Bush's presidential campaign. Of his role as intellectual godfather of supply-side economics, he said, "We were a group of people who fit a time and place. To expect us to fit another time and place is not to understand us."

Dennis B. Levine, the young investment banker whose testimony about Ivan Boesky spawned the Wall Street insider trading scandal, struck a plea bargain deal with federal prosecutors in which he pleaded guilty to four felony counts, was fined $362,000, and returned $11.6 million in illegal profits. After serving less than a year of a two-year prison term, he was paroled and then gave a lecture to Columbia University Business School students. His subject: white-collar crime.

Arthur Liman returned to his law practice in New York. Among his new clients after the Iran-contra affair was Michael Milken.

Edwin Meese continued to live and work in Washington, where he was a fellow at the conservative Heritage Institute and a consultant. He also lectured, wrote a nationally syndicated newspaper column, and was writing a book that he said would combat inaccurate reporting about him during the Iran-contra affair.

Michael Milken was indicted on ninety-eight instances of fraud, racketeering, and illegal insider stock trading. After his indictment prominent business executives, bankers, and lawyers from around the country raised $150,000 to purchase full-page ads in leading newspapers headed "Mike Milken, We Believe in You." In a plea bargain deal, struck just before additional criminal charges were to be filed against him, Milken on April 14, 1990, agreed to plead guilty to six lesser felony counts and pay a six-hundred-million-dollar fine. The plea deal, which closed the largest criminal prosecution in Wall Street history, was criticized because it left Milken immensely wealthy and didn't require him to give information on other cases until after he was sentenced. In a statement Richard C. Breeden, chairman of the Securities and Exchange Commission, said: "Despite the efforts to mold public opinion, Mr. Milken's admissions today demonstrate that he stood at the center of a network of manipulation, fraud and deceit." Milken's sentence was ten years in jail.

George Mitchell was elected majority leader of the U.S. Senate by his fellow Democrats. Among those he defeated was Daniel Inouye.

Walter Mondale left Washington to practice law in his native Minnesota but did not run for the U.S. Senate, as had been expected.

John Nields returned to his Washington, D.C., law practice. He was among the lawyers active in assisting growing numbers of homeless.

Lyn Nofziger's conviction on charges of illegal lobbying at the White House in the Wedtech scandal was overturned by a U.S. court of appeals panel because of what the two to one court majority called "ambiguity" in the conflict of interest law under which Nofziger was tried. Later the full court of appeals unanimously rejected a prosecutor's request to reconsider the ruling reversing Nofziger's conviction.

Manuel Antonio Noriega, after surviving two coup attempts, a defeat by Panamanian voters, which he declared invalid, and repeated public appeals for his overthrow by President Bush, was deposed by a U.S. military invasion just before Christmas 1989. Noriega surrendered to American authorities after days of sanctuary inside the Vatican Embassy in Panama City, was charged, and was brought back in shackles to the United States, where he awaited trial. He threatened to expose secrets about high U.S. knowledge of drug trafficking and make further embarrassing Iran-contra revelations.

Oliver L. North was convicted by a Washington, D.C., jury of falsifying and destroying documents, accepting an illegal gratuity, and aiding and abetting the obstruction of Congress, but acquitted of nine other more serious charges and given a three-year suspended sentence. He was ordered to perform twelve hundred hours of community service in a Washington, D.C., drug prevention program. His lawyer portrayed him as a "sacrificial lamb" who obeyed the orders of his commander in chief and was fired to spare Reagan political harm. Though the judge warned the jury not to be influenced by his lawyer's argument that North was only following orders, jurors said they believed North's sincerity and did not want him to go to jail. Thus, like the country, they accepted a Nuremberg defense rationale about North's activities. Judge Gerhard Gesell also observed that while North's notoriety had caused him many difficulties, "it has also made you a rich man." North was then being paid twenty-five thousand dollars per lecture while appearing regularly before wealthy conservative groups throughout the country. On July 20, 1990, a U.S. Court of Appeals panel overturned North's conviction by a two to one vote and ordered the case sent back to the trial court for a new set of extensive hearings. This raised questions whether convictions of any Iran-contra defendants who received grants of immunity for their congressional testimony would ever stand. The two judges voting to overturn North's conviction were Reagan appointees with strong conservative credentials.

John Poindexter's lawyers said in court that the former presidential national security adviser regularly briefed Vice President Bush about secret Iran-contra operations and that President Reagan had authorized many of the activities for which Poindexter was indicted. The judge ruled that for his trial Poindexter was entitled to Reagan's personal papers and diaries, but not those of Bush. On April 7, 1990, the jury found him guilty on all five criminal counts involving conspiring to mislead Congress, obstructing congressional inquiries, and lying to lawmakers. Two months later he was sentenced to six months in prison. In sentencing him, Judge Harold H. Greene warned of the dangers of high government officials using national security to mask deceit and wrongdoing. Not to give a jail term, the judge added, "would be tantamount to a statement that a scheme to lie and obstruct Congress is of no great moment" and would "encourage others in positions of authority and secrecy to frustrate laws that fail to accord with their notions of what is best for the country, and to carry out their own private policies in the name of the United States." Up to that point none of the Iran-contra defendants had served time in jail, all having won suspended sentences and even praise from judges.

Ronald Reagan continued to live in Bel Air, California, where he purchased the mansion leased to him by friends, gave speeches, and worked on his memoirs. Seven months after he left office, he underwent surgery to remove fluid on his brain caused, doctors said, when he was thrown from a horse while riding in Mexico. In her memoir, published late in 1989, his wife, Nancy, confirmed that she had relied on an astrologer's advice for scheduling of presidential trips and news conferences, meetings with heads of state, and an assessment of how well Reagan and Mikhail Gorbachev would get along. In his first book published after the presidency, *Speaking My Mind,* Reagan said of the Iran-contra scandal that "in looking back I wonder if this whole thing wasn't a setup, a sting operation, by the Iranians." After being ordered by the judge to give videotaped testimony in John Poindexter's criminal trial, on more than one hundred occasions Reagan testified that he could not recall details about Iran-contra. The prosecutor assailed him for winking toward Poindexter from the witness stand and accused him of giving "biased" testimony in order to protect Poindexter.

Oral Roberts, whose televangelist Tulsa ministry faced mounting debts of more than twenty-five million dollars, was forced to close both his City of Faith Hospital and medical school and sell a married student housing complex near the Oral Roberts University campus and five ministry-owned houses, including those in which he and a son lived.

Warren Rudman remained a senator from New Hampshire, with close ties to the Bush White House, but he also continued to display his independence by voting against his party and President Bush on a constitutional amendment plan to make flag desecration a crime. In July 1990 Bush nominated a Rudman protégé to the U.S. Supreme Court to fill a vacancy left by Justice William Brennan's sudden retirement, a move that liberal critics feared would signal a potential historic shift to the right by the Court. Judge David H. Souter was Rudman's assistant, and later his deputy, when Rudman was New Hampshire's attorney general in the 1970s. As a U.S. senator Rudman had been instrumental in recommending Souter for appointments to the bench.

Richard Secord, in a plea bargain deal in November 1989, pleaded guilty to a felony charge of lying to Congress when he said that no money raised by the Enterprise had gone to Oliver North during the Iran-contra affair. On January 24, 1990 he was given a two-year probationary sentence and ordered to pay a fifty-dollar court fee, thus continuing the no-jail-time record in Iran-contra cases.

David Stockman left government service and became a senior partner in the Blackstone Group, a private investment bank that helped engineer Japan's Sony Corporation take-over of Hollywood's Columbia Pictures. He was reported to earn more than two million dollars a year and lived in Connecticut's fashionable Fairfield County.

Jimmy Swaggart remained on the air after he acknowledged involvement with a prostitute. Despite bad publicity and increased public skepticism, a Gallup survey in late 1989 reported that the number of Americans who watched religious television and the number who contributed to televangelists remained stable.

Donald J. Trump fell on hard times after the junk bond market collapsed and was forced to battle bankers and other creditors for payment of outstanding loans. In the summer of 1990 bankers put together a rescue package designed to keep Trump solvent for another twelve months. He received $65 million in new loans and was able to defer interest and principal payments on about $1 billion of his $2 billion debt. Trump was forced to withdraw his most ambitious take-over bid of $7.5 billion for American Airlines after airline stocks fell sharply amid fears of the viability of junk bonds in October 1989 and later put the Trump Shuttle up for sale. Early the next year, New York news coverage of Trump's pending divorce suit overshadowed momentous events in Moscow, Eastern Europe, and South Africa. It was described in the press as "Trump v. Trump, the divorce," and as "the first great celebrity trial of the nineties." Trump's next book, *Trump: Surviving at the Top,* reflecting his change in fortune, became another best seller at the end of 1990.

Paul Volcker, former chairman of the Federal Reserve Board, campaigned for public service as head of a bipartisan commission and continued to cite statistics showing uninterest in public service careers at Harvard's Kennedy School of Government, where he had studied.

E. Bob Wallach, close friend and law school classmate of former Attorney General Edwin Meese, was sentenced to six years in prison and fined $250,000 in connection with the Wedtech influence-peddling scandal. In sentencing him, the judge assailed Wallach's behavior, saying: "Major government contract awards were being made because of your influence at the back stairs of the White House. . . ." During Wallach's trial Meese was cross-examined sharply about his friend's activities and testified he had only a "general" or "dim" recollection of their key conversations.

Jude Wanniski operated a consulting business out of New Jersey and published an annual *MediaGuide* that awarded high ratings to "movement conservative" journalists and low ones to liberals.

NOTES AND SOURCES

Among the sources for this book is a historical treasure in the form of extensive tape-recorded oral history interviews of the Reagan governorship years in California. Transcripts from these tape recordings were checked for accuracy by the subjects after interviews had been conducted by scholars at various branches of the University of California system. The recordings and transcripts are maintained on the Berkeley, Davis, Los Angeles, Claremont, and Fullerton campuses. They are indispensable to an understanding of the attitudes and values that were commonly shared by the Reagan group in California and later came into play in Washington. Many of the California events described in those interviews eerily foreshadow those of the Reagan presidency.

Interviewing for the Reagan Gubernatorial Era series began in 1979, a year before Reagan's successful presidential campaign. The project was funded by the California legislature as part of a continuing state-financed California History Documentation Project established to tape-record autobiographical interviews with persons significant in the history of California and the West. In addition, the oral history project drew upon and supplemented research by such participating programs as the Hoover Institute at Stanford University, which houses the Ronald Reagan Papers, the California State Archives in Sacramento, and work resulting from grants by the National Endowment for the Humanities, the Rockefeller Foundation, and the Bay Area State and Regional Planning Project. Interviewed for the oral history project were Reagan himself, key aides and operatives who subsequently came with him to Washington, and the group of wealthy conservative businessmen who first were so instrumental in pressing Reagan to become an active political candidate and later played leading roles in financing, staffing, and shepherding his political career from Sacramento in the sixties to the White House in the eighties. Some of the interviews were with people who had significant dealings with Reagan in the early 1950s when he was beginning to move from actor to corporate spokesman and political commentator. All are revealing for their insights into social, economic, and political views that so clearly were held strongly by Reagan and many of those who later helped establish the standards of his presidency in the 1980s. Where quotation marks from these Reagan aides involved in the California years are used in the narrative, they are taken directly from transcripts of the oral history interviews. Unless otherwise cited, the material that forms the basis of the narrative beginning with Ronald Reagan's inaugural day on January 20, 1981, and then depicts scenes around the United States comes from my interviews while traveling across the country in the months just before that inauguration. Most of the subsequent events described in this book, such as the Iran-contra congressional hearings, are also the product of personal reporting and interviews. Months after the hearings ended, for instance, I conducted lengthy retrospective interviews with leaders of that committee, both Republicans and Democrats, the key attorneys and staff investigators. All were tape-recorded, as were virtually all the other interviews (such as those on Wall Street) from which I have drawn material presented herein. In the fall of 1988, during the closing months of the last presidential election of the Reagan years, I traveled again to the same locations described early in this book and reinterviewed many of the same people to whom I had spoken at the beginning of the decade. Their assessments of the eighties are described in the segment that begins with George Bush's inauguration on January 20, 1989.

Manuscript source citations not otherwise attributed follow.

NOTES

Quotes before **PROLOGUE**

"It was a period of moral slump . . .": from Samuel Hopkins Adams, *The Incredible Era: The Life and Times of Warren Gamaliel Harding* (Boston: Houghton Mifflin Company, 1939), p. 186.

"Reagan runs continuously . . .": from Garry Wills, *Reagan's America. Innocents at Home* (New York: Doubleday & Company, Inc., 1987), p. 2.

BOOK ONE: WASHINGTON, JAN. 20, 1981

1. The Capital

page 19. "When you gotta pay . . .": quoted by Colman McCarthy, *Washington Post,* February 1, 1981, G-2.

19. "They give you . . .": Ward Sinclair and Bill Peterson, *Washington Post,* January 21, 1981, pp. A29–32.

20. "looked like furry . . .": Elisabeth Bumiller, *Washington Post,* January 19, 1981, p. B1.

20. "furs swallowed . . .": ibid.

20. "a perfumed herd . . .": ibid.

20. "There are 10 times . . .": ibid.

20. "A bacchanalia of . . .": ibid.
20. "As the ragged outcasts . . .": ibid.
21. "A couple of years . . .": ibid.
21. "Well, this is . . .": Megan Rosenfeld and Joseph McClellan, *Washington Post,* January 20, 1981, p. B1.
23. "This is what . . .": Sinclair and Peterson, op. cit.
23. "It's sort of . . .": ibid.

2. The Loser

page 25. He made detailed handwritten notes . . . : Carter's diary notations are published verbatim in his memoir, *Keeping Faith: Memoirs of a President* (New York: Bantam Books, 1982), pp. 9–13. Other direct Carter quotes cited in this chapter are also from his memoir.
26. Reagan "had had a long night, was sleeping . . .": ibid. p. 11.
26. Footnote: Deaver described that scene . . . : Michael Deaver, *Behind the Scenes* (New York: William Morrow and Company, Inc., 1987), pp. 98–99.
30. "The twentieth century will be . . . ": quoted by John Dos Passos, *U.S.A.: The 42nd Parallel* (Boston: Houghton Mifflin Company, 1930), p. 5.
38. ". . . a Reagan victory . . .": Deaver, *Scenes,* p. 99. Deaver added: "There is no doubt in my mind that the euphoria of the hostage release would have rolled over the land like a tidal wave. Carter would have been a hero, and many of the complaints against him forgotten. He would have have won."
39. Carter "looked at himself in the mirror . . .": Carter, *Faith,* p. 13.
39. Reagan reflected on the physical change . . . : Deaver, *Scenes,* p. 100.
40. "Mr. Jordan, the president wants you": Hamilton Jordan, *Crisis: The Last Year of the Carter Presidency* (New York: G. P. Putnam's Sons, 1982), p. 16. Jordan, as White House chief of staff, had access to transcripts of calls.

3. The Winner

page 42. Two girl friends, who had dated him . . . : Anne Edwards, *Early Reagan: The Rise to Power* (New York: William Morrow and Company, Inc., 1987), p. 142. Hers is the best account of Reagan's family and upbringing.
43. "As a kid . . .": ibid., p. 62.
44. "You know why . . .": ibid., p. 64.
45. "Literally flushed with . . .": Wills, *America,* p. 78

4. The New America

page 59. "There is a legend . . .": Edwards, *Early Reagan,* p. 540.
60. "Disabled by ground fire . . .": ibid. p. 541.
61. "I discovered that night . . .": ibid., p. 90.

5. The New Conservatism

page 65. "The neutral, umpire state . . .": Arthur S. Link, *American Epoch: A History of the United States Since the 1890's* (New York: Alfred A. Knopf, 1955), p. 69.
66. "In our own day . . .": Richard Hofstadter, *The Age of Reform: From Bryan to F.D.R.* (New York: Alfred A. Knopf, 1955), p. 3.
67. "No nation in history . . .": full text of "A Time for Change" speech quoted in Edwards, *Reagan,* p. 561.
75. "No doubt the precise line . . .": Hofstadter, *Reform,* pp. 13–14.

6. The Great Reaction

page 78. Parody of *Macbeth* called *MacBird!* . . . : from Richard Harwood and Haynes Johnson, *Lyndon* (New York: Praeger Publishers, 1973), p. 124.

8. A New Era

page 94. "If you don't like Mr. Truman . . .": reported by Martin Schram, who was present, *Washington Post,* January 21, 1981.

BOOK TWO: AMERICA, JAN. 20, 1981

9. The Cabal

page 99. "a tattered snake skin . . .": Jude Wanniski, "We Will All Be Supply Siders," in his letter to the editor, *Washington Post,* July 27, 1981.
99. "argue for a reduction . . .": ibid.
100. "Over and over again . . .": David A. Stockman, *The Triumph of Politics: Why the Reagan Revolution Failed* (New York: Harper & Row, Publishers, 1986), p. 48.
100. "pixie air . . .": John Brooks, "Annals of Finance: The Supply Side," *New Yorker* (April 19, 1982), p. 142.
102. "Now I kept thinking . . .": ibid., p. 100.
102. "I ran to New York . . .": ibid.
104. "We called the group . . .": ibid., p. 104.
104. "an economic doctrine . . .": Evans and Novak, *Washington Post,* June 8, 1978.
105. "thoroughly hosed him . . .": Stockman, *Education,* p. 10.
108. "minimalist government . . .": ibid., p. 8.
108. "I was about to meet . . .": ibid., p. 45.
109. "cussed a blue . . .": ibid.
109. "Meese seemed . . .": ibid.
109. "saying very little . . .": ibid.
109. "Reagan's performance was . . .": ibid.
110. "was always a Trojan Horse . . .": William Greider, "The Education of David Stockman," *Atlantic* (December 1981).
110. "a blueprint for . . .": Stockman, *Politics,* pp. 65–68.
111. "What it is sure to do . . .": Brooks, *New Yorker,* p. 130.
112. "the inequality of riches . . .": Merle Curti, *The Growth of American Thought* (New York: Harper & Brothers, Publishers, 1943), p. 637.
112. "so frequent was the use . . .": Frederick Lewis Allen, *Only Yesterday: An Informal History of the Nineteen-Twenties* (New York: Harper & Brothers, Publishers, 1931), pp. 179–81.
112. "to serve our stockholders . . .": ibid., p. 130.
113. "Taxes were to be . . .": Charles A. Beard and Mary R. Beard, *The Rise of American Civilization* (New York: Macmillan Company, 1930), vol. 2, p. 701.
113. "Search and you shall . . .": George Gilder, *Wealth and Poverty* (New York: Bantam Books, 1981), p. 41.
114. "shrill moral exhortations . . .": Robert Claiborne, "The Feminist Menace," "Book World," *Washington Post,* January 13, 1974.
114. "promethean in its . . .": quoted by Henry Allen, *Washington Post,* February 18, 1981.
114. "ESP is important to me . . .": from an interview with Gilder by Henry Allen, *Washington Post,* February 13, 1981.
115. "Capitalism begins with . . .": Gilder, *Wealth,* p. 42.

10. Rustbelt

page 122. "The investment in . . .": William T. Golden, ed., *Science and Technology Advice to the President, Congress and Judiciary* (New York: Pergamon Press, 1988), p. 95.

11. Sunbelt

page 129. "Growth is a . . .": author's interview with Jay W. Forrester, published "Outlook," *Washington Post,* June 8, 1975.

BOOK THREE: THE TEFLON YEARS

13. Electronic Culture

page 139. "designed each presidential . . .": Donald T. Regan, *For the Record: From Wall Street to Washington* (New York: Harcourt Brace Jovanovich, 1988), p. 248.

141. "Television is just . . .": quoted by Bernard D. Nossiter, "The F.C.C.'s Big Giveaway Show," *Nation* (October 26, 1985), pp. 402–4.

146. "for perfect love . . .": Ruth Rosen, "Search for Yesterday," in *Watching Television,* ed. Todd Gitlin (New York: Pantheon Brooks, 1986), p. 42.

147. "the cross-fertilization of sports . . .": James Michener, *Sports in America* (New York: Fawcett Crest, 1977), p. 430.

14. Myths and Realities

page 154. "the literature of the spirit . . .": Joseph Campbell, with Bill Moyers, *The Power of Myth* (New York: Macmillan Company, 1988), p. 3.

164. "The leaders of . . .": William Manchester, *The Glory and the Dream: A Narrative History of America, 1939–1972* (Boston: Little, Brown and Company, 1973), vol. 1, p. 491.

166. "Calvin Coolidge still believed . . .": Allen, *Yesterday,* p. 182.

15. Privatizing

page 168. "wily stalkers of . . .": Howard Kurtz, *Washington Post,* January 5, 1983.

169. "If they're going . . .": *Wall Street Journal,* April 18, 1986, p. 1.

171. "During 1981, 1982 and . . .": from summary findings, House Energy and Commerce Subcommittee report, August 30, 1984.

171. "protect the source . . .": Cass Peterson, *Washington Post,* April 10, 1987.

174. "advocates for Wedtech . . .": Mary Thornton, ibid., May 26, 1987.

175. "introduce the company . . .": George Lardner, Jr., ibid., April 18, 1987.

176. "everything that was taking place . . .": George Lardner, Jr., ibid., July 2, 1988.

177. "A few yards from . . .": from "This Week with David Brinkley," ABC-TV, June 16, 1988.

178. "the increasingly troubled . . .": *Conduct and Accountability: A Report to the President by the President's Blue Ribbon Commission on Defense Management* (Washington, D.C.: U.S. Government Printing Office, June 1986), p. 1.

181. "You could hear it . . .": Bill McAllister and Chris Spolar, *Washington Post,* August 6, 1989.

182. "set up and . . .": Edward T. Pound and Kenneth H. Bacon, *Wall Street Journal,* May 25, 1989.

183. "There's not a . . .": David Johnston, *New York Times,* August 13, 1989, p. E-1.

183. "For conservative pro-Reagan . . .": James J. Kilpatrick, *Washington Post,* August 11, 1989.

191. "unmistakable evidence . . .": Paul Volcker, "The Quiet Crisis," Francis Boyer Lecture, delivered at the American Enterprise Institute, Washington, D.C., December 2, 1987.

16. God and Mammon

page 196. "Almost without our . . .": Jeffrey K. Hadden and Anson Shupe, *Televangelism: Power and Politics on God's Frontier* (New York: Henry Holt and Company, 1988), p. 40.
197. "one cannot possibly . . .": ibid., pp. 35–36.
198. "is founded on . . .": Gilder, *Wealth,* p. 310.
198. "metaphors for grace . . .": A. James Reichley, *Religion in American Public Life* (Washington, D.C.: Brookings Institution, 1985), p. 18.
198. "The free enterprise . . .": ibid., p. 17.
202. "The local stations . . .": Frances FitzGerald, *Cities on a Hill: A Journey Through Contemporary American Cultures* (New York: Simon and Schuster, 1986), p. 125.
202. "The greatest part . . .": Alexis de Tocqueville, *Democracy in America* (New York: Colonial Press, 1900), vol. 1, p. 304.
206. "All mass movements . . .": Eric Hoffer, *The True Believer: Thoughts on the Nature of Mass Movements* (New York: Harper & Row, Publishers, 1951), p. xi.

17. The Insiders

page 215. "There are no easy . . .": quoted in *Newsweek* (January 4, 1988), p. 42.
222. "any predator . . .": Connie Bruck, *The Predators' Ball: The Junk-Bond Raiders and the Man Who Staked Them* (New York: American Lawyer/Simon and Schuster, 1988), p. 17.
223. "The gospel according to . . .": ibid., p. 17.
226. "We have created . . .": "Greed on Wall Street," *Newsweek* (May 26, 1986), p. 45.

18. Deregulation

page 228. "seem out of . . .": *Newsweek* (March 9, 1987), p. 49.
232. "brash young traders . . .": Eric N. Berg, Kurt Eichenwald, and Julia Flynn Siler, *New York Times,* January 30, 1989, p. D6.
233. "Some of the agents . . .": ibid.

19. The Ledger

page 243. "economic and political power . . .": Thomas Byrne Edsall, "The Return of Inequality," *Atlantic* (June 1989).

20. Secrets

page 257. "the most important place . . .": Walter LaFeber, *Inevitable Revolutions: The United States in Central America* (New York: W. W. Norton & Company, 1983), p. 271.
257. "The Reagan administration . . .": ibid., p. 284.

22. April Again

page 275. "kept tugging at . . .": Daniel Patrick Moynihan, *Came the Revolution: Argument in the Reagan Era* (New York: Harcourt Brace Jovanovich, 1988), p. xxv.
277. "Dear Bill . . .": ibid., pp. 178–79.
279. "What we had here . . .": ibid., p. 185.

27. Crash

page 372. "The snow of twenty-nine . . .": F. Scott Fitzgerald, "Babylon Revisited," *The Stories of F. Scott Fitzgerald,* ed., Malcolm Cowley (New York: Charles Scribner's Sons, 1954), p. 402.
373. "There is a . . .": John Kenneth Galbraith, "The 1929 Parallel," *Atlantic* (January 1987), pp. 62–66.

374. "[T] he infinitely benign . . .": ibid.
374. "These lie in . . .": ibid.
375. "As people in the summer . . .": Allen, *Yesterday,* pp. 309–10.
386. "What crashed was . . .": *Time* (November 2, 1987), pp. 20–21.

28. Reckoning

page 389. "There is more . . .": Michael Barone and Grant Ujifusa, *The Almanac of American Politics 1988* (Washington, D.C.: National Journal, 1988), p. xxv.
392. "According to the admitted . . .": Henry Adams, *History of the United States During the Administrations of Thomas Jefferson* (New York: Library of America, 1986), vol. 1, pp. 99–100.
393. ". . . a collection of essays . . .": William T. Golden, ed., *Science and Technology Advice to the President, Congress and Judiciary* (New York: Pergamon Press, 1988).
394. "Whoever it was . . .": quoted by Thomas B. Edsall, *Washington Post,* January 20, 1989.
394. "Let me tell you . . .": Henry Eason, "A Southerner in Reagan's Country," *Atlanta Weekly* (September 1981).
401. "The stern truth is . . .": Charles M. Haar, *New York Times,* October 18, 1988.
406. "It's not my . . .": Mark Hertsgaard, *On Bended Knee: Ronald Reagan and the Taming of the Press* (New York: Farrar Straus Giroux, 1988), p. 62.

BOOK FOUR: AMERICA, JAN. 20, 1989

32. Rustbelt and Farmbelt

page 429. "Change can lead . . .": *Technology and the American Economic Transition: Choices for the Future* (Washington, D.C.: Congress of the United States, Office of Technology Assessment, May 1988).

32. Wall Street

page 432. "Students coming out . . .": Sarah Bartlett, *New York Times,* December 25, 1988.
436. "I'm not interested . . .": Cindy Skrzycki, *Washington Post,* December 18, 1988.
436. "The pressure to . . .": ibid.
436. "One of the . . .": ibid.
437. "These are odd . . .": James Grant, *New York Times,* January 14, 1989.

33. Washington

page 438. "We prefer not . . .": Bernard Weinraub, *New York Times,* January 19, 1989.
446. "From Reaganomics . . .": Donnie Radcliffe, *Washington Post,* January 23, 1989.
447. "In the friezes . . .": Frances FitzGerald, "Memoirs of the Reagan Era," *The New Yorker* (January 16, 1989), pp. 71–83.
450. "a sort of financial . . .": *American Agenda: Report to the Forty-first President of the United States* (Washington, D.C.: American Agenda, November 8, 1988), vol. 1. Most of the statistics cited herein about the American condition at the end of the eighties are from this report, a product of extensive studies and reports by distinguished business, economic, political, and academic figures, many of whom were to play major roles in the Bush administration.

450. "We must borrow . . .": ibid.
452. "Seriously underprepared . . .": ibid.
454. "I have always thought . . .": from an interview with General Hutton in the *Seattle Times,* published via the Associated Press in the *New York Times,* September 1, 1989.
459. "He spans our lives . . .": Wills, *America,* pp. 1–2.

EPILOGUE

page 464. "There is no greater fatuity . . .": quoted by Senator J. William Fulbright, speech, "The Cold War in American Life," at the University of North Carolina, April 7, 1964, reprinted in full in Haynes Johnson and Bernard M. Gwertzman, *Fulbright: The Dissenter* (New York: Doubleday & Company, Inc., 1968), p. 288.
471. "In considering why . . .": from an address, "Have Celebrities Replaced Heroes?," by Dr. J. S. Holiday, before the Commonwealth Club, San Francisco, August 12, 1988.
472. "The ordinary American . . .": Gunnar Myrdal, *An American Dilemma: The Negro Problem and Modern Democracy* (New York: Harper & Brothers, Publishers, 1944), p. xlvi.

BIBLIOGRAPHY

To paraphrase Dr. Johnson, I have ransacked a library to make this one book, and herewith are set out some of those volumes from which I have drawn. It is not an all-inclusive list: the social, economic, and political literature on the Reagan period alone would require a volume to describe. In the text I have tried to credit main sources when cited directly or indirectly. Here I have arranged bibilographical sources and works consulted (excluding newspapers and periodicals) into four main categories. First are works of general and American history, mainly nonfiction. The second category embraces the Reagan era of the eighties. In it I have included memoirs and other works from the Carter presidency because that period cannot be separated from the one that follows and, of course, because it also set the stage for Ronald Reagan's presidency. Third are works bearing on supply-side economics and conservative economic ideology. The fourth and final category pulls together works about the Iran-contra affair and the general subject of covert operations that form an important part of my own effort.

1. GENERAL AND AMERICAN HISTORIES

Adams, Henry. *History of the United States During the Administrations of Thomas Jefferson, 1801–1809.* 2 vols. New York: Library of America, 1986.

———. *Democracy: An American Novel.* New York: Harmony Books, 1981.

———. *The Education of Henry Adams.* Boston: Houghton Mifflin Company, 1918.

Adams, Samuel Hopkins. *The Incredible Era: The Life and Times of Warren Gamaliel Harding.* Boston: Houghton Mifflin Company, 1939.

Allen, Frederick Lewis. *Only Yesterday: An Informal History of the Nineteen-Twenties.* New York: Harper & Brothers, Publishers, 1931.

———. *Since Yesterday: The 1930s in America, September 3, 1929–September 3, 1939.* New York: Perennial Library, 1972.

———. *The Big Change: America Transforms Itself, 1900–1950.* New York: Harper & Brothers, Publishers, 1952.

Beard, Charles A., and Mary R. Beard. *The Rise of American Civilization.* New York, New York: Macmillan Company, 1930.

Beer, Thomas. *The Mauve Decade: American Life at the End of the Nineteenth Century.* New York: Alfred A. Knopf, 1926.

Bernstein, Carl, and Bob Woodward. *All the President's Men.* New York: Simon and Schuster, 1974.

Brandon, Henry. *Special Relationships: A Foreign Correspondent's Memoirs from Roosevelt to Reagan.* New York: Atheneum Publishers, 1988.

Broder, David S. *The Party's Over: The Failure of Politics in America.* New York: Harper & Row, Publishers, 1972.

———. *The Changing of the Guard: Power and Leadership in America.* New York: Simon and Schuster, 1980.

———. *Behind the Front Page: A Candid Look at How the News Is Made.* New York: Simon and Schuster, 1987.

———, and Stephen Hess. *The Republican Establishment: The Present and Future of the GOP.* New York: Harper & Row, Publishers, 1967.

Bryce, James. *The American Commonwealth.* 2 vols. New York: Macmillan Company, 1899.

Campbell, Joseph, with Bill Moyers. *The Power of Myth.* New York: Doubleday & Company, Inc., 1988.

Caro, Robert A. *The Years of Lyndon Johnson: The Path to Power.* New York: Alfred A. Knopf, 1982.

Carroll, Bob; Pete Palmer; and John Thorn. *The Hidden Game of Football.* New York: Warner Books, 1988.

Commager, Henry Steele. *The American Mind: An Interpretation of American Thought and Character Since the 1880's.* New Haven: Yale University Press, 1954.

Cousins, Norman. *"In God We Trust": The Religious Beliefs and Ideas of the American Founding Fathers.* New York: Harper & Brothers, Publishers, 1958.

Curti, Merle. *The Growth of American Thought.* New York: Harper & Brothers, Publishers, 1943.

Drew, Elizabeth. *Washington Journal: The Events of 1973–1974.* New York: Random House, 1974.

———. *Politics and Money: The New Road to Corruption.* New York: Macmillan Company, 1983.

Fitzgerald, F. Scott. *The Great Gatsby.* New York: Charles Scribner's Sons, 1925.

Forrester, Jay W. *Collected Papers of Jay W. Forrester.* Cambridge: Wright-Allen Press, Inc., 1975.

Fulbright, J. William. *The Arrogance of Power.* New York: Random House, 1966.

Furnas, J. C. *Great Times: An Informal Social History of the United States, 1914–1929.* New York: G. P. Putnam's Sons, 1974.

Galbraith, John Kenneth. *The Affluent Society.* Boston: Houghton Mifflin Company, 1958.

———. *The Great Crash, 1929.* New York: Avon, 1980.

Garreau, Joel. *The Nine Nations of North America.* Boston: Houghton Mifflin Company, 1981.

Gibbon, Edward. *The Decline and Fall of the Roman Empire.* 3 vols. New York: Heritage Press, 1946.

Gitlin, Todd, ed., *Watching Television.* New York: Pantheon Books, 1986.

Goldman, Eric F. *Rendezvous with Destiny: A History of Modern American Reform.* New York: Vintage Books, 1956.

———. *The Crucial Decade—and After: America, 1945–1960.* New York: Vintage Books, 1960.

Gunther, John. *Inside U.S.A.* New York: Harper & Row, 1947.

Hamilton, Alexander; John Jay; and James Madison. *The Federalist: A Commentary on the Constitution of the United States,* ed. Henry Cabot Lodge. New York: G. P. Putnam's Sons, 1904.

Harwood, Richard, and Haynes Johnson. *Lyndon.* New York: Praeger Publishers, 1973.

Hodgson, Godfrey. *America in Our Time.* New York: Doubleday & Company, Inc., 1976.

Hoffer, Eric. *The True Believer: Thoughts on the Nature of Mass Movements.* New York: Harper & Brothers, Publishers, 1951.

Hofstadter, Richard. *The Age of Reform: From Bryan to F.D.R.* New York: Alfred A. Knopf, 1955.

Johnson, Chalmers. *MITI and the Japanese Miracle: The Growth of Industrial Policy, 1925–1975.* Stanford: Stanford University Press, 1982.

Johnson, Haynes. *The Bay of Pigs.* New York: W. W. Norton & Company, 1964.

———. *In the Absence of Power: Governing America.* New York: Viking Press, 1980.

———, and Bernard M. Gwertzman. *Fulbright: The Dissenter.* New York: Doubleday & Company, Inc., 1968.

Kearns, Doris. *Lyndon Johnson and the American Dream.* New York: Harper & Row, Publishers, 1976.

Kempton, Murray. *Part of Our Time: Some Ruins and Monuments of the Thirties.* New York: Simon and Schuster, 1955.

Kennedy, Paul. *The Rise and Fall of the Great Powers: Economic Change and Conflict from 1500 to 2000.* New York: Random House, 1987.

Leighton, Isabel, ed. *The Aspirin Age, 1919–1941.* New York: Simon and Schuster, 1949.

Liebling, A. J. *The Press.* New York: Ballantine Books, 1964.

Link, Arthur S. *American Epoch: A History of the United States Since the 1890's.* New York: Alfred A. Knopf, 1955.

Lippmann, Walter. *Public Opinion.* London: George Allen & Unwin, Ltd., 1922.

———. *A Preface to Morals.* New York: Macmillan Company, 1929.

Lukas, J. Anthony. *Common Ground: A Turbulent Decade in the Lives of Three American Families.* New York: Vintage Books, 1986.

Manchester, William. *The Glory and the Dream: A Narrative History of America, 1939–1972.* 2 vols. Boston: Little, Brown and Company, 1973.

Moyers, Bill. *Listening to America: A Traveler Rediscovers His Country.* New York: Harper's Magazine Press, 1971.

Myrdal, Gunnar. *An American Dilemma: The Negro Problem and Modern Democracy.* New York: Harper & Brothers, Publishers, 1944.

Nixon, Richard. *Six Crises.* New York: Doubleday & Company, Inc., 1968.

Parrington, Vernon Louis. *Main Currents in American History: An Interpretation of American Literature from the Beginnings to 1920.* 3 vols. New York: Harcourt, Brace and Company, 1927.

Peirce, Neal, R. *The Megastates of America: People Politics and Power in the Ten Great States.* New York: W. W. Norton & Company, Inc., 1972.

Reedy, George E. *The Twilight of the Presidency from Johnson to Reagan.* New York: New American Library, 1987.

Rugoff, Milton. *America's Gilded Age: Intimate Portraits from an Era of Extravagance and Change, 1850–1890.* New York: Henry Holt and Company, 1989.

Schlesinger, Arthur M., Jr. *The Age of Roosevelt: The Crisis of the Old Order, 1919–1933.* Boston: Houghton Mifflin Company, 1957.

———. *A Thousand Days: John F. Kennedy in the White House.* Boston: Houghton Mifflin Company, 1965.

———. *The Cycles of American History.* Boston: Houghton Mifflin Company, 1986.

Schell. Jonathan. *Observing the Nixon Years: "Notes and Comment" From the New Yorker on the Vietnam War and the Watergate Crisis, 1969–1975.* New York: Pantheon Books, 1989.

Sheehan, Neil. *A Bright Shining Lie: John Paul Vann and America in Vietnam.* New York: Random House, 1988.

Sloat, Warren. *1929: America Before the Crash.* New York: Macmillan Publishing Company, 1979.

Stone, I. F. *The Haunted Fifties: 1953–1963.* Boston: Little, Brown and Company, 1989.

———. *In a Time of Torment: 1961–1967.* Boston: Little, Brown and Company, 1989.

Tocqueville, Alexis de. *Democracy in America.* 2 vols. New York: Colonial Press, 1900.

Toffler, Alvin. *Future Shock.* New York: Random House, 1970.

Tuchman, Barbara W. *The Guns of August.* New York: Macmillan Company, 1962.

Twain, Mark, and Charles Dudley Warner. *The Gilded Age.* 2 vols. New York: Harper & Brothers Edition, 1899.

White, Theodore H. *The Making of the President, 1960: A Narrative History of American Politics in Action.* New York: Atheneum Publishers, 1961.

———. *The Making of the President, 1964.* New York: Atheneum Publishers, 1965.

———. *The Making of the President, 1968.* New York: Atheneum Publishers, 1969.

———. *The Making of the President, 1972.* New York: Atheneum Publishers, 1973.

———. *Breach of Faith: The Fall of Richard Nixon.* New York: Atheneum Publishers, 1975.

———. *In Search of History: A Personal Adventure.* New York: Harper & Row, Publishers, 1978.

Wilson, Woodrow. *The State: Elements of Historical and Practical Politics.* New York: D. C. Heath & Co., Publishers, 1898.

Winship, Michael. *Television.* New York: Random House, 1988.

Woodward, Bob, and Carl Bernstein. *The Final Days.* New York: Simon and Schuster, 1976.

2. THE REAGAN ERA

Anderson, Martin. *Revolution.* New York: Harcourt Brace, Jovanovich, 1988.

Barnet, Richard J. *The Lean Years: Politics in the Age of Scarcity.* New York: Simon and Schuster, 1980.

Barrett, Laurence I. *Gambling with History: Reagan in the White House.* New York: Doubleday & Company, Inc., 1983.

Batra, Dr. Ravi. *The Great Depression of 1990.* New York: Simon and Schuster, 1987.

Beckwith, Colonel Charlie A., and Donald Knox. *Delta Force.* New York: Harcourt Brace Jovanovich, 1983.

Bell, Terrel H. *The Thirteenth Man: A Reagan Cabinet Memoir.* New York: Free Press, 1988.

Besen, Stanley M.; Thomas G. Krattenmaker; A. Richard Metzger, Jr.; and John R. Woodbury, eds. *Misregulating Television.* Chicago: The University of Chicago Press, 1985.

Blumenthal, Sidney, and Thomas Byrne Edsall, eds. *The Reagan Legacy.* New York: Pantheon Books, 1988.

Boskin, Michael J. *Reagan and the Economy: The Successes, Failures, and Unfinished Agenda.* San Francisco: ICS Press, 1987.

Boyarsky, Bill. *The Rise of Ronald Reagan.* New York: Random House, 1968.

Bruck, Connie. *The Predators' Ball: The Junk-Bond Raiders and the Man Who Staked Them.* New York: American Lawyer/Simon and Schuster, 1988.

Brzezinski, Zbigniew. *Power and Principle: Memoirs of the National Security Adviser, 1977–1981.* New York: Farrar Straus Giroux, 1983.

Burrough, Bryan, and John Helyar. *Barbarians at the Gate: The Fall of RJR Nabisco.* New York: Harper & Row, 1989.

Cannon, Lou. *Reagan.* New York: G. P. Putnam's Sons, 1982.

Carter, Jimmy. *Keeping Faith: Memoirs of a President.* New York: Bantam Books, 1982.

Christopher, Warren; et al. *American Hostages in Iran: The Conduct of a Crisis.* New Haven: Yale University Press, 1985.

Deaver, Michael, K., with Mickey Herskowitz. *Behind the Scenes.* New York: William Morrow and Company, Inc., 1987.

Dobson, Ed, and Ed Hinson. *The Seduction of Power.* Old Tappan: Fleming H. Revell Company, 1988.

Drew, Elizabeth. *Portrait of an Election: The 1980 Presidential Campaign.* New York: Simon and Schuster, 1981.

———. *Campaign Journal: The Political Events of 1983–1984.* New York: Macmillan Company, 1985.

———. *Election Journal: Political Events of 1987–1988.* New York: William Morrow and Company, Inc., 1989.

Dugger, Ronnie. *On Reagan: The Man & His Presidency.* New York: McGraw-Hill Book Company, 1983.

Duignan, Peter, and Alvin Rabushka, eds. *The United States in the 1980s.* Menlo Park: Addison-Wesley Publishing Company, 1980.

Duke, Paul, ed. *Beyond Reagan: The Politics of Upheaval.* New York: Warner Books, 1986.

Edsall, Thomas Byrne. *The New Politics of Inequality.* New York: W. W. Norton & Company, Inc., 1984.

———. *Power and Money: Writing About Politics, 1971–1987.* New York: W. W. Norton & Company, Inc. 1988.

Edwards, Anne. *Early Reagan: The Rise to Power.* New York: William Morrow and Company, Inc., 1987.

Erickson, Paul D. *Reagan Speaks: The Making of an American Myth.* New York: New York University Press, 1985.

FitzGerald, Frances. *Cities on a Hill: A Journey Through Contemporary American Cultures.* New York: Simon and Schuster, 1986.

Friedman, Benjamin. *Day of Reckoning: The Consequences of American Policy Under Reagan and After.* New York: Random House, 1988.

Gerston, Larry N.; Cynthia Fraleigh; and Robert Schwab. *The Deregulated Society.* Pacific Grove: Brooks/Cole Publishing Company, 1988.

Golden, William T., ed. *Science and Technology Advice to the President, Congress and Judiciary.* New York: Pergamon Press, 1988.

Gorbachev, Mikhail. *Perestroika: New Thinking for Our Country and the World.* New York: Perennial Library, 1987.

Greider, William. *Secrets of the Temple: How the Federal Reserve Runs the Country.* New York: Simon and Schuster, 1988.

Hadden, Jeffrey K., and Anson Shupe. *Televangelism: Power and Politics on God's Frontier.* New York: Henry Holt and Company, 1988.

Haig, Alexander M., Jr. *Caveat: Realism, Reagan, and Foreign Policy.* New York: Macmillan Company, 1984.

Harris, Louis. *Inside America.* New York: Vintage Books, 1987.

Harwood, Richard, ed. *The Pursuit of the Presidency 1980.* New York: G. P. Putnam's Sons, 1980.

Hertsgaard, Mark. *On Bended Knee: Ronald Reagan and the Taming of the Press.* New York: Farrar Straus Giroux, 1988.

Hobbs, Charles. *Ronald Reagan's Call to Action.* Nashville: Thomas Nelson Publishers, 1976.

Jordan, Hamilton. *Crisis: The Last Year of the Carter Presidency.* New York: G. P. Putnam's Sons, 1982.

LaFeber, Walter. *Inevitable Revolutions: The United States in Central America.* New York: W. W. Norton & Company, 1983.

Laqueur, Walter. *The Age of Terrorism.* Boston: Little, Brown, and Company, 1987.

Lekachman, Robert. *Visions and Nightmares: America After Reagan.* New York: Macmillan Company, 1987.

Lewis, Michael. *Liar's Poker.* New York: W. W. Norton & Company, Inc. 1989.

Light, Paul, C. *Baby Boomers.* New York: W. W. Norton & Company, Inc. 1988.

McElvaine, Robert S. *The End of the Conservative Era: Liberalism After Reagan.* New York: Arbor House, 1987.

Magaziner, Ira C., and Robert B. Reich. *Minding America's Business: The Decline and Rise of the American Economy.* New York: Harcourt Brace Jovanovich, 1982.

Marsden, George, ed. *Evangelicalism and Modern America.* Grand Rapids: William B. Erdmans Publishing Company, 1984.

Mayer, Jane, and Doyle McManus. *Landslide: The Unmaking of the President, 1984–1988.* Boston: Houghton Mifflin Company, 1988.

Michener, James A. *Sports in America.* New York: Fawcett Crest, 1977.

Moldea, Dan E. *Dark Victory: Ronald Reagan, MCA, and the Mob.* New York: Viking Press, 1986.

Moynihan, Daniel Patrick. *Came the Revolution: Argument in the Reagan Era.* New York: Harcourt Brace Jovanovich, 1988.

Murray, Charles. *Losing Ground: American Social Policy, 1950–1980.* New York: Basic Books, Inc., 1984.

Noonan, Peggy. *What I Saw at the Revolution.* New York: Random House, 1990.

Opinion Research Corporation, *Implementation and Enforcement of Codes of Ethics in Corporations and Associations.* Princeton: Opinion Research Corporation, 1980.

Palmer, John L., ed. *Perspectives on the Reagan Years.* Washington, D.C.: Urban Institute Press, 1986.

———, and Isabel V. Sawhill, ed. *The Reagan Experiment: An Examination of Economic and Social Policies Under the Reagan Administration.* Washington, D.C.: Urban Institute Press, 1982.

———. *The Reagan Record: An Assessment of America's Changing Domestic Priorities.* Washington, D.C.: Urban Institute Press, 1984.

Pell, Eve. *The Big Chill: How the Reagan Administration, Corporate America, and Religious Conservatives Are Subverting Free Speech and the Public's Right to Know.* Boston: Beacon Press, 1984.

Phillips, Kevin P. *The Emerging Republican Majority.* New York: Arlington House, 1969.

———. *Mediacracy: American Parties and Politics in the Communications Age.* New York: Doubleday & Company, Inc., 1975.

———. *Post-Conservative America: People, Politics and Ideology in a Time of Crisis.* New York: Random House, 1982.

Prestowitz, Clyde V., Jr. *Trading Places: How We Allowed Japan to Take the Lead.* New York: Basic Books, 1988.

Quigley, Joan. *"What Does Joan Say?": My Seven Years as White House Astrologer to Nancy and Ronald Reagan.* New York: Birch Lane Press/Carol Publishing Group, 1990.

Reagan, Nancy. *My Turn: The Memoirs of Nancy Reagan.* New York: Random House, 1989.

Reagan, Ronald. *Speaking My Mind.* New York: Simon and Schuster, 1989.

Reeves, Richard. *The Reagan Detour.* New York: Simon and Schuster, 1985.

Regan, Donald T. *For the Record: From Wall Street to Washington.* New York: Harcourt Brace Jovanovich, 1988.

Reich, Robert B. *Tales of a New America.* New York: Times Books, 1987.

Reichley, A. James. *Religion in American Public Life.* Washington, D.C.: Brookings Institution, 1985.

———, ed. *Election American Style.* Washington, D.C.: Brookings Institution, 1987.

Reutter, Mark. *Sparrows Point: Making Steel—The Rise and Ruin of American Industrial Might.* New York: Summit Books, 1988.

Schlesinger, James. *America at Century's End.* New York: Columbia University Press, 1989.

Smith, Hedrick. *The Power Game: How Washington Works.* New York: Random House, 1988.

Sobel, Robert. *The New Game on Wall Street.* New York: John Wiley & Sons, 1987.

Speakes, Larry, with Robert Pack. *Speaking Out: The Reagan Presidency from Within the White House.* New York: Charles Scribner's Sons, 1988.

Straub, Gerard Thomas. *Salvation for Sale: An Insider's View of Pat Robertson's Ministry.* New York: Prometheus Books, 1986.

Thomas, Tony. *The Films of Ronald Reagan.* Secaucus: Citadel Press, 1980.

Vance, Cyrus. *Hard Choices: Critical Years in America's Foreign Policy.* New York: Simon and Schuster, 1983.

Walter, Ingo, ed. *Deregulating Wall Street: Commercial Bank Penetration of the Corporate Securities Market.* New York: John Wiley & Sons, 1985.

Wells, Tim. *444 Days: The Hostages Remember.* New York: Harcourt Brace Jovanovich, 1985.

Wills, Garry. *Reagan's America: Innocents at Home.* New York: Doubleday & Company Inc., 1987.

Wolfe, Tom. *The Bonfire of the Vanities.* New York: Farrar Straus Giroux, 1987.

3. SUPPLY-SIDE ECONOMICS

Friedman, Milton. *Capitalism and Freedom.* Chicago: University of Chicago Press, 1982.

Gilder, George. *Wealth and Poverty.* New York: Bantam Books, 1981.

Greider, William. *The Education of David Stockman and Other Americans.* New York: E. P. Dutton, 1982.

Kemp, Jack. *An American Renaissance: A Strategy for the 1980's.* New York: Berkley Books, 1981.

Laffer, Arthur B., and Jan P. Seymour. *The Economics of the Tax Revolt.* New York: Harcourt Brace Jovanovich, 1979.

Mundell, Robert, A. *Man and Economics.* New York: McGraw-Hill, Inc., 1968.

Roberts, Paul Craig. *The Supply-Side Revolution: An Insider's Account of Policymaking in Washington.* Cambridge: Harvard University Press, 1984.

Stockman, David A. *The Triumph of Politics: The Inside Story of the Reagan Revolution.* New York: Avon, 1987.

Wanniski, Jude. *The Way the World Works.* New York: Basic Books, 1978.

4. THE IRAN-CONTRA AFFAIR AND COVERT OPERATIONS

Bradlee, Ben, Jr. *Guts and Glory: The Rise and Fall of Oliver North.* New York: Donald I. Fine, Inc., 1988.

Cockburn, Leslie. *Out of Control: The Story of the Reagan Administration's Secret War in Nicaragua, the Illegal Arms Pipeline, and the Contra Drug Connection.* New York: Atlantic Monthly Press, 1988.

Cohen, William S., and George J. Mitchell. *Men of Zeal: A Candid Inside Story of the Iran-Contra Hearings.* New York: Viking Press, 1988.

Dinges, John. *Our Man in Panama: How General Noriega Used the United States—and Made Millions in Drugs and Arms.* New York: Random House, 1990.

Eddy, Paul, with Hugo Sabogal and Sara Walden. *The Cocaine Wars.* New York: W. W. Norton & Company, Inc., 1988.

Emerson, Steve. *Secret Warriors: Inside the Covert Military Operations of the Reagan Era.* New York: G. P. Putnam's Sons, 1988.

Franck, Thomas M., and Edwin Weisband, eds. *Secrecy and Foreign Policy.* New York: Oxford University Press, 1974.

Gutman, Roy. *Banana Diplomacy: The Making of American Policy in Nicaragua, 1981–1987.* New York: Simon and Schuster, 1988.

Kempe, Frederick. *Divorcing the Dictator: America's Bungled Affair with Noriega.* New York: G. P. Putnam's Sons, 1990.

Kwitny, Jonathan. *The Crimes of Patriots: A True Tale of Dope, Dirty Money, and the CIA.* New York: W. W. Norton & Company, Inc., 1987.

Ledeen, Michael. *Perilous Statecraft: An Insider's Account of the Iran-Contra Affair.* New York: Charles Scribner's Sons, 1988.

Martin, David C., and John Walcott. *Best Laid Plans: The Inside Story of America's War Against Terrorism.* New York: Harper & Row, 1988.

Marshall, Jonathan; Peter Dale Scott; and Jane Hunter. *The Iran-Contra Connection: Secret Teams and Covert Operations in the Reagan Era.* Boston: South End Press, 1987.

Prados, John. *Presidents' Secret Wars: CIA Pentagon Covert Operations Since World War II.* New York: William Morrow and Company, Inc., 1986.

Report of the Congressional Committees Investigating the Iran-Contra Affair. With Supplemental, Minority, and Additional Views. November 1987. Washington, D.C.: U.S. Government Printing Office, 1987.

Shannon, Elaine. *Desperados: Latin Drug Lords, U.S. Lawmen, and the War America Can't Win.* New York: Viking Press, 1988.

Subcommittee on Narcotics, Terrorism and International Operations, U.S. Senate Foreign Relations Committee, *Drugs, Law Enforcement and Foreign Policy.* 2 vols. Washington, D.C.: U.S. Government Printing Office, 1989.

Tower, John; Edmund Muskie; and Brent Scowcroft, *Report of the President's Special Review Board.* Washington, D.C.: U.S. Government Printing Office, 1987.

Turner, Admiral Stansfield. *Secrecy and Democracy: The CIA in Transition.* New York: Houghton Mifflin Company, 1985.

Wise, David, and Thomas B. Ross. *The Invisible Government.* New York: Random House, 1964.

Woodward, Bob. *Veil: The Secret Wars of the CIA, 1981–1987.* New York: Simon and Schuster, 1987.

ACKNOWLEDGMENTS

Unfortunately it is impossible to thank all of those to whom I owe a debt for this book. During conversations in homes and offices all over the country, hundreds of people have shared their thoughts about America with me. So did numerous officeholders in and out of Washington. I am grateful to them all. Years ago, when I was a graduate student at the University of Wisconsin, Professors Howard K. Beale and Thomas LeDuc, among others, provided inspiration in the tradition of Frederick Jackson Turner, Merle Curti, and other great American historians from that institution. I owe a special debt to three newspaper editors. At the *Washington Evening Star,* Newbold Noyes, its editor, and Charles B. Seib, its managing editor, first made it possible for me to travel throughout the country and report on America. At the *Washington Post,* Benjamin C. Bradlee, its executive editor, continued to send me on reporting trips around the country and for years has been a constant source of encouragement and support, personally and professionally. Among other colleagues, David S. Broder, America's best political reporter, provided wise insights and warm friendship on many national journeys that began when we both were on the *Star* and that continued for years on the *Post.* Among other *Post* colleagues from whose knowledge I have profited during trips around the country, I am particularly grateful to Thomas Byrne Edsall, Dan Balz, Margaret Engel, Bill Peterson, and Paul Taylor. For support and counsel, I am also indebted to Howard Simons, the *Post*'s late managing editor and my collaborator in another book project; to Leonard Downie, Jr., its current managing editor; and to Robert G. Kaiser, in charge of the paper's national coverage, to whom I am especially grateful for his invaluable assistance in sharpening my Iran-contra coverage. Among others on whose good judgment I have relied for years are Richard Harwood and the late Laurence Stern. For years, too, my fellow television panelists on "Washington Week in Review"—Charles Corddry, Paul Duke, Charles McDowell, Jack Nelson, and

Hedrick Smith—contributed to my understanding of international, national, and political currents. Timothy Dickenson, a Renaissance man in every sense of the term, provided much stimulus during many conversations about the Reagan years. Lucy Shackelford was of immense help in handling a number of final, and critical, research tasks. I'm also grateful to Jennifer Belton, director of information services at the *Washington Post,* and to Harris Worchel and Kim Klein of the *Post*'s photo library for assistance in obtaining illustrations. Among friends to whom I could always turn for guidance and criticism were Cathy A. Ball, Christie Basham, Noel Epstein, Al Horne, and Jean Kirk. In Washington, D.C., the Brookings Institution, with its wealth of resources and talented people, contributed immeasurably to this book project by appointing me a guest scholar for two years during the research for this effort. Among many helpful scholars there, I am particularly grateful to Thomas E. Mann, director of Brookings's Government Studies Program, and to Barbara D. Littell of its Center for Public Policy Education. At the Bancroft Library, the University of California, Berkeley, I am indebted to Gabrielle Morris, coordinator of the oral history project dealing with the Reagan gubernatorial years, for much kind assistance. At Berkeley, too, Ray Colvig, Eugene C. Lee, and Nelson Polsby helped in many ways. For help in television research, I am grateful to the library and information center of the National Association of Broadcasters in Washington, D.C., and to Walt Wurfel and Sara Fitzgerald. Olwen Price relieved me of the burden of sorting through countless hours of tape recordings of interviews and transcribed them with dispatch and competence. The faith, judgment, and unfailing optimism of Eric P. Swenson, my editor at W. W. Norton & Company, once again made me realize that a writer can never adequately acknowledge the debts he owes to a good editor. At Norton, I'm grateful for the support of its chairman, Donald S. Lamm, and especially appreciative of the editorial criticism of Carol Houck Smith, with whom I was fortunate to work again. Finally I wish to acknowledge the indispensable part that Tucker Malarkey, my researcher and editorial assistant, played in creating this book. For more than two years she was a partner in *every* aspect of this work and contributed to it in more ways than I can enumerate. She deserves credit for whatever strengths it has. Quite literally, this book could not have been written without her.

H. J.

November 1990
Washington, D.C.

Index

ABOUT THE AUTHOR

Haynes Johnson, a Pulitzer Prize winner in journalism, as was his father before him, has been a reporter, a columnist, an editor, and a television commentator and is the author or coauthor of nine other books, among them the best seller *The Bay of Pigs* and *In the Absence of Power.* After three years in the U.S. Army during the Korean War, in 1956 he began his newspaper career on the *Wilmington* (Delaware) *News-Journal* and the next year joined the *Washington Evening Star,* where he earned a national reputation for his reports on American life and the Pulitzer Prize for distinguished national reporting for his coverage of the civil rights conflict in Selma, Alabama. Since 1969 he has been on the staff of the *Washington Post* and currently writes a column on national affairs. Johnson was born in New York and holds a master's degree in American history from the University of Wisconsin. He has taught at Princeton University, has been a commentator on NBC's "Today" program, and appears regularly on the "Washington Week in Review" television program broadcast nationally over PBS.